D1614501

THE

PUBLICATIONS

OF THE

SURTEES SOCIETY

VOL. 214

Hon. General Editors

R. H. BRITNELL and M. M. HARVEY

THE

PUBLICATIONS

OF THE

SURTEES SOCIETY

ESTABLISHED IN THE YEAR
M.DCCC.XXXIV

VOL. CCXIV

SUNDERLAND WILLS AND INVENTORIES 1601–1650

EDITED
BY
JOAN BRIGGS, RITA McGHEE
JOHN SMITH, JENNIFER TINDALL
ANN TUMMAN, XENIA WEBSTER

THE SURTEES SOCIETY

THE BOYDELL PRESS

First published 2010

A Surtees Society Publication
published by The Boydell Press
an imprint of Boydell & Brewer Ltd
PO Box 9, Woodbridge, Suffolk IP12 3DF, UK
and of Boydell & Brewer Inc.
Mt Hope Avenue, Rochester, NY 14620, USA
website: www.boydellandbrewer.com

ISBN 978–0–85444–069–6

ISSN 0307–5362

A catalogue record for this book is available
from the British Library

Details of other Surtees Society volumes are available
from Boydell & Brewer Ltd

The publisher has no responsibility for the continued existence or
accuracy of URLs for external or third-party internet websites
referred to in this book, and does not guarantee that any content
on such websites is, or will remain, accurate or appropriate.

Papers used by Boydell & Brewer Ltd are natural, recyclable
products made from wood grown in sustainable forests

Printed in Great Britain by
CPI Antony Rowe, Chippenham and Eastbourne

CONTENTS

PREFACE

This collection includes all the surviving wills and inventories for Sunderland, Bishopwearmouth and Monkwearmouth in the period 1601 to 1650. The great majority are in the keeping of the Special Collections at Durham University Library. For access and for the laborious tasks of fetching and carrying, thanks are due to Dr Sheila Hingley, the sub-librarian in charge of heritage collections, and the members of her staff, who also gave much helpful advice.

The work was undertaken to support research into the history of Sunderland being prepared by the Victoria County History Trust of Durham. The editors and team leaders of the project, Dr Gill Cookson and Dr Christine Newman, commissioned and encouraged the work which was done under the aegis of the National Lottery Fund's enterprise, England's Past for Everyone.

The work of transcribing was done by volunteers who have in the past three years transcribed all the wills and inventories for Sunderland for the period 1549–1700. They are Mrs Joan Briggs, Mrs Rita McGhee, Mr John Smith, Ms Jennifer Tindall, Mrs Ann Tumman and Miss Xenia Webster. Mr Stuart Miller, responsible for this and other groups of volunteers, kept a friendly and helpful eye on all their work. Miss Elaine Naylor and staff at the Washington Library welcomed the group to accommodation in the library for their weekly meetings. Finally, the work has benefited from the warm encouragement, infinite patience and exacting oversight of Professor Richard Britnell, who with Dr Margaret Harvey, as joint-editors of the Surtees Society, also provided indispensable assistance in transcribing the Latin endorsements of the documents.

H. J. Smith

EDITORIAL METHOD

Punctuation and the use of capitals have been regularized, except that the seventeenth-century convention of writing ff for a capital F has been preserved where it occurs. Abbreviations and contractions have been extended throughout. The following conventions have been used in preparing the text for publication:

[*illegible*]	editorial comment
[........]	text missing because of damage to the document
be[queath]	damaged or abbreviated English text restored by the editors
<bequeath>	uncertain reading
{bequeath}	text deleted
\bequeath/	text interlined
ad*ministrati*o	abbreviated Latin text extended by the editors

All values in the inventories have been rendered in uniform columns of pounds, shillings and pence and translated from Roman into Arabic numerals. Where the Roman forms occurred elsewhere in the wills or inventories they have been left.

The documents in the text have been numbered 1 to 90, and these numbers are used in the introduction to refer to the document or the individual concerned.

Eighty-eight separate individuals witness these documents by signing their full names, including Margaret Halyman (73). This is noticed editorially in every case. Those who signed with their initials are also identified: some used both initials, IM for John Marley (55), PS for Peter Sharpe (75); and some used one initial, R for Roger Thornton (79), A for Anthony Weatherhead (80), T for William Thompson (60, 64) and M for James Morre (74). They include M for Margaret Curtes (49) and H for Humphrey Harrison (62, 75). Twelve signed with a cross but most others with what is described here as a 'symbol' which in some cases is consistently used: John Johnson (31, 34, 42), the blacksmith, always drew a horseshoe with nail-holes, as a witness, as an appraiser and, finally, as a testator. William Potts used a shape like Σ but in the four cases (36, 55, 65, 69) it changed its orientation. The description 'symbol' is used also to cover marks which were little better than random scratches.

Almost all the documents of this period have recently been assigned reference letters and numbers in a still continuing programme of listing and filming. These references are given at the end of each of the documents but it is still usual to call for them by year and personal name. All the documents are listed by the year of probate even if written in an earlier year.

ABBREVIATIONS

DPR1   Durham Probate Records 1
WI Durham *Wills and Inventories from the Registry at Durham, Part IV*, ed. H. M. Wood, Surtees Society 142 (1929)

INTRODUCTION

Sunderland in the earlier seventeenth century was in transition from a small fishing village on the south side of the River Wear. It was part of the parish of Bishopwearmouth with the hamlets of Ryhope, Silksworth, Barnes and Grindon. Monkwearmouth was a totally separate parish on the north side of the Wear, incorporating Hylton, Southwick and Fulwell.

The sources

This edition comprises all the surviving documents of probate for the parishes of Bishopwearmouth and Monkwearmouth from between 1601 and 1650, but does not include the bonds taken to ensure proper administration. All but a few of these records are to be found in the Special Collections of Durham University Library. During the Commonwealth and Protectorate all wills were proved in London and are now in the National Archives at Kew; and two of these, both from 1649, are included in this collection (89, 90). Finally, one estate in the collection, that of Henry Rand (18) in 1614, was proved at the Guildhall in the City of London, the base of the East India Company with which he sailed.

The probate records in this collection are amongst the 484 probate documents transcribed by the England's Past for Everyone volunteers for the period 1549–1700. These are chronologically distributed as follows.

1549–1550	1
1551–1575	29
1576–1600	46
1601–1625	34
1626–1650	56
1651–1675	114
1676–1700	204
1549–1700	484

These figures bear only a very approximate relationship to the growth of Sunderland. The apparent decline from the period

1576–1600 to 1601–25 is because the registers of wills, which ensure
their survival in copy form, cover much less of the later period. A
considerable number of Sunderland wills and inventories made in
the years 1601–50 have disappeared. A check on the number actually
presented for probate is possible by consulting the probate act
books,[1] which briefly record the proceedings on all estates proved. It
is at present not possible to consult all the act books, because of their
condition, but those for the years 1601–7, 1614–19 and 1614–25 yield
the following statistics.

	Proven	Extant
1601–1607	26	6
1614–1619	17	13
1614–1625	40	18

The Bishopwearmouth registers, for the first half of the period
1601–50, record the burials of 405 men and women who could have
qualified as testators. This figure excludes persons described as wife,
son or daughter, or as belonging to other locations or nationalities,[2]
various strangers, sailors and sojourners. Testamentary documents
survive for only twenty-seven of those burials in the years 1601–25.

This volume contains the documentation for ninety-one individuals of Bishopwearmouth and Monkwearmouth for the period
1601–50, twelve of whom were women. One document is for the
estate of a man and wife, Robert and Jane Thompson (83). The documents comprise.

Wills with an inventory	43
Wills with inventory and renunciation	1
Wills without an inventory	9
Nuncupative wills with an inventory	9
Nuncupative will without an inventory	1
Letter accepted as a will	1
Inventory only	17
Inventory with renunciation	1

1 Durham University Library, Special Collections, for the period 1607–50,
Probate Act Books 8, 10–17.
2 London (one), Lynn (one), Boston (two), Kent, Lincolnshire, Yorkshire and
Northumberland, together with three Dutchmen and a Frenchman, various
strangers, sailors and sojourners, and Anthony of Barnes, a black Moor.

Declarations of account with an inventory	3
Declarations of account without inventory	5
Total	90

The provision in the Fees for Probate Act of 1529 that fees should only be charged on estates above £5 has been read, incorrectly, to mean that no estate below that value qualified for probate.[3] Estates worth less than £5 were proved. The inventory of Thomas Watt (56) amounts to no more than 17s. However, it is true that only a few of those dying left estates for probate. Thus, the act book for 1614–25 shows that only thirty-six of the 226 persons buried in those years at Bishopwearmouth were the subject of testamentary proceedings, no more than 17 per cent. In Darlington, in roughly the same period, the percentage was 27 per cent of potential testators. Sunderland, as a new and fast-growing industrial and commercial settlement, probably had an exceptionally large number of poor people, quite unable to leave an estate worth disposal or valuation.

Wills normally take no account of landed property, which was the responsibility of other institutions: manorial courts, the bishop's halmote court or the civil courts. However, there are several examples of testators designating heirs to land.[4] Clearly, wills were the means of making intentions and preferences known even if without legal finality.

Dating the wills

There are sixty-four wills for the whole period 1601–50 and the registers of Bishopwearmouth church can supply burial dates in thirty-eight cases. In addition, three wills are dated after the recorded burial date. If the dates can be relied upon, only a few can be described as last-minute compilations: five are dated the day of burial or of death. Another fifteen may have been sick-bed compilations: five dated within seven days of burial or death, five within a fortnight and five within a month. In eighteen of the thirty-eight cases, burial occurred after a month or more had elapsed. Ten wills are dated over six months before burial.[5]

---

3   21 Henry VIII, c. 5. The error is commented on in Tom Arkell, 'The Probate Process', in Tom Arkell, Nesta Evans and Nigel Goose, eds, *When Death Do Us Part: Understanding and Interpreting the Probate Records of Early Modern England*, Local Population Studies Supplement (Oxford, 2000), p. 12.

4   Arkell, 'The Probate Process', p. 8.

5   For a similar calculation, see S. Coppel, 'Will Making on the Deathbed', *Local*

Moreover, the dating of wills very near the time of death appears suspect in some cases. The widow Alice Wilkinson (15) was buried on the very day her will is dated, 29 August 1613. The will was nuncupative or by word of mouth. It had to be written out and it was actually witnessed on 4 September, five days after her death. It has much detail and names fourteen beneficiaries, quite an achievement for someone at the very point of death. Perhaps it was composed for her some days before the 29 August. Relatives, neighbours, ministers or scribes would surround and prompt the dying person, reminding him or her of whom and what they should remember, surely leading to some nagging and badgering. The Act of Henry VIII, concerning Uses and Wills, spoke of declarations elicited from 'such persons as be visited with sickness, in their extreme agonies and pains, or at such time as they have scantly had any good memory or remembrance ... at which times they being provoked by greedy and covetous persons lying in wait about them, do many times dispose indiscreetly and unadvisedly their lands and tenements; ... and many other inconveniences have happened, and daily do increase among the king's subjects, to their great trouble and inquietness, and to the utter subversion of the ancient common laws of this realm'.[6]

An example comes from 1604, a year of serious epidemic in Sunderland. The annual average of burials in Bishopwearmouth doubled. In that year, Anthony Gefferson of Ryhope (5) was 'lijnge in a coove in the feild sicke in the visitation'. He was in effect quarantined, either voluntarily or by action of the neighbourhood. The curate and two worthy householders approached him, and, no doubt from a safe distance, asked, 'whoe should have his portion of goods if he died'. He then left £1 10s to the poor and made specific bequests to at least eight people, several of £1, 15s and 10s. However, two days later, his interrogators returned, 'to gather somethinge more perfitly from him'. He now repudiated what he had said before, limiting bequests to 5s each and the remainder to his brother. Not content, Mr Richard Clement, the curate, 'willed him to give somewhat more to his uncle Christopher for he was but a poore man'. Anthony, now perhaps understandably exasperated, replied, 'Take it you all and give it where you will.' These 'were the last words that he used touchinge the premisses'. This occurred on 25 July, and Anthony was buried on the following day.

Population Studies, 40 (Spring 1988), p. 38.
6   27 Henry VIII, c. 10.

The role of the clergy

Although until 1858 probate was a service provided by the church, the part played by clergymen at the death-bed, and in the compilation of wills, appears to diminish up to the mid-seventeenth century. Some two-thirds of the wills made between 1551 and 1575 (17 out of 25) were witnessed by men in holy orders. Between 1576 and 1600, the proportion dropped to less than a quarter (8 out of 38), between 1601 and 1625 to less than a third (7 out of 23), and between 1626 and 1650 to less than one sixth (6 out of 41). Among the last six cases, three clergymen, including the Frenchman Isaac Basire, chaplain to both Charles I and II, as well as the Puritan curate, Richard Hicks, and Thomas Waite, were involved in the will-making of the rector John Johnson (80). They acted as colleagues rather than spiritual guides, rather as two ship-carpenters did for the will of William Huntley, ship-carpenter (84).

The rise in lay literacy may account for this decline in the clerical role, but the unpopularity of clergy may also have been a reason. Anti-clericalism was an important influence in the Protestant Reformation and two popular acts of the Reformation were those regulating probate fees and mortuaries.[7] Mortuaries were a traditional levy upon the estate of a deceased person, sometimes amounting to their second best beast. This was regulated to take the form of a small fixed sum. In the neighbouring probate jurisdiction, the Act to avoid Exactions taken by Spiritual Men in the Archdeaconry of Richmond (1534)[8] gives some idea of the aggrieved feeling that ecclesiastical probate jurisdiction could arouse. The Act declared that many inhabitants of the archdeaconry 'have been long time sore and grievously exacted and impoverished by holders of benefices and spiritual promotions there, by taking in the name of a pension or of a portion from every person who dies, sometimes the ninth part of his goods and chattels and sometimes the third part'. In Sunderland, especially, from the mid-1620s, powerful persons of pronounced anti-clerical views came to dominate the town, notably George Lilburne of Sunderland and George Gray of Southwick. George Lilburne, although son-in-law and brother-in-law of two clergymen, was particularly notorious with the Durham clerical establishment for his opposition to Church policies and indeed, after 1626, appeared more frequently than local clergymen as a witness of wills

---

7   21 Henry VIII, c. 5 and c. 6.
8   26 Henry VIII, c. 15.

or appraiser of inventories or in other associated roles such as arbiter. He wrote out at least one will and an inventory too.

From 1595 until 1632, Francis Burgoine was the rector of Bishopwearmouth but the only time his name is mentioned in these documents is as a creditor. His curate, Richard Clement, participated in the making of three wills before taking up his appointment as vicar of Dalton-le-Dale in 1605. He it was who had the delicate task of extracting the dying wishes from the unfortunate Anthony Gefferson (5). The will of Ralph Fletcher (12) in 1612 was witnessed by the curate Randulph Bentley, a man who styled himself a minister, perhaps implying that he was inclined to favour Puritan rather than Laudian church practices. Walter Marshall took on the role of curate in 1620 following the death of Bentley, but we have to wait nine years for his name to appear, as an appraiser of the blacksmith, John Johnson (42). The fact that John Johnson was a churchwarden at the time may account for Marshall's involvement. In November 1622, Walter Marshall did take certain notes by direction of Agnes Ayre for drawing up her last will and testament. She lived another twenty-one months after that time and Marshall was informed that she disposed of her estate other than by the notes she had given him.[9]

Inventories

An important step in the process of probate was the drawing up of an inventory of the assets and possessions of the deceased, assessing their value.[10] Inventories were often very detailed in respect of farming assets, including the value of leases and farm implements. House furnishings were likewise amply described. The account of the widow of William Freeman (81) in 1644 tells a story of losses at the hands of the Scottish army and Sir William Armyne, the parliamentary commander; the inventory is actually a schedule of plundered goods. The account of Robert and Jane Thompson (83) is a very full record of losses by occupation, billeting and assessments during the war. Inventories are, however, disappointingly summary where clothing and books are concerned. Drury observes that there

9 The National Archives, Durham Chancery Depositions, Durh 7/23, Thomas Ayre vs. Robert Ayre, 1625 (there are no piece numbers).
10 For an authoritative account see J. Linda Drury, 'Inventories in the Probate Records of the Diocese of Durham', *Archaeologia Aeliana*, 5th series, XXVIII (2000), pp. 177–91.

was a conflict of interest in the compilation of inventories, between family members who might want only a brief valuation and the non-family beneficiaries who wanted a full list.[11] Nevertheless, inventories are now regarded as unique for what they reveal of the work and living conditions, and the vocabulary, of ordinary people.[12]

Normally four men of probity and good acquaintanceship with the family, including kin, creditors and debtors too, describing themselves usually as 'four indifferent men', would view the assets of the deceased and value them. The nephew and son-in-law of Thomas Burdon (38) were among the appraisers of his inventory in 1626. Two creditors were among the four appraisers of George Collier of Monkwearmouth (41) in 1629. William Oliver of Monkwearmouth (21), who died in 1615, was a chapman, an itinerant trader, which probably accounts for his having two inventories in the one document, one taken at Morpeth by three individuals there and one at Bishopwearmouth by three other individuals.

It is likely that inventories were drawn up within earshot of potential beneficiaries and different kinds of pressure might be applied as the appraisers went about house and yard in their work. The long statement by the four 'prisers' of the assets of Richard Bartram the butcher (13) suddenly abandons its impersonal tone as his widow, it seems, feelingly interpolates, 'Item, a cubbord w[hi]ch my said husband gave to my maid, Barbara Taylier, 3s 4d, and of money, £1 6s 8d'. The inventory-makers say, somewhat oddly, at the commencement of the inventory of Robert Huntly of East Burdon (32) in 1622, 'Imprimis, foure oxen, presented to them & conscionably prised at £14 13s 4d'. Possibly they were defending that particular valuation or maybe they were disowning it.

Some individuals were especially trusted in this work: John Johnson, blacksmith and churchwarden (42), was appraiser of nine inventories before his death in 1629. He clearly was a man of trust in the locality. When in 1623, Robert Ayre of Tunstall went to George Lilburne's house to discuss selling some property, he took Johnson with him 'as an indifferent man betwixt them', to whom the articles

---

11 Drury, 'Inventories' pp. 178, 183.
12 See Edmund Weiner, 'The Language of Probate Inventories', and Barrie Trinder, 'The Wooden Horse in the Cellar: Words and Contexts in Shropshire Probate Inventories', in Arkell, Evans and Goose, eds, *When Death Do Us Part*, pp. 255, 268.

of agreement could be confided.[13] John Shepherdson the elder was another trusted individual. He was appraiser of eight inventories. He was probably the son of the John Shepherdson who had been witness and appraiser of nine wills and inventories before 1596. Shepherdson and Johnson both signed with a mark, which indicates that literacy was not the primary qualification.[14] In Johnson's case the mark was a carefully drawn horseshoe.

The process of probate

The documents for probate were then taken to the diocesan court at Durham, meeting usually in the Galilee chapel of the cathedral, but also occasionally and more conveniently at principal towns in the county. The court met every fortnight. Executors and witnesses of the will would travel from their homes to Durham, produce the documentation, including an inventory of goods and possessions, and be sworn to its truth. Those who appeared and were sworn as witnesses are often indicated in the documents by the endorsements *juratus* for a male person or *jurata* for a female. George Lilburne was paid 14s 4d for his trouble in riding to Durham about the administration of the estate of Ralph Wells (49) in 1632. The court, if no matters of contention arose, would then grant administration and tuition too, where minors were concerned. The letters of administration and the tuition for Thomas Wilson of Bishop-wearmouth (17), in 1614, cost a total of 29s. If the will was a nuncupative one, made by word of mouth, the witnesses would sometimes have to make formal depositions before the consistory court. It does not appear that depositions were made in the consistory court for any of the nuncupative wills in this collection although Gefferson's two word-of-mouth statements were contradictory and their proving seems to have taken up to two years. The will of Jane Smart (69) is accompanied by a list of inter-rogatories, showing some question arose over the circumstances of the will-making. The costs of proving Alice Wilkinson's will were only 19s, which suggests that proving it was straightforward. In the case of Henry Rand (18) there was no will. It was his last, very personal letter to his parents which was produced for light on his

---

13 National Archives, Durh 7/21, George Lilburne vs. Robert Ayer, 1623.
14 See David Cressy, *Literacy and the Social Order: Reading and Writing in Tudor and Stuart England* (Cambridge, 1980), pp. 10, 13, 189.

wishes.[15] In his case as in others, letters of attorney could also be produced.

Subsequently the administrator was expected to produce a statement of what had been spent and the balance after all debts and obligations were met. Recent writing regards such documents, known as declarations of account, as the most authentic statements of the actual value of an estate.[16] However, they do not survive in great number. In this collection there are three with an inventory and five without, for only eight of the ninety estates.

Family and kinship
The structure of the family has long been under discussion[17] and probate records have a bearing on the question of whether the family had an extended or nuclear structure, how wide was the kinship circle, and how widows ranked and fared.

Nine of the sixty-four Sunderland wills were by single persons, of which only one was a woman, Margaret Goodchild (10). The majority of these single people make parents or siblings their executors, to whom they also left their goods and property. Leases of their land were usually left to brothers. Sisters on the other hand were left animals or sums of money. The one spinster represented in the collection, Margaret Goodchild (10) who died in 1610, left £80, her share of her late gentleman father's wealth. She divided her legacy by giving her brother £20 and to each of her three married sisters £13 6s 8d (20 marks). She appears to have accepted the principle of male primacy among her siblings. Wife, children, parents, brothers and sisters, in that order, are the beneficiaries of almost every will.

Of these sixty-four wills, fifty-two were of married men. Thirty-nine show that their wives survived them. Twelve of these widows were sole executors of their husbands' estates. Widow and son were joint executors in five cases. Gabriel Marley (9) in 1609 made his two daughters his executors although they appear to have been minors because he states that his second wife is to be tutor to them, while she remained a widow. He provided his estate with a double safe-

---

15 Jeff and Nancy Cox, 'Probate 1500–1800: A System in Transition', in Arkell, Evans and Goose, eds, *When Death Do Us Part*, p. 25, refer to less orthodox testamentary documentation accepted.
16 Ibid., pp. 35–6, 103–9.
17 Ralph A. Houlbrooke, *The English Family, 1450–1700* (London, 1970); Lawrence Stone, *The Family, Sex and Marriage in England 1500–1800* (London, 1977; 2nd edn, London 1990).

guard, in effect. The children of his first marriage were made executors to protect their interest and were protected too against the consequences of his widow's possible remarriage. Marley's will was generous also to his mother and his siblings.

These wills show that the majority of the married children had set up their own households. They were not far distant from their parents, however, and occasionally the testator asks that sons and married daughters perform services for the surviving parent. Anthony Watson (19) left his wife two acres of arable land in each of the three cornfields of Ryhope, and pasturing for two cows and ten sheep in ox and sheep pastures there. He required of his son George that he should in due season plough, sow and harrow that land, and lead home the corn in harvest. George was also required every year to bring to her dwelling house in Ryhope two fothers of coal, two of whins and two of hay, which she was to buy. George Middleton (1) gave to his sister, Constance Middleton, half an acre of land in every field in Silksworth, and his son was to carry the compost to her grounds, plough them, and bring home the corn. Robert Watson of Bishopwearmouth (3), in 1603, directed that his executor should pay for a new cupboard for his sister and have it made 'of such woode as I have about the hows'. However, George Middleton (1) appeared to fear some contention in his family when he declared, 'I disire my said wiffe, as evere there was anie love betwene us, to stande good mother to my said sonne and quietlie to suffer him to mowe and occupie all such landes as are alreadie sett forth unto his use duringe her liffe'.

The Sunderland wills appear to confirm the view that the nuclear family was then predominant. Outside the immediate family of husband wife and children, there are only token bequests to other relatives. In these nuclear families there were on average three to four surviving children. Only two men appear to have had large families. Thomas Burdon (38) who died in 1626 had six sons and two daughters. Edward Lee (47), gentleman, had eight children. Only five of the sixty-four wills mention godchildren.

Wives and widows
Although there was some variation among English dioceses, a widow in Durham was generally entitled to a third of her husband's wealth.[18] In this collection, the thirds were a minimum entitlement.

---

18   Cox and Cox, 'Probate 1500–1800', pp. 19, 21.

Only three of the fifty-two married testators left their widows no more than the third and the rest of their goods to children and grandchildren. Eight widows were left all the testator's goods, moveable and unmoveable. Six testators left both house and farm jointly to the wife and eldest son.

The common law normally viewed the property or assets of the bride as wholly her husband's upon marriage[19] but Chancery and ecclesiastical law could take a different view.[20] The inventory of Thomas Jordan (6) in 1606 states 'Item, to Elizabeth Jordan his late wife, due by a bond £20'. It also states he owed his wife another £50. A local woman, Alice Smith, bought land in Middle Herrington after the agreement to marry her husband John. She had free disposal of it after marriage.[21] There were cases too of concealment from the husband. In 1624 there was a Chancery action concerning Gillian, the wife of a local man, Christopher Glover, who possessed divers sums of money kept in private, unknown to her husband, intending to dispose of them to whom she pleased.[22] These exceptions are few but show that the rule was not absolute. Primogeniture normally ensured that land and houses went to the eldest son but wills often modified this rule, chiefly by assuring the widow's needs of maintenance.

Earnest testamentary avowals of affection between husband and wife may be viewed with the same scepticism as the pious utterances which come at the very beginning of all wills. However, the idea that marriage was arranged solely on a contractual basis, with acquisition of property as the *raison d'être*, seems not to be the whole story. The fact that a number were sole executors of their husbands' wills although having adult children clearly points to trust between spouses. Marriage as an economic contract does not exclude the growth of mutual love and respect. Affection and trust were expressed by most of those dying. They believed they were going to meet their Maker and falsehoods at that time were totally inappropriate. Examples of loving reference occur in the first and last of the wills in this collection. In 1601, George Middleton of Silksworth (1)

19 Ibid., p. 22.
20 A. L. Erickson, *Women and Property in Early Modern England* (Abingdon, 1993), p. 5 and passim.
21 The National Archives, Durh 7/17b, John Smith vs. William Hill, 1619.
22 The National Archives, Durh 7/22, Oswald Glover vs. John Harrison, 1624.

refers to Margaret, 'my well-beloved wiffe' and, more ambiguously, makes a request to his wife 'as evere there was anie love between us'. In 1649, William Bowes (90) in his will, made before he travelled an uncertain world of war and revolution, refers to 'my deare and most true deserving wife' and trusted to her the upbringing of his only son 'for further legacie and token of my truest affection'. This trustworthy and deserving wife had been fourteen years old when they married and was not yet twenty-one when she became a widow.[23] These words, coming not in the formulaic beginning of the wills but at the very end, seemingly express absolute trust in the ability of these widows to manage the capital, properties and other goods they leave behind. In the majority of cases the wife is sole executrix because the children are under age or the couple are childless. Peter Marley (45) was an exception: his children were grown up but still he made his wife sole executrix. Wives returned this trust. Alice Smith, none of whose three children had been born alive, when asked as she lay upon her deathbed who should have her land, gave what seems to be a surprised and indignant response: 'Who but my husband? For none should have it but he during his life.' Scandalous exceptions of course occur: in 1604, James Lankaster of Bishopwearmouth was suspected of having two wives living; and Alexander Brown of Bishopwearmouth was charged that he kept a woman in his house as his wife and 'hath now put her away and sayeth she was not his wife'.[24]

A curious case is that of Edward Dearnley (35) and Margaret, the wife of Edward Burne (4). Dearnley and Mrs Burne were presented at the archdeacon's court in 1600 for an immoral relationship (*pro incontinencia vite*). They had to make several journeys to Durham City for the hearings.[25] They were eventually cleared on the oath of three neighbours, but had to pay the costs of the hearings. Despite this hurtful charge, Edward Burne, in his will of 1606, spoke unreservedly of his trust in his wife and appears to defend her against enemies within the family, asking 'to be buryed whereever yt shall please Margret, my wyff, whom I make myne executrix ffully & wholy of all my goods & cattels movabell & unmovonbill [*sic*], to use

23 Robert Surtees, *The History and Antiquities of the County Palatine of Durham*, 4 vols (London, 1816–40), IV, p. 112.
24 Durham University Library, Special Collections, Archdeacon's Act Book, DDR/A/ACD/1/1, f. 164.
25 Ibid., ff. 6v, 11, 13.

at her will & pleasure, and she to deaill with my kynred, John Hall &
Marke Watson, acordyng as thay do behave them towards her, they
beyng my neaves [nephews]'. He was buried on 12 May 1606. Five
years later, on 16 May 1611, the widow Burne married Dearnley, her
old co-accused.

Bequests to the poor
The period 1601–50 opens with the passing of the Act for Relief of
the Poor,[26] a mighty embodiment of principles and rules which
lasted, in amended form, until 1929. England had learnt to fear the
poor. They were seen as a source of delinquency and rebellion. Their
numbers were growing as a result of changing economic conditions.
They moved about the country in shoals and private charity could
no longer cope. Under the new act, each parish appointed overseers
and levied a rate to manage the poor. Nevertheless, until 1625 more
testators of Sunderland were giving to the poor. The increase in the
number of poor must have excited compassion as well as alarm.
Thirty-eight testators (seven of them women) made charitable
bequests to the poor. Four testators remembered the poor of parishes
elsewhere. Christopher Dickinson (71) bequeathed equal amounts of
6s 8d to the poor of Scarborough and Sunderland 'besids what my
wife giveth at my funerall'. Henry Hilton (76) bequeathed to the
poor of thirty-six parishes, including several in the south of England.
    The largest and most detailed bequest to the poor was that of
Henry Hilton, Esquire (76), starting with £24 yearly for ninety-nine
years for distribution in thirty-six parishes and townships: fifteen in
County Durham, thirteen in Sussex ('where I now live') and six in
Surrey. The responsibility for his complex and generous bequest lay
with the Lord Mayor and four senior aldermen of the city of London.
The amounts bequeathed range from this down to the 3s bequeathed
to the poor by Elizabeth Burdon (14) in 1612. As a percentage of a
total estate the most generous donation appears to be the £3 6s 8d
which the sick maid Margaret Goodchild (10) gave in 1610. Richard
Morgan (33) in his will bequeathed 6s 8d to the poor of Sunderland
but his inventory shows 10s was actually given. The inventory of
Thomas Jordan (6) shows a sum of £4 14s 2d for funeral expenses
and for the poor which suggests a random scattering of money
among those attending his burial. George Middleton (1) in 1601

26   43 Elizabeth, c. 2.

directed the £2 he left for the poor 'to be devided amongst them as my wyff shall think good'.

For the earlier period, 1551–1600, wills and inventories survive for seventy-six estates. Fourteen make bequests to the poor. Of the fourteen, ten are in the quarter century 1576–1600. One testator bequeathed to the poor of five other parishes as well as to Bishopwearmouth and Monkwearmouth. The amounts ranged from 2s to £4. The bequest for the poor of seven parishes asked that they receive 3s 4d in bread. Another testator bequeathed '6 wether shepe and a tupe' and a third bequeathed wheat (quantity not given) or 5s in money. Of the fourteen testators giving to the poor, the estates of seven have surviving inventories which allow some comparison to be made of their generosity towards the poor. They range between 0.32 per cent and 1.6 per cent of their total values.

Of the total 320 wills and inventories of the period 1651–1700, only five make bequests to the poor. William Wood in 1661 bequeathed £13 6s 8d for funeral expenses and for the poor. His wealth amounted to £51 of which 26 per cent is dedicated to these purposes. Peter Green, the ship's purser, in 1667 bequeathed £5 of his total wealth of £35 or 14.3 per cent. There are only two wills of a total of 214 in the quarter century 1676–1700 which make bequests to the poor. George French in 1687 left £20 for poor widows and children of clergymen, and a house in Newcastle to the poor of Cockfield. Finally, Robert Dodgson in 1693 left 10s to the poor of Bishopwearmouth.

It thus appears that giving increased in the period 1576–1625, with a noticeable slump towards 1700. This possibly reflects a new awareness of the poor, followed by complacency as the legislation of the period 1601–12 took effect. In the three main periods, 1551–1600, 1601–50 and 1651–1700, most of the bequests are set out in the wills but are sometimes also seen in the inventory. However, in the period 1651–1700, the much higher percentage of inventories without wills (55 per cent) compared with 1601–1650 (27 per cent) makes it quite possible that bequests in the later period have been understated.[27] (See table on following page.)

---

27 See the discussion in Nigel Goose and Nesta Evans, 'Wills as an Historical Source', in Arkell, Evans and Goose, eds, *When Death Do Us Part*, pp. 50–3.

Bequests to the poor relative to wealth 1601–50*

	Year	Bequest	Estate	%
Robert Watson	1603	20s	£177	0.56
William Scurfield	1607	20s	£27	3.70
Gabriel Marley	1609	10s	£68	0.73
Margaret Goodchild	1610	£3 6s 8d	£80	4.16
Nicholas Bryan	1611	15s	£209	0.35
Ralph Fletcher	1611	10s	£47	1.06
Elizabeth Burdon	1612	3s	£32	0.46
Anthony Watson	1614	5s	£74	0.33
William Pattinson	1615	20s	£195	0.51
Thomas Chilton	1615	20s	£156	0.64
Thomas Hilton	1616	14s	£83	0.84
John Thompson	1616	40s	£212	0.94
Thomas Roxby	1619	10s	£57	0.87
Robert Huntley	1622	10s	£199	0.25
Richard Morgan	1623	10s	£52	0.96
Agnes Thompson	1623	40s	£54	3.70
Mathew Bulmer	1626	10s	£63	0.79
William Burdon	1627	13s 4d	£17	0.39
John Johnson	1629	16s	£90	0.88
Thomas Roxby	1633	5s	£112	0.22
Allison Holme	1634	40s	£198	1.01
George Shepherdson	1635	20s	£114	0.87
Nicholas Thompson	1636	£10 0s	£54	18.5
Christopher Dickinson	1639	13s	£61	1.05
John Hilton	1639	20s	£153	0.65
Reginald Fawcett	1639	40s	£334	0.60
Richard Halliman	1640	10s	£26	1.92
William Thompson	1640	10s	£80	0.62
William Potts	1642	6s	£64	0.46

* Those leaving precise sums and whose valuations are known.

Creditors and debtors
In a society without banks, and in which ready money was in short supply, loans by private persons were the only source of credit.[28] Several Sunderland testators were owed large sums, suggestive of money-lending. George Fell of Ryhope (2) in 1602 left household and

28 Peter Spufford, 'Long-Term Rural Credit in Sixteenth- and Seventeenth-Century England: The Evidence of Probate Accounts', in Arkell, Evans and Goose, eds, *When Death Do Us Part*, p. 213.

farm goods valued at £82 1s 4d, but at least thirty-nine persons in fourteen other localities owed him over £130. His debtors include some persons of gentlemanly rank. George Shadforth (28) had thirteen debtors for a total of £543 3s 4d, including the coal owner, landowner and Newcastle magnate, Sir Henry Anderson, who owed him £200, and other gentlemen such as Mr Raph Fetherston (£100), the Durham lawyer Thomas King (£80) and Mr Robert Cooper, the bishop's attorney-general (£40). Shadforth himself owed £900 to Mr George Collingwood. Ralph Wetslett of Barnes (22), also had debtors and creditors of rank. Farming or trading transactions may explain the debts but the parties may have been brought together by lawyers who knew about the the assets of the one and the needs of the other. However it was, persons of higher rank were not above stooping to borrow.

The need for credit and the ability to provide it went from top to bottom of the social ladder. Thomas Wilson (17) was owed £4 by his landlord's wife and 1s by the widow Wilkinson. Three-quarters of the value of the modest estate of Anthony Hedley of Fulwell, labourer (39), was in the hands of others. Thomas Page, labourer (59), was owed £60 6s of his small estate of £69 13s 4d by various debtors, including George Lilburne, gentleman, who owed him £20 and was a witness to his will. The greater part of the estate of Richard Sharper, yeoman (85), was in five bills of obligation and five bonds, ranging between £2 and £20. Elderly persons, no longer at work, might well have been persuaded that they ought to help others. It is likely that widows, especially, were expected to lend their money. In 1613 Elizabeth Smith of Fulwell (16) had two debtors, one of them a knight, Sir John Claxton, who owed her £20. Among the twelve creditors of Robert Scurfield (46) were four women to whom he owed £34 18s 8d.

Money was, of course, lent within families. Robert Watson (3) had members of his own family among his nineteen creditors. He owed his brother Anthony £18 18s 4d and his brother William £16 6s 10d 'upon an accounte which I doe refere to his owen reckninge and concience'. He both employed his sister Isabel and borrowed from her: he owed her £12, 'as doth appeare by a bill of my hande', £1 8s 'of lent money', and a further £1 10s for her wages. The inventiory of Isabel Richardson (65) records that her daughter-in-law Isabel, formerly wife of her late son Thomas Richardson and now remarried, owed her £5, 'as by a pare of articles betwean her & me, with som others, it doth & may appear'. Thus legal instruments were employed to secure debts within the family. Elizabeth Smith (16), who was owed £40 by her son, Thomas Smith of Waldridge, directed the sum to be paid to her two daughters, thereby putting the debtor under some pressure. Debts within families may not always have been voluntarily contracted. Among family borrowers, expectations would be high and the sense of obligation to repay perhaps lower than usual.

Portions became involuntary loans. A child's allotment by a will, a portion, would be confided to some individual, usually of the family, to be held, and used, until the child came of age. Evidence of holding on to portions or delay in paying them appears frequently. At the time of his death in 1626, Thomas Burdon (38) was owed £9 by Cuthbert Maltby, as part of his wife's portion, which makes it seem that much time had elapsed since it was due. Thomas Bulbe of Hilton (27) took action in Chancery in 1615 to make John Brough pay his wife £6 13s 4d, which was part of her portion.[29] To avoid suits they had referred the case to five arbiters who decided £4 should be paid in two instalments of £2 but it was never paid. Bulbe died in 1617 which may mean that his wife was already of mature years and had not yet been paid her portion.

Houses
Not until the end of 1630 do references occur in wills and inventories to house building, ownership or letting. In December 1630 the Sunderland businessman Edward Lee (47) had four tenants including William Menorie, who paid him a rent of £1 per annum, and Maurice Prescott (62) who paid him £6 for a year-and-a-half rental for his house.[30] The first testaor to mention construction work taking place is cordwainer Thomas Dickenson (50). In March 1632 he bequeathed his daughter, Elizabeth, his house in Sunderland 'which he lately builded', while 'the rest of his howses in Sunderland' were left to his two-year-old son John. Thomas Watt, labourer (56), did not mention building work when he made his will in 1633, but he owned eight houses in addition to his own home. His married daughter Ann lived in one, William Watt lived in another, and Cuthbert Roxby (probably a member of his wife's family) paid him a yearly rent of £1 5s. In January 1640, the town councillor and mariner

29 The National Archives, Durh 7/13, Thomas Bulby vs. John Brough, 1615.
30 For Lee see Maureen M. Meikle and Christine M. Newman, *Sunderland and its Origins: Monks to Mariners*, Victoria County History (Chichester, 2007), pp. 104, 107, 109, 123.

Christopher Dickinson (71), stated in his will that he was having a house built but realised it might have to be sold to pay his debts. He also had houses rented to John Read, William Nicholson and Mr John Pemerton, with one having a lease valued at £13 6s 8d. James Ryder (70) referred specifically to rents arising out of houses as he made his bequests. Another town councillor, the blacksmith William Potts (79), was a multiple-property owner.

Rooms

Thirty of seventy-three inventories for the period 1601–50 gave the actual number and names of the rooms, together with a list of their contents. In the decade 1601–10, no more than three rooms per house were enumerated whereas in the following decades, 1611–20 and 1621–30, the number increased to between four and seven. During the last two decades, 1631–40 and 1641–50, five to ten rooms are commonly enumerated. Among his five rooms, Reginald Fawcett (73) possessed a 'flower chamber', which hints at the exquisite but was actually a room for storing flour.

In the early decade of 1601–10, the three rooms listed for Robert Watson, yeoman of Bishopwearmouth (3), were used as much for storage of farm implements and crops harvested, 'malt & pease in the chamber' together with 'parcels of stufe'. Only 11 per cent of his total wealth was in the form of household goods, 'two ammeries, a cawell, cheares, stowles, a table, brasse, pewter, & all other things plased in the forehowse' and 'a kettell and a copper pott'. In the last decade, Robert Bowes (55) of South Biddick's household goods were almost 25 per cent of his total wealth and he owned several books of devotion as well as '6 glasse plates and 2 cheanye dishes'.

The following list of named rooms, and the items they seem most likely to contain according to the inventories, may well overlook the rearrangement of goods for the convenience of the appraisers, but if people were still living in the house things were probably left much as they were.

Hall (twenty-four houses):
forms, chairs, cupboard, tables, stools, beds, bedclothes, feather-beds, blankets

Parlour (sixteen houses):
tables, forms, cushions, pewter ware, pairs of bars, salts, reckon crooks, racks, bedsteads, bedding and bed hangings, coverings

Chamber (twelve houses):
beds, sheets, napkins, a kettle, brass pots, candlesticks, salts, spoons, a chamber pot, pressers, tables, cupboards, bedsteads, purses and apparel, chests

Hall house (five houses):
cupboards, spences, pressers, bedsteads, tubs

Chamber within the hall (five houses):
beds, table, sheets, napkins, kettles, brass pots, candlesticks, salts, spoons, chamber pots, pressers, cupboards, bedsteads, purses and apparel, chests

Great chamber (four houses):
tables, forms, bedsteads, feather beds, mattresses, bolsters, cods, happins, coverlets, chests, linen sheets, table napkins, pressers, baskets, spinning wheels, ale stands, tubs

Middle chamber (three houses):
feather beds, chests, spinning wheels, buffet stools, chair, coverlets, blankets, woollen mattress

Milkehouse (4 houses):
butter, cheeses, trays, milk houles, skeels, butter kits, milk siles, leaven tubs, stands and barrels.

Buttery (3 houses):
kettles, trenchers, wooden bowls, trays, skeels, earthenware mugs, kettles, trenchers, wooden bowls, trays, skeels, earthen mugs

One may wonder at the scale of accommodation in Alice Hall's Bishopwearmouth house. In July 1603 it was presented at the archdeacon's court 'that she keepeth evil rule in her house & receiveth into her house men's sons, daughters & servants unlawfully whereby they provoked to lust, incontinent life & evil behaviour in the nighttime & upon Whitsonday last did carry & allure & receive to her house in time of divine service above forty persons that came not to the church'. Given the modest size of houses and their two or three rooms, she was perhaps hosting an outdoor event.[31]

---

31 Durham University Library, Special Collections, Archdeacon's Act Book, DDR/A/ACD/1/1, fo. 144.

Total value of household goods
expressed as a percentage of total wealth

	No. of rooms	Value of contents			Total wealth			% of total
1602 George Fell	2	£7	0s	0d	£83	11s	4d	8
1603 Robert Watson	3	£7	18s	8d	£228	4s	10d	3
1606 Edward Burne	3	£22	8s	0d	£35	11s	9d	63
1611 Nicholas Bryan	4	£32	15s	0d	£209	3s	11d	15
1612 Richard Bartram	5	£16	19s	4d	£20	3s	4d	84
1615 William Pattinson	5	£29	18s	6d	£195	16s	10d	15
1615 William Oliver	4	£7	11s	8d	£7	19s	10d	95
1617 George Shadforth	4	£62	14s	6d	£674	8s	8d	9
1623 Richard Morgan	2	£3	17s	8d	£52	4s	4d	6
1623 Agnes Thompson	1	£32	2s	10d	£54	18s	6d	59
1626 Edward Dearnley	3	£25	2s	9d	£36	6s	10d	69
1626 Charles Booth	4	£28	5s	0d	£80	9s	0d	35
1629 John Johnson	2	£17	8s	4d	£90	17s	8d	19
1630 Peter Marley	6	£166	13s	4d	£206	6s	2d	81
1631 Robert Scurfield	4	£18	9s	4d	£306	4s	4d	6
1631 Edward Lee	9	£165	4s	6d	£167	9s	6d	99
1632 Thomas Dickenson	5	£11	13s	1d	£24	15s	0d	46
1633 John Harrison	5	£60	14s	8d	£60	14s	8d	100
1635 Robert Bowes	10	£45	18s	6d	£174	5s	0d	26
1635 George Burgoyne	5	£31	8s	4d	£475	11s	2d	7
1635 Geo. Shepherdson	6	£15	13s	1d	£114	1s	5d	13
1635 Thomas Whitehead	3	£15	14s	10d	£15	14s	10d	100
1638 James Ryder	5	£68	9s	8d	£91	9s	4d	75
1639 Chris. Dickinson	4	£23	12s	10d	£61	16s	10d	38
1639 Reginald Fawcett	3	£82	17s	8d	£334	6s	0d	25
1639 John Hilton	3	£4	16s	0d	£153	8s	2d	3
1640 William Thompson	7	£50	16s	7d	£162	14s	9d	31
1642 William Potts	3	£63	9s	8d	£64	9s	8d	98
1644 William Freeman	5	£34	14s	2d	£171	18s	4d	20
1646 Samuel Smaithwaite	1	£15	9s	0d	£67	11s	0d	23

Total wealth ranges from £7 19s 10d to £674 8s 8d of which six totals are under £50, nine are under £100 but above £50 and thirteen are over £100.

Clothing

The common image of seventeenth-century clothing, derived from portraits and television productions showing the powerful and the wealthy, is of rich materials, highly decorated.[32] Very few portraits were made of working people, so that inventories are invaluable for their constant reference to the apparel of ordinary people. However, the references are usually disappointingly summary: the simple phrase 'purse and apparel' sufficed. Such dismissive usages could conceal a range of quality and quantity of clothing. The apparel of Edward Lee (47) was worth £15, and that of George Shadforth (28) £13 6s 8d; that of Thomas Roxby (31), Robert Huntley (32) and Edward Dearnley (35) was appraised at £1 10s each. Only a very few inventories appear to record entire wardrobes. Examples in this text are the inventories of well-to-do women, Elizabeth Smith (16) and Elizabeth Lee (48), while the very long inventory of Raph Wells (49) has randomly placed items, perhaps acquired by the same transaction as the 'pawned petticoat'. Thomas Bulbe (27) had three pair of breeches, two doublets, two jerkins, two pairs of stockings, one cloak and two hats, valued at £2 5s, which were probably an entire and, in contemporary terms, an ample wardrobe.

Elizabeth Smith's inventory lists sixteen smocks and four petticoats, four gowns, two waistcoats, three felt hats, twenty-two patclothes, fourteen 'crutches' (probably kerchiefs) and an old cloak. Also listed are eleven shirt bands and six crossclothes. Her four gowns were probably the fitted English gown with plain sleeves. Sleeve patterns varied: they were puffed, paned or dropped. Her two waistcoats were jackets which fitted the waist and were shaped over the hips. Only unmarried women could have unbound hair. Hair was usually plaited, and could then be covered by a cross-cloth: this was a triangular piece of linen of which the bias edge was laid on the forehead and the triangular point at the back. Over the cross-cloth a coif or hat was worn. It was considered unseemly for married women to expose their throats: partlets and neckchiefs were therefore used to fill the neckline. These could be the 'crutches' and 'patclothes' mentioned in her inventory. The edges of garments needed to be protected and strips of material were placed around hems and sleeves. This could be the function of her eleven shirt-bands and her two safeguards.

---

32 For example, see Aileen Ribeiro, *Fashion and Fiction: Dress in Art and Literature in Stuart England* (New Haven and London, 2005).

Most people's clothes were made for them. One or two inventories mention spinning wheels, but it is likely that the cloth to be made into clothing was mostly bought; yarn was spun and cloth woven by persons practised in the skills needed. The materials in question – various types of wool and linen – were for the most part produced in Britain; silk and cotton had to be imported, so that fabrics made from these threads were more expensive. Pure cotton fabrics called calicoes were woven in India and the East. They were reaching England by the 1600s, but were expensive. Europeans did spin cotton thread, but it was weak and so used as a weft thread in fustian. Raw cotton was used as a padding in, for example, doublets. Linen was mixed with wool to produce linsey-wolsey, which had a linen warp and a woollen weft and was loosely woven. William Pattinson (20) had 'two yeards of linsey-wolsey' and six yards of woollen cloth, together worth 12s in 1615. The majority of fabrics were not dyed. Though it is rare for colours to be specified, cloth dyed with natural dyes was likely to be white, black russet, green or blue. If they were dyed by professional dyers the chief colours were black, blue, white and red.[33]

During the sixteenth century fashions changed slowly and it was possible to hand down most clothes and goods. From 1604, the sumptuary laws prescribing the nature and quality of dress for the ranks of society were no longer being renewed. By the end of the seventeenth century, it was pointless for families to keep a wardrobe to be handed down because clothes grew out of date. However, bequests of clothing were also a way of being commemorated[34] and clothing was sometimes itemised in wills when a gift was made of it. Thus Percival Vipond (7) gave a doublet to his brother; a pair of breeches to Michael Watson and 'the rest of his apparell he gave to the poore woman that kept him' (probably Grace Tailor who is a witness to his will). Ralph Fletcher (12) gave to Richard Watson 'all my wearinge apparell or clothes which I used one my backe'. In his inventory it was valued at £1. These two references tell of the low quality of most apparel and explain its summary treatment in inventories. By contrast, cloth in the form of bedding is described in much detail in most inventories and was valued far more highly.

---

33 See Audry Barfoot, *Everyday Costume* (London, 1961) and N. Mikhaila nd J. Malcolm-Davies, *Tudor Tailor* (London, 2006).
34 Keith Thomas, *The Ends of Life* (Oxford, 2009), pp. 127, 137–8, 252.

Books

Books occur in only nine of the seventy-four inventories. In two, the references are to bibles, which may have been the only book in the households of William Pattinson (20) and George Shepherdson (60). In the opinion of Cressy, the possession of bibles is no indicator of literacy.[35] There was a greater quantity of devotional literature in the household of Robert Bowes (55), where two bibles, a psalm book and five prayer books are enumerated. Thomas Jordan of Ferryboat (6) and lessee of the same, had two book almeries valued at 2s and books valued at £1 17s 6d. Together with the quality and quantity of his furniture, these suggest a man of culture in a rather surprising location. His collection of books was the most highly valued in all the wills

Occupations

This collection of wills and inventories yields little direct evidence of the development of Sunderland before 1630. The most wealthy testators were still agriculturalists. Then in the period 1631–40 Edward Lee, gentleman, coal owner and merchant (47), rises to the top, and in the last twenty years, men of commerce and the coal trade are the most well-to-do. Across the whole period 1601–50, forty-five testators engaged in farming, ten in trade and crafts, and seven in maritime occupations. In addition there were seven gentlemen and a clerk in holy orders. The occupations of nine others are unknown. Of the women, one woman was described as a gentlewoman, eight as widows and one as a spinster. The gentlemen were mostly living by agricultural rents; the five, whose occupations cannot be determined with certainty, were very probably retired from farming. Henry Rand (18), who died far from Sunderland, at Cape Verde on an East Indiaman, and Bernard Crosby (89), who brought over 5 hundredweight of currants from Zante, seem exceptional in being of the new age of overseas expansion and trade. George Lilburne, who occurs variously as a witness, creditor or appraiser in a number of wills, is always described as a gentleman, but a hostile witness observed that 'his trades are infinite, chaundler, grocer, mercer, linen draper, freitore to ships, farmer of collieries, farmer of land, keelman, brewer, &c'.[36] However, farmers and

---

35 Cressy, *Literacy and the Social Order*, pp. 50–1.
36 Thomas Triplett to Edward Hyde, 15 January 1640/1, in Bodleian Library, Clarendon MSS 19, 1496. For Lilburne, see H. L. Robson, 'George Lilburne, Mayor

tradesmen were also deeply involved in a number of industries at this time and in the development of the river and the coal trade. Drury points to the inadequacies of self-description among persons in trade who may be using status or guild membership as, say, butchers or tanners, rather than the occupations they actively pursued.[37]

Farming

This traditional industry was itself undergoing a modernisation which played a vital part in supporting economic and demographic growth in this period.

Rank and status were closely linked with ownership and occupation of land. The title of gentleman normally implies possession of landed property, and the titles of yeoman, husbandman and labourer usually denote lesser landholders. The distinction between these last three titles is the subject of much discussion but documents in this collection show no clear divisions of wealth between husbandmen and yeomen. Thus George Fell, husbandman (2), left an estate valued at £289 9s 8d and Robert Watson, yeoman (3), left a gross amount of £255 18s. However, the evidence of this collection is that the term husbandman fell into disuse at the end of the sixteenth century. In the period 1549–1600 there are eleven husbandmen leaving estates and eight yeomen. In the period 1601–50, there is only one husbandman and he appears right at the beginning of the period, in 1602. In the period 1651–1700, there are thirty yeomen making wills but no husbandmen.[38] Labourers were undoubtedly low in the scale of wealth: the three who left estates between 1601 and 1650 were men of extremely modest means, including Thomas Watt (56) whose estate was valued at 17s.

Inventories offer more information on farming than on any other subject: livestock, crops and implements are enumerated and valued. Livestock is valued by generation and sex; thus among sheep there were tups, ewes, wethers, shearlings, hogs and lambs but there is no mention of breed. Pet names for oxen and cows sometimes appear in the wills when bequeathed: 'a black cowe called Allblack', although

of Sunderland', *Antiquities of Sunderland*, 22 (1960), pp. 86–132; Meikle and Newman, *Sunderland and Its Origins*, especially p. 108.

37 Drury, 'Inventories', pp. 185–6.

38 In Cressy's opinion, the term yeoman was used loosely in Durham diocese, *Literacy and the Social Order*, p. 125.

the wills for the period 1549–1601 yield better examples, 'ij° oxsen, the one bronne called Burnette, and one read looke haucked, called Proudlook', and 'on oxe called the Captaine'. Sheep are the most numerous of stock and probably were the most systematically reared. Two farmers may have been chiefly dairymen, Thomas Wilson (17) and Charles Booth (37), but cows are usually in twos or threes in the inventories and may also be the only beast possessed by poor or elderly householders. The travelling tradesman, the chapman William Oliver (21), had a cow at Bishopwearmouth and another at Morpeth.

The farming was predominantly mixed, with fairly equal values of crop and stock. Farmers who were exclusively stock-rearing or cultivating crops were unusual. Percival Vipond (7) and William Scurfield (8) are exceptions for they had only livestock. The great majority grew some wheat, oats, peas and some rye as staples. Perhaps because they were being carefully and thoroughly harvested, gleaning was forbidden in Bishopwearmouth fields.[39] In several cases the value of crops exceeds that of livestock, if not by much, but teams of draught oxen are commonly the most valuable of their stock and their value should be considered an adjunct of arable husbandry. Bulls were kept by several farmers whereas in other, poorer, localities only one farmer might keep a bull which he hired out, or farmers collectively might share a bull. Poultry or pullen, in small quantities, such as the 'tenn hennes and a cock, 3s 8d' belonging to Thomas Chilton (23), are to be found in many farmyards. He also had a 'turkey henn', which in 1615 was probably an American novelty, though one is found elsewhere in the county at that date. Geese and pigs were also kept in small quantities. Farming tools and equipment are also enumerated in detail in the inventories.

Bishopwearmouth leases and copyholds were the property of the bishop, who was inclined to leave things as they were, but Monkwearmouth belonged to the Durham dean and chapter, who were very ready to drive hard bargains. George Gray of Southwick and his friend Anthony Smith acquired a reputation as trouble-makers for their organisation of dean and chapter tenants to resist attempts to raise rents.[40] When the term of his lease expired, a tenant

---

39 Durham University Library, Special Collections, DHC1/1/75, fo. 264.
40 *Calendar of State Papers, Domestic, 1639–40* (London, 1877), pp. 499–500, 510, 538; *Privy Council Registers*, 12 vols (London, 1967–8), IX, p. 354; XII, p. 75.

probably faced demands for a higher lump sum for renewal and an increased rent. However, so long as his term continued he had the freedom of bequeathing his lease or of selling it. He could sub-let if he wished. A few of the testators had leases in other parishes: George Shadforth (28) has been noticed with his lease of Murton in Dalton-le-Dale; Mathew Bulmer (36) of Sunderland had an eleven-year lease of meadow ground in Weardale, up to fifty miles away, valued at £7, and other ground there too.

Leases of farms and other agricultural properties are mentioned and valued in several wills. Their values range from £5 to £600. Even the lower of these two values represents a very important and profitable asset. Most leases were for fixed terms of years and were probably valued for the years remaining. William Burdon (40) had the lease of three roods of arable in each of the three fields of Ryhope and pasture rights in the ox pasture and the fallows. His lease was valued at £5, having three years to run. No other statement of unexpired time for a local tenancy is to be found. George Shadforth (28) had leases of property at Tunstall in Bishopwearmouth and Murton in a neighbouring parish that were valued at £600 and £40 respectively. Unexpired time may account for some of the difference but it is as likely that, at a time of bitter dispute between landlords and tenants, the one is a lease recently altered to a commercial rate and the other still unimproved. The total values of the stock, crop and implements on the two farms, at £274 7s 0d and £204 13s 0d, differ by not enough to explain the disparity in the values of the leases.

Coal trade

In 1589 Robert Bowes of Barnes, grandfather of William Bowes (90), leased a strip of land along the river bank at Bishopwearmouth and invested in ten salt pans to produce salt by evaporation, using the low-grade coal from the pit he had sunk at Offerton.[41] By 1609, Wearmouth was shipping out 12,000 tons of coal a year compared with Newcastle's 250,000 tons, but by the 1680s its shipments were equivalent to a third of those of Newcastle.[42] The inventory of Edward Lee (47) of 1631 shows that he held the lease of a colliery at Urpeth and on Chester Moor. Lee would have shipped his coal to Sunderland but the colliery of Samuel Smaithwaite (82) of

---

41 Meikle and Newman, *Sunderland and Its Origins*, pp. 96–102.
42 Ibid., p. 119.

Monkwearmouth Hall, lay within the grounds and lordship of Plessey, in Northumberland, and would have been shipped out of the port of Blyth. Plessey Hall was owned by the Widdrington family who also owned Monkwearmouth Hall, the home of Smathwaite and his wife Mary, Robert Widdrington's daughter.[43] Ralph Wells (49), a very considerable tradesman of the town, in 1632 sold coal of different qualities from his Sunderland premises, some at 2s 9d per chalder and some at 9s 0d. In July 1644, when Parliament restored the Wearside collieries to its supporters, such as George Lilburne and George Gray, a maximum selling price was imposed of 14s per chaldron of 'Sunderland measure' for the best coal and 12s for the worst.

The parish registers show how numerous keelmen had become at the beginning of the century, in the period 1601–25. A total of thirty-six separate individuals in this occupation are named, chiefly as the fathers of children being baptised. That they were busy as well as numerous is implied in the presentment to the archdeacon's court in November 1603 of seven of them because 'they cast their keeles & rowe & worke on the Sabbaoth daies'.[44] The parish registers, in the same period, mention far fewer other trades: three carpenters and two pipers, four fishermen, amongst the old-established occupations, and two salters among the newer.

The sea

The port and industrial town of Sunderland was emerging from the two parishes, north and south of the River Wear, Monkwearmouth and Bishopwearmouth. The beginnings were modest. In 1559, Wearmouth was described as a creek of Newcastle, little haunted by merchants and merchandise, and in 1564, economic activity appears to have been only that associated with seven fishing cobles. Buildings and inhabitants were said to be in great decay. From the late sixteenth century, Sunderland and the Wear were sharing in the new prosperity of Newcastle and the River Tyne, due to the spectacular expansion of the coal trade and associated industries such as salt-making; the Wear was attracting entrepreneurs and capital discouraged or excluded by the monopoly conditions on the

---

43 Ibid., p. 104.
44 Durham University Library, Special Collections, Archdeacon's Act Book, DDR/A/ACD/1/1, fo. 158.

Tyne.[45] The wills and inventories which follow tell little of this story before 1650. Five testators have shares in ships and two testators only can be clearly identified as fishermen. The two mariners and the ship's carpenter do not appear before the end of the period. In the period 1601–50 only 8 per cent of the occupations of testators are connected with the sea. In the period 1651–1700 they amount to 26 per cent. Quays and shipyards had developed and Sunderland was a principal port of export. By the 1660s the collier fleets from Sunderland were a sight to behold.

Funerals
Funerals were an important opportunity to demonstrate status and worth. The dying were anxious that their funerals be done properly.[46] Percival Vipond (7) willed 'that he might be honestlie brought forthe'. Matthew Kelly, labourer (68), asked that £4 8s 'shall be imployed for my honest & credible bringinge forthe, at my buryall'. The location of burial was also relevant to upholding social distinctions.[47] The chancel was normally reserved to those of quality and to the clergy. William Bowes of Barnes (90) required 'my bodie … to be interred in the buriall place of my mother, within the chancell of the church of Bishop Wearmouth'. About twenty persons asked to be buried in the church and some specified the whereabouts. Thomas Chilton (23) wished 'my body to buried in the church of Munckewarmounth, in the north end of my oune stall under the great stone' and Anthony Hedley, labourer (39), 'my bodye to be buryed in the churche of Monnckwarmouthe, on the south syde of the fonte'. Henry Hilton (76), esquire, in requiring no excessive display, nonetheless proposed a very important location for himself: 'I bequeath my body to the earth to be decently interred, without all vaine pompe and glory, in some parte of the cathedral church of St Paule's, London, as neere the place where the tombe of Doctor Dunne is erected, as conveniently maybe, in such sort and manner as my executrix and executors hereafter named shall thinke fitt'. Moreover, he wanted 'a faire tombe like in fashion to the tombe of the said Doctor Dunn as may be'. Others of rank were more modest. John Johnson, rector of Bishopwearmouth (80), assigned his

---

45 Meikle and Newman, *Sunderland and its Origins*, p. 103.
46 Clare Gittings, *Death Burial and the Individual in Early Modern England* (London, 1984), p. 89.
47 Thomas, *Ends of Life*, p. 150.

body to the earth from whence it came; and Edward Lee, gentleman
(47), committed his body to the earth, to be buried in decent and
christianlike manner. Most people were buried in the churchyard,
though whether a burial was within the church or outside in the
churchyard seems not to have been a matter of great moment.
Gabriel Marley (9) asked to be buried in the churchyard, 'as near my
wife & children as possablie may be'. Mathew Bulmer (36) left the
choice of church or churchyard to the disposing of his executors.
George Wilson (86) gave his body to the earth whence it came and
desired it may be buried in the church or churchyard, 'wheather it
shall please my frinds'.

These requests must have covered a wide range of religious scru-
ples: bells were rung at the funerals of George Shepherdson (60),
William Pattinson (20) and Thomas Dickenson (50) but it was likely
that others would have declined such an accompaniment and other
features of the Roman Catholic past. Commemorative bequests, obits
and masses were no longer lawful. In only one case is a funeral
sermon mentioned in a funeral account, that for William Thompson
(75). But funerals still featured much that was traditional. The distribution of doles continued until a very late date,[48] although seen
more and more as encouraging improvidence. Examples such as that
of the churchwarden, John Johnson (42), who gave the poor of the
parish 16s to be bestowed upon them at his burial, have already been
discussed. Another pre-Reformation tradition, that of giving the best
beast of the deceased to the priest, was regulated in Henry VIII's
reign and commuted to a standard payment of 10s which frequently
appears in the inventories, named a mortuary.[49]

Gittings observes that as the religious element in the funeral ritual
diminished, the social aspects increased. An important part of the
funeral was the social gathering, the eating and the drinking, which
followed the burial not only of adults but children too, and even the
burials of paupers and poor travellers.[50] Funerals were among the
occasions 'enlivening' parochial life, along with weddings,
churchings and christenings.[51] Food was the most expensive single

48 Gittings, *Death, Burial and the Individual*, p. 161.
49 Christopher Hill, *Economic Problems of the Church* (Oxford, 1956), pp. 90,
171–2.
50 Gittings, *Death, Burial and the Individual*, pp. 57, 61, 80.
51 Thomas, *Ends of Life*, p. 220.

cost of a funeral and usually amounted to half the total spent.[52] At Sunderland funerals of the period it appears to have been even more than that. Expenses at the funeral of George Shepherdson (60) were £10 10s 4d, of which £7 11s 4d (72 per cent) was spent on food and drink. The funeral of William Thompson (75) cost £6 3s 8d, of which £4 18s 8d (69 per cent) was for food and drink. The complaint of a woman of Kent that in this district funerals were celebrated too well appears to be borne out. Jane Beale of Kent said her husband had died in 1645 'at or about Sunderland in the north parts of England' and that more was spent on his funeral 'than needed to have been if he had died at or near home'.[53]

Conclusion

This collection of wills and inventories provides only some of the evidence of Sunderland's growth. At the beginning of the period, it is more a record of the mortality of an older Sunderland. As activity at the port increased, Sunderland grew in size and importance. By the 1630s, the bishop granted the town a charter, in recognition of a new Sunderland. Of the first town council, two aldermen, Robert Bowes (55) and George Burgoyne (58), and five councillors, William Thompson (75), William Potts (79), William Freeman (81), William Huntley (84) and John Potts (87), left estates included in this collection.

In the last ten years of the period, the Civil Wars and the Revolution from 1640 severely disrupted the economic and social structures of Sunderland. Northumberland and Durham suffered a longer and possibly more destructive period of war than any other county: a one-year-long Scottish occupation during 1640 and 1641, a three-year royalist occupation from 1642 to 1644, then a period of fighting in Sunderland's vicinity from January to May 1644, followed by three years of Scottish occupation to 1647. However, it is evident from the wills and inventories of the following period, 1651 to 1675 and forward to 1700, that Sunderland's recovery was portentously rapid, as Macaulay observed of the growth of the wealth of the nation as a whole in that time.[54]

---

52 Gittings, *Death, Burial and the Individual*, p. 157.
53 Ibid., p. 103.
54 Thomas B. Macaulay, *The History of England*, 4 vols (London, 1864), I, p. 133.

LIST OF THE WILLS

WILLS AND INVENTORIES

1. George Middleton of Silksworth, Bishopwearmouth, 1601

[........] of perfect memorie [........] followinge, ffirst, I bequeath my soule in[........] creator and maker [........] to be saved by the precious death and bloodsheed of [........] scaviour onelie and by no other m[........] or waies. Secondly, I bequeath my bodie to be bur[........] Wermouth church. Item, I give unto my [........] & heire, George Middleton, my greate presse in the [........].[1] Item, I give unto my said sonne my bedsteade and table that stand in the parlor, after the death of Margarett, my wiffe. Item, I give unto Margaret Middleton, my welbeloved wiffe, all the reste of my goodes moveable and unmoveable, both within and without my house. I {bequeath} give my three farmes, which lye altogether on the southside of the towne and are nowe in the occupation of John Glen, William Wilkinson, Sampsone King, clerke, and Stephen Sommer, together with the pastures that are nowe in John Gibson's hands, to be solde to the best valewe for the paiemente of my debtes, and xl^{li} porcion apeece for fyve of my children, and if anie thinge remaine of the price of the said landes over and besides the paiements of my debtes and the aforesaide porcions of xl^{li} a peece for fyve of my children, namely, Addame Middleton, Elizabeth Middleton, Barbarie Middleton, Susan Middleton and Gilbert Middleton, my will and pleasure is that the same be given to the use of Margarett my wiffe. Item, I give unto the poore of the parishe xl^{s}, to be devided amongst them as my wiffe shall thinke good. Item, I give unto Barbarie Selbie and to Margarett Selbie, my daughter's children, three poundes to be equallie devided betwene them and to be paide when as my wiffe shall thinke best, either when they come to aige or before. Item, I give unto Cicilie Rose vj^{s}viij^{d} and a house to dwell in rente free att the appointemente of my wiffe and eldest sonne, so longe as she

---

1 The beginning of this document is badly torn.

lyves. Item, I give unto my sister Custannce Middleton, alias Custaunce,[2] half an acre of lande in everie feilde as they be nowe sett forth to be plowed by my sonne and heire for hir use duringe hir liffe. Item, my will is that my said sonne & heire shall leade forth hir compasse <unto> the said lande and carie home hir corne so longe as she shall live. Item, I give unto my said sister one cowe gate in the fallow more so long as she shall leve. Item, I give unto my said sister Custannce \alias Custaunce/ Middleton x[s] in money, to be paid unto hir by my wiffe, presently after my death. Item, I give to James Whithead, the sonne of Heughe Whithead, deceased, xx[s], to be paide by my wiffe when as she shall thinke good. Item, I give unto my goodsone Henry Wycliffe, sonne of John Wycliff of Ufferton, x[s] to be paid by my saide wiffe when he shalbe of lawfull yeares. Item, I give all the reste of my landes, besids those which I have appointed to be solde for such uses as are before specified, unto George Middleton, my sonne and heire, after the death of Margarett, my wiffe. And also I disire my said wiffe, as evere there was anie love betwene us, to stande good mother to my said sonne and quietlie to suffer him to mowe and occupie all such landes as are alreadie sett forth unto his use duringe her liffe. And also I charge my said sonne George Middleton, uppon my blessinge, to be a duetifull and a lovinge childe unto his said mother. Lastlie, I make this my last will & testamente, revokeinge thereby all other will or willes whatsoever as I have heretofore made, to what intent or purpose soever they have bene made. And I make Gilbert Middleton, my youngest sonne, and Elizabeth Middleton, my daughter, executors of this my last will and testamente. And I make Richard Middleton of Tunstall, gent., and Henry Whithead, gent., supervisors of this my said will, trustinge that they will see the same fulfilled and performed accordinge to the trewe intent and meaninge of the same. And in witnesse hereof, I have hereunto subscribed my hande, Januarie the xxviij[th], 1599, reade and subscribed in the presence of these witnesses, Robert Hutton, Robert Selbie, Henrie Whithead, Thomas Swalwell, Thomas Wilson, John Glen and Richard Clement, curate of Bishop-wermouth.

Source: DPR1/1/1601/H8/1, parchment 1m. Text is missing at the beginning of the will because of a tear.

---

2   This may be the intention of the clerk, but it is difficult to distinguish between the spelling of the two forms of 'Custannce' here and later.

2. George Fell of Ryhope, Bishopwearmouth, husbandman, 1602

In the name of God, Amen, the xth daye of July, in the yere of our Lorde God 1602, I, George ffell of Ryop in the parishe of Bishopwermoth in the countie of Durhame, husbandman, beinge sicke of bodye but of goode & perfitt remembrannce (thankes be unto almightie God), doe make my last will & testament in manner & forme followwinge. ffirst, I bequeathe my soule into the hands of almightie God, my maker & redeemer, and my bodye to be buried in the parishe churche of Bishopwermothe. Item, I give & bequeathe unto Anne, my wyfe, and George, my eldest sonne, the whole house & farment in Ryop which I nowe dwell in, and all the whole stynte upon the said farment, that is to saye, the corne, catle, gressinge, waynes, yockes, soomes & all other things belonging to the same howse or farment (excepting only suche parcels of howesalstuffe as I shall give in this my last will & testament); and the said howse & gooddes to be equallye devided betwyne Anne, my wyfe, and my said sonne George. Item, I give unto Anne, my wyfe, and George, my sonne, all my ffreeleage in Seahame, in as free & ample maner as I nowe holde it, with all appertinances therewith belonginge, to be equally devided betwyne them, and the longest lyver of them to have bothe the lease in Ryop and the freeholde in Seahame, and after their decesse, to the heires of my sonne George, and if he dye without issue then the same to remayne unto my sonne John & his heires, and if he dye without issue then to my sonne Edwarde & his heires, and if he dye without issue then to the right heires of me, the testator. Item, I give & bequeathe unto John, my sonne, all the right, tytle & interest which I nowe have, or by covenant I & my sonne John ar heareafter to have, in my neighbour John Burdon's ffarment, togeather with all the stinte I have upon the said farment, that is to saye, all the corne, catle & other thinges whatsoever I have in or upon the one moitie or halfe of the said farment at this presente. Item, I give & bequeathe unto Edwarde, my sonne, a yocke of stotts which ar at Broodebery, a graye fillye which is at Seahame and all the dettes, some or somes of money, whatsoever the be, which ar due & owinge unto me by any person or persons whatsoever at the makinge of this my last will and testament. And my will is that my executors shall recover my dettes at theire owen costes & charges for my said sonne Edwarde. Item, I give unto my three sonnes, George, John and Edwarde, six of my best brasse pottes, to either of them towe pottes, & the same to be equally devided betwyne them by the oversears of this my last will and testament. All the rest of my gooddes not given or bequeathed, I doe give & bequeathe unto Anne my wyfe and George, my sonne, and doe make them my full, whole & sole executors, and I doe ordayne & appoynte for my owversears of this my last will and testament, John Sotforthe of Mourton, Edwarde [........] and Robart ffoster of Ooldes.

Wittenesse [........]

of this [........]   Rich[........]

Rich[........]   Robar[........]

An inventory of the gooddes & chattles of George ffell of Ryop in the parishe of Bishopwermothe in the countie of Durhame, husbandman, deceased, praysed by us George Sheperdson, George Burdon, William Thomson and Anthoney Watson, the xviijth daye of Auguste in the yeare of our lord God 1602, and in the yeare of the raygne of our soveraigne ladye Queene Elizabethe, the xliiijth.

	£	s	d
Imprimis, six drafte oxen, price	14	0s	0d
Item, fyve key, one whye, three stottes & fower calves	10	0s	0d
Item, xxxviij yeowes, lammes & hoggets	6	6s	8d
Item, towe olde maires & one foale	3	0s	0d
Item, towe stottes at Broodeberye & a graye fillie	6	13s	4d
Item, an olde sowe		8s	0d
Item, the croppe of corne in the grounde	28	0s	0d
Item, the haye		13s	4d
Item, plowe geare & wayne geare, yocks & some	7	0s	0d
Item, the lease of the farment in Ryoppe	10	0s	0d
Item, the ingeare in the hale & chamber & within the hacke, with his apparrell & pullyne about the howse	7	0s	0d
Item, the haye in Seehame feilde		13s	4d
Some	43	14s	8d

The gooddes and stynte upon John Burdon's farment

	£	s	d
Imprimis, six oxen, the price	10	0s	0d
Item, three key & a stotte	4	0s	0d
Item, an olde horse & a maire	2	0s	0d
Item, the crooppe of corne upon John Burdon's ffarment	23	0s	0d
Item, the haye		6s	8d
Some	39	6s	8d

The whole some of the dettes and gooddes specified in the
inventorye is cclxxxix^{li} ix^s viij^d

George Sheporson [*full name signed*]
George Burdon [*marked with a symbol*]
Wi[lliam] Tomson [*marked with a symbol*]
[Anthony] Watson [*marked with a symbol*]

Dettes owynge to George ffell at the makinge of this his will as
followethe,

Robart Dale, sonne of George Dale of Dawton	13	0s	0d
Adame Holmes of Wermothe	13	13s	4d
William Hocheson of Whitborne	13	15s	0d
Widoe Partis of Ryop	5	6s	0d
Robart Burdon of Ryop	7	12s	4d
James Bee of Isingeton	3	10s	0d
Mr Walker of Litlethorpe	4	15s	0d
Thomas Plunton of Eastbolden	4	12s	0d
Robart M[ar]shall of Coldhaselton	3	10s	0d
William Walker of Silkesworthe	2	17s	0d
William Walker more for a bole of corne which Robarte Morye hade	1	4s	0d
John Browen of Great Chilton	1	0s	0d
William Pottes of Gatesheade	4	0s	0d
Mr Richarde Midleton of Tunstall	9	0s	0d
Robert Watson of Wermothe	3	0s	0d
Thomas Oxnarde of Mounton	1	9s	0d
John Roxbie of Hilton	1	0s	0d
Dame Dawson of ffromygate in Durhame	1	1s	0d
William Jervice of Clapworthe	2	0s	0d
Robart Fowell of Durhame, bocher	2	5s	0d
William Smithe of Wermothe	7	0s	0d
Richarde Smithe of Hartlepoole		11s	0d
Diglis the smithe of the Pans		3s	4d
Richarde Youne of Seahame		16s	0d
Widoe Leddall of Seahame		18s	6d
George Wardon of Ishingeton & odde money	5	0s	0d
Edwarde Harper of Westowe	5	6s	8d
James Hazin of Ishington		9s	0d
Bell Pithie of Westboldon, wydoe	2	0s	0d
Sr Thomas Easterbie of Seaham, vicar	1	15s	0d
Raphe Moysier of Ryop	2	0s	0d

Rowelande Chamer of Seahame	1	4s	0d
John Rowesbie of Sunderlande		10s	8d
Robart Bee of Sunderlande	1	12s	0d
Robart Curtice of Seaham [........]	2	13s	4d
[Mo]re Robart Curtice of Seaham for [........]	1	1s	4d
[........]ilton of Seaham for a yew [........]			
[........] Warde of Sunderla[........]		7s	0d
[........]echild [of Sun]derland [........]		6s	6d
[........]day [........]		9s	4d
[........]		10s	0d
[........]³		23s	0d

Source: DPR1/1/1602/F1/1–3, paper 3ff.

3. Robert Watson of Bishopwearmouth, yeoman, 1603

Jn the name of God, amen, I, Robart Watson of Bushopwermoth, sicke in body but of goode and perfitt rememberance, do make this my last will & testament, the iiij[th] day of Maye, 1603, in maner and forme followinge. ffirst, I committe my soule into the hands of almightie God, my maker, trustinge assuredly to be saved by the death & passion of our lorde Jesus Christ, And my body to the earth whence it came. Item, I give to the poore of Bishopwermoth parishe xx[s]. Item, I give to every one of my bretheren's children one ewe & one lambe. Item, I give & bequeath unto my brother Antoney Watson the lease of my tenement and ffarmeholde in Ryop. Item, I give unto my brother William Watson all my parte of corne nowe sowen & growinge on William Smith's farme at half parte. Item I give & bequeath to my sister Isabell Watson one browen why nowe pasturinge on Ryop Moore. And further my will is that my said sister shall have a newe cupborde made her at the cost of my executor of such woode as I have about the howse. Item, I give to my brother George Watson my best branded cowe. Item, I give to John Rokesby of Sunderlande his towe daughters, to either of them, one yewe and one lambe. All the rest of my goodes & chattles, my debte, legacies & funerall expences payd & discharged, I give to my brother

---

3 Names of witnesses to the will, and the end of the inventory, are badly damaged by a tear.

Antonye Watson, whome I make the only executor of this my last will and testament. Witnesses hereof
Christopher Wharton, William Smith, John Tomson, Robert Chilton of Newebotle [*no signatures or marks*]
Richarde Clement [*full name signed*]

An inventorye of the goodes of Robart Watson of Bishopwermothe in the countie of Durhame, yeomann, who deceased the vj[th] daye of Maie, anno Domini 1603, and in the first yere of the raigne of our dreade soveraigne lorde Kinge James, praysed by George Sheperdson, John Sheperdsonn, Nicholas Briant and George Borden as followeth.

The inventory of his goodds in Ryoppe

Imprimis, seven oxen att the price of	13	0s	0d
Item, one stotte		18s	0d
Item, a browen whye given to Isabell Watsonn	1	0s	0d
Item, a horse, a maier & a fillye	3	13s	4d
Item, xiiij sheepe prised att	3	5s	4d
Item, the wheat and pease in the barne and garthe	2	13s	4d
Item, the whole croppe of his corne now growinge upon the grounde	28	0s	0d
Item, one corne arke, with the lockes and keaies		15s	0d
Item, an oxe harrowe and a horse harrowe		11s	0d
Item, a longe waine, towe old shortte weaines, a plowe and a plowe beame	1	8s	0d
Item, iiij soomes, iiij yockes, ij shackels, a paire of horsegeare furneshed, a masterswingletre & a horse some, ij paire of linne pinnes, ij coulters & a socke		15s	0d
Item, a paire of waine ropes, muckforkes, spades and shoveles		2s	4d
Item, a boue and a quiver of showteinge shaftes		4s	0d
Item, a peare of bounden whelles, a peare of stinges, an old coope waine & wheeles, and an old horse harrowe which was parcell of Thomas Aiers' portione given by legacie as appearethe by his father's will	3	0s	0d
Item, the lease of the ffarmett in Ryoppe	15	0s	0d

Some lxxiiij[li] v[s] iiij[d]

An inventorye of his goodes in Warmouthe

Item	£	s	d
Item, six oxen and a branded stotte	17	6s	0d
Item, two oxen which Thomas Roxbie haith for his legacie which was oweinge unto him	6	0s	0d
Item, a branded cowe given to George Wilsonn	1	13s	4d
Item, six kyen, thre calves	12	0s	0d
Item, two calves of a yeare olde	1	0s	0d
Item, two stagges and a fole of a yeare olde	4	6s	8d
Item, one baie maire which Thomas Roxbie haith for his legacie	2	13s	4d
Item, two maires and a nagge	6	0s	0d
Item, viij gelde sheappe, price	1	16s	8d
Item, xxiiij ewes & a suckeinge lambe	6	0s	0d
Item, xviij lambes	2	0s	0d
Item, two sowes, price		14s	0d
Item, the wheatte in the garthe	7	0s	0d
Item, the pease in the barne & garth	2	13s	4d
Item, all the corne upon the grounde belonginge to the seate howse & the fyne of the parsonage lande[4]	48	0s	0d
Item, the corne of towe acres of lande which he had to havers with William Smithe	4	0s	0d
Item, of haye & pastors in the howsefielde	3	0s	0d
Item, ij longweines & iij coopeweines with linne pinnes	2	10s	0d
Item, two oxe harrowes and one horse harrowe		15s	0d
Item, five ploues		8s	4d
Item, six soomes		12s	0d
Item, two curters and three sockes		5s	6d
Item, thre boltes and thre shakells		2s	4d
Item, thre old axes		1s	4d
Item, fyve muckforkes		3s	0d
Item, six corneforkes & two spaides		2s	0d
Item, two paire of waine ropes, iij teddars		3s	0d
Item, six yeockes		4s	0d
Item, ij paire of horsegeare, with all furniture		2s	8d
Item, ij paire of longe waine blaides		12s	0d
Item, all woode wrought and unwrought about the howse	1	6s	8d

---

4 This and the following three items are taken from the copy of the damaged original.

Item, the haye in the barne		6s	8d
Item, the fyrecoles		2s	0d
Item, two ammeries, a cawell, cheares, stowles, a table, brasse, pewter, & all other things placed in the forehowse	1	10s	0d
Item, a kettell and a copper pott		13s	4d
Item, a paire of waineblaides, vij bordes and tenn railes lyinge now in the staggarthe		6s	8d
Item, the malt and pease in the chameber	1	16s	0d
Item, parcells of stufe in the chameber		13s	4d
Item, his apparell	1	0s	0d
Item, a coke and thre henes		1s	0d
Item, thre sackes and ij pookes		3s	4d
Item, ploughes, waines, yockes, somes and other instruments of husbandrye att the wido Aire's house of Tunstall, a legacie given to her sonne Thomas Aire	3	5s	4d

Some cliij^{li} xix^s vj^d

Debtes which others owe to the testator

Imprinis, William Smyth of Warmothe	1	9s	0d
Item, Robart Burden of Warmothe		8s	0d
Item, Alice Pasmore of Warmothe		4s	0d
Item, Mr William Whiteheade	20	0s	0d
Item, Mr George Whiteheade	2	0s	0d
Item, Christofer Richardsonn	1	13s	4d
Item, Robarte Gennisyn of Sunderlande		12s	0d
Item, Richarde Bartonn		11s	8d
Item, William Davie of Sunderland		16s	0d
Som	27	14s	0d

Somma totalis cclv^{li} xviij^s x^d

Debts owinge by the saide testator as followeth

Imprimis, to my brother Anthonye Watsonn	18	18s	4d
Item, to Robarte Maven	2	10s	0d
Item, to Raphe Johnsonn	3	8s	0d
Item, to thexecutors of George Fell late of Riop	3	0s	0d
Item, to George Bee of Ryop	3	0s	0d
Item, to William Burdonn	2	13s	4d
Item, to thexecutors of Robarte Parsmoure late of Ryope	2	0s	0d
and a bushell of pease		3s	4d

Item, to William Watsonn my brother I owe upon an accounte which I doe refere to his owen reckninge and concience	16	6s	10d
Item, to John Sheperdson thelder of Warmoth	1	11s	0d
Item, to John Sharpe		3s	4d
Item, to my syster Isabell Watsonn as doth appeare by a bill of my hande	12	0s	0d
Item, I owe to my cosinge Thomas Aire his childe's portion, which appeareth by his father's will and testament, the some of		[no entry]	
Item, to George Burdon of Ryop			9d
Item, to Thomas Kinge for strawe		6s	0d
Item, to the stewarde of the parsonage for strawe		3s	4d
Item, to Raphe Reade of Silkefourth	1	0s	0d
Item, to my sister Isabell of lent money	1	8s	0d
Item, I owe my syster for weiges	1	10s	0d
Item, to Richarde Flecher of Durhame		4s	4d
Item, to the poore people[5]			
Item, his ffunerall expenses			
Item, for provinge the will			
Item, for a mortuarie and lairstall			
Item, to Mr Clement for charges about the will			
Item, the rent of his ffarme			

Summa debitorum lxxviij^{li} xvij^s iij^d

Summa totalis debitis deductis clxxvij^{li} j^s vij^d

Source: DPR1/1/1603/W5/1, 4–5, 8, paper 3ff., parchment 1m.

4. Edward Burne of Sunderland, yeoman, 1606

The 20th day of Aprell, 1606

In the name of God, amen, I, Edward Burne of Sunderland in the contey of Durham, yeoman, being in good & perfyt memory, do mak this my last will & testament \in maner & forme followinge/. ffyrst, I bequayth my sowll unto almighty God, my savauer & redeemer, and my bodey to be buryed whereever yt shall please Margret, my wyff, \in the churche of Warmouth/ whom I make myne executrix

---

5 This and the following entries are not found in the paper copy and are in a different hand.

ffully & wholy of all my goods & cattels movabell & unmovonbill, to use at her will & pleasure and she to deaill with my kynred, John Hall & Marke Watson, acordyng as thay do behave them towards her, they beyng my neaves. In wytnese wheareof, I have mayd this my will & therto have set to my hand, [*marked with a scratch*]
In the presence of William Hutton and Mathew Burnne
Thies words interlined was done in the presents of us who is underwryten
Mathew Burn, the mark of [*marked with a symbol*]
William Hutton [*full name signed*]
Robart Goodchilde, the mark of [*marked with a symbol*]

An inventorye of such goods and cattells as did beelonge unto Edward Burne late of Sunderland, deceassed, & praysed this present 26th Junij, 1606, *videlicet*:

Inprimis, ij kyne praysed att	4	0s	0d
Item, one yonge heyffer praysed att	1	0s	0d
Item, one browne mayre praysed att	2	0s	0d
Item, one stand bed & a trindle bed in the lowe parler		10s	0d
Item, one table & iij formes in the same parler		10s	0d
Item, one carpett cloth for the same table in the parler		4s	0d
Item, iiij payre of lynn sheetts & vj payre of pyllew-beers	2	0s	0d
Item, vj payre of straken shetts, iij pyllowbearers	1	10s	0d
Item, iiij dussen napkins		6s	0d
Item, iiij table clothes		4s	0d
Item, ij ffether bedds with ij mattresses, ij coverings, ij blanketts, ij happyngs, ij boulsters & ij pillowes, with bedsted & coverings	3	13s	4d
Item, one bedsted, with a mattrisse, a boulster, ij coverings, one happyng, tow blanketts	1	10s	0d
Item, one presse, with lockes and keyes to it		10s	0d
Item, one counter		3s	4d
Item, one tubb, with tow formes		8s	8d
Item, one dance chest		4s	0d
Item, iiij fur chestes		6s	0d
Item, one tubb, ij formes & thre chayres in the hall		13s	4d
Item, one cubbartt in the hall howse		8s	0d
Item, tow spences in the hall howse		5s	0d
Item, xxiiij peeces of pewter	1	10s	0d
Item, iij candelsticks, iij saltes, ij chamer potts		4s	0d

Item, iij small brasse pottes		12s	0d
Item, towe iron pottes		2s	0d
Item, thre spytts, a payre of racketts, one dripping pann, a \<grid\> iron, iij racking crokes, a payre of tonges & a porr		10s	0d
Item, tow kettells of brasse		10s	0d
Item, tow guyl fatts, a maskinge fatt, a stonne trowe		13s	4d
Item, a maulte arke		4s	0d
Item, iiij barrells and a ganntree		6s	8d
Item, iij quarters of a fyve man botte, with ankers, masks, shott sayles & oares	7	0s	0d
Item, vij heringe nettes ffor fyshinge	1	0s	0d
Item, xj peec of tramell lynes	1	2s	0d
Item, vj peac of halver ffor the sayd bott		12s	0d

Somma £35 11s 9d

Debts oweinge unto the sayd Edward Burne as followeth

Inprimis, William Shipperson of Sunderland	2	0s	0d
Item, Rychartt Shipperson of Sunderland	3	0s	0d
Item, Mr Gilford Lawson of Washington	10	0s	0d
Item, Heugh Byrd & Rychartt Branlynge	3	8s	10d
Item, William Walton	2	0s	0d
Item, William Whytthed of Brighowse	4	6s	8d
Item, Robertt Jennings of Sunderland	1	2s	6d
Item, Raphe Hylton		16s	0d
James Lyell of Barmston	1	10s	0d
Item, William Jarvice of Lynn	1	13s	0d
Item, Mr Henry Parkinson	5	0s	0d

Som of the debtes £34 0s 7d

The totull of all added together is	69	12s	4d

Per me Arthere Manninge [*full name signed*]
Robertt Barkus [*full name signed*]
Signum Robert Goodchild [*signed with a symbol different from that on the will*]
Signum Robert Bee [*marked with capital initials R B*]

Source: DPR1/1/B14/1–2, paper 3ff.

5. Anthony Gefferson of Ryhope, Bishopwearmouth, 1606

July 23th, 1604

Anthonie Gefferson of Ryop, the day and yere above written, lijnge in a coove in the feild sicke in the visitation, uttered these wordes followinge (being questioned and demannded by us, whose names ar underwritten) whoe should have his portion of goods if he died. The poore shall have xxx^s; William Pattison's children xx^s a peece; Anthonie Watson's children xv^s a peece; Margery Nicholson of Hilton xx^s; John Pattison x^s; Christopher Pattison x^s; Andrewe Pattison v^s; the rest my brother Robart and his w[........]^6

Richarde Clement
Raphe Moyser
John Ranson

July 25th, 1604

Twoe dayes after, the foresaid persons cominge to visit him againe and to gather somethinge more perfitly from him, did put him in mynde of his former words which he then denied, sainge 'Nor fyve shillings apeece for a remembrance, my brother shall have the rest'. Then Mr Clement willed him to give somewhat more to his uncle Christopher for he was but a poore man, to whome he answered, 'Take it you all and give it where yo[u] will', which were the last words that he used touchinge the premisses.

Source: DPR1/1/1606/J2/1, paper 1f.

6. Thomas Jordan of Barnes Ferry or Ferryboat, 1606

May it please your worship to understande that we, Elizabeth Jordan, late wife of Thomas Jordan, late deceased intestate, and John Jordan, sonne of the said Thomas, doe heerby utterlie renownce, forsake and quite claime all such right and propertie as we or either of us have or cann pretende in or unto all or any the goods, chattles and other rightes of the said Thomas Jordan, intestate, ffor and in consideracion of certaine bondes and articles made betweene the said intestate in his lifetyme and ffrancis Jordane, eldest sonne of the said Thomas, which the said ffrancis, since his death, haith

---

6   Three words are cropped.

undertaken to ratifie and confirme, and with which we hold ourselves sufficientlie satisfied, advanced and preferred.

And, theirfore our desier is that the sole and proper administracion of the said interstate's goodes, chattles and other rights whatsoever may be (att your worship godlie discretion) committed solelie and properlie unto the said ffrancis, which heerby we shall and will seeme (soe much as in us is) to ratifie and confirme. Wittnes our handes this seconde of Januarie, anno Domini 1606.

The signe or marke of
Elizabeth Jordan [*marked with a scratch*]
Jo[hn] Jordan [*marked with a cross*]

An inventorie of all the goodes and chattles, moveable and unmoveable, [of Thomas Jordan][7] late of Barnes fferry al[ia]s fferryboate, deceased, praised the nenith daye of September in the fowerth yeare of the reigne of our sovereigne lord James, by the grace of God, of England, ffrannce and Irelande, kinge, defender of the faith &c., and of Scotelande, the ffortith, by John Shepperdsone, Thomas Smithe, Robarte Guy and William Guye

Inprimis, att Boldon, one cowe, one oxe and fifteene young beastes, praised to	20	0s	0d
Item, seven calves	3	10s	0d
Item, a baye mare and a baye fillye	2	13s	4d
Item, fower sowmes, one coulter, one socke & a shakle		10s	0d
Item, two cowpwaines, one paire of wheales, a longewaine with axellnailles, hoopes.and wheales, one paire of stinges, one axeltree, two ploughes, twoe yokes, half a dozen bowes, one oxe harrowe and one horse harrow	2	13s	4d
Item, haye in the house and yarde	5	0s	0d
Item, one arke		13s	4d
Item, wheate and peaze now groweing, with all the other corne their	15	0s	0d
Item, att the fferrye boate, twelve kyne	27	0s	0d
Item, the reversion of the boate lease, beinge halfe a yeare	3	10s	0d

---

7 Omitted from the manuscript (MS).

Item, three brasse potts, one iron pott, two kettles and fower panns	2	10s	0d
Item, eleven dublers, five pottin dishes, fower sawcers, two tunnes with a cover, five candlesticks, a latyne ladle, a laver and a basen of brasse	1	6s	8d
Item, a longe table with a frame, a cupborde, a forme and a cheasetroughe	1	5s	4d
Item, two booke almeries		2s	0d
Item, a gunn, a reckon crook, a chimney and two spitts		12s	0d
Item, two arkes		15s	0d
Item, two almeries	1	0s	0d
Item, one bedsteade with hangeings	1	0s	0d
Item, five double coverietts and one single coverlett	3	0s	0d
Item, five happings		10s	0d
Item, neine paire of lynneing and harden sheates	3	0s	0d
Item, two boardecloathes		4s	8d
Item, two lynneing towels		5s	8d
Item, two pillowbers		2s	0d
Item, five napkinns and one diaper napkin		2s	3d
Item, haye att the boate	4	10s	0d
Item, two fetherbedds and two boulsters	2	0s	0d
Item, one paire of double and one paire of single blanketts		6s	0d
Item, one other bolster and one codd		3s	0d
Item, a black mare	1	10s	0d
Item, a beehive		5s	0d
Item, thirtie three cheases	1	0s	0d
Item, eight stoone of butter	1	4s	0d
Item, fower axes, one addes, three wimbles with other iron stuffe and a greate sledge or hammer with a spade and a shovell		16s	0d
Item, his apparell with other his furniture	3	6s	8d
Item, two oake trees, one ould footeboate, one longe ladder, a paire of cowpewaine soales and other woode		7s	8d
Item, three forkes			6d
Item, three swine		15s	0d
Item, three chistes, one cownter and one cawell		5s	0d
Item, two rideing saddles		2s	0d
Item, one seinge glasse			4d
Item, fower yardes of white cloathe		4s	0d
Item, a chaire and two cushones		2s	6d

Item, tubbs, barrels, skeales, cheasvatts, milke bowles			
and syles	1	0s	0d
Item, one lute		5s	0d
Item, fower silver spoones, with other ringes and jewels		16s	0d
Item, milne pickes and a givelack		2s	6d
Item, a lease of the fowerth parte of Biddick house till			
May daie next	2	5s	0d
Item, his bookes	1	17s	6d
Item, tinn spoones			6d
Item, a spineing wheale, three paire of cardes, a flaskett,			
fower pannyers or maundes and a glasse caise		3s	4d
Item, sacks, poakes, one wallet, three hand towels and			
one stoone of towe		3s	4d
Item, the lease of the mylne	6	13s	4d

Summa bonorum cxxvj^{li} ix^{s} xj^{d}

Debtes oweinge to the said Thomas Jordane att his death

Inprimis, owen to him by Mary Lumley	25	0s	4d
Item, for jeaste att Boldon	1	4s	8d
Item, for his cottagers rents their		5s	4d
Item, for rent of a fowerth parte of Biddick house	2	5s	0d

Summa debitorum xxviij^{li} xv^{s} iiij^{d}

Debtes which he did owe att the tyme of his death

Imprimis, for hay att ffoorde	4	0s	0d
Item, for jeaste att ffoorde	1	4s	0d
Item, for the fferrieboate rent	3	10s	0d
Item, for the milne rent		18s	0d
Item, for the rent of Boldon and Biddick house		19s	11d
Item, for a rent for a fourth part of Biddick house	1	5s	0d
Item, for the hinde and servants wages	1	0s	0d
Item, for the hind and smithe's waiges at Boldon		2s	6d
Item, to Elizabeth Jordan, his late wife, due by			
a bonde	20	0s	0d
Item, for funerall expences and to the poore	4	14s	2d
Item, for his mortuarie and larestall		16s	8d
Item, to the said Elizabeth, his late wife	51	0s	0d

Summa lxxxix^{li} x^{s} iij^{d}

Source: DPR1/1/1603/J3/1–3, paper 4ff., inventory sewn.

7. Percival Vipond of Monkwearmouth, 1607

A note of the last will of Percey Veponte, late of the parish of Monnckwermouth, disceased, which he made the xxjxth of Julie last, anno Domini 1607, in the presence of these wittnesses whose names are herunto subscribed, disposinge his goods nuncupativelie, by word of mouth, as ffolloweth. ffirst, he willed that he might be honestlie brought forthe & that the money which he had in his chest, *videlicet* 3ˢ, vˢ which was owinge to him by Rychard Sparrow, one cowe which he had at Hilton, & xxvjjˢ which was owinge to him by Richard Walton of Wellgill in Alstonmor, should be all bestowed upon the poore of the parishe of Monckwearmouth, his funerall charges & other duties deduckted out of it & discharged. Item, his will was that Raph Lumley, or Mychaell Lumley, his sonne, should have the said cow if it pleased them for xxvjˢ viijᵈ & if they did refuse hir at that price then she was to be sold to whome as would give most for hir. Item, the foresaid xxvijˢ which was owing him by 2° men of Alstonmore for sheepe, he willed that Gabriel Marley should demand the same & receive it when the daies of payment comes. Item, he gave a dublett to his brother; a payre of breeches to Mychaell Wattson & the rest of his apparell he gave to the poore woman that kept him. Also his will was that all the goodes which was in his brother's hands should rest in his said brother's hands & therefore he would dispose no parte of it to any other.

Wittnesses herof

Robert Berleyⁱᵘʳᵃᵗᵘˢ, his mark [*marked with a symbol*]
Rychard Sparrowⁱᵘʳᵃᵗᵘˢ, his mark [*marked with a rough circle*]
{Grace Taler}
Grace Taler, mark [*marked with two parallel diagonal strokes*]

Administratio bonorum &c. data Richardo Vepont, fratri dicti defuncti [*seven or eight illegible words*]. Obligatur de {soluend'} distribuend' bona &c. secundum arbitracione dicti judicis (solutis debitis et legatis etc.)

An inventorie of all the goods and chattalls of Percivell Vepont, late of the parish of Monkwearmouth, deceased, praised and valewed by iiijᵒʳ honest men the xxvjᵗʰ daie of August, 1607, videlicet Richard Teasdaill, George Richeson, Thomas Hutcheson and Richard Lee as followeth

Inprimis, v kyen and two calves	5	5s	0d
Item, xxx olde sheepe	4	13s	0d
Item, xv lambes	1	5s	0d
Summa bonorum £11 4s 0d			

Debtes owinge to the deceased

Inprimis, Richard Teasdaill for one cowe	1	0s	0d
Item, Thomas Richeson for v yowes		14s	2d
Item, George Walton of Nenthall		13s	0d
Item, Anthonie Walton of Nenthall		18s	8d
Item, Richard Walton of Welgill	1	7s	0d
Summa debitorum £4 12s 10d			

Summa totalis bonorum et debitorum £15 16s l0d

Signum Richardi Vepont [*marked with a symbol*]

More goodes and debtes bestowed at the testator's ffunerall

Item, one cowe price	1	2s	0d
Item, in his purse		3s	0d
Item, owing by Richard Sparrow		5s	0d
[*A marginal note beside his last item says* 'paid']			
Some £1 10s 0d			

Source: DPR1/1/1607/V2/1–2, paper 2ff.

8. William Scurfield of Grindon, Bishopwearmouth, yeoman, 1609

In the name of God, amen, the xxvth daye of {July} November, 1607, I, William Scurffeild of Grindon in the countie of Durham, yeoman, being sicke in body but perfitt in remembrance, thanks be to God, maiketh this my last will and testament in manner and forme followinge; ffirst, I give and bequieth my soule into the hands of almightie God throughe Jesus Christ, our lord, by whose death and passion, I trust to be saved; and my body to be buried in the church or churchyeard of Bushoppwarmouth. ffirst, I give and bequieth unto the poore of the parishe which are most nedful at the daye of my death or buriall xx^s. Item, I give and bequieth unto my sonn in lawe James ffarrowe, and to Allice, his wiffe, my doughter, and theire children, the some of five pounds over and above their

porcion which I have already paid to the said James & Allice, of which v^li James ffarrowe is oweing xx^s. I am contented to forgive him x^s thereof, so my will is he allowe that xxs which he is oweing me. I will that the other iiij^li be paid to them or wether of them that shalbe liveing at a yere's end after my death. Item, whereas my sonne in lawe John Thompson is oweing me fiftie shillings I forgive him x^s thereof; and I give to him and his wiffe Ellen and theire children the some of five pounds, videlicet xls which he is oweing and iij^li more be paid to him or his wife or children two yeres after my death. Item, I give and bequieth unto my sonne Rowland Scurffeild five pounds to be paid three yeares after my death. Item, I give and bequieth unto the laite children of John Dixson, that is to say Elizabeth, Marye, Jane & Issabell, to every one of them, xxs a peece. All the rest of my goods, my debts, legac[ie]s & funerall expenc[e]s dischardged, I give unto my sonn Robert Scurffeild, whome I maike my full and sole executor of this my last will and testament. In witness whereof I have hereunto sett my hand and seale the daye and yere abovesaid, in the presence of these witnesses
William Scurffeild, marke [*marked with a symbol*] [*seal*]
Peter Dentonn [*full name signed*]
Robert Grey [*full name signed*]
Thomas Maultland [*full name signed*]
William Cooke, marke [*marked with a symbol*]

An inventory of the goods and chattells of William Scurfeild, laite of Grindon, deceased, and praised by Peter Denton, Robert Guy, William Cooke and James ffarrowe as followeth

Imprimis, his apperell and his bedd he lay in	4	0s	0d
Item, thre kyne and two quyes	11	0s	0d
Item, xxx^o ewes and other shepe	9	0s	0d
Item, one maire which he raid upon	4	0s	0d
Soma xxvij^li			

Source: DPR1/1/1609/S3/1–2, paper 2ff., and seal. A summary of the will, without the inventory, is printed in WI Durham, pp. 24–5.

9. Gabriel Marley of Hilton, Monkwearmouth, 1609

The 20 of June, anno Domini 1609

In the name of God, amen, I, Gabrell Marley of Hyltone in the parish of Munkewearmouth, do maik this my last will and testament in manner & form following. Firste, I bequeth my soulle unto almightie God, trusting to be saved by his mercie, through the merits of his sone, Jessus Christ, my savioure and redemer, and my body to bee buried in my parish church yeard as near my wife & children as possablie may be. Item, I gyve to the pore of our parish x^s to be bestowed imediatly after my death by the curate & church wardenes. Item, I gyve to my mother Elizabeth Marley a cowe, to choise wher she will among them I have, and the begger of two sowes which ar about my house. Item, I gyve to my brother Samuell Marley all my apparell, exceipt my grene cloke which I gyve unto my brother Peter Marley upon conditione that he shall gyve my syster Alse Marley xx^s. Item, I gyve my brother Samuell al my worke gear in my shope, exceipt my great stedye and instead of that, I gyve hime the stedye at Lamsley, which was my father's, and fortie shillings of money. Item, I gyve my brother Thomas Marley a yeowe and a lame. Item, I gyve my wife Doritie Marley a spangde whie, which goes at Belsay, and hir thirdes of all my goodes, according to the custome of the lawe. All the rest of my goodes, theis my legeses, my deibtes & funerall expences discharged & paid, I gyve to my two daughters Frances Marley and Jane Marley, whom I maik my sole executors to and for their owne use and comoditie. Item, I make supervisores of this my will John Stobes of Newcastle, gentlemane, and Reignold Wright of Litle Thorpe, yeomane, whom I dissir to se this my will discharged and performed, as I have apponted. Item, I comit the tuitione of my two childrene unto my wyfe so longe as she shall remayne a widowe; and as sone as she marieth agayne, to the above named John Stobes and Reinold Wrighte.

Witness[e]s hereof, Samuell Marley & William Wrangham [*no signatures or marks*]

An inventori of all the goods and chatles, moveables and umoveables, which was Gabrell Marley of Hilton's, deceased, prissed by theis fower men, that is to say, Richard Gibson, Robert Barley, Robert Hilton, Richard Sparro

Imprimis, his apparell	4	0s	0d
Item, two oxen	6	13s	4d

Item, fower kye	7	0s	0d
Item, fyve whies	7	6s	8d
Item, on bule, on bule stirke, on whie stirke	2	6s	8d
Item, on gelding, two mares, on fole, on litle colte	11	0s	0d
Item, fyften yowe shepe & syxe oge shep	3	13s	4d
Item, two swine, that is to say, on hoge & on sewe		[........]	
Item, wheat, beig, pease & otes	8	[........]	
Item, wheat, peas & ry, which grewe at Boldone	5	0s	0d
Item, hayes		10s	0d
Item, plowes & plowe gear, wayne & wayne geare	1	3s	4d
Item, on cupbord, on kawell, on table, on form, on stoole, on longe settle, on chare	2	0s	0d
Item, thre chestes & a coffer		6s	0d
Item, on old ambery, thre olde bedes		5s	0d
Item, on spining whele, 3 tobes, 3 barels, on chirne, 3 skeles		7s	0d
Item, on old tobe, a cheste, two bordes		2s	0d
Item, coles, an old kettle, two other kitles, a pane, a skimmer		15s	0d
Item, two potes, a frying pane & other implementes		6s	0d
Item, aleven puder dublers, 2 sauser, a poting dish		10s	0d
Item, fower candlestickes, thre saultes		3s	0d
Item, a pecke, kanes, dishes, drinking potes, temses		2s	0d
Item, fower chimey bares, tonges, crakes, a speete		12s	0d
Item, two trwes, with other implementes		2s	0d
Item, bedding, with a windowclothe & a socke	2	3s	0d
Item, ganders, gesse & hense		2s	6d
Item, in the smidye, a stedy, a payre of bellowes, a vice, hamers & other implementes	2	6s	8d
Item, two chistes, ane arke	2	6s	8d
Item, two grindstones, with crakes & implementes		4s	0d

Somma totalis is thre score & seven poundes nynten shillings syxe pence, whereof the legeses is xiij^{li} iij^{s} iiij^{d}

Deibtes owen unto the said Gabrell Marley

Item, William Wray of Whittle, gentlemane	1	3s	0d
Item, William Sanders of Lamesley	2	0s	0d
James Atkinson of Munkwearmouth		8s	4d
William Sothren of Heworth	2	0s	0d
Item, Mathew Bankes of Usworth	3	0s	0d

Item, John Foster of Newcastle	1	15s	0d
Item, Mr John Delavall	1	10s	0d

Som xj^{li} xvj^s iiij^d

Deibtes which the said Gabrell oweth

Imprimis, to Francis Jordone	9	0s	0d
Item, to John Waultone of Durham	1	0s	0d
Item, to George Waulton	4	0s	0d
Item, the lordes rente	2	0s	0d
Item, to Robert Hilton & Richard Thomson	1	12s	6d
Item, to Peter Hotchone	1	0s	0d
Item, to Mr Wauller	1	0s	0d
Item, to Margret Wilkinson		19s	6d
Item, to Elizabeth Marley		5s	0d
Item, to John Lockey		6s	0d
Item, to Nychollas Waulton		7s	0d
Item, to Henry Hope		3s	0d
Item, to Richard Foster		3s	0d
Item, to Christopher Hopper		10s	0d
Item, to Annas Gibson		1s	3d
Item, to Margret Hotchone		2s	0d
Item, for fyve chesses		1s	3d
Item, to Margret Snadone		3s	4d
Item, to sherers		2s	6d
Item, to Richard Sparro		6s	0d
Item, to ffrancis Jordone for corne	3	13s	4d
	22	18s	7d

Som of deibtes which he owith is xxvj^{li} xviij^s vij^d

Somma totalis, the deibtes and legeses deduckted, is xxxix^{li} xiiij^s

Source: DPR1/1/1609/M3/1, 3, 5, paper 5ff. There are two copies of the will and the inventory. The second copy of the will is identical to the one printed above except for differences of spelling and the omission of the witnesses' names.

10. Margaret Goodchild of Ryhope, Bishopwearmouth, 1610

In the name of God, amen, the xix daye of September in the yeare of Lord God 1610, I, Margaret Goodchilde of Ryhope in the parishe of Busshopwermoth, sicke of bodye but of good & perfect remembrance (thankes be geven to almyghtie God) do make this my last will and testament in maner and forme followinge. ffyrst & especiallye, I commend my soule to the handes of my lord & saviour Jesus Christ, by whose merites, death and passion I trust to be saved, and my bodye to be buryed within the church off my parishe Busshopwermoth. Item, I geve & bequeath to my brother Robert Goodchyld twentie pound of lawfull Englyshe money, to be payd to hym forth of my goodes that of right belongeth to me for filiall & chylde's portion. Item, I gyve & bequeath to my sister Agnas Gybson twentie marke of Englyshe monye, to be likewyse payd forth to her of my goodes that of right belongeth to me. Item, I gyve and bequeath to my syster Jane Huntlye twentie marke off lawfull Englyshe monye to be payd to her forth of my goodes & portion that belongeth to me. Item, I gyve and bequeath to my syster Joane Sheperson twentie marke of lawfull Englyshe monye to be payd to her out of my goodes & portion that belongeth to me. Item, I geve to be distrybuted & geven to the poore thre pound syx shillinges eight pence to be in like sort paid forth of my goodes. The rest and resydue of all and singuler my goodes that of right belongeth to me for my portion of my father John Goodchyldes goodes deceassed, I do whollye gyve and bequeath to my ffather & mother, George Sheperson and Marye Sheperson. And do also make my ffather & mother, George Sheperson & Marye Sheperson, executors of this my last will & testament.

Wytnesses at the makinge hereof, Anthony Watson, Wyllym Burdon, George Sheperson with others [*no signatures or marks*]

An inventory of all such goodes and chattles as Margaret Goodchild late of Rihoop, deceased, dyed possessed of and which was dewe unto her fourth of her father John Goodchilde his goodes late of Rihopp, deceased, which Margaret dyed whilst she was sole and unmarried

Inprimis, dew to the said Margarett for her filiall
    porcion and administrator parte of her said father's
    goodes   80   0s   0d

Payed fourth of the said goodes as followeth

ffirst, for phisick and other necessary thinges for her in her sicknes who did languish a yeare and a halfe before she dyed	5	0s	0d
Item, for her funeral expenses &c	3	10s	0d

Summa viij^{li} x^s

Sic restat de claro iij^{xx} xj^{li} x^s

Source: DPR1/1/1610/G4/1–2, paper 2ff. A summary of the will, without the inventory, is printed in WI Durham, pp. 47–8.

11. Nicholas Bryan of Monkwearmouth, yeoman, 1611

In the name of God, amen, the xvjth daie of August, anno *regni* Regis Jacobi &c nono, anno Domini 1611, I, Nicholas Bryan of Muncke Warmouth in the county of Durham, yeoman, sick in body, but of good and perfecte remembrance, praised be almightie God, do make this my last will and testamente in manner and forme following, that is to saie; ffirst and principally, I commend and committ my soule into the hands of almighty God, my maker, hopeing assuredly by the death and passion of my saviour Jesus Christ to have lif everlasting, and my body I commend to thearth from whence it came, and the same to be buryed within the parish churche of Muncke Warmouth aforesaid. Item, I gyve and bequeath unto the poore of the parish of Bushopp Warmouth aforesaid [*sic*] the some of x^s and to this parish of Muncke Warmouth v^s. Item, my will and mynd is that my sonne Thomas Bryan and his heires, shall have enioy all my lands, tenementes & hereditaments whatsoever, lying and being in the towne, territories and fields of Bushopp Warmouth, and that my brother Michaell Bryan shall have the tuicion and govermente of the said Thomas Bryan during his minorety, and that my said sonne shalbe broughte upp & kepte at schole wheareby he maie learne some knowledg the better to understand <therronafter>. And my will and mynd is that my said sonne Thomas Bryan shalbe broughte upp & kepte with and by my said ffarme and the profitts thereof, and whatsoever surplusage shalbe hadd or receyved over and above his mayntayneannce for the said ffarme for and during the tearme & space of twelve yeares the same shalbe paid by the said Michaell Bryan unto my fyve children, Barbarie, Isabell, Margarett, Nicholas & Michaell Bryan, to be equally devided amongst them as they and every or any of them shall come to lawfull yeares of age, at the discrescion, vewe and judgemente of John Smith the elder, boocher, Roberte Beckwithe, merchannte, Thomas Richeson and Raphe Reade, yeomen, for the increasing & amending of their childe's porcions. Item, my will and mynd is that my brother Thomas Roxby and Agnes his wif shall have the tuicion and govermente of my said two sonnes Nicholas and Michaell Bryan and of their porcions for and during their minoreties, hopeing they wilbe a ffather & mother unto them, and will kepe them at schole as my hope is in them. Item, I gyve and bequeath unto the said Nicholas Bryan, my sonne, a browne cowe, and unto my said sonne Michaell Bryan a black cowe called Allblack. Item, I gyve and bequeath unto Elinour Wrenn and Margarett Wrenn, to either of them, sixe shillings eighte pence for a token. Item, my will and mynd is that my mistris Mrs Barbara Riddell shall have the tuicion & govermente of my daughter Barbara Bryan during her mynorety. Item, my will and mynd is that Roberte Beckwith, merchannte, and his wif shall have the tuicion and govermente of my daughter Isabell Bryan and her childe's porcion for and during her minorety. Item, my will and mynd is that my ell ffather John Smith, boocher, and Margarett, his wif, shall have the tuicion and govermente of my daughter Margarett Bryan and of her porcion for & during her minorety. Item, I gyve and bequeath unto Dorothy Richeson, daughter of Thomas Richeson, a French crowne for a token. Item, I gyve and bequeath to every one of my brother Michaell his sixe children three shillings foure pence. Item, I gyve and bequeath unto my said sonne Thomas Bryan my bowe and quiver with the arrowes thearein. Item, my will and mynd is that if it shall please God to take to his mercy my said brother Michaell Bryan before my said sonne Thomas shall come to lawfull yeares of age, that then such of the said foure men before named, (videlicet) John Smith, Roberte Beckwith, Thomas Richeson & Raph Reade, as shalbe willing to take my said sonne Thomas shall have the tuicion and govermente of him and of his said lands, and he to do & performe in every respecte as formerly my said brother Michaell is to do & performe by this my will & mynd. Item, I gyve and bequeath unto Anne Smithe, the doughter of the said John Smithe, fyve shillings for to buy her an apron with all. All the rest my goods, cattells & chattells whatsoever, moveable and unmoveable, my debtes, legacies & funerall expences paid and discharged, I gyve and bequeath unto my said children, Nicholas Bryan, Mychaell Bryan, Barbara Bryan, Isabell Bryan and Margarett Bryan, whome I make and ordeyne executors of this my last will & testamente, renouncing

& forsaking all former wills by me formerly made. And I make & ordayne the said John Smith, Roberte Beckwith, Thomas Richeson & Raph Reade supervisors of this my last will and testamente, and I gyve and bequeath to every one of them fyve shillings for a token. Item, I gyve and bequeath unto my sonne Thomas Bryan foure iron somes, three long waynes with iron assill, nailes & hopes, foure cowpe waynes and all my plowghes and plowghe geare and all wood for that purpose, as harrowes & iron pynnes & hoopes. Witnesses heareof, John Smith, Michaell Bryan, Thomas Richeson and ffrancis Leighton, vicar.

Signum Johannis Smith, <elder> [*marked with a symbol*]

Thomas Richardson [*full name signed*]

Signum Michaeli Bryan [*marked with a symbol*]

And ffrancis Leighton, clericus [*marked with an ornate symbol*]

[*On the reverse, occur the names*] Barbara, Isabel, Margaret, Thomas, Nicholas, Michael

An inventory of all the goodes & catles that Nicholas Bryan of Munckwarmouth died possesst, uppon the 24 of September, 1611, praist by fower indeferint men, videlicet John Shipperson, Thomas Hilton, John Thomson, John Johnson

Inprimis, 8 oxen	32	10s	0d
Item, 3 stotes	6	0s	0d
Item, 10 kye	21	0s	0d
Item, 12 younge catle	13	10s	0d
Item, 5 horses & meares	15	0s	0d
Item, 51 sheepe of all sortes	15	0s	0d
Item, 19 swine	4	13s	4d
Item, 4 geis		4s	0d
Item, one beid, a table and formes in the hall	2	10s	0d
Item, in the pairler <&> 2 chambres, 5 bedes, a table	2	10s	0d
{Item, all the beeding woollen}			
Item, 3 fether beedes and one overseale \coverleed/[8], with all the coverleeds and coodes	8	10s	0d
Item, 6 paire of lin sheites, 4 pair of harden sheites, 6 bord clothes, 6 diber napkins, 20 other table napkins, 20 cood pillibers, on head sheit & fringe about the beed	7	0s	0d

---

8   The insertion 'coverleed' seems to be a gloss on 'overseale'.

Item, 4 ketles and a bayson with <ewer>	3	0s	0d
Item, 5 brass pots and arne poot	3	0s	0d
Item, 2 dozen & 5 puder dubles	1	9s	0d
Item, i dozen of banketin dishes		12s	0d
Item, ii lever and a baising		2s	0d
Item, 7 puder candlestikes		7s	0d
Item, 3 brasse candlestikes		3s	0d
Item, 4 flouer potes		4s	0d
Item, i potle pote & 2 quart potes		4s	0d
Item, 4 puder potes, 2 pint pots		6s	0d
Item, 3 puder chyrnes		2s	0d
Item, 2 puder pecis		2s	0d
Item, 3 saltes		1s	0d
Item, a chamber pot & a posset dish		2s	0d
Item, his reparell	5	0s	0d
Item, on bowe and quiver		10s	0d
Item, 6 silver spounes	7	10s	0d
Item, 2 dong waynes	1	10s	0d
Item, 2 short waynes	1	0s	0d
Item, 20 somes	1	10s	0d
Item, 3 pair of horse geir		3s	0d
Item, 15 geirt yokes		8s	0d
Item, on copp wayne		5s	0d
Item, 2 paire of plowe arnes, 2 axes & <twoe> spaides, i assell naill		8s	0d
Item, 3 grappes with other arne forkes		1s	6d
Item, 2 wayn hopes			8d
Item, 3 plowe beimes		3s	0d
Item, 14 assell trees		1s	0d
Item, 14 wayn fellows		3s	6d
Item, 9 moud bordes		2s	3d
Item, 10 plowe heades		1s	0d
Item, 11 arrow boules		2s	0d
Item, 4 wayne overens		2s	0d
Item, 1 arne chimnay		10s	0d
Item, a paire of tanges and a pore		1s	4d
Item, implements in the loft		6s	8d
Item, 4 wayne hoopes assell nailes		6s	0d
Item, the arke in barne		13s	4d
Item, 3 wayne blaydes		10s	0d
Item, a paire siles		3s	4d

Item, 2 ooxen harrowes & 4 horss harrowes		16s	0d
Item, al the corne and grain at Bishopwarmoth	53	0s	0d

£2009 [*sic*] 3s 11d

Item, half the mylne for three years and about fyve monethes to come	12	0s	0d
Item, <a> corne	1	6s	8d

Suma totalis ccxxvij^{li} x^s vij^d

Source: DPR1/1/1611/B14/1–5, paper 5ff.

12. Raphe Fletcher of Bishopwearmouth, yeoman, 1611

Anno Domini 1611°   5 March

In the name of God, amen, I Raphe ffletcher of Bishopp Wermouthe in the countie of Durham, yeoman, sicke and weake in bodie but of good and perfecte memorie, God be thanked therfore, do constitute and ordaine my last will & testament in manner & forme following. Firstly, I bequieth and recommend my soule into the handes of almightie God, my creator & redeemer and savior, and my bodie to be buried in the church yeard of Bishopp Wermouth. First, I bequeath and give to bee distributed to the poore, 10^s. Item, I give unto Richard Watson all my wearinge apparell or clothes which I used one my backe. Item, I give to my son John ffletcher (all the rest of my goodes not bequeathed, and my funerall charges being deducted also) I saye all the rest of my goodes. I leave for my son John whatsoever I did owne, possesse and inioye, whom I do make my onelie executor of this my last will & testament. In witnes wherof, I the said Raphe ffletcher have set to my marke.

Raphe ffletcher, marke [*marked with a symbol*]

Witnesses herrof, Randulph Bentley, minister; John Tompson, William Robinson, Richard Tompson [*no signatures or marks*]

An inventorie of all such goodes and chattells as Raph ffletcher, late of Bishoppwarmouth in the county of Durham, yeoman, dyed possessed of, taken this xvith day of Aprill, 1612, by these men, prizers thereof, vid*elicet* John Sheperdson, John Thompson and William Robinson.

Inprimis, ffower oxen	12	0s	0d
Item, ffower kine and thre stirckes	7	0s	0d
Item, thre horses and mares worth	5	0s	0d
Item, fiften old shepe & eight lambes	2	13s	0d
Item, of land in the field ffowerten acres of every			
grayne which ly together	14	0s	0d
Item, of corne in the barne	1	16s	0d
Item, waynes, donng, ropes, harowes, plewes with all			
the geare & furniture thereto	2	0s	0d
Item, two bedd steads		5s	0d
Item, a cupbord & a cawell		13s	4d
Item, ffower chests		4s	0d
Item, a lavere tubb and skeiles & other tymber		1s	8d
Item, two kettles, a brasse pott & pewter vessell		13s	0d
Item, his working tooles		5s	0d
Item, his bedclothes		5s	0d
Item, potts, racks and an iron grate		13s	4d
Item, chares, tubbs and stooles & a table		3s	4d
Item, his wearing apparell	1	0s	0d

Summa xlviij^{li} ij^{s} viij^{d}

Source: DPR1/1/1612/F2/3, 5; will, paper 4ff., inventory, parchment 1 m.
There are two copies of the will in the same hand.

13. Richard Bartram of Sunderland, butcher, 1612

A true coppie of an inventorie taken of all the goods and chattelles of
Richard Bartrum of Sunderland in the countie of Durham, butcher,
the 21° daye of August, anno Domini 1612, by theis prisers, William
Hardcastell, John Hallyday, Thomas Scarbroughe and Thomas
Richardson

Imprimis, those things in the halle one cubbord, armerie	10s	0d
Item, 6 peuter platters with 4 candlesticks & 3 salts		
called double saltes	14s	0d
Item, one chamber potte, a cup & little measures	1s	4d
Item, 2 brazen candlestickes	1s	0d
Item, one forme, 7 buffet stooles of firre	3s	0d
Item, one carpet cloth	1s	4d
Item, an iron chimney, 3 paire of reckens, a pair of		
tongs and a pur	8s	0d

Item, 2 painted clothes		3s	0d
Item, in the chamber, within the halle, bed clothes,			
one featherbed, a bouster, 2 cods, 2 coverlids,			
2 blankettes, an happing	2	6s	8d
Item, in an upper chamber, bedclothes, a coverlidde,			
a boulster, a cod, twoe happings		10s	0d
Item, sixteene yards of unbleached harden		5s	4d
Item, 5 paire of linne sheetes	1	4s	0d
Item, 6 pillow beares		6s	0d
Item, 3 pair of hearden sheetes		6s	0d
Item, 6 bord clothes		10s	0d
Item, 6 short table clothes		2s	4d
Item, twoe dozin table napkins		6s	8d
Item, 3 chestes, little ones, and a ioined forme		6s	0d
Item, in another upper chamber, a coverlid, twoe			
happinges and a servants bed and 3 bedsteads,			
twoe formes and a table with a frame	1	0s	0d
Item, in an inner parlor, a table & 2 formes		6s	0d
Item, in the kitchin, 2 brasse potts, 2 fish pans and a			
litle pan		16s	0d
Item a great kettell	2	5s	0d
Item, twoe halfe hundred waights & 2 pound waightes		5s	0d
Item, twoe spits, a fryeing pan, of plate two pair of pot			
hoockes and range		6s	8d
Item, brewing vesselle and washing tubbes		14s	0d
Item, a tempse, a seeve, 6 peuter spoones		12s	0d
Item, a spade, a stang, a pair of stinges and ston lide		1s	0d
Item, a syde table in the buttrie		1s	0d
Item, a sow		8s	0d
Item, a cubbord which my said husband gave to my			
maid, Barbara Taylier,		3s	4d
and of money	1	6s	8d
Item, a chaffing dishe, 7 peuter dishes, 5 sausers		8s	0d
Item, 6 kanns, a cup, 2 jugge peper querns, twoe			
boulles, 2 trese		3s	0d
Item, 6 boulles of malte	3	0s	0d
Item, 2 dozen of trenchers		1s	0d
Item an old sword		2s	0d
Item, hoppes		10s	0d

Sume is £20 3s 4d

Debts due unto Richard Barton, late of [Bisho]ppwarmouth within the countie of Durham, butcher, deceased, at the houre of his death

Imprimis, by James Bentley, smith		15s	0d
Item, by Richard Smith, salter		9s	0d
Item, by Raiphe Preston, sailer		13s	0d
Item, by William Bule, salter		4s	0d
Item, by Robert Wilkinson		5s	0d
Item, by Richard Miller	1	0s	0d
Item, by Richard Browne, salter		9s	0d
Item, by Richard Porrett		7s	0d
Item, by Raiphe Allison		7s	0d
Item, by John Leadbeater		5s	0d
Item, by Jhane Roksby of Sunderland		11s	4d
Item, by Thomas Sparrow	2	0s	0d
Item, by Thomas Scarbrough		3s	3d
Item, by John Shipperdson	11	11s	0d

Debts owinge by Richard Bartram of Sunderland, butcher, deceased, att the houre of his death, videlicet:

Imprimis, unto Thomas Arras of Seham	3	15s	0d
Item, unto John Johnson of Warmouth	3	9s	0d
Item, unto Edward Harle, tanner	2	0s	0d
Item, unto John Browne of Warmouth	1	0s	0d
Item, unto Widow ffell of Ryeopp	2	0s	0d
Item, unto Cuthbert Wilson of Warmouth		9s	0d
Item, unto Richard Morgane of Sunderland		14s	0d
Item, unto Thomas Lambert of Duresme	1	3s	0d
Item, unto James Goslinge of Richmond	2	10s	0d
Item, unto Thomas Wright of Whitbume	3	0s	0d
Item, unto Robert Dinge		12s	0d
Item, unto Charles Boothe		17s	0d
Item, unto [blank] Easterbye, widowe	1	0s	0d
Item, unto William Willson	16	0s	0d
Item, unto John Halliday	9	13s	8d
	47	13s	8d

Source: DPR1/1/1612/B4/1–2, paper 2ff.

14. Elizabeth Burdon of Ryhope, Bishopwearmouth, 1612

This being the eight of November, anno Domini 1612,[9] in the name of God, amen, I, Elizabeth Burdon, late wife of George Burdon of Ryop, latelie deceased, beinge in good and perfect remembrannce, doe make this my last will and testament in maner and forme followinge. ffirst, I committ my soule to almightie God, my maker and redeemer, and my bodye to be buried in my parishe churchyard of Weremouthe. I give and bequeath to the poore of my parish att my dyeinge daye iij[s] iiij[d]. I give to Robert Burdon a gimmer lambe. Item, I give to Allice, my daughter, a gimmer lambe. I give to Elizabethe, my daughter, a gimmer lambe. I give to George Burdon, my sonne, a gimmer lambe. I give to Edmund, my sonne, a ewe and a lambe. I give to Allison, my youngest daughter, a ewe and a lambe. I give to my godson Thomas Gowland and Marye his wife a bushell of wheat and a bushel of peese. I give to the saide Edmund and Allison, to either of them, fortye shillings in money. All the rest of my goodes, moveable and unmoveable, belonging to my thirdes, I give to my five children above named, that is to say George Burdon, Edmund, Allice, Elizabeth and Allison, whom I make full executors of this my last will and testament. And I make supervisors of this my last will and testament William Burdon, Thomas Burdon, Anthony Surrett. These three above named I desire them for God's sake to take my thre youngest children and there goods till they come to be of xxj yeares of aige, that is to say, William Burdon to have tuicion of Allison and her portion, Thomas Burdon George with his part and Anthonye Surret to have tuicion of Edmund and his part and portion.

Elizabethe Burden's marke [signed with a symbol]

Witnesses of the same,
William Burdon, his marke [*marked with a scratch*]
Thomas Burdon [*full name signed*]
Anthonye Surrett [*full name signed*]
Johne Renardsonn [*full name signed]*
Anthonye Watson [*full name signed*]

xv° Januarij 1612

An inventarie of the goodes and chattels of Elizabethe Burden, late wife of George Burdon, late of Ryop within the parishe of

---

9   The words 'This being ... 1612' are from the first draft of the will.

Bishopp Weremouth in the countye of Durham, wedowe, deceased,
praised the fifteenth daye of Januarye by these ffower honest men
William Thompson, Anthony Watson, John Renardson and William
Burden

In primis, seaven oxen praised att	16	0s	0d
Item, ffyve kyne praysed att	8	6s	0d
Item, three younge beastes praised att	2	0s	8d
Item, a mare and a horse praised att	4	0s	0d
Item, eighteen old sheepe and foure hogges	6	6s	8d
Item, ffower swyne praised att	1	0s	0d
Item, all manner of corne within the barne & garthe	1	0s	0d
Item, the corne on the ground beinge eight bowles	4	0s	0d
Item, hay in the barne	2	0s	0d
Item, ploughe and plough geare, waine and waine geare, yooke and soome, and all other implements thereunto belonginge	4	0s	0d
Item, beddinge, woolinge and linninge, blankets, sheats, happins, codpillowbers and coddes, brasse and pewter with other implements within the house	6	4s	0d
Item, the pulleyne about the house		3s	4d

Suma totalis lxxiiij^{li} viij^{d}

Source: DPR1/1/B16/1, 3; will, paper 1f., inventory, parchment 1m.

15. Alice Wilkinson of Bishopwearmouth, widow, 1613

The last will & testament of Alice Wilkinson, late wif of Richard
Wilkinson of Bishopwermoth in the county of Durham, deceased,
upon the xxix^{t} day of August anno 1613, uttered by her upon her
death bed in the presence of thos whose names are subscribed,
videlicet John Hilton & Richard Bee. Imprimis, she the said Alice did
bequeth her soule to almightie God, & her body to be buryed in the
parishe churche of Bishop Wermoth aforesaid. Also she did give &
bequethe to her two daughters Elizabeth & Margaret Wilkinson all
hir housould stuffe. Item, to Richard Wilkinson, her sonne, all her
parte of the hawver corne then growing which should have bene
divided betwene them. Item, more to her said two daughters two
whies of two yeares old & upwards. Item, to eache of the foure
children of the said Richard Wilkinson, videlicet John, Thomas,

Raphe & Isabell Wilkinson, one boule of wheate. Item, to Isabell Hilton, daughter of John Hilton, one boule of wheate & one ewe. Item, to John Hilton, sonne of the said John Hilton, one boule of wheate to buy him bookes. Item, to the three childrene of Adam Wilkinson every one a sheep. Item, to Richard Bee, her servant, one stirk of a yeare & a half old. All other her goodes & chattells whatsoever, her debts legasies, childe's portions & funerall expences being paid, she did make her sonne Robert Wilkinson & Margaret Wilkinson, hir daughter aforesaid, her full & sole executors of this her last will & testament. In witnes whereof the said John Hilton & Richard Bee have hereunto sett there handes & marks the fourth day of September, 1613.

John Hilton [*full name signed*]
Richard Bee, mark [*marked with a symbol*]

Ane inventory of all the goodes and chattles latelie belonginge to Ales Wilkinson, wedo, and late wife of Richerd Wilkinson, deceased, departed the xxixth daye of August, praised by foure men, John Thomson, John Shipperson, William Robinson and John Johnson, the xx^th of September, anno Domini 1613

Imprimis, foure oxen	17	10s	0d
Item, three kine	5	13s	4d
Item, three whye stirkes given by legasie	3	0s	0d
Item, one oxe strike	1	0s	0d
Item, thre ewes and two lambes	1	2s	0d
Item, five swine	1	16s	8d
Item, wheate in the barne and garth	20	0s	0d
Item, bigg in the barne and garth	10	0s	0d
Item, oates in the garth	3	6s	8d
Item, pease in the garth	8	6s	8d
Item, hay in the barne and garth	2	10s	0d
Item, wheat and pease strawe		3s	0d
Item, one coupe wayne, one longe wayne, one plowe with yokes and somes, and oxe harrow, two horse harrowes, two shalkles and two boltes, and coulter and socke, one old wayne wheele with two irone hoopes and one paire of horse geare	3	1s	4d
Item, foure old bedsteedes, one table, certeine broken bordes & other rotten peeces		13s	4d
Item, a pressor, a paire of wayne stinges, with other geare in the byer		5s	0d

Item, one iron chimney		15s	0d
Item, two stone troughes		2s	6d
Item, thre cubbordes and one chare	3	0s	0d
Item, halfe a score of pullen yonge and old		3s	4d
Item, twentie six pewter dublers, 3 pewter potts and 3 pewter salts	1	10s	0d
Item, seaven brase potts, one brase morter and one iron pestle	2	5s	0d
Item, thre kettles	1	13s	0d
Item, foure paire of lin sheetes, foure paire harden sheetes	2	5s	0d
Item, six piliberes and six towels		10s	0d
Item, her apparell	2	13s	4d
Item, five hand coverlets	1	6s	8d
Item, two mattresses, 6 codds, 3 blanketts and five cushens	2	13s	4d
Item, a chist, a chirne, certeine old tubes, two riddles, two paire of temses, two sives, two heckles, two pokes and a sacke, one old wyndo cloth, thre skeeles, six meeles, one milksile, two barrels and one washinge tube	1	10s	0d
Item, a speete, a paire of tongs, two muckforks, on corne forke, a spade, a muckhack and a sithe		6s	0d
Item, a kilne haire		13s	0d
Suma totalis	99	14s	2d

Debtes owing by the testator & first for child's portions

Imprimis, to Robert Wilkinson for his portion	5	0s	0d
Item, to George Wilkinson	1	6s	8d
Item, to Richard Wilkinson	3	10s	0d
Item, to Adam Wilkinson	1	10s	0d
Item, to Thomas Wilkinson	2	10s	0d
Item, to Elizabeth Wilkinson	5	0s	0d
Item, more owing to her	2	0s	0d
Item, to Margaret Wilkinson	1	0s	0d

Other debts

Item, to Mr. John Catherick for grasse	3	0s	0d
Item, to Richard Bee for wages		12s	0d
Item, owinge to Thomas Bee	1	0s	0d
Item, oweing to John Johnson		2s	4d
Item, more for a mortuary		10s	0d

Item, for a Lairstall	6s	8d
Item, to the poore	6s	8d
Item, for charges about the proving of the will	19s	0d

Suma de*bitorum* £28 14s 0d

Source: DPR1/1/1613/W7/1, 3, paper 5ff.

16. Elizabeth Smith of Fulwell, Monkwearmouth, 1613

xvj[th] die Decembris, anno Domini 1613

In the name of God, amen, I, Elizabeth Smith of ffulwell, sick in bodye but in good and perfect remembrance, do make this my last will and testamentt in manner and forme following. ffirst, I commit my soule to God, my maker and redeamer, and my body to be buried in the parish church of Chester in the middle alley neare unto my two sonnes. Item, I give unto my daughter Elizabeth Lumley, wife unto Michaell Lumley, and Ellinor Peele, ffortie pounds, to be divided equally between them, which is in my sonne's Thomas Smythe's hand. Item, I give unto my said daughter Elizabeth one beddstead, one ffether bedd, one mattresse, one caldren, one ketling, two great chists, the best bedd covering, one silver salt, two diper towells and one silver spone. Item, I give to my godsonne Michaell Lumley one silver spone. Item, I give unto Barbarye Lumley my coffer. Item, I give unto Elinor Peele all my pewter vessell, two brasse potts, one litle ketling, one posnett pott, one cupborde, one trundle bed, nyne happings, two coverletts, thirteen ffether codds, two ffether bedds, thre mattresses, ffoure pare of blanketts, twelve payre of sheets, one chayre being at Walridge, and all my apparrell, wolling and lynnen, tenne codd pillobers, two lynnen towells, thre tableclothes, twelve table napkins and thre cushings. Item, I give unto my daughter Jenett Peele one peece of gould being twentie two shillings. Item, I give to my daughter Anne Clerk one peece of gould, two and twentye shillings. Item, I give unto my daughter Grace Maddison one peece of gould, twentie two shillings. Item, I give unto Lionel Maddison, sonne unto Raiphe Maddison, one peece of gould being two and twentie shillings. All the rest of my goods, movable and immovable, I give unto my daughter Elizabeth Lumley and Elinnor Peele, whome I make executors of this my last will and testamentt. Item, I give more unto Ellinor Peele one peece of gould being two and twentie shillings.

Witnesses hereof, Thomas Carnabye, Christopher Highe, Margarett
Chilton, William Bowrye, Reynold ffawcett [*no signatures or marks*]

An inventorye of all the goods moveable and unmoveable of
Elizabeth Smythe of ffulwell, deceased, praysed by George Colyer,
Reiginald ffawcett, Robert White and George Wilson, the xxxth daye
of December, 1613.

In primis, pewther vessell, great and litle, fortye peece,			
two pewther candlestickes, three brass candlesticks,			
two chamber potts and one salte praysed to	3	2s	0d
Item, one great chiste		10s	0d
Item, twelve yeards of white clothe	1	4s	0d
Item, one cupborde	2	6s	8d
Item, one beddsteade	2	13s	4d
Item, two fether bedds, and two bowlsters	2	13s	4d
Item, tenn fether coods	1	0s	0d
Item, fower matrisses	1	10s	0d
Item, fower payre of blankitts	2	10s	0d
Item, eight payre of lining shetes	3	10s	0d
Item, eight payre of harden shetes	1	13s	4d
Item, tenn cood pillibers		15s	0d
Item, one bedd covering	5	10s	0d
Item, two coverletts		16s	0d
Item, nyn happings	1	13s	4d
Item, two carpinclothes		13s	4d
Item, two diper towells		16s	0d
Item, two lining towells		5s	0d
Item, twelve table napkines		6s	8d
Item, three table clothes		9s	0d
Item, three felt hatts	1	6s	0d
Item, sixtene smockes	1	4s	0d
Item, twelve apparans		8s	0d
Item, fowrtene curtches		10s	6d
Item, six crosclothes		2s	6d
Item, twentie two patclothes		10s	0d
Item, a leaven shirte bandes		4s	4d
Item, fower petticots	2	1s	4d
Item, one gowne	2	6s	8d
Item, one other gowne	1	13s	4d
Item, one other gowne		12s	0d
Item, one other gowne		10s	0d

Item, one waste cote		2s	6d
Item, one great caldron, one ketle, fower little			
pannes and mortis	1	5s	0d
Item, two safeguards and a old cloke		8s	0d
Item, one waste cote		10s	0d
Item, two yetlings		16s	0d
Item, three bras potts and a posnett pott	2	0s	0d
Item, one great chiste		8s	0d
Item, one gould ring	1	10s	0d
Item, one cofferr		6s	8d
Item, one silver salte	1	0s	0d
Item, two silver spones		10s	0d
Item, three milche bowles, one milche syle, fyve dishes		1s	8d
Item, one capcase		3s	0d
Item, one payre of curtins		3s	0d
Item, one payre of bras scales		1s	4d
Item, one other payre of curtins		2s	0d
Item, one hurle bedd		3s	0d
Item, three quishings		8s	0d
Item, one chaire		2s	6d
Item, gould in hir chiste	5	10s	8d
Item, money in the same chiste	7	19s	6d
Item, one cowe branded	2	0s	0d

Som lxxij^{li} xv^s x^d

Debts owing to the said Elizabeth

In primis, Thomas Smythe of Walridge	40	0s	0d
Item, Sir John Claxton, knight	20	0s	0d

Somma cxxxij^{li} xv^s x^d

Signum George Colyer [*marked with a symbol*]
Reignald ffawcett [*full name signed*]
Signum Robert White, [*marked with a symbol*]
Signum George Wilson, [*marked with a cross*]

Source: DPR1/1/1613/S10/1–4; will, paper 2ff., inventory, paper 2ff. sewn.

17. Thomas Wilson of Bishopwearmouth, 1614

An inventorie of all the goodds, chattles and debts which belonged to Thomas Wilson of the parishe of Bushop Wermouthe, deceased, prised the sixth day of September, 1614, by Christofer Wharton, George Shadforthe, Robert Scurefeild and Thomas Burden

Imprimis, viij oxen	44	0s	0d
Item, twelve kine and one bull	30	0s	0d
Item, fower little whyes	5	6s	8d
Item, seaven calves	4	13s	4d
Item, eight mayres, one colt & a foale	30	0s	0d
Item, three score & ten old shepe	21	0s	0d
Item, forty eight lambes	8	0s	0d
Item, one sowe and vj pigges		10s	0d
Item, thirteene geese		8s	8d
Item, the other pooltrye		4s	0d
Item, all the corne on the grounde	40	0s	0d
Item, all the haye	10	0s	0d
Item, all the waynes and wain geare, plowghes and plowghe geare	10	0s	0d
Item, corne in the barne & in the howse	2	0s	0d
Item, the lease of his farme in Silkesworth holden of Mr Sayre	40	0s	0d
Item, butter and cheese	2	0s	0d
Item, beefe and backon		10s	0d
Item, five brasse pottes, a little posnet, three ketles, three pannes and a little yetling	4	3s	0d
Item, all the pewter dublers, saltes, sawesers and candlestickes	2	10s	0d
Item, two cuppbordes	2	10s	0d
Item, a table, a longsettle, stooles & chayres	1	0s	0d
Item, one iron chimney, two reckon crookes a payre of tonges & other impleements		10s	0d
Item, two spitts, a choppin knife and a droppin pan		5s	0d
Item, shelves for laynge cheeses on		2s	0d
Item, one arke		13s	4d
Item, two spinninge wheeles		2s	0d
Item, the milk vessell as skeeles, chirnes, bowles, cheese fatts, two cheese presses, milk shelves, wodd dishes & dublers	1	0s	0d
Item, fower bedsteades	1	2s	8d

Item, one little cawell and a shelf for clothes to ly on		2s	0d
Item, three chestes & a little old counter		8s	0d
Item, in beddinge	6	13s	4d
Item, in linnen, straken, & harden webes	6	13s	4d
Item, in wollen clothe	1	13s	4d
Item, fower tempses		1s	4d
Item, sackes, poakes, window clothes, scuttles, sives and riddles		10s	0d
Item, table clothes and napkins	1	0s	0d
Item, his apparrell & furniture	4	0s	0d

Somma 283^{li} 11^s

Debts dewe to the deceased

Imprimis, by Mrs Elsabethe Sayre	4	0s	0d
Item, by John Tomson of Wermouth		4s	0d
Item, by Wedowe Wilkinson		1s	0d
Item, by Robert Allen		10s	0d
Item, by Alice Earr		10s	0d

Somma debitorum v^{li} v^s viij^d

Somma totalis 288^{li} 16^s 8^d

Debts owinge by the deceased

Imprimis, to Mrs Dorythie Sayre	20	0s	0d
Item, a mortuary dew to the parson of Bushop Warmowthe		10s	0d
Item, the letters of administracion & the tuicion	1	9s	0d

Source: DPR1/1/1614/W3/1, parchment 1m., indented.

18. Henry Rand of Sunderland, 1614

Cape de Verd, this xijth of Maie, 1614

Lovinge ffather & mother, my umble deutie remembered unto yow, trustinge in God yow be in good health, both of yow, with my bretheren & sister, & desiringe your dailie blessinge & prayer to God for me, & likewise that all the rest of our good ffrends & kinsfolke be in good healthe as I was at the makinge heareof, thankes be to God. This is to certifie yow that wee are in saftie heare in Ginne, amonge the neegers, at a place called Capp de Vard, some ix^C leagues from

England southward. The cause of our cominge to this place is because our admarall haith sprunge hir maine mast & so wee came heare to helpe it. Wee were 7 dayes in saffe in Barbare as wee came alonge, thinkeinge to have met with soom masts butt wee found none & so we stoode alongst for this place. We came in to this road on Maie daie in the afternoone. I have noe other newes to write unto yow of at this tyme butt that I am in good healthe, thankes be to God; and, as for my full intente for this voage, I did nott write unto yow as yett but now I doe to the full. I had sartaine thinges by my cozin James Rand's procuremente, which is for the preserveinge of my healthe, as I hope, when wee shall come into the hote cuntre, which amounteth unto some 40 shillinges, the which I would have yow take no care for the discharginge, for yt shalbe betweene my cozin James Rand & I, for it was of his kindness that I should have such thinges with me; and for the discharginge of him I have write in a letter to him, & this to yow, that, yf it please God to take me to his mersie before that we come home againe, that he shall have v^{li} & whatsoever is more, eyther in wages or ventur or whatsoever els hollie to be yours or at your disposinge, save my sea clothes & they to be at my own disposinge or to whom I shall appoynte them for. I owe nothing to anie one in the world as yett save to James Rand, I thank my God. But yf God be so mercifull as to bringe me home amonge my ffrends againe, I shalbe more bownd to gloriefie his name, and then I will se him discharged for this my debt. Butt now as it is fittinge & my deutie that yow should know this, therefor I would have yow take it in good part everie kind of way, both yow & my mother, & nott to be greved anie kind of way but have patience & give God thankes for all his maniefold mercies, for wee injoy more of them then wee deserve ten thousand tymes. Therefor be of good cheare & fainte nott; yow know that He our God in England shalbe our God also in the East Indies yf wee serve him unfainedlie. Therefor, I saie with St Paule, lyfe is unto me deathe & deathe is to me advantadge, for yf it be his will to take, it is in vayne to withstand and yf it be his will to lett raine, it is in vaine to seke to kill. Therefor, live or die, his will abide wee must. And God grant we may all do his will. Therefor, good ffather and mother, let me intreete yow that this my goinge may nott seeme greevas unto yow, so besecheinge God to poure his blessinges uppon yow and to guid yow & us all with his good angell unto that haven wher we maie injoy everlastinge reste, for His sonn's sake that with his blood hathe dearelie bought us, amen. I pray yow remember my deutie to all our good ffrends &

acquaintance in gennarall, your lovinge sonne till deathe, Henrie Rand.

Decimo octavo die mensis Octobris, anno Domini 1614, per *magist*rum Edmundum Pope, legum d*oc*torem, surro*gatum* ven*erabi*lis viri m*agist*ri Tho*mae* Rydley, legum etiam d*oc*toris, comissarij gen*era*lis &c., em*isi*t comissi*onem* m*agist*ro Radulpho Rand, cl*eri*co, avunculo ex paterno latere Henrici Rand, celebis, dum vixit de Sunderland, in com*itat*u Durham, Eboracen*se* provinc*ie*, et deceden*tis* in partibus transmarinis seu in alto mare, haben*tis* tempore vite et mortis suarum nonnulla bona, iura sive cred*itores* infra dioc*esim* London ac iurisdictionis r*eve*rendi p*at*ris d*omini*, d*omini* Joh*ann*is, permissione di*vi*na London, epi*scop*i, defuncti, ad administrand*um* bona &c. iuxta t*e*norem schedule continen*tis* testament*um* pred*icti* deff*uncti* racione quod nullos in eodem sive ead*em* nominaverit ex*ecuto*res sive ex*ecuto*rem de bene &c. ac de pleno &c. in persona m*agist*ri Georgij fforman, n*ot*arii publ*i*ci procu*rato*ris d*icti* Radulphi iur*e* &c., salvo iure de et cum consensu et assensu Joh*ann*is Rand proc*urato*ris nat*ura*lis et l*egi*timi d*ict*i defunct*i* ac legatarij principalis in huiu*s* schedula sive testamento nominat*i* commissioni pred*icto* con-sentien*tis*, prout per quandam schedulam sigillat*am* et subscript*am* manu propria d*ict*i Joh*ann*is Rand in pr*ese*ntijs nonnullorum testium fide dignorum apparet.

Be it knowne unto all men by their pr*ese*ntes that I, John Rand, of Sunderland in the countie of Durham, yeoman, have ordayned, made, constituted, deputed, assigned and aucthorized, and by theis p[rese]ntes, do ordayne, make, constitute, depute, assigne, aucthorize, and in my stead and place, put my welbeloved in Christe Raphe Rand, of Gayton in the countie of Surra, clarke, my true, lawfull and undoubted attorney for me and in my name, to aske, levye, recover, receyve, accepte, take upp and demaund of the right worshipful Sir Thomas Smyth, knight, governor of the righte worshipful company of merchanntes trading the East Indies, or of any other person from the said companye aucthorized, all such waiges as are dew and belonging to me, being the executor and administrator of my sonne Henry Rand, maryner, deceased, either for or in respecte of any adventure to him dew till the tyme of the death of him, the said Henry, with the profittes theareof or by any waies or meanes whatsoever for his late beinge in the good shipp called the Little Darling, or in any other shipp in her companye to the East Indies, gyveing, and by theis presentes grannting unto my said attorney, full power, good righte and lawful aucthoritie in the lawe in the premisses, to wyne, yssue, make tryall, praie judgemente and execucion, condempne and ymprison and oute of prison againe to delyver, release and discharge, and upon composicion or agreemente, acquitannces or any other lawful discharges for me and in my name to make, assigne, seale and as my deed or deeds to delyver, attorneyes, counsellors or solicitors, one or moe to make, retayne and appointe and them againe to revooke and displace, and finally to do, saie, execute, conclude, determyne and fully finishe as well the whole premisses as also all and every other matter, thinge or cause whatsoever that cann, shall or maie be needfull and requisite to be done in or aboute the said premisses by vertue of theis presentes, and I do covennante and promise by theis presentes to ratifie, confirme, approve and allowe all and whatsoever my said attorney shall doe or procure to be done on or aboute the said premisses by vertue of their presents. In witnes wheareof I, the said John Rand, have heareunto sett my hoond and seale the seaventhe daie of June, in the twelfte yeare of the raigne of our soveraigne lord, James, by the grace of God king of England, ffrannce and Ireland, defender of the faieth, etc, and of Scotland the seaven and fortith.

John Rand [*seal*]

Signed, sealed and delivered unto Edward Rand, master and maryner, for and to thuse and behoof of the said Raphe Rand, in the p[rese]nce of

Thomas Humfraye
Edward Rand
John Coolson
Thomas Watson, notary publicq
Anthony Normann, servien*tis* dicti notarij

Sources: Corporation of London Libraries, Guildhall Library MSS, will registers, 9171/22, ff. 365r–v. The original of this letter, in Corporation of London Libraries, Guildhall Library MSS, original wills, 9172/27/365, is endorsed: To my lovinge ffather John Rand at Sunderland or ells wher give this I praie yow I pray yow deliver this letter, with the other, at the Plow in Chepside to my cozin James Rand
The wages is xxvj[li]

19. Anthony Watson of Ryhope, Bishopwearmouth, 1614

In the name of God, amen, I, Anthony Watson of Ryop in the parishe
of Bushop Warnouthe, sick in bodye but of good and perfect
memorye, do make this my last will and testament in manner forme
followinge. First, I commend my soule into the handes of allmightie
God, trustinge to have of him remision and forgivnesse of of all my
sinnes and life everlastinge, throwghe the meritts of the deathe and
passion of his welbeloved sonne Jesus Christe, my onely saviour and
redemer, and my bodye to the earthe. I give to the poore people of
the parishe of Bushopwarmouthe five shillinges. Item, I give to my
wife Alice Watson for and duringe her life naturall, the house that
John Hobson of Ryop dwellethe in, with the garthe thereto
belongeinge. Also, I give to her two acers of arrable land in everye of
the three corne fieldes in Ryop, to be sett forthe unto her, forthe of
my farme in Ryop, by Christopher Wharton and John Sheperson, for
and duringe her life, without payinge any rent therefore. Also, I give
to my said wife pasturinge for two kye and ten sheepe in Ryop oxe
pasture and sheep pasture without paying any rent for theim. And
my will is that my sonne George Watson shall freely and without
any payment, in dewe season, well and sufficiently plowe, sowe and
harrowe the arrable land above said, and lead home the corn in
harvest to such barne and stackgarthe in Ryop my said wife shall
appoint. And this service of husbandrye to be done to her dureinge
her life. And my will is that my sonne George Watson shall yearely,
as longe as my said wife shall live, bringe her, to her dwellinge
howse in Ryop, two foothers of coles and two foothers of whinnes
and two foothers of hay, she payinge for the coles at the pitt, for
fellinge of the whinnes and payinge for the haye, and makinge it
ready for leadinge. Item, I give to my son George Watson my yonge
gray mayre. Item, I give and bequeathe to William Browen and to
John Browen, my daughter's children, to eyther of them, a yowe and
a lamb. Item, I give and bequeathe to my sonne in law Ambrose
Moyser and to my dawghter Alice, his wife, to eyther of them, a
yowe and a lamb. All the rest of my goods and chattles, moveable
and unmoveable, my debts payd, I give and bequeathe to my sonne
George Watson, whom I make my full executor of this my last will
and testament. Published as the last will and testament of Anthony
Watson, the nyenteenth day of December, 1614, in presence of
Christopher[juratus] Wharton, Robert Awd, John Dobson[juratus]
Thomas[juratus] Ayre [*no signatures or marks*]

An inventorye of all the goodes and chatles which belonged to Anthony Watson of Ryop of the parishe of Bishop Warnouthe priced the 29 day of December, 1614, by Nicholas Tomson, Robert Goodchild, Thomas Roxebye and John Fell.

Inprimis, vj drawght oxen	17	0s	0d
Item, iiij mayres	7	0s	0d
Item, iij kyne & one stirk	6	13s	4d
Item, xxv sheepe	5	0s	0d
Item, hay and strawe	3	0s	0d
Item, corne in the barne & stackgarthe	20	0s	0d
Item, corne sowen on the ground	5	0s	0d
Item, viij swine	1	6s	8d
Item, one arke	1	0s	0d
Item, ploughes and waynes, yoakes and sowemes, with all theire iron furniture and ploughe and wayne timber, with horse harrowes and oxen harrowes	5	0s	0d
Item, all manner of howseholde stuffe	3	6s	8d

Somma lxxiiij^{li} vj^s viij^d

Debtes dewe to the testator

Imprimis, Raiphe Moiser	2	10s	0d

Debtes which the testator was indebted to others

Imprimis , to Edward Fell	3	14s	0d
Item, to Margerye Tomson	6	0s	0d
Item, to Robert Burdein	2	0s	0d
Item, to John Browen	14	0s	0d

Somma xxvij^{li} xiiij^s

Source: DPR1/1/1614/W4/1–2, parchment 2mm.

20. William Pattinson of Bishopwearmouth, 1615

In the name of God, amen, I, William Pattinson of Bushope Warmouth, feelling myself to be sicke in bodye but of good and perfecte memorye, do make this my last will and testamentt in manner and forme followinge. First, I commend my sowl in the handes of amightye God, my maker, trustinge to have forgiveness of all my sinnes and in heaven life everlastinge, thorough the merittes and mediacion of Jesus Christ, my onely savioure and redemer, and my bodye to be buried in the parishe churche of Bushope Warmouthe. Item, I geve and bequeath unto the poore people of Bushopewarmouthe parishe xx⁵. Item, I geve and bequeath unto my sonne Robertt Pattinsonn my bible, and my will is {that in consideracion of such things as I have formerlie geven unto my sayd sonne Roberrt Pattinson} that he shall have no partt or filliall portion of the rest of my goods & chattelles. Ittem, I geve and bequeath unto my wife Alice Pattinson for the educacion and bringinge upp of my youngere children the lease of the howse and landes yett endureinge which I have of the reverend father in God, the lord bushope of Durham. All the rest of my goods and chattels moveable and unmoveable, nott bequethed, my debtts & funerall discharged, I geve and bequeath to my wife Alice Pattinson, to my sonnes Christofor Pattinson, John Pattinson, William Pattinson, and to my daughters Issabell Pattinson, Marye Pattinson, and to the child or children that my wife is nowe conceyved withall, all whom I do mak my executores of this my last will and testament. Also my will is that if any of my sayd children shall dye before they have lawfull power to dispose of ther childe's porcion & the goods and chattells due to them by this my last will and testament, that then ther childe's porcion and partt of the sayd goods & chattells shalbe equalye devided amongst the rest of of my younger children. In testimony hereof, I have hereunto sett my hand and published this my last will & testament, the 26ᵗʰ daye of October in the yeare of our lord, 1614 and

William Patteson [*full name signed*]

in the presence of these
John Shipperdsonⁱᵘʳᵃᵗᵘˢ [*full name signed*]
John Thompson his mark [*marked with a symbol*]
Anthonye Newby [*full name signed*]
John Hillton ⁱᵘʳᵃᵗᵘˢ [*full name signed*]

Ane inventory of all the goodes & chattells lately belonging to William Pattinson of Bishopwermothe in the county of Durham, yeoman, deceased, as it is valued & prised by these foure men, videlicet John Thomson, John Shepperson, iunior, Anthony Newbie & John Johnson, the xxvjº day of January, anno regni Regis Jacobi &c., duodecimo, anno Domini 1614

Inprimis, ten oxen, price	40	0s	0d
Item, nyne kine	20	0s	0d

Item	£	s	d
Item, six horses & two foles	14	16s	8d
Item, one sowe & seaven young swyne	2	10s	0d
Item, fortie & one sheep of ewes & others	10	10s	0d
Item, wheate in the barne & stackyards	10	10s	0d
Item, pease in the barne & stackyards	16	0s	0d
Item, bigg in the barne & garth	8	13s	4d
Item, oates in the barne & garthe	6	0s	0d
Item, wheate & rye battens in the barn & garth		13s	4d
Item, all the hay and strawe threshed	3	6s	8d
Item, all the wheate sowen one the ground, being by estimacion xx acres	30	0s	0d
Item, long waynes, cowpwaynes & wheales, two oxe harrowes & two horse harrows	4	3s	4d
Item, thre plowes with there irons, yokes, somes & horsegeere with other furniture thereto belonging	1	13s	4d
Item, dunge forkes, corne forkes, spades, sholves & rakes		6s	6d
Item, newe wooden ploughe geere & wayngeere	1	0s	0d
Item, thre ladders		1s	0d
Item, sixe wayne ropes		2s	0d
Item, ten boules of pease in the lofte	2	16s	8d
Item, two cupbords in the halle house & two pressers in the chamber	4	6s	8d
Item, a litle cupbord in [the][10] chamber		5s	0d
Item, iiij° bedsteedes, one old counter, a little cupbord & a fflannders chiste	2	0s	0d
Item, five tubbes, two basketts, & a hopper		2s	8d
Item, sixe boules of oate malt	1	6s	8d
Item, in the parlor, a short table with a frame & three buffett formes		6s	8d
Item, in the kitching, v barrs, iij tubbes, v° skeeles, thre cannes, ij dussen trenches, one spynninge wheele & a paire of wooll cards, two skeppes, ij battledoors, one paire of yarne windle blaydes a stone trough		10s	0d
Item, two kettles, a brasse pan & iij brasse potts	1	10s	0d
Item, in the hall house, pewter dublers, candlesticks, potts, & other small peeces one the cupbord heeds	1	13s	4d
Item, ij mattresses, sixe coullered coverleds, iiij°			

---

10 Omitted from the manuscript text.

happings, foure blanckets, ten bolsters and coddes & a carpett	4	16s	8d
Item, furniture and apparell belonging to his body	3	0s	0d
Item, a paire of saye bedd couurtaynes		8s	0d
Item, five paire of sheetes & one od sheete lynning	1	15s	0d
Item, five straken sheetes & thre bord clothes		13s	4d
Item, xj pelowbers, one towell & one vallance for a bedd		10s	0d
Item, a dussen table napkins		5s	0d
Item, hanginges about a bedd in the parlor & a covering for the bed & sixe cushings		12s	0d
Item, sixe yeardes of woollen clothe & two yeards of linsey woolsey		12s	0d
Item. a table in the hall with a frame, two buffet formes formes, ij chayres, a truckle bed & a cheesbord		13s	4d
Item, in the halle ane iron chimney, & in the parlor a paire of barres, ij recken crookes, a paire of racks, a speete & a frying pann		16s	0d
Item, ane axe, a porr & a paire of onges		1s	0d
Item, ane arke		6s	8d
Item, a kilne haire & a paire of malt whernes		13s	4d
Item, one cock, iiij henns, ij capons & ij geese		3s	4d
Item, ij yeardes & iij q[ua]rters of brode clothe		16s	6d
Item, a window clothe, v sacks & two pokes		6s	8d
Item, one lease holden of the lord bishop of Durham	3	6s	8d
Item, vij riddles & sives, viij milke boules, iiij cheese fatts, ij woodden dublers & one chirne		4s	0d
Some of the goods prised in this inventory is	195	16s	10d

Debts oweing to the testator

Imprimis, Edward Dearnley for viij bowles & 3 peckes of malt	4	3s	8d
Item, William Pasmore for a horse		7s	6d
Item, John Thomson, keelman, for a litle house	3	17s	0d
Summa of the debts owing to the testator is	8	8s	2d

Summa totalis of all the goods belonging to the testator	204	4s	0d

Debts owing by the testator

Imprimis, to Mr Airye of Hougton	8	0s	0d
Item, to Roger Scurfeild	4	10s	0d
Item, to John Ireland of Harrington	11	17s	0d

Item, to Jasper Thomson	2	6s	8d
Item, to George Halliday	1	0s	0d
Item, to Raphe Pattinson, maister	1	8s	10d
Item, to John Pattinson	1	11s	0d
Item, to Elizabeth Thomson		8s	6d
Item, to Christofor Thomson		2s	4d
Item, to Elizabeth Hilton	1	6s	6d
Item, to servants for wag[e]s	2	1s	9d
Item, to Richard Pattinson		16s	0d
Item, to John Johnson for worke		18s	6d
Item, for the lord's rent	1	1s	0d
Item, for a mortuary		10s	0d
Item, for a lairstall		6s	8d
Item, to the minister, clark & seggerston		2s	2d
Item, for ringing the bells		3s	0d
Item, to the poore	1	0s	0d
Item, for the funerall expences	1	0s	0d
Item, to Mr Christofor Wharton		15s	0d
Item, for a bowle of pease to the said Christofor Wharton		6s	8d
Item, for a boule of wheat to the ffery bote		10s	0d
Item, for a boule of malt to Richard Robinson		10s	0d
Summa of the debts owing by the testator	42	12s	1d
So rests	161	11s	11d

Source: DPR1/1/1615/P4/1, 3, paper 4ff.

21. William Oliver of Monkwearmouth, chapman, 1615

An inventory of the goods & chattels of William Oliver late of Monkwarmouth, chapeman, deceased, taken & praysed by fower indifferent men this last of August, 1615, as ffolloweth:

Imprimis, att Morpeth a brand[e]d cowe	1	6s	8d
Item, one meare price	2	5s	0d
Per Cuthberte Ogle			
Gawen Smith			
Bartram Gard			
Item, att Bushopp Warmouth one branded cowe, worth	1	10s	0d
Item, one table in the hall with a fframe		6s	8d

Item, one fforme & two chaires, worth	2s	0d
Item, vj pewter platers, one salt seller & two candle sticks, worth	3s	4d
Item, two spynning wheeles, worth	2s	0d
Item, in one chamber within the hall, one bedstead, one chyst and a coffer	5s	0d
Item, one flocke bedd with a happyng coverlett & one bolster	7s	4d
Item, three paire of lynnen sheets, two pillowe beares, one borde cloath, 3 table napkins, & two hand toules, worth	17s	0d
Item, in the hall one racking crooke & three iron barres, worth	1s	6d
Item, in the chamber over the hall, a litle ould bedstead & a litle table without a frame, one flock bedd, one happing & a coverlett & a code, worth	6s	8d
Item, more one bedstead for servannt, two sheets & a happing, worth	3s	4d
Item, in the kitchen, one brasse pott, two pannes, one frying panne, one barrelle, one stand for drinks, one flackett, 4or drinking cannes	7s	4d
Item, two greene chaires, worth		8d
Item, one skeele, one milk syle & two bouls		8d
	4 13s	2d
Summa totallis	7 19s	10d

John Shipperdson, younger [*no signature or mark*]
William Hardcastell [*no signature or mark*]
Thomas Potts [*no signature or mark*]

Owing per bill from Richard Winter of Berwick as appeareth	4	0s	0d
Owing more per a note from John Lowris of Berwick as appeareth	1	16s	0d

Exhibitum per uxorem &c., 2 Septembris, 1615

Source: DPR1/1/1615/02/1, paper 2ff.

22. Ralph Wetslett of Barnes, Bishopwearmouth, 1615

A true inventorie of all the goods and chattels moveable and unmoveable of Rauph Wheisletts layte of Barnes, deceazed, praysed by these fower indeferent and honest men, the xxv[th] September, 1615, Robert Skurffeild, John Johnsonn, Rauph Reede, Mathew Kelley.

Imprimis, xj kyne and whies	32	10s	0d
Item, hay standinge in the housefeild	1	10s	0d
Item, fiftie sheepe	14	8s	0d
Item, sixteene lambs	2	8s	0d
Item, one meare	1	10s	0d
Item, three stirks or calves	2	0s	0d
Item, swyne	2	0s	0d
Item, geise		10s	0d
Item, pulleine, henns & cocks		5s	0d
Item, bees		10s	0d

Summa ys lvj[li] xj[s]

Houshould stuffe

Item, one coubert, one counter, one calle and one presser {with one longe table}	2	0s	0d
Item, brasse and pewder vessell	2	0s	0d
Item, two cheares, with chists		11s	0d
Item, wood vessell	1	15s	0d
Item, fower bedsteeds		2s	6d
Item, coverletts, happens and blankets	2	0s	0d
Item, one matterisse and blanketts		16s	0d
Item, linninge and harden sheets	2	4s	0d
Item, table clothes and napkings		7s	0d
Item, two speets, one paire of thongs, with pott kilps, reckens & iron barrs		7s	0d
Item, all his worke geare		13s	4d
Item, butter and cheise		10s	0d
Item, chese bourds & weabaulks		2s	0d
Item, his apparell, purse and other furniture	2	13s	4d

Summa ys xvj[li] xiiij[d]

Debts owne to the deceazed

M[r] Ralph Bowes, esq.,	2	13s	4d
Rauph Pallesser	1	6s	8d

Anthonie Bakon		11s	0d

Summa ys iiij^{li} xj^s

Debts owne by the deceazed

To Mr Humfray Whartonn	4	14s	0d
To Thomas Smith	4	10s	0d
{To Robert Skurfeild	2	0s	0d}
To Mr Tempest	1	18s	0d
To George Cragge		4s	4d

Summa ys xiij^{li} vj^s iiij^d

Funerall expenc[e]s	2	0s	0d

Source: DPR1/1/1615/W11/1, paper 2ff.

23. Thomas Chilton of Fulwell, Monkwearmouth, 1615

[*Version A*] In the name of God, amen, I, Thomas Chilton of Foulwell in the parish of Munckewarmounth, doe make this my last will amd testament in manner and forme following: first of all, I give and bequith my soule to almighti God, my redemer and saviour, and my body to buried in the church of Munckewarmounth, in the northend of my oune stall under the great stone. Imprimis, I give and bequeth to the poure xx^s to be payed within thre mounths after my death. I give to my daughter Barbary Browne chilldren xx^{li} amongst theme as foloweth: to Willam Hollalye viij^{li} and a selver spone, and to Margaret Hollalye vj^{li}, and to the rest of the chilldren that she hath to Thomas Browne vjli, to be devided amongst theme equily, every one alyke. Allso I give unto my daughter Jeane Huichinson chilldren xx^{li} as foloweth, that is, to Thomas Huichinson x^{li} and a sillver spone, and to the rest of these chilldren x^{li}, to be devided amongst them, every one a lyke. Allso I give unto my daughter Elsabeth Huntlay chilldren xx^{li} as foloweth: to Raphe Huntlay hyr eldest son a selver spone, and the twentye pounds to be devided amongst theme, everyone alyke. I give unto Mighell Jurdison chilldren, to eviry one of theme, a yeowe and a lame, and to his eldest son John Jurdison a selver spone. Allso I give to Thomas Coulson chilldren, to every one of theme, a yeowe and a lame. And for all the rest of my goods and chattelles, moveble and unmoveble, my debtes, bequeths, funeralles descharged, I give unto my most welbeloved and trustye wife Margerit Chillton, whome I make my whole and sole executor for to dispose to the plesure of God and the health of my soule, anno Domini 1613, dayted the xxjst day of August. Item, I give more unto Thomas Hutcheson, after the death of my wife, a plough with coulter and socke, a longwayne, cowpewayne, yooks and sowmes for the same. Item, I give more unto Willyam Hollalye my sworde which Michaell Jurdison hath.

Thomas Chilton, his m[ar]ke [*marked with a scratch*]

Witnesses heareof when the testator did acknowledge the same to be his last will when the same was redd unto him aboute a weeke before he dyed,
Reignold ffawcett ^{iuratus}, Anthony Younge^{iuratus}, Cuthbert Thompson, his marke [*no signatures or marks*]

[*Version B*] In the name of God, amen, I, Thomas Chilton of ffulwell in the parish of Munckwarmothe, doe maik this my last will and testament in manner & forme followinge: ffirst of all, I give & bequeath my soule to almighti God, my redeemer and saviour, and my bodie to be buried in the church of Munckwarmothe in the north end of myn owne stall, under the great stone. Inprimis, I give and bequeath to the poore xx^s to be paid within three months after my death. I give to my daughter Barbara Browne children xx^{li} amongst them, as followeth: to William Hollaley viij^{li} and a silver spoone, and to Margaret Hollaley vj^{li}, and to the rest of the children that she hath, to Thomas Browne vj^{li}, to be devided amongst them equallie, everie one a like. Alsoe, I give unto my daughter Jane Hutchinson children xx^{li} as followeth: that is, to Thomas Hutchinson x^{li} and a silver spoone, and to the rest of these children x^{li}, to be devided amongst them, everie one a like. Alsoe, I give unto my daughter Elisabeth Huntleys children xx^{li}, as followeth: to Raph Huntley, her eldest sonne, a silver spoone, and the twentie poundes to be devided amongst them, everie one a like. I give unto Michaell Jurdeson children, to everie one of them, an ewe and a lambe and to his eldest some, John Jurdeson, a silver spoone. Alsoe, I give to Thomas Colson children, everie one of them, an ewe and a lambe. And for all the rest of my goods & chattels, moveable and unmoveable, my debts, bequeaths & funerals discharged, I give unto my most welbeloved & trustie wife Margaret Chilton, whome I maik my whole & sole executor for to dispose to the pleasure of God and the health of my soule, anno Domini 1613, dated the xxjth daie of August. Item, I give more unto Thomas Hutchinson, after the death of my wife, a plough with coulter & socke, a longe waine, coope waine yokes and somes

for the same. Item, I give more unto William Hollaley my sword,
which Michaell Jurdeson hath. Witnesses hearof, when the testattor
did acknowledg the same to be his last will, when the same was reed
unto him aboute a week before he died, Reginald ffawcett, Anthonye
Younge, Cuthbert Thompsonn.

Concordat haec copia cum originali exh*ibita* per me, *Robertus*
Newhouse, notararius

An inventorye of all the goodes and chattles moveable and
unmoveable of Thomas Chilton, late of ffulwell, deceased, praysed
by fowre indefferent men, videlicet Robert Tayllor, Reignald
ffawcett, Michaell Lumley and Anthonye Young, this xxviij[th] day of
November, anno Domini 1615.

Imprimis, ten oxen, with all the hay a boute the howse or tenement	45	0s	0d
Item, vj kyen and two whyes	13	6s	8d
Item, vj young stirkes	3	13s	4d
Item, fyve horses and mears	10	0s	0d
Item, in sheepe ould and young, thre score and three	11	16s	0d
Item, in swyne xvj	3	10s	0d
Item, corne in the stackyarde and in the barne	30	0s	0d
Item, wheate and rye sowne in the field	20	0s	0d
Item, waines and wayne geare, plowes and plowe geare, yookes, and sowmes, oxen harrowes, horse harrowes	4	10s	0d
Item, one cupborde, two bedd steads, two chistes & one arke	2	13s	4d
Item, one brew lead, a stepe stone, with other stone troughes	1	0s	0d
Item, fowre bowles of malte	2	0s	0d
Item, two ketles, two pannes and an iron pott		10s	0d
Item, eight pewther dublers, one cham[b]er pott, one candlesticke and a chaffing dishe		10s	0d
Item, vij silver spones	1	1s	0d
Item, one table, a longsetle, one forme, one spence, one chaire and one buffitt stole	1	0s	0d
Item, one chimney, one spete, a porr, a payre of tongs, a payre of racks & a rackingcroke		15s	0d
Item, tenn hennes and a cock		3s	8d
Item, two geese, three ducks and turkye henn		4s	0d

Item, tubbes, stands, skeeles, bowls, dishes, a chirme & trenchers		6s	6d
Item, one gavelocke, one hacke, a stone hammer, two axes & a how		6s	0d
Item, one window clothe, with ridles and seves, sackes & pookes		3s	4d
Item, for forkes, shovels, spades		4s	0d
Item, fowre payre of shetes, two codpillibers, eight coverlets and happings, sex fethercodds	1	13s	4d
Item, his apparell, with his furniture	2	0s	0d

Somma totallis clvj^{li} xv^s ij^d

Debts oweing to the testator

In primis, Richard Tayllor for a bowle of malte	13s	4d
Item, Thomas Brome for a bowle of malte	13s	4d

Somma xxvj^s viij^d

Debts which the testator is oweing

In primis, to Mr Dean and the Chapter for the martinmes rent	2	15s	9d
Item, to Mr Hilton	7	0s	0d
Item, to Cuthbert Thompson for his wage		4s	4d
Item, to John Smyth for his wage		7s	8d
Item, to Thomas Gowland		10s	0d
Item, to Mr Hedworthe	4	0s	0d
Item, to Margarett Thompson		2s	0d
Item, for two stone of lint		14s	0d
Item, for a mortuarye and a layre stalle		13s	4d

Somma xvj^{li} vij^s j^d

Somma de claro cxlj^{li} xiij^s ix^d

Reignald ffawcett [*full name signed*]
Mickhell Lumley [*full name signed*]
Anthony Younge [*full name signed*]

Source: DPR1/1/1616/C5/1–4. Two copies of the will, parchment 1m. and paper 1f.; inventory, paper 2ff. sewn.

24. Thomas Hilton of Bishopwearmouth, yeoman, 1615

The 28 of Aprill 1614

In the name of God, amen, I, Thomas Hilton of Bishopwermoth in
the county of Durham, yeoman, sick of body but of whole and
perfite remembrance, thanks be to God, make this my last will &
testament in maner and forme following. ffirst, I bequeth my soule to
almightie God & my body to be buried in the parishe churche of
Bishopwermothe. Item, I bequyth to the poore of that parishe xiiij^s.
Item I give to my sonne John Hilton all the ploughe & waynegeare
with all the tymber for buylding or for ploughe & wayne, also all
yokes & somes & all wayne & ploughe geere, with ane iron chimney
in the halle house, a steepe stone, & a table in the halle house which
shall remain as airloomes. Item, to Thomas Hilton, sonne of John
Hilton, one grete brasse potte. Item, I will that Thomas Aire shall
have foure oxen, foure kine & xx ewes \with so many/ lambes, two
horses & a fillie, two whies, the one of 2 one other of 3 yeares old,
two calves, item one lode of rye, item so muche corne of every
grayne as will sowe his farmhold in Tunstall, the ground plowed &
maid redy. Item, William Thomson & Adam Middleton is to leve the
ffarmhold at Mayday next after the date hereof & to deliv[e]r up all
suche implements of husbandry as they received at their entry, & in
consideracion of all former articles & covenants they ar to have at
their departure the some of xiij^li of lawful English money. Item, I will
that all suche houshold stuffe as I or my wif have provided for the
mariage of Thomas Aire & my daughter Ann shalbe deliv[e]red unto
them freely. All the rest of my goods & chattels undisposed of by this
my last will, moveable & unmoveable, my debts, legases & funerall
expences paid, I bequethe to my wif Elizabeth Hilton & my said
sonne John Hilton, whom I make my full executors of this my laste
will & testament. In witnes hereof, I, the said Thomas Hilton have to
these presents sette my hand the day & yeare abovesaid.

Thomas Hilton's mark [*marked with a scratch*]

Post scriptum
Item, I leve & committ my daughter Elizabeth Hilton to the custody
& tuition of my wife & my sonne to be by them well & sufficiently
manteyned & governed, with meate, drinke, apparell, lodging & all
other needfull necessaries during her life naturall.

Debts owing the Thomas Hilton

Imprimis, my sonne John Hilton for half the crope			
one the ffarmhold now growinge	23	6s	8d
Item, Rob[e]rt Burdon for a bushell of wheate		8s	0d
Item, Mr George Whiteheed	4	0s	0d

Debtes owing by Thomas Hilton

Imprimis, to my sonne John Hilton	10	0s	0d
Item, to Robert Huntley	18	0s	0d

Witnesses hereof

John Shepp[er]son, senior, mark [*marked with initial capitals I S*]
John Johnson's^iuratus mark [*marked with a symbol, a horseshoe*]
Tho[mas] Sparrow^iuratus [*full name signed*]

Ane inventory of all the goods and chattells lately belonginge to Thomas Hilton of Bishopwermoth in the county of Durham, deceased, as it is valued & prised by these foure men, videlicet John Thompson, John Sheperson, junior, William Robinson & John Johnson, the 22 daye of May anno regni Regis Jacobi &c, decimo tertio

Imprimis, thre oxen	13	0s	0d
Item, iiij kyne	7	0s	0d
Item, xx sheepe	5	10s	0d
Item, iij horse & mares	7	0s	0d
Item, x lambes		13s	4d
Item, thre oxe stirks	1	13s	0d
Item, one sowe & two pigs		12s	0d
Item, two longe waynes, thre cowpe waynes, iiij plowes, j oxe harrow & three horse harrowes, iij ladders, iiij somes, two shalles, vj yoks, two coulters & two socks	3	16s	8d
Item, seaven acres of wheat sowen & growing	9	6s	8d
Item, foure acres of bigg growing	5	6s	8d
Item, seaven acres of pease growing	5	5s	8d
Item, thre acres & a half of oates growing	2	0s	0d
Item, on oxe sold at Durham	4	0s	0d
Item, one table & a chimney	1	0s	0d
Item, one cupboard, one spence & a cawell	3	0s	0d
Item, iij kettles, iij panns		16s	8d
Item, xiiij pece of pewter dishes, ij brasse potts, j dussen pewter spoones, one mortar & pestell, one pinte potte, thre candlesticks & iij saltessellers	1	13s	4d

Item, two bedsteeds, one old arke & flanders chist, one counter, one cawell	1	0s	0d
Item, ij chistes, nyne tubbes, one chirne, nyne milke bowells, 3 skeeles, thre barrells, six sives & riddles, one hopper, one pecke & one wooden bottle, with one greete washing boule	1	10s	0d
Item, one kilne haire, one windowcloth, iij sacks, iiij pokes, two temses & j heckle		10s	0d
Item, ten coverleds, two paire of blanketts, six bedd codds, two paire of linn sheets, two paire of stakin sheets, half a dussen napkins	3	6s	8d
Item, his apperell & furniture	2	0s	0d
Item, one boule of wheate		10s	0d
Item, ij boules of pease		10s	0d
Item, v bushells of haver malt		10s	0d
Item, iiij bacon flitches & one beefe flitchs	1	3s	0d
Item, iiij cushons, two chaires and thre chesebords		3s	4d
Item, iij hens & a cock		1s	4d
Summa of this inventory is	83	7s	8d

Debtes owing to the testator			
Imprimis, by Mr Georg Whithead	4	0s	0d
Summa totalis of all goods & chattels	87	7s	8d

Debts owing by the testator			
Item, to Robert Huntley	18	0s	0d
Item, to Peter Grene	1	16s	8d
Item, to Elizabeth Hilton	1	0s	0d
Item, to John Scott	1	0s	0d
Item, for the lord's rent	1	0s	5d
Item, to Ales Pattinson	1	3s	0d
Item, to Nichollas Huntley		6s	0d
Item, for ffunerall expences	1	16s	8d
Item, to John Johnson		2s	0d
Item, to Robert Huntley	1	5s	0d
Item, to Richard Holboume for ewes	2	10s	0d
Item, to Richard Huntley	1	16s	0d
Item, for a boule of malt		10s	0d

Summa debitorum 32^{li} 5^s 9^d

Source: DPR1/1/1615/H10/1, 3, paper 4ff.

25. Anthony Smith of Tunstall, Bishopwearmouth, 1616

Februarie 22th, 1615

In the name of God, amen, I, Anthonie Smithe of Tunstall and parishe of Busshopp Warmouthe, beinge sicke in bodye but of perfecte minde & memorie, doe make this my last will & testament, in manner & forme followeinge. ffirst, I committ my sowle to allmightie God, my maker & readeamer, and my bodye to be buried in the parishe churche of Busshopp Warmouthe aforesaide. Item, I give to my tow dawghters Luce & Margarett Smithe, to eyther of them, twentie poundes. Item, I give to Hughe Smithe & to his heires malle my howse or tenement in Sunderlande, and faillinge of his heires malle I give the said howse or tenement in Sunderland aforesaide to my sonne Richarde Smithe & his heires for ever. Item, I give to my saide sonne Hughe Smithe tenn poundes in money. Item, I give to my tow dawghters aforesaide, all my househoulde stuffe, excepteinge a great cawell & an arcke, the chimneye & one great poott,which I will shall remaine to my sonne Richarde Smithe. Item, I give to my sonne Richarde Smithe the lease of my ffarme & all my ploughe & and plowe geare, waine & waine geare, which I have aboute my farme. \And my will is that the abovesaid legaccies given to my children severally, shall stand and shall be to everie of them in full satisfaction of their filiall porcions./ Item, I give to William Thompson, my dawghter's sonne, xx^s. Item, I give to Issabell Herreson, xx^s. Item, all the reste of my goods, moveable & unmoveable, my debtes paide & my funerall expenses discharged, I give them to my sonne Richarde Smithe, whome I make my executore of this my laste will. And I requeste Thomas Rookesbye to be supervaysor of this my said will to see it executed. Witnesses hereof, Robert Ayre^{iuratus}, William Thompson, Rauphe Huntley, Thomas Ayre & George Shadfourthe.

Executio dicti defuncti ad usum dicti executoris et [*one word illegible*] est commissa Thome Rowesbie [*three words illegible*] Richardo Smith \16 annorum/ execut' {Hugh et [*illegible*]}

Septimo Martij, 1615
An inventarie of all suche goods & chattelles of Anthonie Smithe, late of Tunnstall & parishe of Busshopp Warmouthe dyed possessed of, praysed by fowre honest neighboures, videlicet Roberte Ayre, Thomas Ayre, William Thompson & George Shadfourthe.

Inprimis, tow oxene, praysed to	6	13s	4d
Item, fowre kyne, price	8	0s	0d
Item, thre stottrelles, price	3	6s	8d
Item, tow calves, price	1	4s	0d
Item, three horsses or meares	6	6s	8d
Item, five sheape, price	1	10s	0d
Item, ffowere swine, price		17s	0d
Item, corne in the stackgarthe & redye to markett	12	6s	8d
Item, corne sowne & to be sowne	12	0s	0d
Item, plowghe & plowghe geare, waine & waine geare	3	6s	8d
Item, all the househoulde stuffe given to his dawghters	5	0s	0d
Item, the lease of his ffarme, praysed to	80	0s	0d

Suma totallis £141 11s 0d

Debtes oweinge by the saide deceased

Imprimis, to Thomas Herresonne	34	0s	0d
{Item, to Roberte Ayre of Tunstall		11s	0d
Item, to Thomas Rookesbye	1	0s	0d
Item, to William Keye of Durham		6s	8d

Summa debitorum £35 6s 8d

Summa de claro, debitis deductis £104 13s 4d

Source: DPR1/1/1616/S11/1–2, paper 2ff.

26. John Thompson of Bishopwearmouth, yeoman, 1616

In the name of God, amen, the xij daye of July, in the yeare of our lord God one thousand six hundreth and sixteen, I, John Thompson of Bushope Warmouth in the countie of Durham, yeoman, being sicke in bodye but of good and perfect remembrance, thankes be to almightie God for the same, do make this my last will and testament in maner and fforme following. ffirst, I commend my soull into the hands of my lord and saviour, Jesus Christ, in and by whose onlye merites, deathe and passion I trust to be saved, and by no other meanes, and my bodie to be buried in the parish church of Bushop Wermouth. Item, I give and bequeath to the pore of Bushop Wermouth parish xl^s. Item. I give and bequeath to my sister daughter Annas Sanderson, x^{li}. Item, I give and bequeath to my sister, wedo Sanderson, iij^{li} vj^s viij^d. Item, I give and bequeath to my sister son, John Bordon, x^{li}. Item, I give and bequeath to my sister in lawe Elsabeth Colson one busshell of wheat to be paid yearly during hir lyfe naturall. Item, I give and bequeath to my man William Curtiss one branded copt why. Item, I give and bequeath to Tomeson Colson on branded why, to be given hir when she is xxj yeares of agge. Item, I give and bequeath to Annas Shiperson one gimer hog. Item, I give and bequeath to Elsabeth Pasmore on gimmer hog. Item, I give & bequeath to Annas Brown on why. Item, I give & bequeath to Annas Shipperson, my brother in lawe his daughter, on blak why going in the faugh. All the rest of my goods and chattells movabell and unmovabell, my debts, legeses and funerall expenses paid, I give and bequeath unto my wife Annas Thomson^{iurata} and my sister son Richard Sanderson^{iuratus} whom I make my executors of this my last will and testament, in witnes herof I have set to my hand in the presence of thes witnesses, the day and yeare above written

Witnesses William Shep[er]son^{iuratus} [*full name signed*]

      John Shipp[er]dson^{iuratus} [*full name signed*]

      Willy[a]m Robbeson^{iuratus} mark [*marked with single stroke*]

[*Endorsed*] 27 Jul[y] 1616, inv*entorium* ad [£]212 10s 4d

A trew inventorie of all the goodes, movabell and unmovabell that John Thompson of Bushop Wearmouth dieid possest of, and prased by these fowre men, John Shipp[erd]son, Addam Holme, John Johnson, William Robinson, this viij daye of July, 1616

Imprimes, xij oxson	54	0s	0d
Item, x kye	20	0s	0d
Item, vj whies	6	0s	0d
Item, one boull	1	0s	0d
Item, xxix ewes	7	0s	0d
Item, xxvj geld sheep	7	0s	0d
Item, xx lames	2	10s	0d
Item, xxv akers of wheat and bigge	37	10s	0d
Item, xxij akers of pees and ottes	22	0s	0d
Item, wheat in the house, pees and malt	2	0s	0d
Item, thre longe waynes with ther wheles	2	0s	0d
Item, thre coupe waynes with ther wheles	5	0s	0d
Item, five horsses and meares	13	0s	0d
Item, two stages and one foolle	3	10s	0d

Item, two cawles		6s	8d
Item, five plowes with ther irones		16s	0d
Item, xij draught yokes		8s	0d
Item, thre soomes, two oxe harrowes, two hors			
harrowes, thre payre of horsgeere	1	6s	8d
Item, xij new oxtrees, thre new beemes		10s	0d
Item, one pare of new <funles>, one ledder		4s	0d
Item, five dunge grapes, two hakes, fowre cornforkes,			
one leepe and one showle		5s	0d
Item, thre newe stinges, two spades, three <stees>,			
two rakes, one cheespres		13s	4d
Item, two ammries	2	0s	0d
Item, two tables, one hossat forme, two hossat stules,			
two chares, one forme		13s	4d
Item, five bras potes, two copper kettels, one yetling,			
two panes, five brase kanddelstix	2	0s	0d
Item, xxiiij peese of puder dublers, xv sassers, one			
quart poot, on pint poot, fower toones, two saltes,			
one puder candlestick	1	0s	0d
Item, one chimler, rakkencrouks, one frienpan, one			
speet, one payre of rakes, one payre of tonges,			
one poor	1	0s	0d
Item, two bedstedes, one flander chist		14s	0d
Item, one fedder beed, one mattres, two blancodes,			
fower hingers, one payre of shetes, six coverledes,			
one covring, thre codes and one bouster	2	7s	0d
Item, one presser		10s	0d
Item, fower chistes, one little tabel		16s	0d
Item, for tobes		6s	8d
Item, thre riddles, one seeve, one peack, one window			
cloth, thre sakes, two pokes, one payre of temses		8s	0d
Item, five payre of leningshetes, six pillevers, two			
bordclothes, two towels	1	13s	4d
Item, thre doblats, thre payre of briches, one clooke			
with the rest of his fornetor	4	10s	0d
Item, thre beef flickes, one bakon flicke		12s	4d
Item, x hennes, one cock, two capons		4s	0d
Item, xxxiiij cheses		13s	4d
Item, five stone of butter		16s	0d
Item, two whistirkes	1	7s	8d
Item, thre beehyves		10s	0d
Item, seven ould swine & six piges	1	10s	0d

Item, two stone and a halfe of wolling yearn	16s	0d
Item, fowre coup waynesoles	6s	0d
Some totalis ccxij^{li} x^s 4^d		

Detes owen to the above named John Thompson as foloing

Thomas Snawdon	1	3s	0d
Richard Barton	2	12s	0d
Thomas Watte		11s	0d
William Stevenson		5s	0d
Thomas Bell		10s	0d
Some of the detes v^{li} ij^s			

Summa totalis bonorum et debitorum £217 12s 4d

Source: DPR1/1/1616/1–2, parchment 2mm.

27. Thomas Bulbe of Hilton, Monkwearmouth, 1616

An inventorye of all the goodes and chatilles of Thomas Bulbe, latte of Hilton, decesed, praised by thes 4 men, Pettere Hocheson, Richard Sparrowe, Roberte Hilton, George Daill, the xixth daie of ffebrearye, anno 1616, as followeth,

Impremes, one cadrone, one cettell, 4 panes	1	12s	0d
Item, syxe pootes, one with anothere	1	10s	0d
Item, one posnoote and a pare of clipes		1s	0d
Item, one poodere pootte, 3 candelstickes, 10 saseres		3s	4d
Item, thre ammeres, 2 caveles	3	0s	0d
Item, one chemleye, 2 rakene rukes, one pare of tonges, one pore, one speate, 2 rakes		14s	0d
Item, one chare, 2 bufyte stoyles, one tabell, one cupstoyll, one cheste, one arke, one longstedell, one chesbord, on planke	2	5s	0d
Item, one ffedere bead, one bostere, on blankete, 3 codes, twoe coverlydes, one hapen	2	0s	0d
Item, ffowere lyinginge shetes, 2 hardene shetes		19s	0d
Item, twoe tubes, 2 churnes, one cheste, one trunke		9s	0d
Item, lose bordes		2s	0d
Item, thre pare of breeches, 2 dublytes, twoe girkenes, 2 paire of stokenes, one cloke, 2 hattes	2	5s	0d
Item, thre kyee	5	5s	0d

Item, haye valued to		10s	0d
Item, one meare, one sadell, one soyde	2	5s	0d
Item, twoe sylvere spoines given unto the childrene, thre swine	1	2s	0d
Item, thre stoynes		3s	4d
Item, twoe whyes	2	0s	0d
Item, tene yowes	4	4s	0d
Item, one arke in the byere		10s	0d
Item, one buttere cite and one pointe potte		1s	6d
The som	31	1s	2d

Debts owinge

Item, due from Williem Hall at Maye daie nexte cominge	8	0s	0d
Due from Williem Townerawe dwelling in me Lord Darsye's parke	2	10s	0d
Due from Thomas Gybscon at Mychellmas nexte	2	0s	0d
Due from Edward Gybscone to be paied at the same tyme	1	0s	0d
Due from Thomas Tesdell at this same tyme		16s	0d
Due from John Bell		2s	2d
Due from Raph Bedlinton in his[11] hande		16s	0d
Due from John Lockey		2s	8d
From Thomas Vasye		2s	0d
Richard Thompscon, due to be paied		6s	6d

More of the same

{Michell Toode for to be paied		10s	8d}
John Thompsoon, due for to be paied		2s	4d
Henerye Curtes, due for to be paied		10s	0d
John Audere of the well house, due for to be paied		2s	0d
The som, £16 0s 6d			

Detees due for to be paied

Nickelles Chesbrouge	4	0s	0d
John Hoppere	2	13s	4d
Raph Brough		7s	6d
Owinge for a stoyne of lyne		7s	6d
The som, £7 8s 4d			

---

11 The manuscript repeats 'his'.

Wytneses of the same
  Peetere Huchescon [*marked with a cross*]
  Richard Sparrowe [*marked with a symbol*]
  Robertt Hilton [*marked with a symbol*]
  George Daill [*full name signed*]

[*Endorsed*] 13 Apr 1616, administratio data Elizabethae viduae. Richardus et Maria filii in minore etate.

Source: DPR1/1/1616/B14/1–2, paper 2ff.

28. George Shadforth of Tunstall, Bishopwearmouth, yeoman, 1617

In the name of God, amen, I, George Shawdfurth of Tonstall within the parish of Bushopp Weremouth, in the countie of Durham, yeoman, sicke in body but of good & perfect remembrance, God be praised therefore, doe make my last will & testament this last day of July, anno Domini 1617, as followeth. ffirst, I give my soule to the hands of almightie God, my onlie savior, and my bodie to be burryed in the parish church att Dalton. Item, my will is that my welbeloved wife shall labour by all meanes possible to procure the wardshipp of my eldest sonne. Item, I give to my second sonne Anthonie Shawdfurth my lease and all my interest of Tonstall for all the yeares therein unrunne & yett to come, in full contentacion of his filiall porcion & all other bequests whatsoever thereof maid by my welbeloved uncle John Shawdfurth to the said Anthonie. Item, I give all the rents & profitts whatsoever arising out of my moitye of Warden Lawe unto my onlie daughter [*blank*] Shawdfurth for the tearme of tenn yeares, for the raising up of five hundreth pounds which I gave hir in full satisfaccion of hir filiall porcion. Item, I give to everie of my sister Isabell hir children xl^s a peece. Item, I give to everie of the children of John Shawefurth of Warden, xx^s a peece Item, I give to Marie Bell xx^{tie} markes. All the rest of my goodes & debts due to me I doe give to my welbeloved wife Isabell Shawdfurth for the true payment of all such debts as I am owing to anie person & for the payment of my legasies in this my will conteyned, and I doe make my said wife sole executrix of this my last will and testament. And I make George Collingwood of Eppleden, esq., and John King of the cittie of Durham supervisors of this my will, and I give unto either of them xx^s for a token.

Witnesses thereof,
George Collingwood [*full name signed*]
John King [*full name signed*]

An inventarie of all the goodes and chattells wherof George Shawdfurth of Tonnstall within the parish of Bushopp Weremouth dyed possessed of praysed by these five men, v*idelicet* Christopher Younge, Edward Daile, Thomas Gregson, Thomas Robeson and Anthonie Ayer, the xix[th] of August, anno Domini 1617.

Att Tonnstall

Inprimis, xiiij kyne, one with another, att l[s] a cowe[12]	35	0s	0d
Item. a bull	2	10s	0d
Item. xxix ewes, att vij[s] a pece	10	3s	0d
Item. viij drawght oxen, att xj[li] a yoake	44	0s	0d
Item. xvij acres of hard corne and xvij acres of ware corne	60	0s	0d
Item. vj lode of ottes, threshed in the barne, att vj[s] viij[d] a lode	2	0s	0d
Item. xx[tie] threaves of wheate, by estimacion, in a stacke, att vj[s] viij[d] a bushell	5	0s	0d
Item. pease on the same stacke, estimated at	1	10s	0d
Item, one meare and a foale	5	0s	0d
Item. one younge meare	2	0s	0d
Item. an other olde meare	1	13s	4d
Item. one bay nagg	3	6s	8d
Item. one other coult	2	0s	0d
Item. one yeare old stagg	1	13s	4d
Item. one old bay meare and a foale	2	10s	0d
Item. two whies	5	0s	0d
Item. ix stottes	24	0s	0d
Item. vij calves and one sturdy calfe	4	4s	0d
Item. a bull stirke	1	6s	8d
Item. xx[tie] tuppes	6	0s	0d
Item. lxxij old sheepe on the hilles, att vij[li] a score	25	4s	0d
Item. xix lambes	4	0s	0d
Item. iiij swyne	2	13s	4d
Item. ij longe waynes, with yrn bound wheles	6	13s	4d
Item. iij old coupe waynes & wheles	1	0s	0d

---

12 50s a cow.

Item. iij ploughes & soomes for them	1	6s	8d
Item. xxx fudders of hay	10	0s	0d
Item. xij geese		6s	0d
Item. xx^{tie} hennes & chickines		6s	8d
Item. xij stone of butter	2	0s	0d
Item. lx cheses, att vj^d a peece	1	10s	0d

In the hall

Item, ij cubbordes	1	0s	0d
Item, xiiij peece of pewther		7s	0d
Item, iiij candlesticks & five saults		10s	0d
Item, ij tables, ij chares, one forme		6s	8d
Item, one paire of barres & ij reckencrooks, ij spitts		7s	0d
Item, a litle longsettell		3s	0d
Item, a muskett, a callever & a dagg	1	0s	0d
Item, a certaine wollen yame		2s	6d

cclxxvij^{li} ix^s ij^d

In the parler:

Item, a cubbord & a portall		10s	0d
Item, a drawing table & 7 buffet stooles		13s	4d
Item, a fedder bedd a truckell bedd & a bedstead, with the furniture	2	0s	0d
Item, one longsettell & a chist		6s	8d
Item, x peece of pewther		5s	0d
Item, a paire of yron barres		1s	0d
Item, a billstaffe, ij swordes, his saddell furnished		10s	0d

In the midle chamber

Item, a fedder bedd furnished & a bedstead	2	6s	8d
Item, a little chist, a spinning whele, a little buffett stoole & a litle chaire		3s	4d
Item, ix coverletts & one blankett	3	0s	0d
Item, a new wollen matteris		10s	0d

In the uper chamber

Item, one side cubbord, with 2 almeries in it		6s	8d
Item, 6 quishions		10s	0d
Item, an almerie & 2 brasse potts		13s	4d
Item, a paire of barres		1s	0d
Item, a fir chist		5s	0d
Item, five lyn webbes conteyning xx^{tie} yerds a peece	5	0s	0d

Item, one harden webb		10s	0d
Item, xvj stone of wooll	8	0s	0d
Item, his apparell	13	6s	8d
Item, in present mony	6	0s	0d
And more delivered to Mr Rober Collingwood &c.	27	0s	0d
Item, vj silver spoones	1	10s	0d
Item, ij dozen & an halfe of table napkins		10s	0d
Item, iiij lyn bord clothes		10s	0d
Item, the lease of Tonnstall		600 pounds	

vj^{C}lxxiiij^{li} viij^s viij^d

Att Murton

Item, 2 wheate stacks, by estimacion, conteyning 46 threaves	10	0s	0d
Item, 4 ote stacks, conteyning, by estimacion, 5^{xx} x^{13} threaves	16	10s	0d
Item, 28 fudders of hay, vj^s per fudder	8	8s	0d
Item, one yron buned wayne	3	6s	8d
Item, an other paire of bune wheles and a paire of old wayne blades & wheles	2	13s	4d
Item, a coope wayne & yron wheles	2	0s	0d
Item, 2 olde coopes & a paire of old wheles & stings		13s	4d
Item, 4 sawen ieasts		10s	0d
Item, 12 axeltrees		9s	0d
Item, plowghes, soomes & yoakes		13s	4d
Item, 4 long wayne blades	2	0s	0d
Item, 4 coope wayne soles	1	6s	8d
Item, certaine wood in the new house	1	0s	0d
Item, 6 oxen	30	0s	0d
Item, xlj olde shepe	12	0s	0d
Item, 6 kyne and one bull	14	0s	0d
Item, thre kyne, one being new calved	6	0s	0d
Item, 3 stotts, 3 quies & a bull stirke	11	2s	0d
Item, 2 calves	1	4s	0d
Item, xv acres of hard corne & xv acres of ware corne	30	0s	0d
Item, liij lambes	8	16s	8d
Item, a lease holden of the church of Durham	40	0s	0d
Item, 2 olde meares	2	0s	0d

cciiij^{li} xiij^s

---

13 i.e. 110, which is (5x20)+10.

Debtes due to the testator			
Item, Sir Henrie Anderson, knight, by bond	200	0s	0d
Item, Mr. Raiph ffetherston	100	0s	0d
Item, Thomas King	80	0s	0d
Item, John Addie	14	0s	0d
Item, William and Peter Denton	28 odds		
Item, Adam Midleton	2	16s	8d
Item, Mr. Robert Cooper of Durham	40	0s	0d
Item, Thomas Gregson	12	0s	0d
Item, Edward Daile	47	0s	0d
Item, James Denton for a yoake of oxen	14	0s	0d
Item, Robert Goodchilde, the price of a cow	3	6s	8d
Item, Barthram Owrde, the remainder of a bond	2	0s	0d

ccccxliij^{li} iij^s iiij^d

Disperet debts			
Item, Roger Lumley & others by bond	64	0s	0d
Item, John Lawe by bond	31	13s	4d
Item, John Hutchinson	11	0s	0d

cvj^{li} xiij^s iiij^d

Debts that the said testator did owe			
Item, to Mr George Collingwood	900	0s	0d

Source: DPR1/1/1617/S3/1–2; will, paper 2ff., inventory, parchment 2mm. sewn. A summary of the will, without the inventory, appears in WI Durham, p. 117.

29. Alice Watson of Ryhope, Bishopwearmouth, widow, 1618

In the name of God, amen, I, Alas Watsone of Ryhoop in the countye of Durham, wedow, being sike of bodye but perfect in remember-ance, doe now make my last will and testament this secunde day of September, anno Domini 1618, in manner and forme following. ffirst I bequeath my soull unto the handes of Jesus Christ who hath bought me with his precious bloude, & by him I hoop to have remissione and forgiveness of my sines. Secundly, I committ my body to be buried in the church of Bushoop Warmouth. And for my goods and chattells, I give and bequeath in manner and forme following. Imprimis, I give and bequeath unto the two sones of John Browne,

William Browne and John Browne, ether of them, ten shillings. Ittem, I give unto Annas Watsone, my maid servant, twenty shillings. Ittem, I give unto Raiph Robsone on ewe lambe, and unto William Watsone another ewe lamb, and unto Jane Robson another ewe lambe. Ittem, I give unto Alesse Moyser, my daughter, one basone and one spininge whelle. Ittem, I give unto Ambrose Moyser three children, Samuell, ffrancie and Elener, twenty shillings. Ittem, I give unto John Stokell, my man servant, five shillings. Ittem, I give unto John Robson, my brother, five shillings. Ittem, I give unto John Stokell, sone of Christofer Stokell, xii^d. Ittem, I give unto George Robson, my brother, tow shillings. And for all the rest of my goods and chattells, funerall expenses being taken forth, I give unto George Watsone, my sone, and unto Ambrose Moyser, my sone in law, which two I mak my executors of this my last will and testament.

Alas Watsone, hir mark [marked with a symbol]

Wittnesses herof,
John ffell, his marke [<i>marked with a symbol</i>]
Edward ffell, his marke [<i>marked with a symbol</i>]
William Shipp[er]dsonne [<i>full name signed</i>]

October
The inventory of all such goodes, as did fall due unto Allice Watson, widow, late of Bishopp Weremouthe, deceased, for her thirdes or widow right of her late husband Anthonie Watson, late deceased, amounting unto the sum of £11 6s 8d

Paid for the funeral expenses of the said deceased   1   0s   0d
{Als}

Source: DPR1/1/1618/W6/1–2, paper 2ff.

30. Adam Holme of Bishopwearmouth, yeoman, 1619

In the name of God, amen, I, Adam Hollme of Bishopp Warmouth in the county of Durham, yeoman, being sike of bodye yeat perfitt in rememberance, doe heere make my last will and testement in maner and forme followinge. ffirst, I bequeth my soull to allmightye God, who hath creatide me, and to Jesus Christ, my savioure, who hath redemide me, by whose death and passione I stedfastley hoop to have pardone and remissione of all my sines, and my bodye to be buried in the parish church yeard of Bishopp Warmouth under the brood stone lying at the south church porch dore. And for all other my goods and chattells, movable and unmovable, I give and bequeath in maner and forme followinge. ffirst, I give unto George Hollme, my second sone, one lease in Ryhoop, houlding one the right reverent father in God, lord bishopp of Durham, with half the crope growing on the said teniment and three oxen, one meare, one long waine, one plough, two yokes & two somes, a coulter and a socke being now at this instant upon the said teniment. Ittem, I give unto my said sone one browne coult folle. ffor my daughter Annas, wheras she being comd to lawfull yeares have receved the full value of one hundreth pownds in full satisfactione of hir child's porcione, yeat I give hir all {the hous} my houshould stuffe, only one bede excepted. And for my eldest sone, Raiph Hollme, he is contented to take fiftye pownds in full satisfactione of his childe's portione at his mother's dying daye. And for all the rest of my goods, moveable and immoveable, I give unto my wif which I make full executor of this my last will and testament.

Adam Holm [*full name signed*]

Witness herof, Randulph Bentley, curat [*full name signed*]
Edward Dayll^{iuratus} [*full name signed*]
William Shipperdsonne^{iuratus} [*full name signed*]
John W<il>son, his marke [*marked with a symbol*]

An inventory of all the goods and chattels moveable and unmoveable which Adam Holme of Bishopp Warmouth in the county of Durham, yeoman, died sezased [*sic*] upon, vewed and praised by thes fowre men, videlicet Edward Daille, John Johnson, Robert Goodchild, and William Shipperdson, the seventh day of Januarie, 1618

Inprimis, six oxen	28	0s	0d
Ittem, six kine	12	0s	0d
Ittem, two stottes	4	0s	0d
Ittem, one why & one stottrell	2	0s	0d
Ittem, foure calfes	2	6s	8d
Ittem, fowre meares	11	0s	0d
Ittem, forty ould sheepe	12	0s	0d
Ittem, twenty sheep hodges	3	13s	4d
Ittem, one foole	1	3s	4d
Ittem, corne in the stackgarth	22	0s	0d
Ittem, corne growing on the grownd	20	0s	0d
Ittem, hay in the garth and barnes	2	13s	0d

Ittem, two longe waines & two coup waines with ther whelles & furniture	7	13s	4d
Ittem, one oxe harrow & one horse harrow		7s	0d
Ittem, two plowes with ther furniture		10s	0d
Ittem, yokes, somes and forkes	1	4s	0d
Ittem, one paire of coupwaine soles		5s	0d
Ittem, plow heades and stiltes		2s	0d
Ittem, xiiijth swine	4	0s	0d
Ittem, corne growingh in the barnes field	4	0s	0d
Ittem, linning cloth	2	0s	0d
Ittem, two bee hives		10s	0d
Ittem, one muskatt & a callever	1	10s	0d
Ittem, his apperrell	5	0s	0d
Ittem, one folle	1	3s	4d
Ittem, the houshould stuffe	47	0s	4d
Ittem, one half crop growing upone one teniment att Ryhoop	13	6s	8d
Ittem, thre oxen, one meare, one longe waine, one ploughe and other implements	15	0s	0d

Suma totalis cclix^{li} viij^s

Legese being deducted ther remaneth clxxxj^{li} iiij^s iiij^d
Dettes beinge deducted ther remaneth clxv^{li} j^s x^d

Dettes owinge by the testatore

Owinge to Mr Burgone for the halfe yeares rent	1	2s	1d
Ittem, owing to Thomas Pige, his man servant	1	0s	0d
Ittem, owing to my sone George for one black horse	4	0s	0d
Ittem, in funerall expences	10	0s	0d

Suma totalis xvj^{li}ij^s vj^d

Source: DPR1/1/1618/H23/1, 3, paper 4ff.

31. Thomas Roxby of Bishopwearmouth, yeoman, 1619

Anno Domini 1619

In the name of God, amen, the sixt day of May in the seveanteenth year of the raign of our soveraigne lord, James, by the grace of God, kinge of England, Skotland, ffrance and Ireland, defender of the faith, &c., I, Thomas Roxby of Bushop Wermouth in the countie of Durham, yeoman, sick in bodie yet in perfect remembrance of minde, God be praised for it, doe make this my last will and testament in manner & forme followinge. First, I bequeath my soule to God the Father, Sonne & Holy Ghost, my creator, redemer & sanctifier, and my body to be buried within the church of Bishops Wermouth. Item, I give to be dealt unto the poore of the parish ten shillings. Item, I give unto Nickolas Bryan, the sonne of Nickolas Bryan, deceased, the iron barrs now standing in the chimney of the forehowse, my best longe wayn and my best cowpwain, five axeltrees and the equall half of all my live shepe yonge & old, to be equally parted betwene him and his brother Michell Bryan, unto whom I doe give the other half of the said shepe. Item, I doe give more unto the said Michell Bryan a black whie calf and twentie shillings in mony. Item, I doe give unto the two daughters of Richard Katchaside each a noble. Item, I doe give unto Nickolas Chambers, my sister's sonne, twentie shillings. Item, I doe give unto Ann Rutley, my sister's daughter, a load of bigge. Item, I doe give unto Robert Watt, the sonne of Thomas Watt, a noble. Item, I doe give unto Marie Wells and Elizabeth Wells, the daughters of Raiph Wells, each ten grotes. Item, my debts & legacies discharged, all the rest of goods, moveable and unmoveable, I doe give unto my wife Annas Roxby, whom I doe make my whole & sole executor of this my last & testament. In the presence of these witnesses whose names ar hearunder written.

John Shipperdson [*full name signed*]
the marke of John Johnson [*marked with a symbol, a horseshoe*]
Raiph Wells [*full name signed*]

The inventory of all the goods & chattells, moveable and un-moveable, of Thomas Roxby, deceased, praysed by thes 4 men hearunder named, this 20th of September 1619

In primis, twoe oxen, praised to	7	10s	0d
Item, five kine and one stott	8	10s	0d
Item, three calves	1	10s	0d

Item, all the sheepe, 7 ewes & 5 hoggs	2	13s	4d
Item, fower swine	1	0s	0d
Item, twoe mares	3	6s	8d
Item, all corn & grain, wheat, big, pees & oates in the barn & garth	20	6s	8d
Item, 2 long wayns & 2 cowpe wayns & forkes	2	0s	0d
Item, one ox harrow & 2 horse harrowes		14s	0d
Item, one plow & plow irons with yoakes and sowmes		15s	8d
Item, hay in the barn	2	2s	0d
Item, one cupboord & a spence	1	6s	8d
Item, 3 kettles, 4 potts & 2 panns	1	6s	8d
Item, 12 peces of pewter & 3 brasse candlesticks		9s	6d
Item, 2 tables, one chaire, 2 formes, one iron chimney, spitt, tonges and two racking crookes, altogether		13s	4d
Item, 3 stand bedds with their furniture		15s	0d
Item, 2 pair linen sheetes, 2 pair courser shetes, 2 pillowbers & 3 towells, altogether		4s	0d
Item, fower chistes		8s	0d
Item, 2 tubbs, 3 barrells, 3 skeles, 3 meeles, 2 skepps, one hopper		5s	0d
Item, all his apparell	1	10s	0d
Item, 4 henns & a cocke		1s	8d
	57	18s	2d

John Shipperdson [*full name signed*]
Richard Katchaside his marke [*marked with a symbol*]
John Johnson's his marke [*marked with a symbol, a horseshoe*]
Robert Ayre [*full name signed*]

Source: DPR1/1/1619/R7/1–2, paper 3ff.

32. Robert Huntley of East Burdon, Bishopwearmouth, yeoman, 1622

A true inventory of all the goods and chattels that Robert Huntley of East Burden in the county of Durrham, yeoman, died, worth or possessed of, as they were presented unto and prised by John Shepherdson, Robert Aire, Thomas Johnson & William Sharpe, yeomen, the fifteenth day of December anno Domini 1622

Imprimis, foure oxen, presented to them & conscionably prised at	14	13s	4d

Item, ten kine	16	0s	0d
Foure stirkes	2	0s	0d
Fifty old sheepe	10	0s	0d
Seaventeen hogges	2	0s	0d
Three horses	4	0s	0d
Wheate standing in the stacke yard	16	0s	0d
Item, bigge in the stacke yard	2	10s	0d
Item, pease in the stacke yard	6	0s	0d
Item, oats in the stacke yard	7	10s	0d
Item, hay & straw	4	0s	0d
Item, plowes & plowgeere, waines & wainegeere, one oxe harrow & a paire of horse harrows	5	0s	0d
Item, three swine		16s	0d
Item, foure cubbords & one spence	5	0s	0d
Item, brasse & pewder	2	13s	4d
Item, one table, two formes, two chaires & other stoles in the forehouse		6s	8d
Item, three chests		3s	4d
Twenty and three paire of lining and straking sheetes & other lining	3	0s	0d
Furniture belonging to beds	4	0s	0d
Foure stone of butter and cheses	1	1s	0d
One window cloth, sackes, pokes, sives & ridles		1s	0d
Wodden vessell		3s	4d
One chimney, with other things about the chimney		5s	0d
Wheate growing on the ground	16	0s	0d
Money lent forth & otherwise due unto him as, namely, in the hands of John Hylton 15^{li}, of Thomas Burdon 25^{li}, of Raphe Perkin 10^{li}, of John Collingwood 8^{li}, of Robert Atkinson 12^{li}, of Elizabeth Johnson 2^{li} 16^{sh}, of Richard Huntley 14 shillings, of Robert Aire 1^{li} 5 shillings	74	15s	0d
His apparel	1	10s	0d
Item, Robert ffoster for a debt		5s	0d
The sume of his inventory	199	17s	0d
The debts to be paid heereout as expressed page 2	30	4s	0d
There remaineth to the widow & foure children	169	12s	4d
Hence deduct the charges for the administration			

Margaret Huntlie vidua
Thomas Huntlie
Eliz[abeth] Huntlie

Ann Huntlie
Isabella Huntlie, Liberi

An inventory of the debts which the within named Robert Huntley, deceased, is found to have due to pay out of his goodes before specified & prised

Imprimis, owing to Edward ffell for rent	5	0s	0d
Item, he was oweing for ffarenton Hall rent	4	13s	4d
Item, to Mr Aray	5	15s	4d
For Silkesworth feild rent	1	5s	0d
Item he was owing to Thomas Aire	3	14s	0d
To Widow Shadforth	3	0s	0d
To John Smith	1	13s	4d
The lord's rent	1	14s	8d
A servant's wages		6s	8d
More to be paide in his behalfe for a mortuary		10s	0d
For a lairestall		6s	8d
To the poore		10s	0d
Funerall expenses	1	10s	0d
For schoolewaiges for his son for writing &c		5s	0d
Summa totalis	30	4s	8d

Source: DPR1/1/1622/H13/1, paper 2ff.

33. Richard Morgan of Sunderland, yeoman, 1623

In the [name of][14] God, amen, I, Richard Morgine of Sunderland by the sea[15] in the countie of Durham, yeoman, beinge sike of bodie yeat perfitt in remenberance, doe make my last will and testement, this eleventh day of Aprill, 1613, in manner and forme ffollowinge. ffirst, I give and bequeth my soull unto almightie God, who hath created me, and to Jesus Christ, my redemer, by whos death and passione I hoop to be saved and have remissione of all my sines, and my bodie to be buried in the perrish churche of Bishoppwarmouth, and for the

---

14 Omitted in the original.
15 In this and other wills Sunderland is described as 'by the sea', 'nigh the sea' or 'near the sea' to distinguish it from Sunderland Bridge: V. Watts, *The Cambridge Dictionary of English Place-Names* (Cambridge, 2004), p. 589. The addition has not been capitalised because it was probably not regarded as part of the name.

rest of all my goods and chattels, moveable and unmoveable, I give and beqieth in manner and forme followinge. In primis, I give to Richard ffell, youngest sone to John ffell, one younge meare tow yeares ould, and one whye, and my best clocke. I give to ffrancis Morgine, sone to George Morgine, seaven powndes to be paied him whenas he shalbe come to lawfull yeares to receive the same. Ittem, I give to John Morgine, sone to George Morgine, five powndes to be paied him wheneas he conmeth to lawfull yeares to receive the same. Ittem, I give to Elezebeth Morgine one cowe and whye stirke of one yeare ould. Ittem, I give to Belle Brice, daughter to Richard Brice, one whye of tow yeares ould. Ittem, I give to Richard Brice one why stirke of tow yeares ould. {And for all the rest of my goods and chattells, moveable and unmoveable, I give to Margerie Morgine, my wife} Ittem, I give to Elezebeth Morgine one cawell, one cubborde in the chamber, one bedstead in the chamber and bedcloth to the same and half of all my puder vessell in the house. Ittem, I give to the pore of Sunderiand vj^s viij^d. Ittem, I give to John Brice one why of two yeares ould. Ittem, I give to the pore of Seham towne iij^s iiij^d. Ittem, I give to John ffell and William Shipperdsone all my sheep now living at Barmstone. And for all the rest of my goods and chattells, moveable and unmoveable, I give to Margerie Morgine, my wif, which I make executrix of this my last will and testament. In witness hereof I have sett to my hand, the daye and yeare above written.

Richard Morgine, his marke [*marked with a cross*]
Witnesse herof
John ffell^{iuratus}, his mark [*marked with a symbol*]
William Shipperdsonne ^{iuratus} [*full named signed*]

Detes owinge to the testator

Ittem, Raiph Perkine of Ryhoop	9	0s	0d
Ittem, Robert Chambers of Hartone	7	0s	0d
Ittem, Anthony Hourd of Offertone	3	13s	4d
Ittem, Mr Robert Roukbie of Weshington for one meare at Whitsonday next to be paied	3	0s	0d
Ittem, Anthony Ourd for one why, to be paied upon the xxvth of March next	2	16s	8d
Ittem, John Read for one cowe iij^{li} to be paied at Candellmes next	3	0s	0d
Ittem, John Wood for iij shepe		15s	0d
Ittem, George Richesone iiij shepe	1	0s	0d
Ittem, Thomas Stafford on shep		5s	0d
Ittem, George Liell two shepe		10s	0d

Ittem, Robert Selbie on shep		5s	0d
Ittem, John Davie		10s	0d
Ittem, Rob[er]t Dixson		5s	0d
Ittem, William Dixson		5s	0d
Ittem, James Care		5s	0d
Ittem, Thomas Tailer on shep		5s	0d
Ittem, Gawen Tayler for cloth		8s	6d
Ittem, Robert Bee for cloth		8s	6d
Ittem, Rowland Chambers		12s	0d
Ittem, Thom[as] Pearson of Harton	1	0s	0d
Ittem, Richard Sones of Seham	1	3s	6d
Ittem, John Horne of Biddick		3s	8d

Jo[hn] ffell de Riop
Nich[olas] Todd de Houghton

An inventorie of all the goods and chattells which Richard Morgine of Sunderland by the sea in the countie of Durham, yeoman, died possessed of, being vewed and praised by fowre men: vid*elicet* Richard Sones, John Ffell, Necholas Tood & William Shipperdsonne, this xxviij[th] of Aprill, 1623.

Inprimis, nine kine	13	6s	8d
Ittem, thre stottes	3	0s	0d
Ittem, thre ocke stirkes	1	10s	0d
Ittem, thre whies	2	6s	8d
Ittem, on coult and one felle	4	0s	0d
Ittem, one ould meare		13s	4d
Ittem, ten shepe	1	0s	0d
Ittem, one ould cartte		3s	4d
Ittem, one rouke of hay at Barnston	1	0s	0d
Ittem, one stake of corne at Seaham and corne in corne [*sic*] in the field	6	13s	4d
Ittem, one lease at Seham of one aker of tillige grownd and certeine pasture gattes	13	6s	8d
Ittem, in the forehouse one cubbord and on cawell with other wood vessell		16s	0d
Ittem, 14th peace of puter, on quart potte, 4 sawsers, on pottinge dish, one salt		13s	4d
Ittem, one kettell, five panes, fowre brase candelsticks, 2 brase pottes, one iron potte, 2 friing panes		13s	4d

Ittem, one table, one chaire, one buffett furme, one dozen trenchers		5s	0d
Ittem, in the chamber one ould spence, on ould cubbord, on kirne & on chist & other wood vessell		6s	8d
Ittem, one paire of line shettes, 2 paire of strakine sheates		13s	4d
Ittem, thre whitt happens		10s	0d
Ittem, his purs and his apperell	1	6s	8d

Sum lij^{li} iiij^s iiij^d

Detes owinge to the testator

Ittem, Raiph Perkine of Ryhoop	9	0s	0d
Ittem, Robert Chamber of Hartone	7	0s	0d
Ittem, Anthony Hourd of Offertone	4	13s	4d
Ittem, Mr Robert Rouxsbie of Weshingtone	3	0s	0d
Ittem, Anthony Hourd of Offerton	2	16s	8d
Ittem, John Read of Barnston More House	3	0s	0d
Ittem, John Wood of Warmouth		15s	0d
Ittem, George Richesone of Warmouth	1	0s	0d
Ittem, Thomas Stafford of Sunderland		5s	0d
Ittem, George Liell		10s	0d
Ittem, Robert Selbie		5s	0d
Ittem, John Davie		10s	0d
Ittem, Robert Dixson		5s	0d
Ittem, James Care		5s	0d
Ittem, Thomas Tailer		5s	0d
Ittem, Gawen Tailer of Sunderland		8s	6d
Ittem, Robert Bee of Sunderland		8s	6d
Ittem, Rowland Chambers of Seaham		12s	0d
Ittem, Thomas Pearson of Harton	1	0s	0d
Ittem, Richard Sones of Seaham	1	3s	6d
Ittem, John Horne of Biddick		3s	4d
Ittem, William Rutter		10s	0d
Ittem, William Dixson		5s	0d

Summa £38 0s 10d

Detts owinge by the testator

Inprimis, owing to John Halleday of Sunderland	8	0s	0d
Ittem, owinge to Sr John Hedworth for rent		17s	6d
Ittem, owinge Elzebeth Morgine for hir wages		5s	0d

Ittem, owinge Bele Brice	3s	6d
Ittem, Richard Brice	3s	0d
Ittem, paied for on coffine	6s	0d
Ittem, for on lairstall	6s	8d
Ittem, for on mortuarie	[no entry]	
Ittem, funerall expences	1 0s	0d
Ittem, given to the pore	10s	0d

Source: DPR1/1/1623/M13/1, 3, paper 3ff.

34. Agnes Thompson of Bishopwearmouth, widow, 1623

In the name of God, amen, I, Annas Thompson of Bishopwaremouth, wido, diseased in body but perfect in minde and of good and perfect remembrance, blessed be God, do make and ordene this my last will and testament in manner and forme as followeth. Imprimis, I bequeath my soule to Christ Jesus, my saviour, hoping through Him to be saved and my body to be buried. Item, I give to the poore of the parish forty shillings. Item, I give to Ann Shepperson, daughter to John Shepperson, a peice of gold, towit twenty two shilings. Item, to John Shepperson, her brother, twenty two shillings. Item, I give to Johan Shepperson, the wife of John Shepperson, eleven shillings. Item, I give and bequeath unto Anos Broun, wido, a black koop whi. Item, I give to Ann Holm, the wife of Raiphe Holm, one fetherbed on wich I nowe lye. Item, I give to Ann Bee, the daughter of Robert Bee, twenty shillings to be paid hir at the aige of twenty on yeares. The rest of my goods and chatles, my funerall expences discharsed, I give and bequeth to Georg Shepperson, Raiphe Shepperson and Christopher Shipperson, my b[r]uther's children, to be equally divided amongst them by Christopher Shipperson[iuratus], Georg Shipperson, Raiphe Shipperson [iuratus], afore named, whom I do make my sole executors to performe thes legacies and all things belonging to my funerall, and this I do frely and of mine owne accord instatute and appoint, being in perfect memory, the 7 daye of May, 1623.
In the presence & hearing of us
William Robinson, his mark [*marked with a symbol*]
John Johnson, his mark [*marked with a symbol, a horseshoe*]

An inventorie of all the goods and chattells that Annas Thomson of Bishopp Warmouth, wedow, died deseased of [*sic*], vewed and

praised this xiijth of May 1613 [*sic*] by fowre men, vid*elicet* William
Robinson, John Johnson, Raiph Holline & William Shepperdson

Inprimis, six kine	9	0s	0d
Ittem, one why & iij calfes	2	6s	8d
Ittem, 14 ewes & 11 lambes	3	0s	0d
Ittem, 11 shep hodges & j toup	2	0s	0d
Ittem, wheat in the barne	1	10s	0d
Ittem, corne in the towne feildes, videlicet tow akers			
of wheat and two of pees & ottes	4	0s	0d
Ittem, iiij swine	1	0s	0d
Ittem, in the forehouse, on cubbord and one ammerie	2	0s	0d
Ittem, one bedstead, one table, 2 buffet formes,			
2 chares, one chest	1	1s	0d
Ittem, one chimney & two reckencrouks & on paire of			
rackes & j paire of tonges		13s	4d
Ittem, 20 peace of puter, one quart potte, on puter			
candelstickes, 5 tunes & 2 saltes, 6 sausers	1	0s	0d
Ittem, iiij bras pottes, 3 kettell, on yetlinge, one paire			
of pott clipes, 4 brase candelstickes	2	6s	8d
Ittem, 4 skelles, 1 firkine & other wood vessell		6s	8d
Ittem, in the chamber, one bedstead, 2 faitherbeds,			
13 codes	2	3s	4d
Ittem, 2 materises & on code		5s	0d
Ittem, one oversea coveringe, 5 hard coverleds,			
5 blanketts, on carpinecloth, 3 ould coverleds	2	8s	0d
Ittem, one peace of russett, 5 yeardes		6s	8d
Ittem, iiij paire of linninge sheates, thre paire of			
hardine sheats, 4 pillebers, 2 towells, 3 table clothes	1	10s	0d
Ittem, 6 yeardes of line, 14 yeards of strakines, 16			
yeardes of hardens	1	3s	4d
Ittem, one spence, one flanders chest, one table and			
other wood vessell in the chamber		13s	4d
Ittem, 3 chestes		11s	0d
Ittem, hir apperrell	4	0s	0d
Ittem, one half stone of woull		2s	6d
Ittem, one halbert		2s	0d
Ittem, in gould	11	10s	0d
Sum totall.	54	18s	6d

Dets owen the said Anas Thomson

Richard Gipson of Hilton oweth	2	0s	0d
Matthew Kelley oweth	2	0s	0d
John Jorland oweth	1	0s	0d
John Taler oweth	1	0s	0d
Richard Roos oweth		12s	0d
Phillip Chipchis oweth	2	0s	0d

Source: DPR1/1/1623/T4/1, 3, paper 2ff.

35. Edward Dearnley of Sunderland, yeoman, 1626

In the name of God, amen, I, Edward Dearnley of Sunderland ny the sea in the countie of Durham, yeoman, being sick in body yett in full and perfect remembrance (praysed be God) make this my last will & testament in manner and fforme following, this xjth day of September in the yeare of our lord God 1623, vi*delicet*: ffirst, I give & bequeath my soule into the hands of Jesus Christ, my onely saviour and redemer, and my body to be buried in Bushopwarmouth churchyard. Item, I give & bequeath to my good ffreind Thomas Teasdaill of the fery boat for a remembrance xij^d of currannt English money. Item, I give to Henry Gibson for a remembrance towards his boat xij^d of like currannt money. Item, I give to my wyff Margareth Dearnley all the rest of my goods moveable & unmoveable, whom I make my full & whole executor of this my last will & testament. In witness whereof I have hearunto sett my hand & seale the day and yeare first written.

Edward Dearnley, his mark [*marked with initial capitals E D*]
Sealed & delivered as my act & dead in the presence of
Henry Gibson [*full name signed*]
Thomas Teasdall [*full name signed*]
William Hardcastell [*full name signed*]
Edward Anderson, his mark [*marked with the initial capital A*]

Januarye the 24th, 1624
A true and perfecte inventorye of the goods and cattells of Edward Dearnlye of Sunderland neere the sea, deceased, valued and p[r]aised by John Shepherdson, William Hardcastle, Thomas Tesdale and Henry Gibson, vi*delicet*:

In the hall house

	£	s	d
Inprimis, two cubbords & xviij peec[e]s of pewter, ij quart potts, ij chamber potts, ix sawcers, a pinte pott & a fill pott, iiij salte sellers & ij candlesticks	3	8s	11d
Item, iiij brasse potts & iij ould dublers, all some of	1	0s	0d
Item, one iron chimney & ij racking crooks, ij iron racks, a porr and a payre tongs		18s	0d
Item, iij spytts, a paire grid irons, a paire tongs, an ould ffryinge pan, a dreeping pan, ij paire of pott kelps		9s	6d
Item, one iron pott, one fishe pan and a little pan, a little ould kettle, all		9s	2d
Item, one firr table with a frame, two formes, ij cheares all some of		11s	2d
Item, one buffett stoole, a paire plaing tables		1s	8d
Item, ij washing tubbes, an owlde sea & three milke bowles & ij water sceeles		2s	10d
Item, a spence with a particion, some		4s	0d

In the great chamber

	£	s	d
Inprimis, one fir table with a frame, two formes, all some of		8s	0d
Item, three bed steads, some of		15s	0d
Item, on feather bed, iij mattresses, iij boulsters and five cods, all is	1	6s	8d
Item, vij happings & iij ould coverletts, all		16s	0d
Item, five ould firr chests, some of		10s	0d
Item, iij payre lynen sheets and five payre streakinge & hearme sheets, all	1	2s	0d
Item, one dozen table napkins, some		3s	0d
Item, one presser & an old cownter		6s	8d
Item, a paire ganntrees, a kerne, iij drincking canns, a baskett, a spining whele, a small ale stand & ij ould tubbs, all		4s	2d
Item, ij ould carpet clothes, some is		2s	0d
Item, his wearinge apparell, some	1	10s	0d
Item, a brew lead, a masking fatt, a tapp stone, a great arcke, ij leven tubbs and ij ould barrells	1	17s	0d

In the little parler

	£	s	d
Item, one ffir table with a frame and ij formes, some of		7s	6d
Item, iiij kyne and a quantytye hay	9	0s	0d

Item, ij bakon fficks, some of	13s	4d
Item, ij henns and a cocke, some of	2s	4d
Item, a deskte, some of	3s	6d

Debts owing to the deceassed

Item, owinge by Tymothy Comen of Durham	10	0s	0d
Item, by Thomas Tesdale, some of	1	0s	0d

Some xxxvj^{li} vj^s x^d

Debts dew by the deceassed

Inprimis, to Edward Lee for iiij barrells & a halfe of beere, some of	2	14s	0d
Item, to Robart Scurfeild of Grynden, some	3	5s	0d
Item, to John ffell of Ryope, some of		14s	0d
Item, to George Thompson, butcher, some		17s	0d
Item, to William Wilson of the Panns, some		19s	8d
Item, to Roger Curye, some of	30	0s	0d

Some indebted xxxviij^{li} vj^s viij^d

Source: DPR1/1/1626/D2/1, 3, paper 4ff.

36. Mathew Bulmer of Sunderland, yeoman, 1626

In the name of God, amen, I, Mathew Bulmer, now of Sunderland ny the sea, in the countie of Durham, yeoman, beinge sicke in body yett in wholle, sound and perfect remembrance (thanks be given to God), doe make and ordeyne this my laste will and testament, the thirde day of November, anno Domini 1625, annoque Regis Caroli &c., Magne Brittanie, ffrancie et Hibernie, primo, in manner and forme following. Inprimis, I doe give and bequeathe my soule into the hands of almightie God, my maker and redemer, by whom I hoap to be saved, and my body to be buryed in the chourche or chourchyarde, att the desposing of my executors. Item, I give to Anne Westwoodd two shillings. Item, I give to Margarett Bulmer, my brother's daughter, ffive shillings. Item, I give to Richard Bulmer, my brother's sonn, two shillings and sixpenc. Item, I give to the poore of Stanhopp parish five shillings. Item, I give to the poore of the chappell of Wardell ffive shillings. Item, I give to Raphe Stobbes of Westgate in Wardell two shillings. Item, I give to everye childe of Henry Bulmer, my brother's sonne, two shillings apece, and I give to the said Henry Bulmer ffive shillings. Item, all the rest of my goods

moveable and umnoveable, my debts, legacies and funerall expenc[e]s discharged, I give and bequeath to Jaine Bulmer, my wyffe, and to William Heppell, younger, of Sunderland afforesaid, whome I make my joynt & full executors of this my last will & testament, revoaking and making of non effect all former wills by me maid. Item, I give to John Potts, sonn of William Potts, of the said Sunderland, the somme of two shillings, and I give to Robert Potts xij^s, and I give to Ursela Armstrong and Barbery Armstronge, to either of them, two shillings. And in witnesse of this my last will and testament, I, the said Mathew Bulmer, have hereunto sett my hand and seale the day and yeare first above written. Mathew Bulmer, his mark [*marked with a symbol*]
Sealed and delivered in the presence of us,
George Lilburn [*full name signed*]
William^{iuratus} Potts his mark [*marked with a symbol*]
William Hardcastell [*full name signed*]

An invotorie of all suche goods and chattells, movable and immovable, as Mathew Bulmer, laite of Sunderlande by the sea, dyed possessed of, praysed by fower men the xxvjth daye of Jullie, 1626, vid*elicet*:

Imprimis, his apperell and money in his purse	1	10s	0d
Item, one leasse for eleaven yeares of a parcell of medowe grounde from John Sheale of Shirwinforde	7	0s	0d
Item, one lease for one yeare of a parcell of grounde from George ffetherstonhalghe	1	0s	0d
Item, in old haye standinge upon the same		12s	0d
Item, one mayer and towe ky	7	0s	0d
Item, in househoulde stufe at Sunderland and att the Westgeate in Wardaile	3	0s	0d
Somme is xx^{li} ij^s			

Debtes owinge to the said Mathew Bulmer

Imprimis, by John Heryson by bonde	9	9s	0d
Item, by William Stobbes by bill	13	4s	0d
Item, by Elsabethe ffetherstonhalghe by bill dew the xiiijth of December nexte	14	6s	0d
Item, by Nicholas ffetherstonhalghe and William ffeatherstonhalghe by bond	6	10s	0d
Somme is xliij^{li} ix^s			

Desperat, item, by Lanclott Mayer	1	0s	0d
Item, by Henrye Carlell		12s	0d

Debtes owinge by the saide deceased			
Imprimis, to Mr Tobye Pilkington	1	0s	0d
Item, to Thomas Toode		10s	0d
Item, to his servante for hir wages		10s	0d
Item, paide for his funerall expences	3	1s	0d

Source: DPR1/1/1626/B7/1, 3, paper 3ff.

37. Charles Booth of Silksworth, 1626

1626 August 18

An inventory of all the goodes and chattells of Charles Bouthe of Silkesworth, late deceased, praised by Barnard Robinson Adam Midleton, Robert Guy, and Robert Scurfeild

Item, three mares and a fole	7	0s	0d
Item, 9 sheepe	2	14s	0d
Item, 10 kyne and a bull	25	0s	0d
Item, 3 quies and 2 stirkes	10	0s	0d
Item, one sowe and 2 shotts		10s	0d
Item, the meadow close and old hay	5	0s	0d
Item, 4 calues	2	0s	0d

The fire house			
Item, one cupbord, with a presse, an old cupbord and a cawle	3	0s	0d
Item, one table, two formes, 2 cawles, with 3 stooles		8s	0d
Item, 10 peece of pewther, 6 sawcers & one pewther candlesticke, 2 pewther salts and one cup of pewther		13s	4d
Item, 2 brasse potts, two brass candlestickes, 2 kettles, 2 old pannes	1	0s	0d
Item, a paire of barres, one reckon, one fryeing pan, a paire of tongs, a spitt and a paire of broyleing yrons		10s	0d

The milke house

Item, 8 stone of butter	1	6s	8d
Item, 30 cheeses		16s	0d
Item, 2 trayes, 10 milkebowles, 3 skeeles, two old butterkitts and milke sile, 2 leaven tubes, 2 kannes, with other bowles and chesfatts		10s	0d

In the chamber

Item, a paire of barres, with a reckon		1s	0d
Item, 3 bedsteades, with an old presse		5s	0d
Item, 2 little chistes and a deske		3s	0d
Item, happings, 3 coverletts, 2 paire of blanketts, 4 featherbeddes	2	13s	4d
Item, 3 quishings		2s	0d
Item, 2 tableclothes of lynnen and one of harden, 2 paire of lynnen sheetes, one towell, 4 table napkins, 4 codwares, 3 harden sheetes	1	0s	0d

In the byer

Item, an old waine, an old cart, an old oxe harrowe and 2 horse harrowes		13s	4d
Item, 3 iron soumes, one cowlter, one socke, 2 paire of forke graines and other iron geere		10s	0d
Item, one gang of felfes, 11 louse bordes, twoe chese presses, with yokes & horse geare, with other wood things, a stone trough and a wood troughe, two old plowes with an old beame, one cole cart & a grindstone	1	13s	4d
Item, in the barne, old hay and new hay, and strawe	1	10s	0d
Item, his apparrell, his purse and all things belonging to his bodie	1	0s	0d
Item, his bookes		10s	0d
Robert Skurfield	10	0s	0d

Summa [*no entry*]

Debts owing to the deceased

Item, George Cuthbertson for one bushel of wheat (paid 2^s 0^d)		7s	2d
Item, Nicholas Smith of Gateshead (paid 30s)	4	12s	0d
Item, Henry Storie of Gateside owes me for a grey mare, price (paid 25^s)	2	13s	4d

Witnesses of this, George Cuthbertson, William Todd of Washington

Item, George Eayre of Silkesworth for horsement and grasse		10s	0d
Item, Roger ffoster of Warmouth, keeleman, for a stone of wooll		9s	6d
Item, John ffell of Newcastle owes me for 10 ewes	2	0s	0d
Item, William Dawson of Durham owes me for halfe a chalder of bigg, whereof there is paid xxxiiijˢ so he owes me		10s	0d
Item, Anthony Crofton owes me		10s	0d
Item, Robert Richardson owes me for hay		8s	0d
Item, Robert Dixon owes me for butter and oates		8s	4d
Item, Elizabeth Tod owes me for butter		4s	6d
Item, Robert Broughe of Herington for butter		8s	4d
Item, Arthure Browell owes me		4s	0d
Item, John Crofton owes me for church rent, malt & house rent	1	13s	8d
Item, Wil[lia]m Thompson of Silksworth owes me as followeth, upon an accompt I paid him xijˡⁱ of which I did owe him xˡⁱ xˢ iiijᵈ, for his wives porcion, and the said William Thompson should have paid Robert Ayre of Tonnstall xxxiijˢ iiijᵈ for a bull	1	10s	0d

Source: DPR1/1/1626/B4/1–2, parchment 2mm. sewn.

38. Thomas Burdon of Burdon, 1626

In the name of God, amen, I, Thomas Burden of Burden, being weak in bodye but in perfect memorye, mayketh this my last will & testament in maner followinge. First, I give and bequeth my soule to almighty God, my mayker and redeamer, hopinge by his pretiouse death and passion to obteyne everlastinge life. Item, my will is that my debtes be payed out of my goodes, before any my children have or receive any parte of my goodes. Item, I give to every of my six sones ten pound a peece and my two eldest sones,[16] Willyam & George, whom I have bound prentises, my will is that they have thair portiones payed with convenient speed after my death; and my other fower sones to be mayntayned by my eldest sone, Thomas, with meat

16 This confusion is as in the original. In fact the eldest son was apparently Thomas.

& cloth untill they be fitt for such trades as God shall dispose them to; and then my will is that my sone Thomas, at convenient tyme, not only pay them iij^{li} vj^s viij^d towardes their byndage but allso pay their portions with spead after to go forward duringe such tyme as they shall not be able to governe it. Item, my will is that, for my two daughters, thay have their severall portions of ten pound a peece when they shall come to yeares of goverment, and in the mean tyme my sone Thomas to mayntyne them. Item, my will is that my sone Thomas have my lease & farme whairin I dwell, with all my goodes, quick & dead, & howse & houshould stuffe as nowe it is, he payinge & dischdeginge my debtes & children's portions, & him I mayke my sole executor, assuringe my self of his care & love to all his bretherin & sisters. This will was mayd the j of October, anno Domini 1626, witnesses, Thomas Burden, the sone of Thomas Burden, & his sister Procter, and his nephew Thomas Johnstone^{iuratus} of Burden, with George Colling- wood^{iuratus}, who wrote the will, the daye & year above written,

George Collingwood [*full name signed*]

23^0 die Januarij, 1626, Georgius Collingwood iurat*us* fuit de veritate huiusmodi test*ament*i, et 27 Januarij pred*ictus* Thomas Johnson iurat*us* fuit de veritate eiusd*em*, unde ad*ministratio*nem et tuitionem[17] liberor*um* pred*ictorum* comiss*a* fuit Tho*me* Burden ex*ecuto*ri in eod*em* test*ament*o nominato, iurato etc.

The inventory of all the goods as well moveable as unmoveable of Thomas Burden of Burdon prayesed by these foure men, Edward Procter, Richard Marshall, Thomas Johnsonne, Richard Huntley.

Imprimis, foure oxen	20	0s	0d
Item, four stoots	17	0s	0d
Item, seavoen kine	18	0s	0d
Item, two stoots & two whyes	7	0s	0d
Item, ij horses, ij meares and on foole	10	0s	0d
Item, foure calves	2	0s	0d
Item, x weathers	5	0s	0d
Item, xxviij ewes, xxx hoogs	16	0s	0d
Item, the cropp one the earth and in the staggarth	20	0s	0d
Item, hay and stray	4	0s	0d
Item, wayne and wheles, plowes with somes, rackes, spads and showles	5	0s	0d
Item, his apperell	2	0s	0d

17 The clerk clearly, and wrongly, puts these words in the accusative case.

Item, all the howsit stufe within the howse and chamber	13	14s	0d
Item, five swine	2	0s	0d
Item, the cock & henes about the hous		3s	0d
Item, the reversion of the lease of the farmhold	5	0s	0d

Sum 144^{li} 10^s

Debts due unto the deceased

Oweing by Cuthbert Maltby for a part of his wives porcion	9	0s	0d

Source: DPR1/1/1626/B8/1–2, paper 3ff.

39. Anthony Hedley of Fulwell, labourer, 1627

In the name of God, amen, the twentithe day of ffebruary in the second yeare of the reigne of our sovereigne lorde, Charles, by the grace of God, king of England, Scotland, ffrance and Ireland, defender of the fayth, &c., I, Anthonye Hedley of ffulwell in the county of Durham, labourer, sicke in bodye but in good and perfect rememberance, all laud and prayse be to almightye God, doe mayke this my last will and testament in manner and forme following. ffirst, I commend my soule to almighty God, my maker and redemer, and my bodye to be buryed in the churche of Monnckwarmouthe, on the south syde of the fonte. Item, I give to Margarett ffoster, daughter unto Anthonye ffoster of ffulwell, one gimmer hogg. Item, my will is that Willyam Hedley, my brother, shall have house rowme for himselfe and his bedd, with my wife soe long as he leiveth, if he and she can agree, and she to pay all the rent for the same. Item, my will is that I may be honestly brought forthe, and all the rest of my goods, moveable and unmoveable, my legasies and funeral expenses discharged, I give unto Ann Hedley, my wife, who I doe mayke executrix of this my last will and testament. In witnes whereof, I have hereunto sette my hand the¹⁸ day and yeare first above written.
Witnesses hereof
Anthony Young^{iuratus} [*full name signed*]
Raphe Lumley^{iuratus} [*full name signed*]

---

18 The manuscript repeats 'the'.

To the right wor(shipfu)ll Mr Doctor Cradocke, Chancelor to the right reverend father in God, Richard, lord bishop of Durham.

Right worshipfull,
Whereas Anthony Hedley, late of ffulwell, deceased, made his will and therein named me, Anne Hedley, his wife, executrix, and forasmuch as I am weake and verie aiged and blinde and so unfitt for travale, [I][19] am willing and desirous that Anthony ffoster, my sister's sonne, may take upon him the execucion of the will to my use. And so referring the same to your worship's consideration, I have hereunto subscribed my marke and take my leave, this xxvij^th of August, 1627.

Anne Hedley, hir marke [*marked with a cross*]
Witnesses hereof
Anthony Younge [*full name signed*]
Raiph Lumley [*full name signed*]

A true inventorye of all the goods and chattels of Anthony Hedlye of ffulwell, labourer, deseased, praised by fower indeferinte men, this two and twentye day of August, 1627.

Imprimis, one cowe	2	6s	8d
Item, fower yowes	1	2s	0d
Item, two old bedsteads, one old cubbord, one old table, two pannes, two dublers, with other smaile impliments		13s	0d
Item, one halfe roode of wheate sowen one the grounde		6s	8d
Item, old haye		10s	0d
Item, two sheepe hogges		6s	8d
Item, three hennes & a cocke		2s	0d
Item, one paire of linninge sheetes and one paire of harne sheetes		8s	0d
Item, one pot, one old candlesticke		2s	0d
The some 5^li 17 0			

Debts oweing to the dead

Inprimis, Richard Waike of Cleadon	6	0s	0d
Item, George Coilyer of Munckweremouth	5	0s	0d
Item, John Kitchinge of Suddicke	3	0s	0d

---

19 Omitted from the manuscript.

Item, David Browne of Bishopweremouth	2	13s	4d
Item, Martin Alleson of South Sheeles		6s	0d
Some	16	19s	4d

The totall some 22^{li} 16^s 4^d

Thomas Taylor [*full name signed*]
George Colyer, [*marked with a symbol*]
Raiph Lumley [*full name signed*]
Anthony Younge [*full name signed*]

Source: DPR1/1/1627/H3/1–3, paper 3ff.

40. William Burdon of Ryhope, yeoman, 1627

In the name of God, amen, I, William Burdon of Ryhoop in the county of Durham, yeoman, being {deaseased} sike and weake of body yeat perfecte of remembrance, do make my last will and testament in manner and forme following, ffirst, I bequeath my soulle unto almightie God, my creator and to Jesus Christ, my redemer, by whose death and passion, I stedfastly beleive to have remission of my sines and my body to be buried in the church yeard of Bishoppwarmouth, and for all the rest of my goods and chattells, I give and bequeath in manner and forme followinge. My will is that, after God hath taken my soull to His mercy, that John ffell the elder of Ryhoop and John Whittans of the same shall se that I be honestly brought forth and buried in the church yeard of Bishoppweirmouth. My will is that ther be given unto the poore of this towne of Ryhoop, xiij^s iiij^d. ffor all the rest of my goods and chattells, moveable and unmoveable, I give and bequeath unto John ffell of Ryhoop the elder and unto John Whittans of the same, which I make joyntly my executors of this my last will and testament, in wittness hearof to this my last will and testament, I have set to my hand and marke this xviijth of November, 1627.

William Burdon, his marke [*marked with a symbol*]
Signed and delivered in the presents of
Jane Whittan, hir marke [*marked with a symbol*]
William Shipperdson [*full name signed*]

Ther is owinge to me, William Burdon, at this time of making this my will, by Edward ffell, five powndes and by Elizabeth Watson, iiij^s.

An inventory of all and the goods and chattels that William Burdon, died deaseased one, being praysed by thes fowre men, v*idelicet* Thomas Roxbye, Edward ffell, Robert Goodchilde & William Shipperdsonne, this first of ffebruarie, 1627.

Imprimis, one cowe, price	2	6s	8d
Ittem, ten shepe, price	2	0s	0d
Ittem, one lease of thre roudes of arable land in every the thre feilds of Ryhoope, with on cow pasture in the oxe pasture, on horse pasture &five sheep gates in the fallowes, to expier thre yeares	5	0s	0d
Ittem, on half aker of wheate in the feild		13s	4d
Ittem, in the testator his purse	1	0s	0d
Ittem, his apperrell with a chest	1	0s	0d
Ittem, wheat in the garth, xx^s	1	0s	0d
Summa	12	14s	0d

Owing to the testator			
Owing by Edward ffell	5	0s	0d
Owing by Wedow Watsone		4s	0d
Summa totallis	17	18s	0d

Paied in funerall expences	1	0s	0d
Paied to the poore of Riuehoop		13s	4d

Thomas Roxbie, his marke [*marked with a symbol*]
Edward ffell, his marke [*marked with a symbol*]
Robert Goodchild [*full name signed*]
W[illiam] Shipperdson [*full name signed*]

Source: DPR1/1/ 1627/B5/1, 2.

41. George Collier of Monkwearmouth, yeoman, 1629

The ffirste day of Aprill 1629

In the name of God, amen, I, George Colyer of Monnckwarmouthe in the countie of Durham, yeoman, sicke in bodye but in good and perfect remembrance, thankes be to God, doe make this my last will and testament in manner and forme ffollowing. ffirst, I bequeath my soule to God, my maker and redemer, and my bodye to be buryed in the parishe churche of Monkwearmouth aforesayd. Item, I give and bequeath unto Raphe Bracke, my goodsonn, one branditt stott of two

years ould and more. Item, I give unto Margarett Brack, my
dawghter and wife to the said Raphe Bracke, one calfe aboute a
quarter of a year ould. Item, I give unto John Bracke, there son, one
bay foole. Item, I give unto my daughter Ann Colyer, for hir child
part or porcion of my goods moveable and unmoveable, thirtye
pounds. Item, all the rest of my goods moveable and unmoveable,
my debts, legacies and funerall expenses discharged, I give and
bequeath to Jane Colyer, my wife, and[20] Thomas Colyer, my sonn,
whome I doe make executors of this my last will and testament.
Item, my will is that Jane Colyer, my wife, is to enioye that my halfe
ffarme which I now dwell on dureing hir lyfetime; and, after her
decease, to com to my sonn Thomas Colyer, if he be then leiveing. In
witnes whereof, I the said George Colyer to my laste will have set to
my hand and seale the day and yeare first above written

George Colyer his marke [*marked with a symbol*] [*seal*]
Sealed, signed and delivered in the presence of
George Devenant [*full name signed*]
Thomas Taylor [*full name signed*]
Sampson Ayre, his marke [*marked with a capital S, reversed*]
Reignald ffawcett [*full name signed*]

Aprill the 13, anno 1629
An inventorie of all the goods, movabell and unmovabell of George
Colyer of Munckwarmoth in the countie of Durham, yeoman,
deseased, praised and valued by theis fower men whose hands ar
heer under writen the day and year above writen.

Imprimis, his halfe of the lease of his farmehould, priced	20	0s	0d
Item, six oxen, priced at	29	0s	0d
Item, two stots, priced	7	0s	0d
Item, fower kie, priced	9	0s	0d
Item, two twinter stirks	2	0s	0d
Item, two wained calves	1	0s	0d
Item, two maires, with one year ould colte	8	0s	0d
Item, thriten ould sheep, with six lambs, priced	3	0s	0d
Item, one sowe, with fower kepinge piges		13s	0d
Item, two brode geese and two ganders, with five hens and one coke		8s	0d

---

20 MS repeats 'and'.

Item, his crope groweing upon the ground this year, priced	20	0s	0d
Item, plough and plough gear, waines and waine gear, with harowes, yokes and sowms, with forks and other implements belonging to husbandre, priced	5	0s	0d
Item, one bowell of wheat, with an other of peas and one of malte	1	10s	0d
Item, two ould cubards, with one tabell and one litell spence, priced	1	10s	0d
Item, two chests, with one arke, priced		10s	0d
Item, one longsedell, one bufet forme, two ould chairs, thre drinke stands, sixe milke bouls, thre skeels, with one washing tub		10s	0d
Item, two bedsteads, with one chirne		6s	0d
Item, fower bras pots, fower bras ketels, with two bras candelsticks	2	0s	0d
Item, thriten puder dishes, one quart pot, thre puder salts, two candelsticks and one litell drinkinge cupe, priceid	1	0s	0d
Item, one paire of bars, two rakinge cruks, one spite, one paire of broilinge irons, with one paire of toongs, priceid		10s	0d
Item, eight coverlids and hapings, fower fether cods, with thre paire of hardin shets, priced	1	16s	0d
Item, one paire of lin shets, with fower cod pilivers and fower towels, priceid		10s	0d
Item, five cushones, priceid		3s	0d
Item, his aparell and forinter, priceid	2	0s	0d
Item, given in legacies unto Ralfe Bracke and his wife and his sonne, one stot, one calf and one foole priceid	3	10s	0d

Debts oweing to the testatur

Imprimis, Mr William Wiklife lent money		10s	0d
Item, Robt Folinsby, which was a det due by Mr Sampson Ewbanke		18s	0d

Debts that the testatur is oweing

Imprimis, to Sampson Aire	5	10s	0d
Item, to John Eliner	5	0s	0d

Item, to An Hedlie	5	0s	0d
Item, to Thomas Taylor for rent	2	10s	0d
Item, to the Dean and Chapter for rent of his own tenament due now at Whitsonday	1	10s	6d
Item, for rent of his part of that farme which was Mr Sampson Ewbank's		15s	4d
Item, for funerall expenceis	2	10s	0d
Item, for repairations in and aboute the tenament	2	0s	0d

Some, dets deducted, 24^{li} 15^s 0^d

George Deventt [*full name signed*]
Christopher Shepperdson [*full name signed*]
Thomas Taylor [*full name signed*]
Sampson Aire, his marke [*marked with a capital S, on its side*]

Source: DPR1/1/1629/C7/1, 3–4, paper 4ff.

42. John Johnson the elder of Bishopwearmouth, blacksmith, 1629

Novamber this sixth in the fifth yeare of King Charles his reigne, 1629 In the name of God, amen, John Johnson thelder of Bishopp Wearmouth in the county of Durham, blacksmith, being weake in body but of perfect remembrance, blessed be God, doe institute, nomynate, declare & publish this my last will and testament in manner and forme followinge. Imprimis, I bequeath my soule unto almightye God, my saviour, through Jesus Christ, my mediator & redeemer, by whose death I hope for everlastine life, and my body to Christian buriall in the church {yard} of Bishopp Wearmouth, & for my goods the which it hath pleased God to lend me I doeth bestow them as followes. Item, I give unto my sonne Richard my golden cow, to be delivered to him presently after my death. Item, I doe give unto his wife one read whey calfe white tailed to be delivered unto hir presently after my decease. Item, I doe give unto his fower children, namely, Thomas Johnson, Richard Johnson, Izabell & Ales, to every of them, tenn shillings a peece as a legacye & to be paid a yeare after his dicease. Item, I give to Izabell Smith, the daughter of Richard Smith of Tunstall, tenn shillings, to be paide a yeare after my dicease. Item, I give unto John Johnson & Elizabeth Johnson, the children of my sonne Christopher Johnson, lately deceased, tenn shillings a peece, to be paide them when they come to the age of one & twenty yeares. Item, I give unto the poore of the parish of Bishopp

Waremouth sixteene shillings, to be bestowed upon them at my buriall. Item, I give unto my sonne John Johnson halfe of the cropp, the which I am to have of the land the which I ploweth for Robart Stephenson of Newbottle. Item, I give unto my wife my bay mare. Item, I alsoe give unto my wife, my debts and legacies beinge paide, the thrids of all my moveable gear & alsoe my funerall discharged. Item, I doth make my wife & my sonne John soale executors to this my will & testament & to see that all my debts, legacies & funerall to be dulye & truly discharged. I doth likewise give unto my wife during hir life naturall the cloase the which I bought of Ralfe Reade, comonly called Pillcodd Hill, my sonne Richard h[aving] the winteringe of two key in the same during hir life, that is, to goe from Michallmas untill May daye, & after hir dicease that then the said [to] come to my sonne Richard & his heires; & to this my will & testament I have harunto sette my hand & seale, the day & yeare above written

       John Johnson, his marke [*marked with a symbol, a horseshoe*]
Sealed, signed in the presence of
Thomas Grainge [*full name signed*]
Richard Johnson [*full name signed*]
Richard Smyth [*full name signed*]
Thomas Johnson [*full name signed*]

An inventory of all the goods & chattels of John Johnson, late of Bishopp Waremoth, deceased, as they were viewed & prised, the sixt day of January, anno Domini 1629, by Walter Marshall, clerke, Raphe Jarvis, Richard Smith and Thomas Johnson, yeomen

Imprimis, six oxen at vj^{li} the yoke & two mares, iiij^{li}	22	10s	0d
Item, six kyne, two stirkes & foure calves in the close	17	0s	0d
Item, the hay in the close, iij^{li}, & straw in the yard, iij^{li}	6	0s	0d
Item, foure stotts & a whye more	8	6s	8d
Item, the corne in the stacke yard	7	0s	0d
Item, foure boules of big malt	1	16s	0d
Item, wheate sowen in the feilds at xx^{s} an acre	8	0s	0d
Item, six swine, xx^{s}, and seaven sheepe, xxiij^{s} iiij^{d}	2	3s	4d
Item, two capons, five hens & a cocke		3s	4d
Item, in the forehouse one ambery & a caule		10s	0d
Item, ten peece of peuder, 10^{s}, one peuder candlesticke, a pint pot & a salt, 2^{s}		12s	0d
Two brasse pots, a posnet, & two brasse candlesticks, a brasse kettle & a greate brasse pan & a little pan & a skummer	1	10s	0d

One table, one counter, two formes, thre chares		6s	8d
Beefe & bacon hanging at the balkes		10s	0d
A pare of bars, two reckon crookes, one frying pan, a speete, one paire broiling irons & a paire of tongs & rackes		6s	8d
In the parlour and loft three bedsteads, one chest & a presser		10s	0d
One mattresse, a downe bed, foure coverlets, two blankets, five happings, seaven cods & bolsters, seaven paire of sheetes & three pillowbeares {& 2 tablecloths}	2	15s	0d
Two kirnes, three skeeles, three drinke barrels, foureteene boules, foure cheese fats, a washing tub & a masking tub & two cans		10s	0d
An arke in the kilne, a woollen whele, one sive, three ruddels, a paire of temses		6s	8d
A kilne haire, a window cloth, six seckes & pokes		13s	4d
His apparel	1	0s	0d
Money owen to him by George Richardson, j^{li} x ^{s} & by others, iiij^{li} x^s	6	0s	0d
Money in his purse		10s	0d
Item, money owen by his son Richard Johnson	1	18s	0d
Summa totalis	90	17s	8d

Walter Marshall [*full name signed*]
Raiph Jervis [*full name signed*]
Richard Smyth [*full name signed*]
Thomas Johnson [*full name signed*]

Source: DPR1/1/1629/J6/1–2, paper 3ff.

43. Sampson Ewbank of Monkwearmouth, 1629

xxvij° Maij, 1629
A declaracion of thaccompt of Barbara Ewbancke alias ffollansby, wife of Robert ffollansbie, adminstratrix of the goods and chattels of Sampson Ewbancke, her late husband, late of Munckwermouthe of the dioces of Durham, deceased, made upon her administering the said goods as followeth,

Inprimis, this accomptant chargeth herselfe to have had and
received of the said deceased's goods and chattels
comeing to her handes, amounting to the sum of thirtie
five pounds of lawfull English money as appeareth by
an inventarie thereof made and by her upon
oath exhibitted into the consistorie court at
Durham appeareth,

Summa patet	35	0s	0d

Out of which this accomptant hathe paid and craveth allowance
as followeth,

ffirst, this accomptant hathe paid or satisfied to the
worshipfull the Deane and Chapter of Durham
the sum of xx^{li} vj^s xj^d for arrearags of rent due at
the tyme of the deceased's death for his farme at
Munckwermouth and since by this accomptant
satisfied, as by acquittance appeareth 20 6s 11d

Item, shee hathe paid or satisfied to Anne Hopper for
the deceased's debt and since his death due upon
bond as by the said bond cancelled appeareth, 6 0s 0d

{Item, shee hathe likewise paid or satisfied for the said
deceased's debt and since his death to Mr John
Hilton, due upon bond, as by the said bond
cancelled appeareth 20 0s 0d}

Item, shee hathe also paid to Robert Lambton of
Durham, for the deceased's debt and since his
death, due upon bond, as by the same cancelled
appeareth, 2 2s 9d

Item, shee hathe also paid to Robert Chambers of
Munckwermouth, for the debt of the said
deceased and since his death, due upon bill as by
the same cancelled may appeare 2 0s 0d

Item, she craveth to be allowed unto her for the
funerall expences of the said deceased, for the
fees of the letters of administracion, with suerties
charges, a speciall commission and other charges
about the same 8 0s 0d

Item, shee prayeth to be allowed unto her for the
drawing, ingrossing and passing of this accompt,
with letters testimonial upon the same and other
charges incident thereunto 1 3s 4d

Summ of her payments & allowances	39	13s	0d

So that it appeareth shee hather fullie administred
  the said deceased's estate goods and hathe paid
  more then the same did amount unto, by the
  summ of   4   13s   0d

Admissemus, W. Easdall

Source: DPR1/1/1629/E5/1–2, paper 2ff.

44. Ralph Watson of Barnes, 1629

A true inventory of all the goods and chattels of Raphe Watson, late
of Barnes, deceased, as they weere vewed & prised the thirteenth
day of October, 1629, & in the fift yeare of the reigne of King Charles,
by Thomas Aire, Richard Smith, Nicholas Todd & Thomas Guy.

Imprimis, fifteene milch kine at 50 shillings a peece	37	10s	0d
Item, one stott & two yonge stirkes	3	10s	0d
Item, fourty & two sheepe	14	0s	0d
Item, hay standing in two ruckes or stackes	4	4s	0d
Item, in the house, one cubbord, xiij^s iiij^d & a spence of vj^s viij^d	1	0s	0d
Item, six peuder dishes & six saucers		8s	0d
Item, two peuder candlestickes & two peuder salts		1s	0d
Item, one greate old brasse kettle & a brasse pot		10s	0d
One reccon crooke, one speete, one frying pan		2s	0d
Three skeeles, one chirne & other woodden vessell		6s	0d
One bedstead, one table, a chare, three shelves of furdale & a wheele		3s	4d
One sithe, one spade, an axe & three rakes		2s	0d
Three happins, three cods & two paire of sheetes		10s	0d
His apparrell & money in his purse	1	0s	0d
Item, foure & fifty cheeses at 12^d a peece	2	14s	0d
Money owen to the said Raphe Watson	1	16s	0d
Sum total	67	13s	4d

Item, there is laid out by the said Raphe Watson, upon
  security of certaine lands in Midle Herrington,
  fourty pounds which he appointed to be divided
  equally amongst his foure children   40   0s   0d
So the whole sum of his estate is   107   16s   4d

There is to be deducted out of this

The funerall expences	1	15s	3d
Item, which he oweth for rent	12	0s	0d
Item, to Raphe Martin	4	0s	0d
Owen to Widow Herrison	6	0s	0d
To John Smith		15s	0d
Thomas Guy	5	6s	8d
Sum debts	30	16s	10d

Which taken out of the goods, there rests   77   19s   6d

Thomas Aire, his marke [*marked with capital initials TA*]
Nicholas Todd [*full name signed*]
Richard Smyth [*full name signed*]
Thomas Guy [*full name signed*]

DPR1/1/1629/W4/1, paper 2 ff.

45. Peter Marley of Hilton, Monkwearmouth, yeoman, 1630

Memorandum, that Peter Merley of Hilton in the county palatine of Durham, yeoman, decessed, about the 16 day of February in the yeare of our Lord 1628, did make \a declaracion of this/ last will and testament in maner and forme following \or words to the like effect/. ffirst, he gave and bequeathed unto his wife Agnes Morley halfe of that his lease in Hilton, to have and to hold the same to her owne use dureing her life naturall, and the other half of the sayd lease he gave, lefte and bequaethed unto his sone Henry Merley to have and to hold to him and his heires, together with the reversion of the other half of the lease after the death of the said Agnes Merley, provided that the sayd Henry Merley shall yearely pay unto his brother George Merley, sone of the sayd Peter Merley, the sume of 5li of good and lawfull English money dureing the life naturall of the sayd Georg Merley. Moreover, he gave, left and bequeathed two partes of all the rest of his goods and chattels unto his two daughters Isabel Merley and Margaret Merley, to be equally divided betwene them. Lastly, it was his will and intention that the remainder of his goods and chattels, being the third parte, should rest and remayne unto his wife Agnes Merley aforesayd which sayd Agnes Merlay he made, constituted and appoynted the sole and universall executrix of this his last will and testament.

Witnesses hereof
George Merley^{iuratus} [*full name signed*]
Cuthbert Merley^{iuratus} [*full name signed*]
in presencia Gabrieli Jackson, notarii publici

And inventoryie of the goods and cattells of Peter Marley of Hilton, decessed, praised on the xxv^d of Apriel by Georg Marley, Cristofer Shaw, Edward Middelton and John Huchanson, 1629

Inprimis, his reparrell	3	6s	8d
Item, in the hallhouse, tow cubertes, xxxij peece of bouder & saussers, eight condelstickes, five saltes, thre drinkinge pottes, one flaginge, one basinge, halfe a dozen poting dishes	3	18s	0d
Item, one table, tow chares, one forme, tow hingers		12s	6d
Item, foure poots with cilpes, tow catels, thre panes, tow drepinpanes, thre speetes, one pare of rackes, thre reckincrooke, tow pare of tonges, one friing pane, one choping knife, one shredinge knife	3	1s	6d
Item, in the parler, tow beedes with firnitories to them, one cobert, one [*blank*], one table with a frame, foure buffet stooles, one pare of iron bares, a pore, and a fire shoale and tow quisinges	9	13s	0d
Item, in the fore loft, tow bedsteades, thre chiest, six coverletes, seaven blanckets, eight codes, one peece of twille, one carpincloth		6 [........]²¹	
Item, in the loft over the halle, nine pare of line sheetes, twelfe pare of harden sheets, a dozen of pillivers, a dozen and a halfe of napkines, foure toules, four table cloths, foure chieste, one trinell bed with clothes, thre <bendes> of lether	8	13s	0d
Item, in the east loft, one chist, tobes, wheeles, markinge, paine, seckes, hopes, white cloth, waine ropes, seves, iron forkes, shoules and spaid, woale, one bushell, a peecke	1	1s	0d
Item, in the milkhouse, carnes, sekles, meales, diches, trinshers, standes and barels		13s	4d
Gese, henes and duckes		5s	0d
Item, ploughe and plow greer, waine and waine garer	6	12s	3d

---

21 Text faded.

Item, eight oxson	28	0s	0d
Item, tenne kine and five cavles	25	0s	0d
Item, sixe stotes	9	0s	0d
Item, five stirkes	6	0s	0d
Item, sixe horses and mares	13	13s	4d
Item, five calves[22]	3	15s	0d
Item, foure score sheepe	23	0s	0d
Item, thirtye one lood of otes	15	0s	0d
Item, winter corne, fiftine akers	25	0s	0d

206^{li} 6^s 2^d

Source: DPR1/1/1630/M5/1, 3, paper 2ff. The will was written by the notary public, Gabriel Jackson, but the inventory is in a different hand.

46. Robert Scurfield of Grindon, 1631

Desember the sixteinth, 1630
A trew inventory of all the goods & chattles of Robert Skirfelld of Grindonn, lait deceassed, praissed by these fower gentellmenn under writtenn, George Lilbourne, George Graye, Robert Tompson & Willi[am] Martine

Imprimis, eight oxenn at eight pounds ten shillings a yocke is	34	0s	0d
More, twentie kine	41	0s	0d
More, tow browne stotts, fower yeare oulds	4	0s	0d
More, five lesser stotts wheareof fower of them at Seatonn Dallevell	6	13s	4d
Sevenn whyes wheareof three of them at Seatonn Dallevell	12	5s	0d
More, tenn stirkes & a bull tow yeare oulds	12	10s	0d
Tenn yonng calves	5	0s	0d
More, tow horses, one meare & tow folles	12	0s	0d
More, five skore & sevennteanne yowes & wethers & six toupes	38	0s	0d
More, fortie hoges	7	0s	0d
Fower swine hogges		16s	0d
More, geasse & paltrie	1	0s	0d

22 MS 'cavles'.

Waines & waine geare, plowes & plough gearr, with other wood belonnging to them	8	0s	0d
The korne in the stack garth & kornn in the feald sowenn	66	0s	0d
Haye in the yard & in the feald	7	0s	0d
The house & grounnd besides the rennt & household stuff	50	0s	0d
	306	4s	4d

Imprimis, in the fore house, one chymnie, one paire of racks, tow rackenn crewks with other small matters belonnging to them and tow cubbords & a spencer	1	10s	0d
More, thirteanne putter dishes, thre candellsticks, one pestell & a morter, with other putter standing uppon the cubbard heades	1	0s	0d
More, one bed stead, tow tables, one chair, tow formes & fower chease bordes	1	4s	0d
More, one muskett with hir furniter		10s	0d
More, in the fore house, one bed, one coverlade, tow happens, one paire of blannckets, tenn hespes of yearnn, with other things	1	0s	0d
In the parler, tenn coverlids & one paire of blancketts	1	6s	8d
More, in the parler, tenn coverlides & one paire of blanncketts	2	0s	0d
More, three paire of lineing sheats, fower paire of stracking sheats, twelff table napkins & six cod pillowes	1	10s	0d
More, one peace of huswife cloth & six cushonns		12s	0d
In the chamber, tow brassenn kettles, tow ironn potts, tow panns, halfe a doozenn putter dishes with other small putter	1	10s	0d
More, six milk skealls, twentie woodenn bouls with other wooden vessel		13s	0d
In the lowe chamber, one chyminie, one bed stead & tow ould arcks, with ould tubes & one paire of teamsses		13s	8d
His apparell & his sword	5	0s	0d
	18	10s	0d

Summa totalis of the testator's goods 378[li] 7[s] 0[d]

Debts oweing to the testator

Imprimis, in corne at Bellford	20	0s	0d
By William Clarrke of Warden Lawe is	9	10s	0d
By Henrie Gibsonn & Mr William Wickliffe	3	6s	8d
By Robert Dickennsonn of Sunnderland	2	10s	0d
A stott to Tow of Sunnderlannd	2	6s	0d
By John Burdonn for a stott	2	6s	0d
By William Browne	3	0s	0d
By Cristofer Readshawe	6	0s	0d
By Lannclot Joblynn	2	0s	0d
By John Thornntonn	1	0s	0d
By ffranncis Milboume	1	13s	0d
	53	12s	4d

Debts which the testator oweth

Imprimis, to Robert Tompsonn of Ryop	24	10s	0d
To Jann Newbie of Sunnderlannd	21	12s	0d
To Rauff Jarvice of Warmouth	10	16s	0d
To Christofer Bee of Houghtonn	15	3s	0d
To Wedo Leacmann of Warmouth	4	6s	8d
To Ann Woodemann of Herringtonn	3	0s	0d
To Thomas Ushaw of Uffertonn	3	0s	0d
To John Gibsonn of Herringtonn	3	0s	0d
To Thomas Aire of Tunstall	10	16s	0d
Margerie Tompsonn of Ryop	6	0s	0d
Mister Collingewood's rennt at Whitsunndaye	25	0s	0d
For his funnerall expennces	8	0s	0d
For his teith to M^r franncis Burgine	5	6s	8d
	140	10s	0d

Suma totallis of the debts owenn by the testator 140^li 10^s 0^d

George Lilburne [*full name signed*]
George Grey [*full name signed*]
William Martin's mark [*marked with a symbol*]
Robert Thompson his marke [*marked with a symbol*]
Administratio commissa Isabelle Scurfield, uxori dicti defuncti

Source: DPR1/1/1631/S5/1 ,2, paper 2ff.

47. Edward Lee of Sunderland, gentleman, 1631

In the name of God, amen, the ffowerteenth day of December, anno
Domini 1630, and in the sixt yeere of the reigne of our soveraigne
lord Charles, by the grace of God kinge of England, Scottland,
ffrannce and Ireland, defender of the ffayeth, &c., I, Edward Lee, of
Sunderland by the sea in the countie of Durham, gentleman, beinge
weake in bodye but of good and perfect minde and memorye
(thanks be given to almightie God) doe make and declare this my
last will and testament in manner and forme followinge, that is to
saye: ffirst and principallie I committ my soule into the hands of
almightie God, my creator, and to his sonne, Jesus Christ, my onelie
saviour and redeemer, trustinge and assuredlie beleevinge through
his mercye and meritts onelie to have free remission and forgivenes
of all my sinns and offences and to be made partaker of the liefe
everlastinge in his glorious kingdome. My bodye I committ to the
earth to be buried in decent and christianlike manner; and as
concerninge that estate which it hath pleased God to blesse me
withall, I give and dispose the same in manner and forme
followinge: that is to saye, ffirst I will that all such debts as I may
happen to owe att the time of my decease be satisfied. Item, I give
and bequeath to my eldest daughter, Marye, ffower hundred pounds
of currant English money, to be paid her by one hundred pounds per
annum ymediatelie from and after my decease out of all the rents
and proffitts of all my messuags, lands, tenements and heredittaments which I nowe have, as well my ffreehould land as all such
which I have and hould by lease, untill shee shall have her said
ffower hundred pounds paid her. Item, I give and bequeath[23] to my
daughter Sara the somme of three hundred pounds of lawfull money
of England, to be likewise paid her by one hundred pounds per
annum out of my said messuags, lands, tenements and heredittaments aforesaid, and the rents and proffitts thereof arisinge from
and ymmediatelie after my said daughter Marye is satisfied & paid
as aforesaid. Item, I give and bequeath unto my daughter Ellen three
hundred pounds of lawfull money of England, to be likewise paid
her by one hundred pounds per annum out of the rents and proffitts
of all my said messuags, lands, tenements and hereditaments
aforesaid, from and ymmediatelie after my said daughter Sara shall
have received her said porcion as aforesaid. Item, I give and

---

23 MS repeats 'and bequeath'.

bequeath unto my daughter Elizabeth the somme of three hundred pounds of lawfull money of England, to be likewise paid her by one hundred pounds per annum out of the rents and proffitts of all my messuags, lands, tenements and heredittaments aforesaid, from and ymmediatelie after my said daughter Ellen shall have received her said porcion as aforesaid. Item, I give and bequeath unto my daughter Jane three hundred pounds of lawfull money of England, to be likewise paid unto her by one hundred pounds per annum out of the rents and proffitts of my messuags, lands, tenements and heredittaments aforesaid, from and ymmediatelie after my said daughter Elizabeth shall have received her said porcion as aforesaid. Item, I give and bequeath unto my daughter Rebecka the somme of three hundred pounds of lawfull money of England, to be likewise paid her by one hundred pounds per annum out of the rents and proffitts of my messuages, lands, tenements and heredittaments aforesaid, from and ymediatelie after my said daughter Jane shall have received her said porcion as aforesaid. Item, I give and bequeath unto my sonne Thomas, my youngest child, the somme of three hundred pounds of lawfull money of England, to be likewise paid him by one hundred pounds per annum out of the rents and proffitts of my messuags, lands, tenements and heredittaments aforesaid, from and ymediatelie after my said daughter Rebecka shall have received her said porcion as aforesaid. And my will and minde is that if any of my foresaid children shall happen to dye or departe this liefe before they shall have received their severall porcions as aforesaid, that then the porcion comminge and growinge due and payable to him or her as aforesaid that soe shall dye or departe this liefe I give and bequeath to my eldest sonne, Edward Lee, to be paid unto him by one hundred pounds per annum out of the rents and proffitts of all my messuags, lands, tenements and heredittaments aforesaid, from and ymmediatelie after all my foresaid children that shall survive shall have paid them their severall porcions aforesaid. Item, I give and bequeath to the poore of Sunderland, where I nowe dwell, the somme of tenne pounds of lawfull money of England, to be given and distributed amongst them att the discrecion of twelve ffreemen of the said towne of Sunderland. Item, I give and bequeath unto the wor[shipful], my lovinge friend ffrancis James of Hetton in the countie of Durham, esquier, ffive pounds of lawfull money of England, and to my lovinge friend Mr Thomas Shadforth of Tunsdell in the said countie of Durham five pounds of currant English money. Item, I give and bequeath unto my lovinge wife Elizabeth the use and benefitt of all

that messuage or ten*eme*nte in the tenure or occupacion of Morrice
Prescott, scytuate and beinge in Sunderland aforesaid, for and
duringe the terme of her naturall liefe. Item, I give and beqeath unto
my said lovinge wiefe and my said sonne Edward (my debts,
legacies & funerall expences first paid and discharged) all that my
brewehouse in Sunderland aforesaid, with all and every thappurten-
nances thereunto belonginge, togeather with all such stocke of
money, corne, graine, debts oweinge, ymplements, howshould stuffe
and other things whatsoever to the said brewhouse belonginge or
apperteynine, to the intent and purpose that my said wiefe and
sonne Edward shall manage and use the said brewhouse in such
manner and fashion as I have formerlie done for the better
mainetenannce of themselves and educatinge and bringinge up of
my children untill they shall have received their severall porcions
aforemencioned. And further I doe give and bequeath unto my said
wieff and sonne Edward the overplus of all such rents proffitts and
comodities whatsoever as shalbe made of all and singuler my
messuages, lands, tenements and hereditaments aforesaid (over and
above the said somme of one hundred pounds per annum afore
reserved for the porcions of my said children) for the better
educatinge and bringinge upp of my said children untill they shall
have received their severall porcions as aforesaid. And after my said
children's porcions shalbe paid unto them as aforesaid, I will and
bequeath all my lands, leases, messuags tenements and herditta-
ments and every of them unto my said sonne Edward and to his
heires & assignes forever, he payinge unto my lovinge wife the third
p[........] all the rents, proffitts and other things that shall arise and be
made of all and singuler my said messuages, loands and tenements
and other things for and duringe the [........] and terme of her naturall
lief. And I doe nominate and appointe my said welbeloved friends
ffranncis James and Thomas Shadford to be executors of this my last
will and testament, desireinge them and eyther of them to see this
my last will and testament performed in all things. And I doe revoke
and disannull all former wills and bequests by me heretofore in any
manner of wise had made or done, and I doe make and ordeine this
to be my last will & testament, in witnes whereof to this my presente
last will and testament, conteyninge six sheets of paper, I have here
setto my hand and seale, *videlicet* to the bottome of every sheete of
paper I have setto my hand and one the topp of them, fixed
togeather with a labell I have putto my seal the day and yeere first
above written.

Edward Lee [*signed with full name*] [*seal*]

Signed, sealed, published and declared to be the last will and
testament of the said Edward Lee in the p[rese]nce of us
Mr William Bachouse ^{iuratus}, notarius publicus [*signed with full name*]
John Ashenden, [*signed with full name and lawyer's device*]
Febr[uar]y, 1630 ^{iuratus} P[........]k

An inventorie of all the goods & chattles, lands & tenements of
Edward Lee of Sunderland nere the sea in the countie of Durham,
gentleman, disceased, as they were praised by us, videlicet Thomas
Peyton, Peter Greene, Raphe Wells, Thomas Hullyard

Imprimis, one mare & two keie with hay, three hoggs,			
a sowe and a brane, and three younge shotts	8	6s	0d
Item, moulte and hops with a bowle tubb, a skreene			
for corne, thirtie corne sackes and other implements	50	0s	0d
Item, a bruing lead with the marshe fatt, gilefatte and			
other bruing vessell belonging to the brew howse	13	6s	8d
Item, one small bruing lead	2	0s	0d
Item, a moulte millne, with the appurtenances	6	0s	0d
Item, beere in the seller, with emptie caske and other			
implements belonging to the seller	6	6s	8d
Item, an iron beame & skales, with the weights			
belonging unto them	1	6s	8d
Item, cooles and fierwood	1	0s	0d
Item, in the pumpe yearde, one cisterne of lead, with			
other things ther	2	10s	0d
Item, in the kitching, seven brase potts, ffive kettls,			
one skellete, ffower brase candle stickes	4	0s	0d
Item, in the kitching, twentie pewter platters, six			
candle stickes, ffower chamber potts, six sawcars,			
two morters with pestells, two fring pans, two			
dripping pans, a paier of rackes, ffive spitts, an			
iron chimny, 2 paier of tongs, a fier showlve, a			
jacke to turne spite & other implements	3	5s	0d
Item, in the kitching, 2 chaires of wood & other			
implements of wood		2s	0d
Item, in the learther, two iron potts		6s	8d
Item, in the little butterie, earthen vessels & other			
small things		2s	0d
Item, in the greater butterie, two fflagons, two pewtar			
potts, 2 saltes, three earthen juggs and other small			
things	2	0s	0d

Item, in the closset over the hall, three chargers of pewter, vj potingers, twentie platters, 3 pie plates, six sallet dishes, twentie ffower trenchers, and twelve sawcors	3	6s	8d
Item, eight dossen of trenchers, with other things		3s	0d
Item, in the upper chamber, one standing bedstead with a feather bedd, a materis, a boulster, 2 pillowes, a rigge, a coverlett, three blanketts, with curtaines and vallance	5	0s	0d
Item, a cambic bedstead, with a bed materis and bowlster, two pillowes, three coverletts and a paier of blanketts	4	0s	0d
Item, two looking glasses	1	0s	0d
Item, a livery cubbard with the cloth and two cushings	1	0s	0d
Item, two window cushings		13s	4d
Item, a small table with two carpitts		6s	8d
Item, a trunke with ffive greene chaires & three small pictures		15s	0d
Item, a closse stoole		8s	0d
Item, a paier of iron bares		6s	8d
Item, in the garrett, a lymbecke, a pewter still, a wollen wheele, a lynnen wheele, 3 old chests, with an old bed stead, a materis, a baskett & other things	1	10s	0d
	119	1s	8d
Item, an old sadle, a bridle, a pillion seat and cloth		10s	0d
Item, in the chamber over the moulte chamber, two servants' bedds with ther clothes, a paier of barres, one closse stoole, two chests, two hempers, with other implements in that rome	1	10s	0d
Item, in the iron chamber, iron instruments & other old iron, with other necessaries		13s	4d
Item, in the hie garrett, a half headed bedstead, with raks & other instruments		10s	0d
Item, in the great chamber, one livery cubbard, with the cloth, bason & ewer	1	6s	8d
Item, a little table with the carpett, 4 chaiers, 4 wrought stooles with a trucke bed, a paier of iron bares with fire pane and tonges, with other small things in the said chamber	2	6s	8d

Item, a trunke, with thirtenne paier of harding sheets, six paier of straking sheets and a bedd stoole	3	3s	4d
Item, in the mydle chamber, a great cheste with a fine table cloth and a dussen of napkings sutable unto it	1	6s	8d
Item, two course table clothes and two dozen of napkings	1	0s	0d
Item, a new table cloth and a dozen of napkings		13s	4d
Item, a shorte dioper cloth, with ffive napkings		6s	8d
Item, two cubbard clothes and two longe towells		10s	0d
Item, a dussen of course table napkings		6s	0d
Item, a dussen of worn table napkings		5s	0d
Item, twelve pillobeeres		16s	0d
Item, a stamell bering cloth, with childe bed lynnen	2	10s	0d
Item, ffive paier of holland sheetes	3	6s	8d
Item, nyne paier of lynnen sheetes	3	12s	0d
Item, twelve course pillowbeeres		10s	0d
Item, six course[24] hand towells		3s	0d
Item, twentie yeards of new lynnen	1	0s	0d
Item, sixtenne yeards of gray holland coste	1	1s	4d
Item, one standing beddstead & a truckell bedd with curtings and vallance, two fether bedd, 2 bowlsters, one matteris, two ruggs two blanketts and two pillowes	5	1s	0d
Item, a ffower squaier cheste, ffive course table clothes, a duzen course napkings & towells and a wallett		6s	8d
Item, a duble salt of silver, a silver bowle and six silver spones	5	0s	0d
Item, two chestes and two chaires	1	0s	0d
Item, a warmeing pan, a paier of barres, one presse, two looking glasses and other small things	1	2s	0d
Item, a muskett with hir furniture	1	0s	0d
Item, brickes and tiles	1	4s	0d
Item, in the hall, a drawing table and two carpetts, six stooles covered with leather and ffower joyned stooles	2	3s	0d
Item, more in the hall, videlicet six small chaiers, a paier of bares with a fier pane and tongs, an old watch	1	0s	0d
	46	7s	4d

---

24 MS repeats 'course'.

Item, eightenne cushens		18s	0d
Item, in Thomas Brome's howse, two and ffortie			
deales	1	5s	0d
Item, in William Ursie's howse, 2 old cubbards,			
a spence, a portale dore & a forme	1	0s	0d
Item, in the stable, 60 spares, two leathers, sixtenne			
oke gice, six learge deales and other small things	1	10s	0d
Item, att Mourice Prescott's howse end, six buntings			
& three peeces of oke wood, with other loose			
things about the howse		15s	0d
Item, a rent of sixtenne pounds per annum, yit to			
come for one yeare of a closse in Streatelam	16	0s	0d
Item, of good debtts, appering by billes and booke	100	0s	0d
Item, in desperate debts, about	30	0s	0d
Item, in redie mony in the howse	228	0s	0d
Item, thirtie firking of butter	24	0s	0d
Item, an old table in the butter seller, a paier of			
bason skales to weigh butter, with other old			
rubish		5s	0d
Item, a creadle of osiers for a childe		2s	0d
Item, his weering apparrell	15	0s	0d
	418	15s	0d

Item, an annuall rent of ffortie shillings from
 Mr Talbutt Lisle for ffower yeares and a halfe yit to come
Item, one lease of Helmeland Row for 26 yeares yit to come,
 which renteth yearely lxxvij^li xiij^s iiij^d
Item, diverse leases about Barmestonne grownds for certaine
 yeares yit to come, which renteth per annum lv^li [25]
Item, a lease of a collery att Urpeth & Chester More, for three
 yeares yit to come, which renteth per annum cleare iiij^li
Item, lease of a waste & a howse bulte thereon, in which
 William Menorie now dwelleth, for 16 yeares yit to come
 which rententh per annum j^li

The some of all the movable goods, besides theis			
annuall rents, in leases above written, is	584	4s	0d
Item, paid for his funerall chargs	32	19s	10d

---

25 This entry is followed by an unexplained sign that might be a 2 or a comma.

Tho[ma]s Peytone [*signed with full name*]
Raiph Wells [*signed with full name*]
Peter Green, his mark [*marked with a symbol*]
Thomas Hullyard [*signed with full name*]

*Source: DPR1/1/1631/L7/1–8, paper 8ff. A summary of the will, without
the inventory, appears in WI Durham, pp. 230–1.*

48. Elizabeth Lee of Sunderland, gentlewoman, 1632

An inventory taken the xxvth of September 1632 of all the goods &
chattells of Mrs Elizabeth Lee, late wife of Edward Lee of Sunderland
neere the sea in the county of Durham, gentlewoman, deceased,
praised by us, Thomas Ball the elder, Roberte Rutter & Richard
Smith

Imprimis, one standing bedd with curtaines & vallance, one feather bedd, one bolster, 2 pillowes, one side pillow, one greene and white rugg, 3 blanketts, a matrice, two paire of sheets & 4 pillowberes	8	0s	0d
Item, on paire of new holland sheetes and a paire of pillowberes	1	0s	0d
Item, six diaper napkins		9s	6d
Item, 4 course diaper napkins		2s	0d
Item, 2 damaske napkins		3s	0d
Item, 2 pewter platters weight 4s at		3s	4d
Item, 2 gownes, one riding cloke & safegard, one greene petticoate & 1 hatt	5	0s	0d
Item, 4 aprons	1	0s	0d
Item, 4 ruffs	1	6s	8d
Item, 4 paire of cuffs		3s	0d
Item, 6 dressings		5s	0d
Item, 2 night railes		4s	0d
Item, 2 old wrought wastcoates and 7 quaifes	1	0s	0d
Item, 2 stomachers & a printed handkeirchief		2s	0d
Item, 4 crosse clothes, 2 quaifes, one laced handkercher, 3 paire of white sleeves & one drawne workequaife		9s	0d
Item, 3 paire of gloves, 2 paire of kimes, 2 purses, 1 maske, 1 peece of gold lace, 1 booke, one lookin-glasse, with other small thinges	1	0s	0d

Item, one silver bowl, 1 silver thimble, one bodkine, one chaine & whistle	2	15s	0d
Item, a jemall ringe of gold, a hoop ring & a small cracked ringe		18s	0d
Item, certain peeces of gold & other quoines of silver amounting to	9	3s	0d
{More, the rent of Prescott's house for a yeare & a halfe	6	0s	0d}
Item, by bonds & booke debts due to her	116	5s	½d
Item, for a blacke truncke		4s	0d
Item, in ready mony	1	11s	0d
Summa totallis	151	3s	6½d

Thomas Ball, senior [*signed with full name*]
Robert Rutter [*signed with full name*]
Richard Smyth [*signed with full name*]

Source: DPR1/1/1632/L3/1, paper 2ff.

49. Ralph Wells of Sunderland, 1632

A note of all such goods of Raiph Wells as was sould the 8th May, 1632

Imprimis, a paire racks, two spitts, two recking crookes, a fire shovell, a porr & a paire of tongs	1	0s	0d
Item, a boule of rye		8s	4d
Item, a basen & a ewer		11s	0d
Item, 2 new candlestickes & a double salt		4s	10d
Item, a smoothing iron		2s	1d
Item, a brasse candlesticke			8d
Item, a brasse morter & pestell		11s	0d
Item, 5 quart pots, 2 pinte pots, 1 gill pot, 2 ½gill pots, 2 tasters, 3 tonns, j double salt, j small salt, j porrenger, 3 chamber pots		19s	8d
Item, two quart gill pots			11d
Item, a chopping knife		1s	0d
Item, two hornes			5d
Item, two candlestickes & a wreath		5s	0d
Item, a taster for butter		2s	1d
Item, a basen		2s	0d

Item, two axes	2s	8d
Item, 6 sawcers	1s	7d
Item, a brasse pan	2s	4d
Item, two skummers & a ladle	2s	5d
Item, a chafing dish		8d
Item, a gird iron, 2 setting sticks, j tosting iron	2s	4d
Item, a bread grate		4d
Item, a paire tongs & a porr	3s	7d
Item, a smoothing iron		5d
Item, an iron shovell	1s	5d
Item, a plate cullender		11d
Item, a quart & a pinte pot of plate		10d
Item, a plate cullender		7d
Item, a dripping pan of plate	1s	5d
Item, a dripping pan of plate		9d
Item, a frying pan	1s	11d
Item, a frying pan		6d
Item, a plate potlid		3d
Item, a pewter candlestick		9d
Item, a brasse candlestick	1s	5d
Item, a paire tongs & a fire shovell	1s	9d
Item, a durtie platt		4d
Item, a paire of brasse skailes & a beam	1s	2d
Item, 2 hay crookes		5d
Item, a gird iron		8d
Item, a candlestick		2d
Item, 3 fruite dishes of pewter, 2 plates, j sawcer	2s	0d
Item, 2 brushes	1s	0d
Item, a broken tobacco dryer		2d
Item, a basket		7d
Item, 2 gammons of bacon	3s	0d
Item 3 fruite dishes	1s	3d
Item, 3 sawcers & a fruite dish		11d
Item, a wicker voyder	1s	0d
Item, a heckel		4d
Item, a nodie sticke		3d
Item, a brasse pan	3s	6d
Item, a small brasse pan	1s	4d
Item, a small brasse pan		9d
Item, a little pan		4d
Item, a brasse pan	2s	2d
Item, a brasse pan	2s	6d

Item, a timpse	1s	8d
Item, skeps		3d
Item, a hollands cheese	2s	8d
Item, an earthen pott		8d
Item, 2 little pewter dishes	1s	0d
Item, an earthen jugg		1d
Item, 4 spoones of plate		2d
Item, an old tubb		4d
Item, an old bowle of wood		8d
Item, 3 rundlets	2s	0d
Item, a little rundlet		6d
Item, 2 dozen & ½ of cheese trenchers, with a boxe	2s	1½d
Item, an old skeele		9d
Item, one halfe butter firkin		4d
Item, 2 muggs		10d
Item, a glasse bottle		4d
Item, 4 prints		4d
Item a leather bottle	1s	1d
Item, a trencher knife		2d
Item, a tinder boxe		4d
Item, an iron pann	4s	6d
Item, 2 earthen fruite dishes		7d
Item, j dozen of trenchers		5d
Item, j halfe dozen of trenchers		2d
Item, an earthen basen		4d
Item, 11^{lb} of pewter at 11d per pound	10s	1d
Item, 3 small juggs	2s	0d
Item, 8^{lb} of pewter at 11d per pound	7s	4d
Item, 6 earthen porrengers	1s	6d
Item, 2 juggs	2s	0d
Item, l jugg & 4 trenchers		3d
Item, 2 earthen fruite dishes		7d
Item, 4 lyons	1s	0d
Item, 19^{lb} of pewter at 11d per libram	17s	5d
Item, a beatment & a stoole		5d
Item, a wooden plater		6d
Item, a wicker flasket		10d

4^{li} 4^s 5½^d

Item, a Turkie worke cushion	3s	4d
Item, 2 looking glasses	3s	4d
Item, 2 cushions	3s	5d

Item, 2 cushions	5s	2d
Item, 5 cushions	14s	4d
Item, 2 guilded cushions	5s	6d
Item, j cushion	2s	6d
Item, a wicker basket		7d
Item, a wicker basket		11d
Item, a glasse with rosewater		10d
Item, 4 glasses	1s	4d
Item, 4 glasses	1s	4d
Item, j great brasse pott	14s	0d
Item, j small brasse pott	5s	9d
Item, j old skeele		4d
Item, j greene chaire		7d
Item, a spining wheele	5s	6d
Item, a chopping board		10d
Item, a spining wheele	1s	3d
Item, 3 chaires		9d
Item, a churne	1s	4d
Item, a flower kitt		6d
Item, a tray	1s	3d
Item, a small tubb		8d
Item, 2 tubbs		8d
Item, a small kitt		3d
Item, a great kettle	10s	3d
Item, a wicker chaire	2s	10d
Item, a greene chaire	1s	3d
Item, 6 old cushions	1s	6d
Item, an iron pott, pot hookes & cover	4s	3d
Item, j old skeele & other things		6d
Item, a musket rest		10d
Item, an old chaire		8d
Item, 4 pictures		4d
Item, 2 old guilded stooles	5s	0d
Item, a tobacco pipe chist	1s	0d
Item, a band boxe		4d
Item, a little basket		4d
Item, a little table & a buffet forme	5s	6d
Item, 3 buffet formes	4s	8d
Item, an houre glasse		6d
Item, an old bottle		6d
Item, 2 old stooles, j old chaire & a paire of pot clips	1s	5d
Item, j glasse case & a paire tables	3s	4d

Item, a paire yarne windles & blaides			8d
Item, for garden seedes			5d
Item, 3 small rundlets		1s	8d
Item, 30^{lb}, wanting 2 ounces, pewter at 10d per ^{lb}	1	4s	11d
Item, j pound black thread		1s	0d

7^{li} 9^s 11^d

Item, a bedstead, a feather bedd, a bolster, 2 pillowes, 2 blankets, 5 curtaines, j paire sheetes & a mattres	7	0s	0d
Item, 2 rundlets		1s	5d
Item, 2 old happings		2s	7d
Item, a white rugg		3s	2d
Item, 2 old codds		1s	8d
Item, 2 pillowes		4s	8d
Item, j pillow		2s	10d
Item, j fetherbed, 2 pillowes, j bolster	2	8s	0d
Item, one coverlid		8s	2d
Item, one old coverlid		4s	0d
Item, one carpet		4s	0d
Item, one old coverlid		4s	0d
Item, a winding cloth		5s	10d
Item, a featherbed & 2 pillowes	1	11s	0d
Item, one coverlid		11s	6d
Item, 3 blankets		8s	4d
Item, one greene rugg		6s	10d
ltem, a mixt coverlid		5s	0d
Item, a featherbed, 2 pillowes & a bolster	2	0s	6d
Item, j white blanket		2s	6d
Item, j coulored happing		3s	0d
Item, j cradle cloth		5s	0d
Item, j old carpet		2s	0d
Item, a long lining table cloth		5s	4d
ltem, one lining table cloth		3s	1d
Item, 11 course napkins		5s	1d
Item, j paire of course sheetes		6s	3d
Item, j shorte tablecloth		2s	8d
Item, j paire course sheetes		7s	0d
Item, a window cloth			10d
Item, j paire of sheetes		7s	2d
Item, j dozen of napkins		5s	2d
Item, j paire of course sheetes		6s	4d
Item, j paire of clouted course sheetes		2s	2d

Item	£	s	d
Item, j old towell			4d
Item, j paire of course sheetes		5s	1d
Item, j old sheete			10d
Item, j towell			7d
Item, j towell		1s	0d
Item, j paire of ragged sheetes		1s	6d
Item, j paire of old pillowbers			6d
Item, j old towell			2d
Item, j old pillowber			6d
Item, j old paire sheetes		3s	2d
Item, a pound of pepper		1s	6d
Item, j old table cloth		1s	0d
Item, 2 old pillowbers		1s	0½d
Item, 2 old pillowbers		1s	8d
Item, j old napkin			1d

18 16 10½

Item	£	s	d
Item, a paire of old sheetes		4s	1d
Item, an old towell			10d
Item, a lining table cloth		3s	4d
Item, an old winding cloth			2d
Item, a short table cloth		2s	2d
Item, 3 happins		5s	7d
Item, a head sheete		3s	6d
Item, an old peice of darnix			3d
Item, white starch		1s	0d
Item, a cupboard & a cloth		8s	0d
Item, 3 mattresses		13s	4d
Item, a bedstead, a bolster, 2 curtains, & a mattres	1	6s	8d
Item, for an old suite of clothes		8s	10d
Item, for a paire shoes		2s	2d
Item, for sheetes & other things		14s	9d
[no entry]		1s	0d
Item, a paire wooll cardes			8d
Item, 3 hangings		4s	6d
Item, a paire of stockings			10d
Item, a coate		7s	1d
Item, a paire cardes			8d
Item, a paire bodies			6d
Item, an old mattresse		5s	4d
Item, an old suite		5s	0d
Item, an old happin		1s	5d

Item, an old happin	1s	0d
Item, a happin	2s	4d
Item, a paire of cardes		8d
Item, a happin	1s	6d
Item, a paire of cardes	[no entry]	
Item, an old happin		8d
Item, 3 old happins	2s	1d
Item, a hatt	1s	1d
Item, 3 paire cardes	2s	0d
Item, a paire stockings		11d
Item, a happin	2s	1d
Item, a paire of cardes		8d
Item, 2 small cods	2s	6d
Item, a fan lid		3d
Item, a paire shoes	2s	4d
Item, a paire shoes	2s	7d
Item, an old coate	4s	4d
Item, an old bolster	2s	8d
Item, a brush		9d
Item, 4 bowles	1s	4d
Item, a paire of old stockings	1s	4d
Item, a skeele & besomes	1s	3d
Item, a hood	1s	7d
Item, a shirt	4s	0d
Item, a shirt	4s	6d

8 7 9

Item, musterseede & a pepper boxe		1s	0d
Item, a boxe & wicker boxes			9d
Item, 2 slivers of lynn cloth		1s	3d
Item, a pott & greese			2d
Item, a swadlin			8d
Item, an old flockbed		2s	2d
Item, a yellow cloth		1s	0d
Item, a pepper box			4d
Item, 2 tables, a bedstead, matts & curtaine rods	1	2s	0d
Item, a paire slipps		1s	0d
Item, a meale tubb		4s	0d
Item, a wheele		1s	7d
Item, a skep			3d
Item, a glass bottle			4d
Item, 15^{lb} & ½ rope at 4d per libram		5s	2d

Item, a bedstead		5s	0d
Item, a swill & a peice of canvas			7d
Item, a runlet			8d
Item, 2 dozen of glasses		1s	2d
Item, a basket & 3 glasses			6d
Item, a trundle bed		3s	8d
Item, a chist		14s	6d
Item, a butter firkin			6d
Item, 2 peeces of a hopp sack			7d
Item, a salt kitt		5s	0d
Item, a glasse bottle			5d
Item, a table		12s	0d
Item, a barrell of beare		12s	0d
Item, 17 dozen glasses at 7d oboli per dozen		10s	7½d
Item, 15 dailes		13s	9d
Item, 5 dailes		4s	7d
Item, a white rugg & an old sheete		4s	2d
Item, j one slitt daile		1s	2d
Item, j little chist		2s	2d
Item, a tubb			6d
Item, 32 barrells at 22ᵈ a peice	3	0s	6d
Item, 4 guilefatts		5s	4d
Item, a trundle bed		4s	6d
Item, a hecke & a forke			8d
Item, for tunnels & swils		2s	1½d
Item, 8 dailes		8s	0d
Item, a cradle & 2 old dailes		3s	5½d
Item, 2 stooles		3s	3d
Item, a forme			2d
Item, 3 firkins		1s	7d
Item, an old tubb			7d
Item, a brake		1s	10d
Item, 2 leathers		5s	4d
Item, 3 dailes		2s	3d
Item, a lanthome			9d
Item, a forke			8d

11 15 2½

Item, 2 little doores		10d
Item, 2 little leathers	1s	6½d
Item, an old forme		10d
Item, an old stoole & a draffe beatment		2d

Item	£	s	d
Item, a paire stangs, slings & canhookes		1s	4d
Item, an old boxe			4d
Item, a paire of old shoes		1s	0d
Item, a paire of old bootes		2s	0d
Item, 2 peices of old planke			10d
Item, 2 things to catch eeles			4d
Item, 2 barrels beare	1	8s	0d
Item, 3 rundlets		2s	4d
Item, 3 great tubbs, 4 small tubbs, j old bucket & j little bowle		5s	4d
Item, for decayed tobacco			8d
Item, j old doore		1s	2d
Item, an old peice wood			1d
Item, a whetstone			3d
Item, a paire woollen cardes			8d
Item, blacke thread			3d
Item, a barrell beare		10s	0d
Item, for old wood & a paire doore lintells		7s	3d
Item, a chalder & a halfe of coles		13s	6d
Item, for feathers		2s	0d
Item, a chist		9s	0d
Item, a short table		7s	6d
Item, 4 whole barrel & 6 half barrel		11s	2d
Item, a stock purse		1s	0d
Item, a paire gamashes & j old booke			6d
Item, a wooden balke & a paire skailes		5s	3d
Item, 5 stone in lead weights		7s	3½d
Item, 6 stone in lead weights		8s	9d
Item, 2 stone in lead weights		2s	11d
Item, an iron balke & a paire skailes		5s	3d
Item, a pillion seate & a cloth		3s	6d
Item, a bushell tubb		4s	6d
Item, j^C wyt & 8^{lb} of hopps at 3^{li}10^s per ^{c}	13	4s	6d
Item, 76 bowles of malt at 7^s per bowle	26	12s	0d
Item, 8 bowles & j bushell of beanes	1	10s	3d
Item, 20 bowles of rye, wanting one halfe peck, at 8^s 4^d per bowle	8	6s	0d
Item, 3 barrels of beare at 14s per barrel	2	12s	0d
Item, 2 kine	5	3s	4d
Item, 3 sowes & 3 hoggs	3	6s	0d
Item, a cocke & a hen		1s	0d
Item, a horse, sadle & halter	3	10s	0d

Item, 3 peckes of wheate	4s	6d
Item, 4 tubbs & a draffe pecke	2s	0d
Item, 6 stone & 5^{lbs} of broad iron	12s	6d
Item, old iron	2s	6d

63 4 5

Item, an old pillion seate			6d
Item, 3^{lbs}& ½ of corke			10d
Item, an iron gavelock		4s	0d
Item, a kitt, a small timpse, a peice sackwebb		1s	4d
Item, a stone morter		1s	1d
Item, a bedstead & seates		7s	4d
Item, two paire of small barrs		5s	6d
Item, old dailes		1s	4d
Item, painted papers		2s	0d
Item, 10 bowles of Margate malt at 7^s 2^d	3	11s	8d
Item, 7 bowles of Scarborough malt	1	19s	6d
Item, for ij^{li} of thred		3s	0d
Item, an old table		3s	6d
Item, a leaven tubb			9d
Item, a paire of timpses			8d
Item, another paire of timpses			10d
Item, 2 skeepes & other things		2s	6d
Item, a peck of barley & a beatment		1s	0d
Item, an old wooden morter			2d
Item, 16^{lbs} thread at 17^d per libram	1	2s	8d
Item, a paire old bootes & shoes		4s	0d
Item, an old tubb & a searcer		1s	2d
Item, a ruler & a sandbox			4d
Item, a <bodkin>, staffe head & 2 old <books>			6d
Item, a leaden inke standish			3d
Item, a ring for keyes			2d
Item, a ¾ barrel bear with caske		10s	6d
Item, two tubbs		3s	0d
Item, 2 iron kettles		7s	7d
Item, 1 dozen trenchers		10s	6d
Item, a small paire skailes & wyts		3s	0d
Item, one lead wyt of 7^{lbs}			10d
Item, 2 paire gold weights		4s	8d
Item, a skoope			6d
Item, 4 old tubbs		2s	0d
Item, an old plate boxe & tobacco			6d

	£	s	d
Item, lead weights		9s	6d
Item, 3 dozen silver buttons		14s	0d
Item, for 9 small bookes		6s	11d
Item, 4 paire cardes		2s	8d
Item, of Jeffrey Nicolls for 24 chalders coles	10	16s	0d
Item, of John Story for j barrel of beare		12s	0d
Item, of James Bentley for 3 half barrels		18s	0d
Item, of John Stelling for halfe a barrel		6s	0d
Item, of Gabriel for a peck of pease		1s	0d
Item, of Mrs Wicliffe for a barrel beare		14s	0d
Item, of Thomas Cooke of Durham for thread	1	1s	3d
Item, of Marmaduke Newton		10s	0d
Item, for a barrel of ships beare & <caske>		7s	6d
Item, for a petticoate which was pawned		8s	0d
Item, of Thomas Rickaby for a debt		15s	0d
Item, of John Story for a barrel beare		14s	0d
Item, of Thomas Taylor for a chalder coles 8s & in payment of a debt due to <Ell> Welles, 11s4d		19s	4d
Item, of Benjamin Langley for Mr Cheyne's debt		2s	4d

30 7 2

	£	s	d
Item, of Robert Arnold for a debt			4d
Item, of John Mempris for a debt	1	10s	0d
Item, of John Burdon upon all reckning		5s	6d
Item, of Richard Wilkinson in payment of a chalder coles		2s	9d
Item, of William Smith		2s	9d
Item, of Dennis for a chalder of coles & other reckonings		16s	6d
Item, of William Snowdon upon his reckoning		1s	10d
Item, of Anthony Taylor upon all reckonings		8s	3d
Item, of William Rutter upon all reckonings		6s	1d
Item, of Gerard Pots upon all reckonings		2s	8d
Item, of Robert Mason in payment of his reckonings		12s	4d
Item, of John Wood upon all reckonings, to 14 Maij	1	7s	9d
Item, of William Roxsby upon all reckonings		18s	8d
Item, of Bess Palmer for a debt		2s	9d
Paid in gold & silver which was found in the chist	87	11s	0d
Item, of Mathew Lambe in payment of a debt	9	0s	0d
Item, of Richard Welsh for ½ barrel ship's beare & <caske>		4s	0d
Item, of Thomas Sharpe for halfe barrel bear		6s	0d
Item, of Thomas Snowdon for 2 barrels beare	1	4s	0d

Julij 16

Item, of James Jepson upon bill	1	10s	0d
Item, for a bushell of pease		2s	8d
Item, of Raiph Marshall upon bill		12s	0d

August 11

Item, of John Robison for a quarter's rent for the house due at Lamas last	6	0s	0d
Item, of Raiph Colson's wife for a boule peese	10	5s	0d
Item, of Mathew Lambe in paymentt of his debt	3	0s	0d
Item, of {M^r} Lilb<urne> for a rigge		7s	0d
Item, of Jochim Bacher for a debt	6	0s	0d

October 8

Item, of John Nicholson for j^lb thread		1s	6d
Item, of Mr Barnes for a paire brasse skales		11s	8d
Item, of Mr Grey for 11 boles pease	1	18s	0d
Item, for pease sold by Elsabeth Wells		11s	6d
Item, for 2 boles of pease of William Pearson		7s	0d
Item, of Francis Newby for iron barres		1s	0d

November 3

Item, for the little guilded cupp		15s	9d
Item, for the white wine cupp	1	4s	9d
Item, for old lead, old bookes, an old sword and other small implements		9s	4d
Item, for a draw table	1	0s	0d
Item, for 2 muskets		4s	0d
Item, for an old sword		1s	6d
ltem, a paire boot hose tops			9d
Item, for j old chaire			9d
Item, for leade		1s	0d
Item, of Geore Robeson the butcher in payment for beare		6s	0d
Item, a presse & an iron chimney	1	6s	8d
Item, an other iron chimney		9s	0d
Item, a table & a frame		8s	0d
Item, for sackes		15s	0d
Item, two silver rings, j gold ring, & a small silver chaine for a currall stalke		17s	0d
Item, a silver bowle	2	9s	6d
{Item, for old sackes		13s	4d}

20

Item, of Christopher Posket for a debt		13s	4d

Item, of John Robinson for a quarter's rent	6	0s	0d
Item, of James Ellerton for a barrel of beare		6s	0d

143^{li} 19^s 8^d

Summa totalis £284 10s 2½d

Debts owen to the testator at the time of his death

By Robert Ayre of Warmouth	3	15s	4d
By Robert Claxton of Chester	1	0s	0d
By John King of Byrlington		11s	0d
By Thomas Iley of Monkewarmouth	2	6s	8d
By Steven Ducke of Byrlington		10s	0d
By William Roxby of Sunderland	1	0s	0d
By Raiph Hogg of Sunderland	1	3s	0d
By Paule Marshall of Scarbrough		10s	0d
By Thomas Travers of Selby	2	0s	0d
By Parcivall Rostell who is dead	4	0s	0d
By John Story of Sunderland, barber	2	0s	0d
By Robert Richardson of Sunderland		12s	0d
By Thomas Grainge of Sundreland		13s	0d
By John Wilson of Monkwarmouth	1	6s	6d
By George Wells, brother of the testator	34	19s	2d

56^{li} 6^s 8^d

Those debts, or the most of them, are desperate debts and will hardly be gotten by any suite and therefore are non inserted as parcell of the inventory, nor yet totally to be neglected if any part thereof can be gotten hereafter.

Moneyes disbursed

Imprimis, to Mr Madison & Mr Langley	10	16s	0d
Item, to John Stelling for his wages	1	16s	0d
Item, to Margaret Redhead for her wages	1	1s	0d
Item, to Gabriel for 2 jorneies hee made for Raiph Wells to Merrington & Newcastle		3s	0d
May 4 1632			
Item, about the administracion at Durham as by a bill of particulars	2	12s	4d
Item, to John Halliwell for a quarter's wages for keeping 7 swine, a horse & 2 kine		3s	4d
Item, to Thomas Taylor for keeling coles, 12^s 4^d, & for part of his binding money which Raiph owed		19s	4d

Item, to Robert Arnold for keeling 3 tides		15s	0d
Item, to Adam Burdon in rye, 8^l 6^s, & in money, 8^l 0^s 6^d			
for a debt Raiph owed him	16	6s	6d
Item, to John Bardon for 4 tides	1	4s	8d
Item, to Richard Wilkinson for 4 tides	1	0s	0d
Item, to William Smith for 4 tides	1	2s	4d
Item, to Dennis Atkinson for 4 tides, 24^s 8^d, & for part			
of his binding which was unpaid, 7^s in all	1	11s	8d
Item, to William Snawdon for 3 tides		18s	6d
Item, to Anthony Taylor for 3 tides		18s	6d
Item, to William Rutter for 3 tides		18s	6d
Item, to Gerard Pots for j tide		6s	2d
Item, to Robert Mason for 2 tides		12s	4d
Item, to John Wood for 3 tides, 15^s, & for part of his			
binding money which was unpaid, 15^s, toto	1	10s	0d
Item, to Willam Roxsby for 3 tides		18s	6d
Item, for Henry Gibson		2s	0d
Item, to John Taylor for hay & other things		5s	0d
Item, to \<Mou\> Leye's wife for bread		2s	0d
Item, to Bess Palmer for hay		5s	0d
Item, to John Stelling & the washer		5s	0d
Item, to Mr Lilburne for charges at Durham &			
\<carrying\>		14s	4d
Item, to Mr Raiph Lambton upon bond	100	0s	0d
Item, to Mr David Myles upon bond	50	0s	0d
Item, to Mr Peter Wells	40	0s	0d
Item, to Thomas Sharpe for a pare shoes		3s	0d
Item, to Thomas Snawdon for meate		18s	2d
22th			
Item, to Mr Mathew for his fee		3s	4d
Item, spent with Mr Mathew at that time			8d
Item, for Mr Freeman's dinner & other charges		1s	2d
24			
Item, spent upon the praisers at Raiph's house		1s	8d
26			
Item, paid for a paire shoes to John Wells		2s	0d
Junij 2do			
Item, for bleeching of lining			7½d
Item, for ropes to Mr March which was owing	1	0s	3d
4			
Item, for two testaments to Florence & Ellenor Wells		5s	4d

	£	s	d
Item, to Dame Taylor for Ellen's board & other necessaries	1	0s	0d
Item, to Sir William Lambton for ½ yeare's rent	1	10s	0d
Item, to George Wells for a rope for which hee paid	1	8s	0d
Item, to George Wells upon Mr Hutton's letter	1	0s	0d
Item, to Mr Lilburne for one jorney & to Mr Freeman for 2 jorneyes to Durham		3s	0d
Item, to Mr Cattrell for children's clothes, as per his bill	1	16s	0d
Item, to Anne Husband for wine at Raiph's buriall	1	0s	0d

July 10

	£	s	d
Item, to Dame Taylor in payment for two children's board	1	0s	0d
Item, for mending John Wells' shoes			4d

13

	£	s	d
Item, paid by Mr Freeman to Mary Wells to buy her clothes	1	0s	0d
Item, paid to Mr Mathew for making a letter of attorney & a release		4s	0d

24

	£	s	d
Item, paid to Dame Taylor for the children's use as per bill		14s	9d

250 19 3^d

	£	s	d
Item, paid more in payment for 2 children's table to Dame Taylor	2	0s	0d
Item, paid for two laier stalles in the church		13s	4d
Item, for a paire of shoes & a paire bodies for Elsabeth		4s	4d
Item, for a sheepe pluck to Rider, 5^d, & for buttons, 5^d			10d
Item, for sope & candles to Martindaile's wife		1s	9d
Item, paid to Mr Madison & the rest of the partners in full discharge of all reckonings betwixt them & Raiph Wells	42	10s	0d
Item, paid to Maurice Prescott in full of a debt		4s	0d
Item, paid for 10 yards kersey for Elsabeth Wells	1	15s	0d
Item, paid for 3 dozen & a halfe lace, at 2^s 2^d per dozen, 7^s 6^d, & silke, j^s		8s	6d
Item, paid for a writt for George Wells		1s	3d
Item, paid to John Burdon for making & mending clothes		5s	6d
Item, to John Wells to buy him clothes		5s	9d
Item paid to George Burgoine for two mortuaries		13s	4d

Item, paid to Dame Taylor in full for the two children's table till Christmas	1	10s	0d
Item, for charges at Raiph's buriall		6s	0d
Item, paid Francis Newby for j^{lb} tobacco for which Ellen Wells did owe him		10s	0d
Item, paid for our charges, 3 children's, Edith Roxsby & a baye & for 3 horse hyre to Durham		9s	10
Item, paid Michael Bryan for wheate, bigg & oates for which Ellen Wells did owe him	1	1s	3d

25 3 6

Item, paid to Mr Maddison & the rest of the partners since our last reckoning, for a bill which proved no bill, by one Beale & Bacon	11	14s	0d
Item, paid to Adam Burdon for binding money & finding clothes for John Wells during his time of apprenticeshipp	8	14s	7d

Summa totalis disbursat*a* £296 11s 4d

Disburs*ata* 296^{li} 11^s 4^d½
Recept*a*   294 10 2½
          2 1 2

Source: DPR1/1/1632/W3/1–6, paper 8ff. sewn.

50. Thomas Dickenson of Sunderland, cordwainer, 1632

Memorandum, that Thomas Dickenson of Sunderland by sea in the county of Durham, cordwayner, being of sane and perfect memorie \the xxijth day of March, 1631/ did make his last will nuncupative in forme following, v*idelicet:* the said Thomas did give and bequeath to his daughter Elizabeth Dickenson one howse in Sunderland, which he lately builded, to hold to her and her heires forever. Allsoe, he gave and bequeathed to his sonne John Dickenson the rest of his howses in Sunderland, to hold to him and his heires forever after the death of Elizabeth Dickenson, wief of the said Thomas, to whome he willed and bequeathed the same for her lief naturall {and ordered and appoynted Robert Dickenson, brother of the said Thomas, to be tutor and guardian of his children aforesaid.}
Wittnesses
Robert Dickinson [*signed with full name*]

Margaret Curtes [*marked with initial capital M*]
Grace Dickinson [*marked with a symbol*]
Mary Dickinson [*signed with full name*]

[*Endorsed*] Isabell, Marie, Ruth, Adeline, Elizabeth, Hester, liberi
[*three words illegible*] Johan' et posthumus natus Elizabetha vidua et
Robertus Dickinson frater.

A true and iust inventory of all the goods moveable and inmoveable
of Thomas Dickenson of Sunderland, deceased, the 23th day of
March, 1631, praised by us, Georg Barnes, John Sheepheardson, John
Robson and Thomas Sharpe, the 14th of May 1632

In the hall

Imprimis, one cubbert	1	0s	0d
Item, the foreside of a buttery and the foreside of a bedd, with a head & a longe setle at the bedside		14s	0d
Item, a table with a foorme, one chaire, fowre buffitt stooles & a falling chaire		16s	0d
Item, one paire of barrs, one spitt, two paire of croakes, with the iron they hang on, one porr, two paire of thongs, two broile irons, one frying pann with certaine other necessaries		13s	4d
Item, two brasse potts		12s	0d
Item, sixteene peece of peuther		16s	0d
Item, three salts, five peuther candlesticks		8s	0d
Item, three cupps & one salt		2s	6d
Item, six sawcers and two sallet dishes		2s	6d
Item, thre quart potts		3s	6d
Item, two chamber potts		2s	0d
Item, three brasse candlesticks		2s	0d
Item, one peuther gill post & halfe a gill pott		1s	0d
Item, twoe litle peuther dublars		2s	0d
Item, one glasse caise and sixteen earthen dublers		3s	0d
Item, three earthen potts		1s	0d
Item, three brasse panns		4s	0d
Item, one ireon pott with kilpes		3s	6d
Item, thre earthen panns			6d
Item, one halbert and a stafe		2s	0d
Item, one latten quart pott & a pinte pott, one tunnell with a butter pott, all of latten		1s	0d

In the parler

Item, one cubbert	1	0s	0d
Item, one table, one chaire, one fourme & a long setle		12s	0d
Item, three cheests		6s	0d
Item, eleaven choussins		9s	0d
Item, one peuther dublar and a wanded glasscaise		2s	0d
Item, one paire of ireon barrs and a reckon crooke & fower plaister pictures		2s	0d

In the chamber

Item, one bedstead and a trundle bedd, two fourmes, one table and a cubbert	1	0s	0d

In the brewhouse

Item, the copper, the tubbes and other brewing vessell	1	10s	0d

In the bread loft

Item, a table, a braike and other necessaries		8s	0d

Moveable goodes

Item, two kine	3	13s	4d
Item, tenn sheepe	2	0s	0d

The bedding

Item, one mattrise, five coddes, two coverlidds, one happin, thre curtaines, thre paire of vallance, two carped cloathes, fower blankets	1	4s	0d
Item, one paire of caises and two paire of temps, a skepp for cloathes and two old bibles		9s	0d

The lynning cloathes

Item, five lynnen sheets, seaven codd pillabies, fowre paire of course sheetes, two linnen table cloathes, thre fleers, thre linnen curtaines and twelve table napkins	2	1s	0d

Other necessaries

Item, one silver spoone		3s	0d
Item, one paire of gold weights		2s	0d
Item, one dozen of trenchers and a halfe and eight peuther spounges		1s	0d
Item, thre furr buckinnes		3s	0d

Item, two litle chaires, two skeels, one salt kilt and one peuther baison		12s	0d
Item, two paire of bootes and a paire of shooes, one peece of leather, and one paire of skoppers		10s	0d
Item, five fir sparrs, thre peeces of oak wood		2s	0d
Item, two coverlids, two codds and a cunter		2s	6d
Item, one cow hide		3s	4d
Item, his apperell	1	14s	0d
Summa totalis	24	15s	0d

George Barnes [*full name signed*]
John Shipperdson [*full name signed*]

A perticuler of moneyes that was owing to Thomas Dickenson
at his death

Imprimis, by William Poskett by a bill	8	0s	0d
Item, by John Sheepheardson	4	0s	0d
Item, by Thomas Todd and William Dawson	4	0s	0d
Item, by Robert Dickenson	1	0s	9d
Item, for sailes that were left by James Denton	3	2s	4d
Item, by Edward Headley		18s	4d
Item, by a note in his debt booke by certaine keale men for bread and beare		7s	0d
Item, by such another note for bread & beare		8s	0d
Item, by Mathew Gest		7s	5d
Item, by James Rider for tyles		7s	0d
Item, by Thomas Welburne		19s	6d
Item, by Christopher Berry		5s	0d
Item, by George Cossen		6s	4d
Item, in moneyes and gold	7	0s	6d
Item, more in gold	2	2s	6d
Summa totallis	33	14s	8d

A perticular of moneyes that Thomas Dickenson was indebted
at his death

Imprimis, to John Husband and his sister Emme Husband		7s	8d
Item, to Richard Cotterill		13s	0d
Item, to John Johnson		11s	0d
Item, to William Poskets	1	0s	0d
Item, to Richard Cowling		7s	0d
Item, to Christopher Berry		6s	0d
Item, to Thomas ffoster		12s	0d

Item, to James Rider	5s	6d
Item, to Michaell Dickenson	5s	6d
Item, to Thomas Alderman	6s	0d
Item, to Christopher Hedley	14s	3d
Item, to Adam Burdon	16s	8d
Item, to the church	14s	9d
Item, to Mr Georg Lilburne	12s	0d
Item, to Mychaell Partridge	6s	0d
Item, to Willyam Hodgson	2s	2d
Item, for victualls and beare for the praisers	3s	0d
Item, for funerall charges	9s	6d
Item, to the ringers	3s	6d
Item, to Mr Hix	5s	0d
Item, for keeping a weake child that was put foorth to be kept with a wife	6s	0d
Summa totalis	7 5s	10d

John Husband and his sister, with the funerall expences {and the praisers' charges} was all satisfied before the praisers did medle or begin to praise any thing and the ringers and church dues.

Source: DPR1/1/1632/D3/1–3, paper 4ff.

51. Thomas Roxby of Ryhope, 1633

In the name of God, amen, I, Thomas Roxebey of Riuehopp, sicke in body but of good and perfect remembrance, thankes be to God, doe make this my last will and testament, the first day of July, anno Domini 1633, in mannner and forme followinge. First, I comitt my soule into the hands of almighty God, my maker, trustinge assuredly to be saved by the death and passion of our lord, Jesus Christ, and my body to be buryed in the churchyard of Bishoppwermouth. Imprimis, I give to Isabell Roxebey, my espoused wife, the comoditie of my tenement of Ruehopp for the space of twelve yeares towards the bringing upp of my children. Item, I give to my wife and to my thre daughters, namely, Elizabeth Roxebey, Anne Roxebey and Alice Roxebey, all my goods and houshold stuffe to be devided equally amongst them. Item, I give to my sonne John Roxeby after the end and expiracion of the said twelve yeares, my lease of the tenement of Riuehopp, & my wife to have the fourth parte of the said tenement after the aforesaid twelve yeares during her life naturall. Item, I {give} will that my {my sonne John} wife Isabell Roxeby at my sonne

his first entrie to the tenement {the sume} shall pay to him the sume of thirtein poundes lawfull mony of England. Item, I give to my sonne John Roxebey plough and plough geare, wain and waine geare which I have about my house. Item, for my funerall expences, I will that my wife doe pay them forth of my goods. Item, I make my sonne John whole executor of this my last will and testament. Item, my mind is that my neihbor John Fell of Riuehopp be supervisor of this my last will, to se these things performed {witnesses hereof}. Item, I give to the poore of the towne of Riuehopp the sume of five shillings. Witnesses hereof,
Richard Smyth [*full name signed*]
John Fell his marke [*marked with a symbol*]
Raph Raynoldson [*full name signed*]

Debts owen to the testator

{Imprimis, Thomas Reede, x pounds}
Item, Thomas Oxnett, xj pounds
{Item, Anthony Page, xlvˢ viijᵈ}
Suma totalis £13 0s 8d

This will was found in the cladinge deske after his death but noe inven*t*orie

Ad*ministrati*o duran*te* minor*e* etate \Joh*annis*/ ex*ecut*oris commiss*a* conc*editur* Isab*elle* vid*ue* ad usum d*icti* ex*ecuto*ris tant*um*. Tuicio d*icti* Joh*annis* ac Eliz*abeth*, Ann*e* et Alic*ie* conc*editur* d*icte* Isab*elle*.

A true and just immentorie [*sic*] of all the goodes and chattels of Thomas Roxbye of Ryhoppe, deceased, praysed by fowre honest neaghbours, John ffell, Edward ffell, Gorgs Watsonne, Thomas Hutchisonne

Imprimis, vi oxen	20	0s	0d
Imprimis, vii kien and 2 whyes and on calfe	17	0s	0d
Imprimis, two meares and on folle	7	0s	0d
Imprimis, two swine hoggs and 3 piggs	1	13s	4d
Imprimis, the korne in the stakeyard and barne	30	0s	0d
Imprimis, two longe waynes and two par of wheales	6	0s	0d
Imprimis, two coup waynes and all the plu and plu gear, {Imp} wayne and wayne geare	3	0s	0d
Imprimis, fortie nine sheape	12	0s	0d
Imprimis, the haye	1	13s	4d

Imprimis, two cubbordes, on spence, two beadstead, on tabell	2	0s	0d
Imprimis, v chistes, 3 cannes, 3 skeales and tubbes and other wooden vessell	1	10s	0d
Imprimis, 3 coverleaddes, 3 happines, 3 blankettes and all the linnen and strakinges and harden and all the rest of the beaden	5	0s	0d
Imprimis, puder and brasse	3	0s	0d
Imprimis, on chimney, on reakincruke, on porre, on speate, on frin panne, on pare of tonges		7s	0d
Imprimis, foure mucke forkes, foure korne forkes		4s	0d
Imprimis, his apperell	2	0s	0d
	112	7s	0d
Deatte oweing for his funeriell	2	0s	0d

John ffell, his marke
Thomas Hutchisonne, his marke
Eadward ffell, his marke
Georges Wattsonne, his marke

Source: DPR1/1/1633/R8/1–2, paper 2ff.

52. John Harrison of Sunderland, 1633

An inventory of the goodes & chattells of John Harrison, late of Sunderland, deceased, as they were appraised by Goerge Lillburne, ffancis Newbye, William Caldwell & John Dickinson, the xij[th] November, anno regni Regis Carolj, Anglie etc., nono, 1633

In the hall

Imprimis, his purse & his apparell	3	6s	8d
Item, one iron chimney, one paire tongs, ij spits, j paire racks & a broile iron		8s	0d
Item, one gird iron, j frying pann, j choping knife, two skummers, a butter taster, with other implements		5s	0d
Item, a cubbard of wainscott, with a vallance & frindge		16s	0d
Item, two cushions, embrodered		6s	8d
Item, 40 pound of thread	2	0s	0d
Item, a table, a fforme, a chaire, a glasse case, a little chaire, a candleboxe & a lanthome		10s	0d

		£	s	d
Item, a cheste, a rundlet of aquavitae, 8 dozen of playing cards & some sope in the chest, with some peices of lyne & tobacco		1	4s	0d
Item, 3 stone & 11^{lb} of pewter		1	19s	9d
Item, 2 pewter potts, ij^{lb} wyt			5s	3d
Item, 8 quart potts, j pinte pott of pewter			11s	4d
Item, 4 chamber potts, j dozen pewter spoones			5s	10d
Item, a brass mortar & j brass candlestick			2s	6d
Item, j gill pott, 5½ gill potts, 3 double salts, 3 tasters, all of pewter			5s	6d
Item, 12 rundlets of strong water		6	0s	0d
Item, a small silver beaker & j small silver taster			15s	0d
Item, j brass pott, j iron pott with hooks & 3 old chafinge dishes			10s	0d

£19 10s 6d

In the butterie

	£	s	d
Imprimis, j new kettle & j old kettle of brasse		18s	0d
Item, 3 wooden bowles, 2 trayes, j dozen trenchers, j old skeele & other wooden things		5s	0d
Item, 5 earthen muggs, with other earthen things		2s	0d

15s 0d

In the parler

	£	s	d
Imprimis, j little iron chimney		2s	0d
Item, 2 little tables		4s	0d
Item, j old bedstead, j rugg, j paire blankets, j fetherbed & bowlster, j paire sheetes, j pillow & pillow beere, all old	1	4s	0d

£1 10s 0d

	£	s	d
Item, 2 servants' bedsteads, with old clothes		16s	0d
Item, a paire skailes, with wooden beames & one stone wyt lead		9s	2d
Item, 5 firkins of butter	3	6s	8d
Item, towe in severall tubs	5	0s	0d
Item, two heads of lyne, j beife tubb, 2 little baskets, with other old tubs		3s	4d

£9 15s 2d

In the great chamber

Imprimis, an iron chimney & a paire tongs		4s	0d
Item, a draw table, sixe joynt stooles, a cover for a table & a bench	1	6s	8d
Item, 2 chaires, j wooden chist, j wooden band.. boxe, j flaskete		13s	4d
Item, 2 pictures, 2 earthen dishes & 2 chalke pictures		10s	0d
Item, 6 checker worke cushions & j list cushion		8s	0d
Item, j bedstead, with curtaines & vallance, j fetherbed, 2 bowlsters, j coverlid, j blanket, j paire sheetes, j pillow & pillow beer	1	13s	4d
Item, 11 lining sheetes, j dozen course napkins, 4 lining pillowbers, 2 diaper cubbord clothes & 2 tableclothes	2	3s	0d
Item, a warming pann of brasse		2s	6d
Item, 13 yards of course cloth & j paire harden sheetes		10s	0d
£7 11s 4d			

In the high garner

Imprimis, 30 yards new course cloth		15s	0d
Item 2 baskets of drinking glasses	6	0s	0d
Item 19 earthen muggs		3s	2d
Item, 8 butter firkins, j old hogshead, other old tubbs		4s	0d
Item, 3 dozen earthen dishes		5s	0d
Item, j bushell of mustard seed		4s	0d
Item, a sive, 2 tempses & a kneding sheet		1s	6d
£7 12s 8d			

Item, j halfe part of a hoy	14	0s	0d
£14 0s 0d			

Suma totallis 60^{li} 14^s 8^d

Debts owing to the testator at the time of his death

By Richard Rotheram for a stone of lyne		7s	6d
per Joseph Lilburne for a quart of aquavitae		1s	4d
per Richard Rotheram for 6 yards of canvas		6s	0d
per Ambrose Mosier for towe		6s	0d
per Henry Gibson for towe		4s	6d
per Widow Dickinson for linning cloth		6s	1d
per Ouswald Towers for a stone of lyne		7s	0d
per Mawdline Hardcastle for a stone of lyne		6s	8d
per George Brees of Yarmoth in lent money	2	4s	0d

per John ffranson of Harling	2	10s	0d
per George Graime for a stone of lyne		6s	8d
per Alexander Dericks for hoopes	4	10s	0d
per Thomas Basnet for lyne		13s	0d
per Robert Moody for course cloth		16s	8d
per William Selbie for lyne		6s	8d
	15	12s	1d

Debs owing by the testator at the time of his death
To Mr Stockin of Yarmoth in part of payment for
a hoy   10 0s 0d

George Lilburne [*signed with full name*]
ffrancis Newby [*signed with full name*]
William Caldwell [*signed with full name*]
John Dickinson [*signed with full name*]
Ad*ministratio* commis*a* Sare vid*ue* &c., Leon*ardus* et Sara liberi &c., in minor*e* etate &c.

Source: DPR1/1/1633/H4/1–2, paper 2 ff.

53. Alison Holme of Bishopwearmouth, widow, 1634

In the name of God, amen, I, Allison Howme of Bushoppwarmouth in the countie of Durham, widdowe, being in good health and perfect remembrance, thankes be to God, doe make and ordaine this my last will and testament in manner and forme followeing. First, I doe willinglie, and with a free hart, render and [........]²⁶ againe my spiritt unto the handes of allmightie God, my creator, nothing doubting but that for his infinite mercies, sett forth in the precious blood of his dearly beloved sonne Jesus Christ, my onelie saviour and redeemer (at that te[rrible] and dreadfull day of generall judgment when all flesh shall be summoned to appeare before his heavenlie tribunall) he [will]²⁷ receive my soule unto his everlasting glory and place it amongst the companie of his celestiall and blessed saints. Item, I commend my body to the earth from whence it came, to be buryed in the church yard of the parish church of Bishopp-warmouth aforesaid, under a great white stone nigh the south porch

26 The manuscript is faded.
27 This sentence, too, is affected by the manuscript having faded.

of the said church. Item, I give unto the poore of Bishoppwarmouth parish aforesaid, the somme of fortie shillings of lawfull English monies, to be distributed amongst them at the tyme of my buryall. Item, I give and bequeath unto my sonne Raph Howme the somme of six poundes thirtene shillings and fower pence of lawfull English money. Item, I give and bequeath unto my daughter Bridgett, nowe wife of William Shipperdson of Morton, the somme of six poundes thirtene shillings and fower pence of like lawfull English money. Item, I give and bequeath unto my daughter Anne, nowe wife of Christopher Shipperdson of Munckwearmouth, the somme of six poundes, thirtene shillings and fower pence of like lawfull English money. Item, I give and bequeath unto Robert Goodchilde, younger sone of Robert Goodchilde of Boldon, the somme of fortie shillings of like lawfull English money. Item, my debts, funerall expenses and sommes abovesaid paid and discharged, I give and bequeath all the residue of my goods and chattels, moveable & immoveable, of what kinde, sorte or quality soever they be, to George Howme, my youngest sonne, whom I make, constitute and ordaine sole executor of this my last will and testament. And if it shall happen that anie ambiguitie, doubt or question doe arise amongst my said children concerning this my last will, then my will is that such ambiguitie, doubt or question shall be expounded, determined and iudged according to the litterall sence and meaneing hereof and no otherwise. And I doe allsoe hereby revoke, adnihilate and make void all former wills or testaments whatsoever by me at anytime heretofore made. In wittnesse whereof I have hereunto putt my hand and seale the third day of March, in the sixt yeare of the reign of our soveraigne lord, Charles, by grace of God, king of England, Scotland ffrance and Ireland, defender of the faith, & in the presence of these witnesses, videlicet:

Alison Howme, signum [*marked with a symbol*]
John ffell, signum [*marked with a symbol*]
Robart ffoster [*signed with full name*]
Robert Daile [*signed with full name*]

An inventory of all the goods and chattells which Alice Holme of Bishopp Wermouth, widow, died seazed of, vewed and praysed by Edward Daill, William Shipperdson, John ffell and Edward Harper, this 14 of October, 1634

Inprimis, hir apperrell	6	13s	4d
Ittem, in redy money	14	0s	0d

Ittem, fowre oxen	23	0s	0d
Ittem, nyne kine	18	0s	0d
Ittem, 2 whyes and on stote	3	0s	0d
Ittem, thre calves	1	10s	0d
Ittem, eightene ould sheep	5	8s	0d
Ittem, seven hoges	1	10s	0d
Ittem, nyne swine	3	6s	8d
Ittem, thre horses and meares	10	0s	0d
Ittem, corne in the stackgarth	73	6s	8d
Ittem, corne growing in the field	30	0s	0d
Ittem, corne in the girdner	2	13s	4d
Ittem, two plowes, on paire of irons, on oxe harrow, on paire of horse harrows	1	6s	0d
Ittem, two long waines, two coup waines, on paire of bunewhels, on paire of worne whells, on paire of stinges & on axeltre	3	6s	8d
Ittem, 3 yookes and 2 soymes and on paire of horse geare		12s	0d
Ittem, coles in the coll holle		10s	0d
Suma	198	2s	8d

Detts owing to the testator

Inprimis, George Younge of Dalton	4	0s	0d
Ittem, Christopher Patteson of Weirmoth	3	0s	0d
Ittem, Richard Johnson of Wearmouth	1	0s	0d
Suma	8	0s	0d
Summa totallis	206	2s	8d

Dettes owing by the testator

Imprimis, in legacies	22	0s	0d
Ittem, in funerall expences	10	0s	0d
Ittem, for the house for rent	5	6s	8d
Ittem, for the Ford Feild rent	3	4s	0d
Ittem, to Raiph Younge for 2 pastus	1	6s	6d
For the lord's rent	1	2s	6d
Ittem, for servants'[28] wages		17s	4d
Suma totallis	43	17s	8d

---

28 Or (less probably) 'servant's'.

All leageces, dettes and funerall expences being deducted, ther
remaneth the some of 162^{li} 5^s 8^d

Edward Daill [*signed with full name*]
William Shipperdson [*signed with full name*]
Edward Harper [*signed with full name*]
John ffell, marke [*marked with a symbol*]

Source: DPR1/1/1634/H9/1; will parchment 1m.; inventory paper 1f.

54. Sampson Ayre of Monkwearmouth, yeoman, 1634

Anno Domini 1634, Appril 7
The last will & testament of Sampson Ayer of Monckwearmouth in
the countye pallatine of Durhame, yeoman.

I, Sampson Ayre, in the town & countie aforesayde (being sick in
bodye, yett, Godd be praised being in perfect memorye) do make
this my last will and testamente, as followith, videlicet: in primis, I
committ my soule unto Godd, the giver of itt, who, I assuredly trust,
will receive itt, att my departure owt of this worlde, through the
mercies & merritts of Christe Jesus, his sonne, my only saviour &
redemer. Next, I committ my body, unto Christian burialle. In
primis, for wordlye goods, I doe bestow them as followeth: in
primis, I do bequeath unto my daughter Allice thirtye powndes, & to
my daughter Isabell thirtye pownds of good & lawfull English
moneye, to be trulye & dulye payde unto them, & eithryer of them,
by Margerye Ayre, my wife (uppon lawfulle demaunde), when my
said daughters shalle come to lawfull yeares of marriage. And,
withall, I doe charge my wife to keepe my foresaid daughters &
maynteine them with convenient apparrell, meate, drincke,
lodgeinge, educatione & all other thinges whatsoever, belonginge or
anye wayes appertaininge unto them. And in consideration of the
premises, I (the foresaid Sampson Ayre) doe make my wife
Margary^{iurata}Ayre my sole exequatrix of all that ever I dye possessed
with (my debts & funeralle rites being payed). In wittness of all
which I have heerunto sett my hand & seale,
     the marke of Sampson Ayre.[*marked with a reversed capital S on its
side*]
In presence of
Francis Todd [*signed with full name*]

Richard Wake^{iuratus} [*signed with full name*]
Richard Quintyn [*signed with full name, and lawyer's device?*]

An inventorye of all the goods moveable and unmoveable of Sampson Ayre of Monckwermouth, desessed, praised by fower indeferent men whose names are underwritten, this xxviij day of Aprill, anno Domini 1634.

Inprimis, nine kyne and fower calves	27	0s	0d
Item, three stots	7	0s	0d
Item, two whyes	3	0s	0d
Item, one horse	1	10s	0d
Item, one swine		7s	0d
Item, two cubbords in the hall	3	0s	0d
Item, one table in the hall with eight joyne stooles	1	6s	8d
Item, fower chares		10s	0d
Item, one cubbord & a table in the kitchinge		13s	4d
Item, one bedstead, two chistes and one little table in the parler	1	4s	0d
Item, two tables, two joyne formes, one old bedstead in the chamber	1	10s	0d
Item, skeeles and tubes and other wooden vessell		13s	4d
Item, in puder vessell	2	10s	0d
Item, two kettles, two brase pots, one iron pott and two pans	2	10s	0d
Item, three chimleys, three spetes, two paire of rackes, one droppinge pan and a rackinge crooke	1	10s	0d
Item, six silver spones	2	0s	0d
Item, one rugg and fower coverlids	1	10s	0d
Item, one featherbed, one bolster, two mattresses and six feather cods	2	10s	0d
Item, fortye six yeardes of lin and twenty yeardes of harne	2	15s	0d
Item, one paire of lin sheets, seaven paire of strakinge sheets, fower cod pillows, three table clothes and one dossen and a halfe of napkins	3	0s	0d
Item, one akcre and a halfe of bigg sowen in a close at Suddicke	2	0s	0d
Item, fower akcre of wheat and bigg and fower akcre of peese and ots sowen	10	0s	0d

Item, a lease of certaine beaste gaites in Symonsid feildes for dyvers yeares yet to come, with one close at Suddicke	35	0s	0d
Item, the lease of his halfe farme	40	0s	0d
Item, his furniture and apparrell	10	0s	0d

Sum 162^{li} 19^{s} 4^{d}

Debts oweinge to the testator

Item, Thomas Newton of Harton	28	0s	0d

Summa totalis 190^{li} 19 4^{d}

Debts that the testator doth owe

Item, to Elizabeth Elmar	30	0s	0d
Item, for his Whitsonday rents	10	0s	0d

Summa clara 150^{li} 19^{s} 4^{d}

Anthony Younge [*signed with full name*]
Thomas Taylor [*signed with full name*]
Robert Chamber [*signed with full name*]
Christopher Shepperson [*signed with full name*]

Source: DPR1/1/1634/A5/1, 3 paper 3ff.

55. Robert Bowes of South Biddick, 1635

An inventorie of the good and chattles of M[r] Roberte Bowes of South Biddicke, deceased, apprised by George Dobson, John Leightly, James Hull and John Duckett

Imprimis, for iij kine, two whyes and a bull	20	0s	0d
Item, viij oxen	24	0s	0d
Item, 13 horses and maires, and two fooles	24	0s	0d
Item, 14 sheepe	3	10s	0d
Item, viij younge beasts	10	0s	0d
Item, for the corne one the ground at the time of M[r] Bowes' decease	22	0s	0d
Item, for plough and plough geare	1	10s	0d
Item, for waynes and waine geare	14	0s	0d
Item, for two tymber tres and 17 planks, and two startes	3	0s	0d

Item, for materiall for makinge up two coupe wayne with {two paire of stinges} two plankes, 3 harrow and two axaltres	2	0s	0d
Item, for 4 beasttynes, whereof 3 of them is already dead and the other likely to dy		3s	4d
Item, for twelve smale oke bordes		3s	0d
Item, for an ould horse tunne		1s	0d
Item, for two axes and an each		2s	0d
Item, for 4 stone hammers and a mattacke		1s	8d
Item, 6 iron houpes		3s	0d
Item, twelve rakes and 4 iron forkes		5s	0d
Item, twenty foure shovelets		12s	0d
Item, for a paire of pincers and other od implements		2s	0d
Item, for 6 free stones		3s	0d

In the hall

Imprimis, one table with 2 drawers and 13 stoules	?	10s	0d
Item, little chair for a childe		1s	0d
Item, one chaire frame		1s	0d
Item, one presse with 3 cubbords	1	0s	0d
Item, one liverie cubbart with a drawer		6s	8d
Item, little spence		3s	0d
Item, one porre, one fireshovell and one paire of iron barres		6s	8d
Item, one wach with a larum	1	0s	0d
Item, a blacke birde and an ould cage		[no entry]	
Item, 2 dozen and vij trenchers of plaine tre ine a box and a dozen chease trenchers and vj ordinarie one		6s	8d
Item, a butter cup and 4 other scales with 2 wodden spones			6d
Item, for <x > cakes of wax		2s	0d
Item, for a stane, a boule and an ould baskett		1s	0d

In the roume over the stable

Imprimis, a table, a coverlitt, a paire of blanketts <and> paire of iron barres	1	0s	0d
Item, a servant bed and bedding that [........]		13s	4d

In the milke house

Item, seckes and pokes, with riddels and ceaves		5s	0d
Item, 2 muges		1s	0d

		s	d
Item, 3 temces and a meale ceane		3s	6d
Item, a pair of temces		1s	0d
Item, vj boules, a kitt and a knocke tubb		4s	0d
Item, 6 trayes, 16 milke boules and 6 chese woods, 2 <synker> and a silling dishe, and a milk sile		10s	0d

In the kitchin

		s	d
Imprimis, v spitts		5s	0d
Item, a paire of iron rackes		3s	4d
Item, a paire of iron barres		6s	8d
Item, two iron reckon crokes and a paire of tonges		5s	0d
Item, a s[k]ummer, 3 brasse laddles, a paire crankes, 2 chaven dishes and a shredding knife and an ould grate		6s	8d
Item, a little iron thinge for rostinge apple one			
Item, 2 fryinge panes, a drippinge pane, 3 iron potts a yetlinge		12s	0d
Item, a pestle and a morter		3s	4d
Item, a skellett		2s	6d
Item, chuppinge knyfe			6d
Item, vij panes		16s	0d
Item, three[29] brasse potts and 2 kettles	1	10s	0d
Item, one cawell		5s	0d
Item, 3 tubbes		4s	0d
Item, 2 weshinge tubbes		1s	0d
Item, 2 tables, 2 furmes and a chease trough		6s	8d
Item, 9 skeales and a hop seane, 2 halfe peckes, a houpe and one ould pecke		4s	0d
Item, 13 wooden dishes and a creminge dishe			4d
Item, one beare flaggin and a little one		2s	6d
Item, 4 chamber potts		4s	0d
Item, 4 candlestickes		4s	0d
Item, two puter salts		2s	6d
Item, a basinge and ure		5s	0d
Item, 2 chargers and 4 larger platters	1	0s	0d
Item, 18 pewter platters of dyvers sorts	1	0s	0d
Item, 6 houle dishes, viij frute dishes, a hand basin & 2 porring dishes		10s	0d

29 This word may be deleted.

Item, 14 cawsers and 13 pewter spownes		3s	0d
Item, for ould pewter		2s	6d

In the little roume under the staires

Imprimis, for 2 funnels and 3 barrels and a gailtre		4s	0d

In the parlor

Imprimis, a little table with drawers		5s	0d
Item, a cradle with 2 pillowes		4s	0d
Item, a liverie cubbers	1	0s	0d
Item, {a bedstead w^th} a feather bedd and bouster, a rugge and a paire of blanketts, {and a truckle}	1	10s	0d
Item, a little truckle bedd, with a feather bedd and bouster, one blankett, a coverlidde and a paire of sheetes	2	0s	0d
Item, a silver porringe dishe and six silver spounes and a silver salte	2	0s	0d
Item, 3 reales			2d
Item, 4 little wodden stoules		2s	0d
Item, {one Fland[e]rs chist}			
Item, 2 little boxes and 2 deskes		3s	4d
Item, 2 thrinne cushens and 2 other cushens		1s	0d
Item, a paire of iron barres and a paire of tonges, and a fire shovels and a little gibb		2s	0d
Item, one broad box		2s	0d
Item, 2 little oulde chaires			6d
Item, a paire of snuffers		1s	0d
Item, a tostinge iron and 2 setting stickes and a smout things iron		2s	0d
Item, for five yardes of copper frynge		1s	6d
Item, 2 lyn table clothes and 2 dozen of napkins	1	4s	0d
Item, 5 cubbert clothes		10s	0d
Item, 10 pillowbers, 3 paire of sheetes	1	12s	0d
Item, 3 shetes of 3 beedes a peice and v pillowbers	1	5s	0d
Item, one pallete sheete, a {damesk} table cloeth, a damesk towell, a dozen of dameske napkins, one square dyper table cloethe and a dyper towell & 6 dyper napkins, one fyne laceworke napkin	4	0s	0d
Item, for a little border for a cubbert with 3 yards of frynge		2s	6d
Item, for the child bedd lyninge		10s	0d

Item, nine harden napkins, 6 harden towells, 2 harden table cloathes, a strakin towell,and a lyn hand towell	8s	0d
Item, 4 paire of sheetes and a single sheetes, 3 lyn shirts with other ould thinges	16s	0d
Item, for the teaster of a bedd of ould velvett 1	10s	0d

In the closett
Imprimis, a voyder and a voyder knife, with a case for the same	1s	0d
Item, for brasse implements	2s	0d
Item, 2 paire wollen cairdes	1s	0d
Item, for 2 heckles	1s	0d
Item, for an ould truncke and 2 boxes	2s	0d
Item, for 2 little bottles of tynn and v wanded bottles, and 3 glasse bottle, and 4 drinkinge glasses, 3 spise boxes, 6 glasse plates, 2 cheanye dishes, a glasse porringer and a preserving glasse, with other little babling thinges	5s	0d

In the roume over the hall
Inprimis, for a hande milne	5s	0d
Item, for 4 ould chistes	5s	0d
Item, for a lyne wheale and other od utensills	2s	6d
Item, for a wollen wheale and other odd utensells	5s	0d

In the midde roume
Inprimis, in a butter baskett, a ringlett and 2 flackitts, with a prent of leade	10s	0d
Item, a v cole and a case with other utensells	5s	0d

In the stoddie
Inprimis, a deske	3s	4d

In the roume over the parlor
Inprimis, one little truckle bedd with a fether bedd, boulster and other clothes	13s	4d
Item, courtins for a bedd and the fringe	10s	0d
Item, for 10 salt fish, one chaire, 2 tables, a liverye cubbert, one ould trunke, and frame for a hand basin {a paire of barres}	13s	4d
Item, two carpitts and 3 cubbert clothes	13s	4d
Item, 6 cushens	10s	0d

Item, curtins for a bedd of lynsiwoollye		6s	8d
Item, for a cott and a suite	2	0s	0d
Item, for a feather bedd teake		15s	0d
Item, for 2 bibles, a salme booke and five prayer bookes and other thinges		13s	4d
Item, for a hatt and a hatt bande		10s	0d
Item, for turkeyes, geasse, cockes, capons and other pultrye	1	0s	0d
Toto	174	?	?

Source: DPR1/1/1635/B6/1, paper 2ff.

56. Thomas Watt of Sunderland, labourer, 1635

May the vij[th], 1633

In the name of God, amen, I, Thomas Watt of Sunderland nere the sea within the countie of Durham, labourer, being sieck of bodie yet perfect in remembrance, thankes be to God, doe make this my last will and testament as followeth. Imprimis, I bequeath my soule unto Jesus Christ, my onely saviour and redeemer, and my bodie to be buried in the church yard of Bishopp Wearmouth. Item, I give and bequeath to my yongest son, John Watt, one coate house in Sunderland aforesaid, now in the occupation of Cuthbert Roxbie, giving the yearely rent of twentie five shillings yearelie. Item, I give to my sonne Phillipp Watt one coate house, now in the occupation of Myles Rauling, in Sunderland aforesaid. Item, I give and bequeath to my sonne Thomas Watt one coate house, now in the occupation of Raiph Simpson, allso in Sunderland aforesaid. Item, I give and bequeath to my daughter Ann {Watt} Hodgson, wife of Thomas Hodgson, one coate house wherin she now dwelleth in Sunderland aforesaid. Item, I give and bequeth to my sonne Robert Watt one coate house, now in the occupation of John Allinbie, in Sunderland aforesaid. Item, I give and bequeath to my daughter Ann Watt one coate house, nowe in the occupation of Elin Thompson, widow, to enter upon after the decease of the said widdow Thompson, in Sunderland aforesaid. Item, I give and bequeath to my son William Watt my seat house in Sunderland and a coate house wherein John Curtus dwelleth. Item, my will is my wife Ann Watt have the disposeing of all these said rentes for the maintinance and bringing up of my said two yongest children, except them rentes which belongs to my son William Watt, for the tearme of five yeares. Item, I give unto my daughter Ann Wat another cote house, now in the occupation of William Watt, the keeleman. Item, all the househould stuffe that belongeth to the house I give it to my wife. And if it shall happen that my wife shall marrie, that then and from thence forth all the other former giftes to be void and of none effect. Item, my will is that my wife shall pay unto my sister Ann Watt twentie shillinges.

Thomas Watt, his mark [*marked with a cross*]

Writen in the presence of us witnesses
John Moverey, his mark [*marked with initials, capitals I M*]
William Watt, his mark [*marked with a cross*]
William Robinson [*marked with a cross*]

A true inventorie of all the goodes & chattells moveable & not moveable of Thomas Watt, late of Sunderland nere the sea in the countie of Durham, labourer, deceased, as followeth, as they were praised by us fower men whose names ar hereunder written

Imprimis, one pare of barres, a reckingcrooke, pare of tonges & an iron pott & pott hookes	3s	6d
Item, one old coupard & a table	10s	0d
Item, a chist	2s	6d
Item, a stone morter, a mell, a tub, a skeele, 2 stone dishes, halfe a doozen of trenchers & a peck	1s	0d

William Dossey [*full name signed*]
Thomas Scarbrough, his mark [*marked with a symbol, a horseshoe*]
William Pottes, his mark [*marked with a capital W on its side*]
John Yonger, his mark [*marked with a cross*]

Source: DPR1/1/1635/W10/1, 2, paper2ff.

57. Mary Shepherdson of Bishopwearmouth, widow, 1635

In the name of God, amen, I, Mary Shipperdson, wedew, of Bishopp Warmoth, being sicke of body but hole and perfect in remembrance, thankes be to God, makes this my last will & testament in manner and forme as followeth. First, I bequeth my soule to allmightie God, my maker & redemer, and by Cristes deeth & pashon I hope only to be saved, and my body to be buryed in the parrissh church of Bishopp Warmoth. Imprimis, I give to the poore of the towne of Bishopp Warmoth and to the poore of the towne ship of Rihop fortie

shillings to be devided at the descression of the overseers. Item, I
give unto Anne Huntly, daughter of Richard Huntley of Burdon, my
grandchild, forty shilings. Item, I give to my sister Anne Curtas,
wedow, all my wering aparrell. For all the rest of my goodes,
moveable or unmoveable, debts and rents, I give unto John
Shipperdson, my sone in law, whome I make my excecutor of this
my last will and testament, who is to discarge all my debts & funerall
expences, this eleuent day of January, anno Domini 1634.
In the presence of us witnesses wherunto I have set my hand
Mary Shipperdson, hir marke [*marked with symbols*]
Witnesses
William Robinson [*no mark or signature*]
Robert Pasmore [*no mark or signature*]
John Curtas [*no mark or signature*]
Thomas Raw [*no mark or signature*]

Source: DPR1/1/1635/S5/1, paper 1f.

58. George Burgoyne of Sunderland, alderman, 1635

June the 15th, 1635
A true inventorye of the goods and chattels belonginge to Mr George
Burgoigne, alderman of Sunderland, deceased the 26th of May in the
yeare abovesaide

In the greate chamber

Inprimis, bookes	1	0s	0d
Item, his apparell and purss	13	13s	4d
Item, 4 paire of sheets, 2 table clothes, 1 carpett	1	13s	4d
Item, 1 seeing glass, 2 chaires		8s	0d

In the little chamber

Inprimis, a servant's bedd	10s	0d
Item, 2 little trunkes, 1 chest, 1 baskett and trenchers	6s	8d
Item, half a dosen stooles	7s	0d
Item, a sadle and furniture	6s	0d
Item, a standish and jack pott	1s	0d

In the lowe parlour

One bedstead, 1 paire of curtaines, 2 ffether beds, 1 bolster, 1 coverlid	5	0s	0d

In the hall

Inprimis, one table, 1 fforme, 2 chaires		6s	8d
Item, ffower chargers	1	4s	0d
Item, 2 quart potts, 2 pinte potts		6s	0d
Item, 3 candlesticks		3s	0d
Item, 2 dosen of sawcers		8s	0d
Item, 5 pottindishes, 1 brass ladle, 1 custorde plate		6s	0d
Item, 1 salt, 1 tun, 1 basin, 4 chamber potts		10s	0d
Item, 1 basin and ewer, 2 cushions, 1 carpett cushion		11s	0d
Item, 3 brass candlesticks, 1 brass morter		10s	0d
Item, 5 jugges, 3 cheney dishes		7s	0d
Item, 1 pair of tiffeney tempsis		2s	0d
Item, 1 quart pott, 1 brass fryin pan, 4 stone platters		6s	0d

In the kitchin

Inprimis, 1 iron chimney, 1 paire of rackes, 2 iron spitts, 1 pair of tongues, 1 porr, 1 rackin crooke	1	10s	0d
Item, 2 brass potts, 1 brass kettle, 1 yetlin	1	2s	0d
Item, 3 driping panes, 1 paire of broylinge irons, 1 chopin knife		8s	0d
Item, 1 table, 3 chaires, 3 skeels, 2 tubbes, 2 bowles, 1 salt kitt, one wooden shovell, 1 lanthorne, 1 little pan, one bowle		13s	4d

In the stable

Haye and oates		5s	0d
	8	18s	0d

In the garner

ffor pease	3	0s	0d
ffor 2 bowles of wheate att Wearmouthe	1	16s	0d
Half a firkin of sope		9s	0d
1 peck and a half peck of strawe		1s	0d
	5	6s	0d

Bushop Wearmouth att the parsonage, in the olde hyndes house and other places

Imprimis, 8 axell trees, 4 ploughe beames		15s	0d
Item, 3 ploughes, 4 ffore yokes, 1 heade yoke		14s	0d
Item, 1 paire of oxe harrowes, 1 paire of horss harrowes	1	10s	0d
Item, 1 pair of oulde wheales		13s	4d

Item, ffor the olde timber and spakes and fellyes,			
1 paire of naffs and wooden hoopes for ffattes		15s	0d
Item, for 4 fore somes, 2 foote somes, 2 bolts and			
shakels, 2 cowters, 2 socks, 1 muck hack and			
some other olde iron	1	10s	0d
Item, 1 dosen plowe heads, 3 corne forkes, 1 hay spade		4s	0d
Item, 1 olde windowe clothe with sives and riddles		2s	0d
Item, 2 paire of wayne roapes		3s	0d
Item, ffor haye		13s	4d
Item, ffor a sythe		1s	6d
Item, 2 oulde coop waynes		8s	0d
Item, 2 paire of oulde bound wheels	2	0s	0d
Item, 2 longe waynes		10s	0d
Item, 3 paire of wayne stinges		6s	0d
Item, 2 hecks and 1 olde cart		8s	0d
Item, ffor a kyll hayre		10s	0d
Item, ffor 2 olde gees and 7 younge ones		7s	0d
Item, ffor 2 sewes and pigges	1	0s	0d
Item, ffor 2 stone and a half of wooll	1	5s	0d
Item, ffor an oulde ark		2s	6d
	13	17s	8d

Source: DPR1/1/1635/B9/1, paper 2ff.

59. Thomas Page of Bishopwearmouth, 1635

Memorandum, that upon the xxviij[th] daie of May, anno Domini 1635, Thomas Page, late of the parish of Bishopp Wermouth, being of perfect minde and memorie, and desirous to make his last will, did nuncupatively make and declare his minde and last will in manner and forme followeing, or in wordes tending to the like effect, vi*delice*t: he did will that his wife should have her thirds of his personall estaite, and did then give to his three sonnes, Thomas, Anthonie and William Page, to ech of them five poundes, and to his eldest and youngest daughters and to his son Henry Page all the rest of his goodes, chattells and creditts, to be equally devided amongest them. In the presence and hearing of George Lilborne, gent., and Robert Knaggs [*no marks or signatures*].

An inventory of the goods of Thomas Page, deceased, as they were prised by Raufe Bulmer, Ambrose Page, Thomas Anderson & Anthony Page, the 10th of Julij, anno Domini 1635

Inprimis, his purse & his apparell	5	12s	0d
One iron chimney, a reckin crook and a payer of tongs		1s	2d
iij lyn sheets and a pillyver		7s	6d
iij old happins		2s	6d
ij pewter dishes, a salt & a candlestick		2s	0d
iij wooden dishes, one cheswood, iij littell boles for mylk		1s	4d
One brasse pott, one iron pott & a frying pan, ij littell pans, a spitt		10s	0d
One old tubb, j old kitt, j stande, one kan, one temse, j peck		2s	0d
One table, one chayre & 2 stooles & a littell fforme		2s	0d
One spinninge wheele and sive		1s	0d
A kawell		2s	6d
A kowe	1	13s	4d
Some is	8	17s	4d

Debts oweing to the testator

Oweing by George Lilburne, gentleman	20	0s	0d
Oweing by Robert Goodchild	20	0s	0d
Oweing by Charles Porter & George Taylor	10	0s	0d
Oweing by Robert Dobson	10	16s	0d
	60	16s	0d

Somma totalis 69li 13s 4d

Raufe Bulmer, mark [*marked with a cross*]
Ambrose Page, the mark of [*marked with a cross*]
Thomas Anderson's mark [*marked with a cross*]
Anthony Page, his mark [*marked with a symbol*]

Source: DPR1/1/1635/P1/1, 3 paper 4ff.

60. George Shepherdson of Bishopwearmouth, yeoman, 1635

A declaracion of the account of Alice Sheppdson, late wife and administratrix of the goods of George Sheppdson, late of Bishopwermouth of the dioces of Durham, deceased, made upon her administring the said deceased's goods as followeth

Inprimis, this accomptant chargeth herself with all
the goods of the said deceased comeing to her hands,
amounting to the sum of cccxvij^{li} v^s xj^d as appeareth
by an inventarie thereof made and by her, upon oath,
exhibitted into the consistorie court of Durham
appeareth   317   5s   11d

Of which sum this accomptant craveth allowance
as followeth ffirst, she craveth to be allowed onto
her for debts, owing by the deceased, the sum of
48^{li} 6^s 9^d which shee is readie to satisfie unto the
severall creditors respectively upon demannde   48   6s   9d
Item, shee craveth to be allowed unto her for the
funerall expences of the said deceased and for his
mortuarie and larestall, amounting in all to the sum of   1   1s   4d
Item, shee praieth to be allowed unto her for
the fees of the letters of administration and
her sureties' chargs in comeing to Durham about
the same, the sum of   1   0s   0d
ltem, for the sixth part of a tithe in Bishopwermouth
due to George Burgoigne by the deceased   11   0s   0d
                                   Summa allocacion*is*   70   8s   3d

Et sic computat*is* computandis et allocat*is* allocandis
restat in manibus huius computan*tis* summa   246   17s   8d

Allocat*ur* per decretum d*omi*ni judic*is* parti computan*ti* totum et
integrum summam,[30] exceptis 10^{li} in pias usus distribuen*dis*

An inventorie of the goodes of George Shepherdson of Bishopwearmouth in the county of Durham, yeoman, who deceased the
one & thirtieth day of May, anno Domini 1635 and in the tenth of the
reigne of our dread soveraigne lord, King Charles, praised by
Thomas Ayre, Raiph Jervis, John Johnson and Michaell Bryan as
followeth

Imprimis, eight oxen at the price   36   0s   0d
Item, nine kine, thre stirkes & two calvs   22   0s   0d
Item, ffive draught horses   18   0s   0d

---

30 More correctly 'tota et integra summa'.

Item, two two yeare ould stags & two foales	5	0s	0d
Item, nine and twentie ewes and hoggs	5	6s	8d
Item, ffifteene lamms	1	13s	4d
Item, ffower swine	2	6s	8d
Item, two longe waines, two cope waines, thre paire of bunne wheles and one paire of new wheles unbund	5	13s	4d
Item, two ploues, two couters, two socks, five somes, six yoakes & thre boults & shakles & two oxe harrowes and two horse harrowes	2	0s	0d
Item, two paire of horse geare, fourtene axeltres, two plough beames, two moult bords, one lathe and other peces of wood		16s	0d
Item, one stacke of wheate in the stackgarth	7	10s	0d

In the hall

Imprimis, one copboare, on ammerei, one table, one forme, two chaires, one long settle and thre bufett stooles	2	6s	8d
Item, one and twentie pueter dishes, two pewter candlesticke, two brase candlesticks, a quart pot and a pinte pot, two litle cups, one salt seller, fower stone platters, one morter & two chamber potts	1	13s	4d
Item, one iron chemney, one paire of tongs, one paire of jackes, one porre, two reconcrooks, one chopping knife & two spitts		16s	0d
Item, thre cheisbords		1s	0d
Item, one bible		10s	0d

In the parler

Imprimis, one spence, one ould cavell, one presser, one counter, one ould chest, tenn boules, six cesefatts, two churnes, two smale barrels, two temces, two paire of wollen cards, one cheese-boule & other smale nesasaries aboute the roume	2	13s	4d
Imprimis, two brasse kettles, tow iron poots, two little panns and one friing panne		13s	4d

In the breuhouse

Imprimis, one ould brewing leade, two greate toobs, two hoppers. two seckes, five pookes, two skeppes, one pekke & six sives and ridles	1	0s	0d

In the milke house

Imprimis, one bedstede, one counter, one table, one
deske, a leavene milke bowels ... 1 ... 0s ... 0d

In the white chamber

Imprimis, one bedsteade, one fether bed, two paire of
shetes, one mattris, fower coverlids, fower fether
coods, two flickes of bacon ... 4 ... 0s ... 0d

Item, in an other rome, twelfe plough heads and two
stilts ... 2s ... 0d

Item, in the byer, fower muke forkes, thre spaids, thre
corne forkes, two axes, one shovel, fower mould
rakes & one paire of waine roppes ... 6s ... 0d
Item, one ould bedstede, two happings, one paire of
sheetes, two sods and one windowcloth, and an
ould kill haire ... 10s ... 0d
Item, fife skeales ... 2s ... 6d
Imprimis, the crope now growing one the ground,
twentie acres of wheate and bigg and twenty
fower acres of pese and oates, at the rate ... 50 ... 13s ... 4d

Item, one musket and a sword ... 13s ... 4d
Item, his apparrell and pursse ... 4 ... 0s ... 0d

Suma 475^{li} 11^s 2^d

Debts owing to the testator

Imprimis, John Hilton ... 20 ... 0s ... 0d
Item, Chistofer Shipperson ... 30 ... 0s ... 0d
Raiph Holmes ... 10 ... 0s ... 0d
Chrisopher Pattison ... 10 ... 0s ... 0d
Mr William Wiklef ... 10 ... 0s ... 0d
John Nicholson ... 6 ... 0s ... 0d
Item, John Pattinson ... 5 ... 0s ... 0d
Item, Robert Wilkinson ... 6 ... 10s ... 0d
Item, George Richarson for a meade ... 2 ... 16s ... 8d
Imprimis, John Moverlie ... 3 ... 7s ... 0d
Item, Christopher Pattison ... 1 ... 4s ... 0d
Item, Richard Cellie ... 1 ... 16s ... 0d
Item, John Bee ... 18s ... 0d
Item, Dennas Atkinson ... 5s ... 3d

Item, Cristopher Henderson		4s	6d
Item, Martin Watson	10	0s	0d
Item, Robert Arnot	2	0s	0d
Summa 114[li] 1[s] 5[d]			

Debts owing by the testator

Imprimis, to Madlen Borgon	10	2s	3d
Item, Richard Smith		10s	0d
Item, Mary Talor	1	0s	0d
Item, John Ceirfeild		2s	11d
Item, Willman Snowdon	6	0s	0d
Item, William Pattison	23	0s	0d
Item, William Gaye	1	0s	0d
Item, Raiph Holmes	5	0s	0d
Item, the lord's rent	2	7s	7d
Item, to John Pattinson ffor soones	1	4s	0d
Totall	48	6s	9d

ffor the funerall expencesse

Imprimis, ffor wine and suger	1	4s	8d
Item, for cheches		7s	0d
Item, ffor coumferts and dide bread	2	2s	0d
Item, ffor beare & bread	1	5s	0d
Item, ffor a boule of wheat		19s	0d
Item, for butter, spises, candles & other nessesaries	1	2s	9d
Item, for the mortuaries & the larestall		16s	0d
Item, for flech		11s	0d
Item, for the poore of the parrish	1	0s	0d
Item, for the buriall, for the coffin & ringing		12s	2d
Totall	10	10s	4d

Imprimis, the wool in the lofte		15s	4d
Item, thre peseese of cloth at the wever, praised	1	0s	0d

Imprimis, an eight part of a ship, praised at the prise of	20	0s	0d
Totall	21	13s	4d

Imprimis, owing by the testator to William Thomson of the Pannes	1	16s	6d

Thomas Ayre [*full name signed*]
Raiph Jervis [*full name signed*]

John Johnson [*full name signed*]
Micheal Bryan [*full name signed*]

The testator's goods amounteth to	317	5s	11d
That the testator oweth amounteth to	60	13s	7d
Suma totallis clerely {256[li] 12[s] 4[d]}			

Administratio comiss*a* Alic*ie* Shippdson, vid*ue*

Note: DPR1/1/1635/S6/1–5, paper 4ff (3ff sewn).

61   Adam Blakeston of Old Burdon, 1635

In the name of God, amen, I, Adam Blakeston of Olde Burden, doe
declare my last will the 3 day of June, 1635, in manner & forme
followinge. Inprimis, my will & minde is, & I doe by this my will
give by legacy unto all my grande children, 40ˢ a peece, that is to say,
to my sonne John Blakston's children, that is to his sonne Adam
Blakeston 40ˢ, & to his sonne John Blakeston 40ˢ, item, to his sonne
Thomas 40ˢ; item, to my sone Thomas Snaden's sonne Thomas 40ˢ;
item, my sonne Robinsonne children, that is to his sonne Thomas
Robinsonne 40ˢ, item, to his daughter Issable Robinsonne 40ˢ, item,
to his daughter Elizabeth Robinsonne 40ˢ. Item, for all the rest of my
goods, I doe by this my will give them equally and proportionablely
to be devided amonghts my 3 children, that is, my sonne John
Blakeston & my daughter Allice Snaden & to my daughter Grace
Robinsonne.
Witnesses hereof, Thomas Robinson and Thomas Snawden [*no marks
or signatures*]

A true inventory of all such goods chattles as Adam Blakeston, late
of Old Burden, dyed possessed of, rated & appraised by Thomas
Shadfoorth of Eppleton, Thomas Glen of Seaton & Nicolas Tode; and
praised[31] the 16 of June, 1635

Inprimis, 9 kine, one with an other at two poundes, thre shillinges & 4ᵈ a peece, in all	19	10s	0d
Item, 19 ewes & lambes at 8ˢ per peece	7	12s	0d

---

31 MS *paised*.

Item, 26 weathers at 8ˢ per peece	10	8s	0d
Item, 10 ewes & one hoge at 5ˢ per peece	2	15s	0d
Item, one steere & one quie at	4	0s	0d
Item, 4 lesser quies at	5	6s	8d
Item, 3 calfes at	1	0s	0d
Item, a black mare	2	10s	0d
Item, 8 milk bowles & one skele		3s	4d
Item, one chare		1s	0d
Item, his purse & apparell	3	6s	8d
	58	8s	8d

In witnes hereof, we have set to our hands the day & yeare above written

Thomas Shadfoorth [*full name signed*]

Thomas Glen, his marke [*marked with a symbol*]

Nicholas Todd [*full name signed*]

Source: DPR1/1/1635/B3/1, 2, paper 2ff.

62. Maurice Prescott of Sunderland, 1635

xiij° November 1635

A declaracion of the accompt of Margerie Prescott, widdow, administratrix of the goods and chattlls of Maurice Prescott, late of Sunderland by the sea of the dioces of Durham, deceased, made upon her administring the said deceased's goods, as followeth, vi*delice*t:

Inprimis, this accomptant chargeth herselfe with the goods of the said deceased cominge to her hands amounting to the sume of xxiij^li xvj^s, as by an inventorie thereof made and by her upon oath exhibited into the consistorie court att Durham appeareth	23	16s	0d

Summa patet

Which sume this accomptant hath fullye administred and craveth allowance as followeth, vi*delice*t:

ffirst, she hath payd or satisfied to Katherine fforton of Gateshead the sume of sixtene pounds for the said deceased's debt and since his death due by bill, dated 7° August, 1631	16	0s	0d

Item, she hath, likewise payd or satisfied unto Richard
Cottrill of Sunderland, aforesaid, for the said deceased's
debt and since his death, the sume of iij^{li} xv^s, by bill
dat^a ultimo die Octobris, 1633, appeareth   3   15s   0d

Item, she hath, likewise payd or satisfied unto Richard
Quinton of the parish of Munkwermouth, gent., the
sume of l^s for the said deceased's debt and since his
death due by bill dated 4º November, 1633   2   10s   0d

Item, she hath, likewise payd or satisfied unto Robert
Chambers of Cleadon, gent., the sume of xliiij^s vj^d
for the said deceased's debt and since his death due by
bond or other specialtie   2   4s   6d

Item, she hath likewise payd to William Caldwell of
Sunderland the sume of xl^s for the said deceased's
debt and since his death due by note subscribed under
the deceased's owne hand   2   0s   0d

Item, she hath likewise payd to Mr John Hilton, the
sume of iij^{li} x^s, parcell of the sume of v^{li} due by bond
or other specialtie for the said deceased's debt and
since his death   3   10s   0d

Item, she hath alsoe paid to James Rider of Sunderland,
butcher, the sume of xx^s for the said deceased's debt
and since his death   1   0s   0d

Summe of her payments and allowanc[e]s   30   19s   6d

Et sic computatis computandis et allocatis allocandis
huiusmodi computans solvit ultra vires bonorum
dicti defuncti   7   3s   6d

Source: DPR1/1/1635/P10/1, paper 2ff.

63   Thomas Kitchin of Southwick, 1635

A declaracion of the accompt of Jane Kitchin, administratrix of the
goods of Thomas Kitchin, late of Suddicke of the dioces of Durham,
deceased, made upon her administring the said deceased's goods as
followeth, videlicet:

Inprimis, this accomptant chargeth herselfe with the
goods of the said deceased comeing to her hands,
amounting to the summe of ccviij^{li} vj^s viij^d as by

an inventorie thereof made and by her upon oath
exhibited into the consistorie court of Durham,
appeareth   208   6s   8d
                    Summa patet

Which summe this accomptant hath fullie administred &
          craveth allowance as followeth, videlicet:
ffirst, she hath paid and satisfied to Elizabeth Mempis
of Moncke Wermouth, the summe of xj^{li} for the said
deceased's debt & since his death due by bond   11   0s   0d
Item, she hath likewise paid or satisfied to Robert
Oliver of Clapheugh the summe of xiij^{li} for the said
deceased's debt & since his death due by bond   13   0s   0d
Item, she hath likewise paid or satisfied to John
Kitchin of Suddicke the summe of viij^{li} for the said
deceased's debt & since his death   8   0s   0d
Item, she hath likewise paid or satisfied to John
Thompson of Suddicke the summe of l^{s} for the said
deceased's debt & since his death due by bill   2 10s   0d
Item, she hath likewise paid or satisfied to Thomas
Belson of Wallerge the summe of xvj^{s} 16s   0d
Item, she hath likewise paid or satisfied to Ann
Byers of Suddicke the summe of xl^{s} for the said
deceased's debt and since his death   2 10s   0d
Item, she craveth to be allowed unto her for funerall
expences the summe of iiij^{li} 4   0s   0d
Item, she craveth to be allowed unto her for the fees
of the letters of administration and her suerties'
charges about the same   1   0s   0d
Item, she craveth to be allowed unto her the summe
of 50^{li} which she is to pay for the filiall porcions of 2
children by her former husband   50   0s   0d

              Some of her payments   90   6s   0d
Et sic computatis computandis [et] allocatis allocandis,
remanet in manibus huius computantis   116   0s   0d

Allocat' Elizabetha Kitchin pro filiali portione   33   6s   8d
Johanna similiter   33   6s   8d
              Residuum parti[bus] computantis
                    Edward Burwell

Source: DPR1/1/1635/K1/1–2, paper 4ff.

64. Thomas Whitehead of Sunderland, fisherman, 1635

A true inventorie of all the goodes & chattells of Thomas Whitehead, late of Sunderland nere the sea in the countie of Durham, ffisherman, deceased as they were praised by fower indifferent men as followeth.

Imprimis, his purse & apparell		10s	0d
Item, in the forehouse, one pare of barres, 2 pare of tonges, one ffrying pan, 2 spittes, a pare of rax, a reckincrooke, a pare of broyleing irons, a pare of bellowes & a little porr, & a ffleshe crooke & a tosting iron		16s	0d
Item, one cupard & an aumrie	1	13s	4d
Item, a chare, a longsettle, 2 tables & a forme		13s	4d
Item, on the cupard head, 6 puter dishes	1	0s	4d
Item, 2 puter candlestickes, 2 brasse candlestickes, 2 saltes, one quart pott, one chamber pott, one chafeindish, one brasse pott, one iron pott, a lampe, an iron pan, 2 little jugges, one bottle, one brush, a can, a grate water skeele & a little barrell		18s	0d
Item, 2 little stooles, one craddle & a buffet stoole, & a little chare		3s	0d
Item, 2 little quishions			6d
Item, one bedstead, 4 happins, a pare of sheetes, one boulster, a cod & a ffeather bed	1	10s	0d
Item, in the butterie, 3 great earthen potts, a callinder, a doozon of trenchers, a band pott, a gallon pot, one old skeele, 3 old tubbes, 2 stooles, with other small implements		10s	0d
Item, in the chamber, one bedstead, j ffeather bed, one boulster, 2 coddes, one blankit, 3 coverlids, one pare of sheetes	2	0s	0d
Item, one counter, one presse, one arke, one chare, 2 fourmes, 3 buffit stooles		16s	0d
Item, coffer & linin, 2 pare of sheetes, 3 pillowes, one table cloth, 2 towells	1	0s	0d
Item, 2 quishons		1s	6d
Item, 3 old tubbs & a peck		2s	6d
Item, one pare of wood rackes & other od things		2s	0d
Item, 2 old chists & a compas		2s	0d
Item, halfe a cobble		6s	8d

Item, 8 piece of summer line	1	2s	6d
Item, 3 piece of string		6s	6d
Item, 5 piece of wint[e]r line		5s	0d
Item, 9 nettes	1	16s	0d
	15	14s	10d

John Husband [*full name signed*]
Robert Yong, his mark [*marked with a five-point star*]
Henry Hirdman, his mark [*marked with an anchor symbol*]
Cuthbert Roxbie, his mark [*marked with a horizontal reversed R*]

27 Nov[ember], 1635
Johanna vidua remanet administratrix et moᵉ introd'

Source: DPR1/1/1635/W14/1, paper 1f.

65. Isabel Richardson of Burdon, widow, 1636

In the naime of God, amen, I, Issabell Richerdson, sick in body but
sounde in mynde & of perfect memory (God's naime be praysed
therfore) do make this my last will & testiment in manner & forme as
followeth. ffirst, I bequeathe my soule into the handes of almightie
God, my creator & maker, hoping to be saved by the pretiouse death
& bloodshed of Christe, my lord, & God, my saviour & redeamer, &
by noe other way or meanes. Secondly, I bequeathe my body to be
buried in Bishop Wermoth church. Item, I give to my grandaughter
Isabell Richardson, the daughter of my late sonne Thomas
Richerdson, the bedstead that now standeth in the forehouse; &
whereas Issabell Huntley, the once wife of my said sonn Thomas &
mother to the said Issabell Richerdson, my granddaughter, is owne
and is indebted to me the sume of five poundes, as by a pare of
articles betwean her & me with som others it doth & may appear, I
do hearby give & bequeath the sayd summe of five poundes to my
said grandaughter, Issabell Richerdson. Item, I give to my said
grandaughter Issabell Richerdson the iron chimney in the forehouse,
the por and tonges to it belonging & one of the reekincrookes. Item, I
give her a yellowe chist now standing in the chamber. Item, I do
make this my last will & testament, revoking hearby all other will or
wills whatsoever that I have heartofore mayd, to what intent or
purpose soever they have been mayd. Item, I give to my two
daughters Barbary Pattison and Issabell Burdon all the rest of my my
goods & chattels whatsoever, movable & immovable, & all my corne
nowe growing & in the earth; & I do make [my] said two daughters

Barbary & Issabel executors of this my la[st wi]ll & testament. And in wit[ness] hearof I have he[reun]to subscribed & set my [hand]e the the fithe[32] day January in the year of our Lord God, one thousand, six hundred, thirtie & five,

Issabel Richerdson, the marke of [*marked with a symbol*]

Red and subscribed in the presence of
George Myddleton [*full name signed*]
John Boukle, the marke of [*marked with a cross*]
William Tomson, the marke of [*marked with a capital T*]

An inventorie of the goods of Issable Richardson of Burden in the county of Durham, widow, who deseased the forth day of March, anno Domini 1636, praised by William Reede, Thomas Ayre, William Thomson, Michael Bryan as followeth

Imprimis, the testator purse and apparrell	3	6s	0d
Item, the corne in the garth with the corne in the house and the corne now growing in the feild	10	0s	0d
Item, fower kine, one why stirke and a mare	13	6s	8d
Item, the hay and the strawe in the house	1	0s	0d
Item, thre shering shepe and thre hogs shepe	1	10s	0d
The houshould stufe in the fore house			
Item, one cubbord, one cauwell, one butterie	1	6s	8d
Item, twenty peter dublers, thre platters, three sallets, one boule, two salts and one tune	1	4s	0d
Item, two cettles, fife panes, one brase pott, one little pott, one posnot pott, fower brase candelstickes	2	0s	0d
Item, one table, one longsettell, one chare, one forme		10s	0d
Item, eight hapings, fower coverlids, one blankett, seaven fether coods	2	3s	4d
Item, one chare, thre stoales, one knop tube, one great bowell, eight milke bowels, aleauen chesfats, two sinkers		6s	8d
Item, given to Issable Richardson, one daughter of Thomas Richardson, deseased, one bedstede, one iron chimny, one por, one paire of tongs, one recconcroke, one yellow chist	3	0s	0d
And fife pounds which is in her mother hand	5	0s	0d

---

32 The manuscript repeats 'the fithe'.

The houshould stufe in the chamber

Item, one bedsteede, one ould fether bed, one long bouster, one fether cod, two blankets, two hapings, one ould coverlid	1	10s	0d
Item, fower paire of linen chetas, thre cod pillevers, one bord cloth, two table napkings, fife paire of harden shets	2	12s	0d
Item, two chests, one ould pecke, thre ridlles, one temce, one ould tub, fower can lids		3s	0d
Item, one pece of linne and one pese of linen yarne		13s	4d
Item, one musket with her furniture		13s	4d
Item, thre stone of butter	1	0s	0d

Debts owing to the testator

Item, John Smith	3	0s	0d

Debts owing by the testator

Item, for the tith		12s	0d
Item, the funerall expesses	8	0s	0d
	62	4s	0d

William Reede, his marke [*marked with a scratch*]
Thomas Ayre, his marke [*marked with the initial capitals, T A*]
William Thomson, his mark [*marked with the initial capital T*]
Michaell Bryan [*full name signed*]

Source: DPR1/1/1635/R5/1, 3, paper 3ff. (inventory sewn).

66. George Thompson of Sunderland, butcher, 1636

Memorandum, that upon the <11th> day of May in the yeare of our lord God, 1636, George Thompson, late of Sunderland in the county of Durham, butcher, being sicke in body but of perfect mind and memory, did by word of mouth make and declare his last will and testament, in manner and forme followeing. Imprimis, he did give his soule to God and his body unto the earth. Item, he did give and bequeath to Joann Thompson, daughter of Thomas Thompson, late of Sunderland afforesaid, ffisherman, three pounds. Item, he did [give] and bequeath to George Harrison, sonne of Humfrey Harrison of Sunderland, butcher, forty shillings. Item, he did give and bequeath unto Humfrey Harrison his three children, vi*delicet* George

Harrison, Humfrey Harrison, younger, and Mary Harrison, the sume of vij^{li} iij^s iiij^d, to be equally devyded and parted amongst them. In the presence and heareing of these witnesses
Richard Grinwell, James Dodshon, Humfrey Harrison [*no signatures or marks*]

A true inventorie taken of all the goods & chattles, moveable & unmoveable of George Thompson of Sunderland in the countie of Durham, butcher, deceased, vewed & praysed by William Potts, Thomas Snawdon & James Liddle, the tenth day of August & in the twelveth yeare of the reigne of our sovereigne lord, King Charles, by the grace of God king of England, Scotland, France & Ierland, 1636

Inprimis, one cowe & a litle hay	2	6s	8d
Item, all his apparell & his furnature	1	0s	0d
Item, in money & debts due to him	12	10s	0d
Summa totalis	15	16s	8d

Item, leaggases given by the said George Thompson, deceased			
Item, given to Joann Thompson, daughter of Thomas Thompson, late of Sunderland, fisherman, deceased	3	0s	0d
Item, given by him to George Harrison, sonn of Umfrad Harrison of Sunderland, butcher	2	0s	0d
Item, more given by him unto Umfride Harrison the children, vi*delicet* George Harrison, Umfride Harrison, junior, & Marie Harrison, to be parted equally amongst them	7	3s	4d
Item, spent at his funerall	2	12s	0d

William Potts, his marke [*marked with a symbol*]
Thomas Snawdon, his mark [*marked with the initial capitals, T S*]
James Liddle, his mark [*marked with a scratch*]

Source: DPR1/1/1636/T4/1, 3, paper 2ff.

67. Nicholas Thompson the elder, of Ryhope, 1636

Memorandum, that on or about the beginneing of the moneth of July, anno Domini 1636, Nicholas Thompson thelder, late of Rhyopp in the parishe of Bishopwermouth of the dyoces of Duresme, being sicke of bodie but of perfect minde and memorie, and desirous to dispose of such worldely goodes as then he had or was possessed of, did in the presence of James Ellert and Jaine Whitton, wife of John Whitton, make declaracion of his minde and last will in manner and forme followeing, videlicet: imprimis, he did give and bequeath unto Roberte Thompson and William Thompson, sonnes of George Thompson, the testator's sonne, two stotts, and to the said George Thompson's wife, one cowe. Item, to John Thompson, son of Richard Thompson, tenne poundes to be delivered to John Ruter, grandfather of the said John, to be by him disposed of for his advantage and profitt. Item, to Elizabeth Thompson, daughter of the said Richard Thompson, one cowe. And to thother three daughters of the said Richard, to ech of them one whye. Item, he did give the summe of tenne poundes lawfull Englishe money to be imployed yearlie by the churchwardens and overseers of the said parishe as a stocke for the use of the poore of the towneshipp of Ryhopp onely. Item, he did give the summe of six poundes to be bestowed upon his funerals. All the rest of his goodes, chattells and creditts whatsoever, he did give and bequeath unto his said sonne Richard^{iuratus} Thompson, whome he made executor of this his last will and testament.

Witness[e]s herof,

James Ellert ^{iuratus}, Jaine Whitton ^{iurata} [no signatures or marks]

An inventorie of the goods & cattels of Nicholas Thompson thelder of Ryhop, lately deceased, praised by fowere honest men, Robert Thompson, William Thompson thelder, William Thompson, younger, and George Watson the xvth of July, 1636

Imprimis, three stotts	9	0s	0d
Item, three kine	9	10s	0d
Item, two whys	1	0s	0d
Item, one swine hog		8s	0d
Item, his purse	16	0s	0d
Item, his apparell	5	0s	0d
Suma totallis	40	18s	0d

Debts oweing to him

Imprimis, by Richard Skeathlocke	4	0s	0d
Item, by William Couteis	2	1s	0d
Item, by John Lowraynce	8	0s	0d
Item, by Richard Thompson thelder		8s	0d
Summa	14	9s	0d

Source: DPR1/1/1636/T6/1, 3, paper 2ff.

68. Matthew Kelly of Bishopwearmouth, labourer, 1636

The last will & testament of Matthew Kelly of Bishop Weremouth

In the name of God, &c., I, Matthew Kelly of Bishop Weremouth within the county palatine of Durham, labourer, being weake in body, but of perfect memory, doe make this my last will & testament as followes. First, I bequeathe my soule into the handes of almighty God & my body to the ground, & for my wordly goodes I bequeathe them thus. For my 10 pounds of mony which remayns in the handes of John Smith, keleman, & Robert Smithe & Richard Smith, heardes of this towne of Bishop Weremouthe, my will is that after my decease it be bestowed upon George Fletcher & Isabell Fletcher, my grandechildren, to eache of them 5 pounndes, & in the meane whyle, till it shall please God they come to age, to remaine in the keeping & usinge of Jarry Potter of the same towne, kealeman, by him to be imployed for there benefitt; & if it soe falle forthe that one of them shall dye, that its parte shall goe to the other childe; & if it shall please God that they shall bothe dye before they come to that age, that then it shall goe to the mother of those children, Elzabeth Ousnet, now wife of Anthony Ousenet of the aforesaide towne, tayler. Alsoe I bequeathe to Matthew Scotte, sonne of John Scotte of this towne, the summe of 5 shillings for a remembrance. In witnesse whereof, I have sett too my hande & seale, this 9th of February, in the year of our Lord 1636.

Matthew Kelly, his marke
[*seal*]

In the presence of us
Richard Hickes
Michaell Bryan

Memorandum, that this is added before the sealing hereof, *videlicet* that the remainder of that mony which is in the handes above

named, being 4 pound & 8 shillings, shall be imployed for my honest
& credible bringinge forthe at my buryall; & if it shall please God
that I dye before the mony be dewe, I leave my daughter in lawe
Elzabeth Ousnet for my exequuter to demande & receive it.

An inventory of the goods of Mathew Kelly of Bishopp Warmoth in
the county of Durham, laborer, who deseased the 29ᵗʰ off December
in the twelft yeare of our lord King Charles, praysed by Michaell
Bryan, Jarrad Poots, Willi[a]m Burton & Anthony Cousnot, as
foloweth, 1636.

Imprimis, his purs & apparell		13s	4d
Item, one coverlid, thre hapings, two shortcods, one boulster, one paire blankets, & one ould fether beed & one pair of ould shetes	1	0s	0d
Item, seaven puter platers & one stone pott & one wodden cale		10s	0d
Item, one fring pann, one cap		1s	0d

In debts owing to the testator

Item	10	0s	0d
Totall	12	4s	4d
his funerall expenses	2	0s	0d
By legasi			5d

Michaell Bryan
Jarrad Pootts, his marke
William Burton, his marke
Anthony Ousnot, his mark

Source: DPR1/1/1636/K2/1, 2, paper 2ff.

69. Jane Smart of Sunderland, widow, 1637

In the name of God, amen, Jane Smart, her last will & testament, first,
I give my soule [to]³³ God & my body to the grave & all the meanes I
have I give as ffolloweth, v*idelicet*, item, to Jane Taylor a greate pott
& a brood pan \called an eitling/. Item, to Elizabeth Taylor my
coffer & what is in it, which stands in the low rowme; more I give

---

33 Omitted from the manuscript.

unto her a dozen napkins sued with blue & 1 drinking napkin & halfe a dozen napkins at bleaching; more 3 Dance potts of the greatest, 1 potle pott, 1 ayle pinte pott, half a gill pott & a table cloke which was he[........]. Item, to Richard Elbroughe 10ˢ. Item, to his sone Michell Elbroughe 10ˢ. Item, to Charles Anderson 10ˢ. Item, to Ambrose Taylor 10ˢ for a token. Item, to George Taylor 10ˢ. Item, to John Anderson a greate chist. Item, to his wife my gould ring which she hath already & ½ a dozen napkins which is at the bleaching. Item, to Margratt Huchison my best gowne & peticote. Item, to An Huchison, which was her <maid's> a gowne & a cote. Item, to Ellioner Lambert, a waste cote & a kirtle. [Item, to] [........] Headly, an owld gowne. Item, to An Shaftoe 2 little Dance potts. Item, to Marg[........] Cooke, 1 litle Dance pott. Item, to Eppie Dwes, 1 Dance pott that wants a knop. More I leave to bury me withal & to pay the cleanshers & what other charges Ambrose Taylor is at, to pay himselfe to the full out of the perticulers heireafter mencioned, videlicet,

Imprimis, 18 puder dishes, 6 or 7 candlestickess, 2 salts, 3 podin dishes, ½ a dozen spounes, 2 quarte, 1 pint & 1 gill pott. Item, a brasse mortar, a pestle, 2 pans, 1 beife pott, a podich pott, a paire of rackes, a iron chimney, a halberd, a bill staffe, a speite, a frying pan, a brand[yron ?], a paire of crankes, a brasse ladle, a pore, a paire of tongs, a paire of tosteing irons, 1 paire of potkilpes & 1 paire of racking crookes. Item, a square table, 1 rowned table, 3 bouffets stooles, 2 standbeds, 1 close bed, 1 fether bed, 2 wainescote chaires, 1 greene chaire, 1 white cheaire, a little table in the buttery, 1 cubbert, 1 chist & a coffer. Item, upon my owne bed, 1 rouge, 1 coverlead, 1 paire of blancketts, 1 roughe gowne, 1 feather bed, 1 boulster, 4 shorte cods & a calfe bed. Item, in the chist a paire of blancketts, 4 coverleades, 2 paire of line sheits, 2 paire of straking sheites & 2 table closes & a silver boule.

Which goods I leave Ambrose Taylor to be full executor & administrator & to despose of his selfe, being payed as he thinkes fitt, giving every child, which I was a witness to, a smale token, given in <perfect> memory before witness, this 4ᵗʰ May, 1637

                    Jane Smarte, her marke [*marked with a capital initial I*]
Witnes
Isabell Headley, her marke [*marked with a symbol*]
Margratt Wilson, her marke [*marked with a symbol*]

Interrogatoria ministranda ex parte Caroli Anderson, testibus productis et producendis ex parte Ambrosij Taylor, executoris pretensi, testes pretensi Janae Smart, vidua, nuper villae de Sunderland iuxta mare, defunctae.

1. Item, interrogetur quilibet testis an ex sua certa scientia sit testatricem predictam [sic] per totum tempus faccionis testamenti predicti sana fuisse memoria.

2. Item, interrogetur quilibet testis an dictum testamentum fuit scriptum ante mortem testatricis, et per quendem, et an testes predicti signavit [sic] huiusmodi testamentum manibus vel signis suis proprijs et in quo loco.

3. Item, interrogetur quilibet testis, in what place the said testatrix made her will and who was present in the same place or roome with her.

4. Item, interrogetur quilibet testis, if {they} \she/ did heare the testatrix dictate unto the clerke the severall bequests contained in the said will and if she was present & did see the testatrix when she did soe dictate & make her said will, and did the clerke write & sett downe the words soe dictated by the testatrix from her owne mouth or from whose.

5. Item, interrogetur quilibet testis, how many daies or houres did the said testatrix live after the makeing of her said will.

6. Item, interrogetur quilibet testis, at whose request or upon what occation she came to be present at the makeing of the said will and what reward she is promised or expecteth to receive for deposeing as a witnes of the said will.

7. Item, interrogetur quilibet testis, quantum valet in bonis suis proprijs <&> re alieno deducto.

DPR1/1/1637/S9/1–2, paper 2ff . The missing and doubtful readings in the will are the result of the manuscript having faded.

70. James Ryder of Sunderland, butcher, 1638

In the name of God, amen, xij[th] day of August, 1638, I, James Ryder of Sunderland[34] in the county of Durham, butcher, beinge sick in bodye but in perfect remembrance, thankes be to God, makes this my last will and testament. ffirst, I bequeath my bodye to be buryed where it shalbe thought ffit by my wife and ffreinds, and my soule to God almightie, hopeing to be saved by {the} his mercy through the

---

34 The manuscript repeats 'of Sunderland', but the repetition is deleted.

merits of his sonne, Jesus Christ, my redeemer. {ffirst} Item, I give to my sonne Marke Ryder ffifteene poundes and to my daughter Joan ffifteene poundes, and if it please God that my wife marye then my wife shall pay to either of them x^{li} more which will make them 25^{li} a piece for their porcions, which shalbe paid to them according as the rents shall arise out of the house and it shalbe paid at {they shall marye} \the tyme of their marradge/ or when they come at lawfull yeares. Item, I geve to my sonne William xiij^{li} vjs viijd and to my daughter Dorathye xiiij^{li} vjs viijd at the tyme they shall come to lawfull yeares, to be paid out of the rent of the houses, but it is intended, if my wife Doratye Ryder do not marrye, then their shalbe but paid to Marke and Joan, eyther of them, the said some of xv^{li} and to William and Doratye, my two yongest children, the said some of xiij^{li} vjs viijd a piece. Ffor all \the rest of / my goodes and estate I make my wife full executrix of this my last will and testament. In witness whereof I have setto my hande and sealethe day and yeare abovesaid,

James Ryder's mark [*no mark*]
Seal

Sealed & delivered in the presence of
George Lilburne [*full name signed*]
George Stevenson [*full name signed*]

August the 28th, 1638
A true inventory of the goods and chattels of James Ridar, late of Sunderland, deceased

Inprimis, his purse and his apparel	10	0s	0d
Item, in the hall, for an iron chimney and other things within the range	1	0s	0d
Item, for 3 chaires, 2 tables and 4 joynt stooles	1	0s	0d
Item, for a cubbert		13s	4d
Item, 10 peeces of puder		13s	4d
Item, 4 puder candelstickes and a brase candlstickes, a flagen, a salt and 2 boales		6s	8d
Item, 9 cushons		4s	6d
Item, in the parler, 2 tables, a chare, a joint stoole, a furme & a livery cubbert		16s	0d
Item, 2 carpencloths, 5 cushons and 2 boxes		10s	0d
Item, in the high chamber, 2 chaires, a table and a furme		10s	0d

Item, a cubbert and such things as is within it	1	0s	0d
Item, for a bedstead with a feather bed and other beding belonging and other beding above the bed with a webb of linen cloth and 5 cushons	4	0s	0d
Item, a trunke and linen therein contained	3	10s	0d
Item, a paire of iron bars		2s	6d
Item, the lease of the house and the appurtenances therto belonging	40	0s	0d
Item, in the flower chamber a servant bed with tubs and meale	1	13s	4d
Item, in the upper chamber a servant's bedd with a loadsadle		10s	0d
Item, for household stuffe in the kitching	2	0s	0d
Item, for worke geare in the shoppe		13s	4d
Item, for spares and deyles	5	0s	0d
Item, for buntings		8s	0d
Item, for 4 kyne	8	13s	4d
Item, for 2 mares	4	0s	0d
Item, for 4 swine	2	10s	0d
Item, for 7 sheepe	1	16s	0d
	91	9s	4d

Prasers
William Dossye [*full name signed*]
Humfrey Herrison [*full name signed*]
Willyam Thompson \for Scurfeild/[35] his marke

Joanna
Marke N[........]
Dorothea
Dorothea[36]

DPR1/1/1638/R16/1, 3, paper 2ff.

---

35 Inserted with two caret marks.
36 These names, which are those of the testator's wife and children, are written to the right of the names of the appraisers.

71. Christopher Dickinson of Sunderland, mariner, 1639

The xiijth daye of October, 1639

In the name of God, amen, the last will & testament of Christopher Dickinson, being sicke in bodie but in perfect memorie, thankes be to God. First, I bequeath my soule to God that created it, & my bodie to the [earth][37] where it shall please God it may lie. Imprimis, I give unto my wife Marie Dickinson the third part of my house lands in Sonderland during hir life & then to returne to my heires; also, after all debtes be discharged, one third part my other goods & chattell to be at hir owne disposing, & the rent of John Read house that he now liveth in for keeping of my daughter Anna Dickinson till she come at age, & my wife Marie to be tutor over hir & my sonne John Dickinson till they be both at lawfull age. Item, I give unto my son John Dickinson, when he cometh at age, the house that now William Nickolson liveth in & the reversion and rent of the house that now Mr John Pemerton liveth in, provided all wayes that the the foresaid house of William Nickolson's house be not of his mother's third; then my will is he should have his choyce where he should thinke be best to chuse for to live in, with the reversion of the other house aforesaid to him and his heires during my leases. Item I give unto my daughter Anna Dickinson hir third part beinge equally devided to hir and hir heires lawfullie begotten, but if it please God she die without isshew then to returne to the next heirs of the foresaid Christofer Dickinson. Item, I give unto my wife Marie Dickinson full tuition of my two children John Dickinson & Ana Dickinson, & do make them all executors if it may stand by law. Item, I give unto Elizabeth Dickinson, daughter of Thomase Dickinson, the sum of twenti shiling to be payd at the end of two years. Item, I do desire the monyes in the house or in the ship may be for the payment of my debts, & if they[38] amount to more my desire is that either that house now in building may be sould, or els the 4th part of the Peter,[39] or the houses theire rent, till my sonne John Dickinson shall come to the age of twentie & one yeares. Item I give unto my sister Ane Hansill five shilling & to all my brother & sisters children xij^d per peece at the end of two yeares, and to the poore of Scarbrough 6^s 8^d, & to the

---

37 The manuscript is illegible.
38 i.e., if the debits exceed the value of the cash in hand. The meaning of this problematic sentence would be helped if 'may be sould' followed 'theire rent'.
39 Apparently the name of a ship.

poore of Sonderland six shillings eight pence, besids what my wife
giveth at my funerall, at the end of two yeares as aforesaid.

Per me, Christofer Dickinson [*full name signed*]

Witnes here of
Georg Humble [*name in the testator's hand*]
John Husband, senior [*full name signed*]
John [........]

The inventorie of the goods and chatles of Christopher Dickinsonn of
Sunderland by the sea in the countie of Durham, mariner, deceassed,
made and approved by Thomas Atkinson, John Hardcastle, Robert
Collingwood and Gorge Humble, the six daye of January in the xv^th
yeare of our gratious Kinge Charles his raign, annoque Domini 1639

Imprimis, readie mony in his purse		[........]	
Item, his apparrell	3	0s	0d
In the hall or forhouse			
Item, one table, one forme, 4 chaires		10s	8d
Item, two glasse cases, iij joynt stooles		6s	0d
Item, one small mappe, the x commandements set in a frame of woode		3s	0d
Item, one seinge glasse, one houre glasse, iij cushinges		6s	8d
Item, xij earthen dishes, iij earthen jugges		3s	0d
Item, one pare of iron barres, 1 reckon croke, j broylinge iron, one fflesh hooke, one smoothinge iron, j fringe pane, one fire shovell, one pare tonges, one rostinge iron, one pare of crankes		12s	0d
Item, two muskets, one sword, one bandeller, one head peece	1	0s	0d
Item, one band pott, one fflagon pott, five puter candlesticks, three salts, 3 taysters, j cupp, nine platters, iiij sallet dishes, six saussers, 4 pottin-dishes, half a gill pott, a quarter of a gill pott, half a dozen tine spones	1	6s	8d
Item, two brushes, one grater			6d
Item, one silver boule, iiij sillver spones	3	0s	0d
Item, one brasse pott, one brasse morter, j iron pestell, two brasse candlestickes, one brasse chaffing dishe, one litle brasse pane and one old brasse kettle		10s	0d

In the parloure

Item	£	s	d
Item, one beed stead with one feather beed, two boulsters, two blankets, one coverlet, one pare of sheets, five curtaines and a vallance	3	0s	0d
Item, one liverie cupbord, one putter basson and sewer, one cupbord cloath, ij cushinges	1	1s	0d
Item, one table, two chists, ij boxes, j casse with glasse botles	1	0s	0d
Item, thre wrought cushinges		10s	0d
Item, five pare of sheets, foure pillows, ij tablecloathes, one dozen napkins	2	2s	0d
Item, one lanthorne, one chamber pott		2s	0d

In the chamber

Item	£	s	d
Item, one beed stead, j feather beed, j boulster, one pillowe, two old hapines, j old coverlet	2	0s	0d
Item, divers bookes		16s	0d
Item, one truckell beed stead, one flocke beed, ij pillows, one pillowbare, ij old hapines, j coverlett		10s	0d
Item, one old table, one old trunke, two old chists		6s	0d
Item, one old sadle one pillion seat		3s	0d
Item, two pare searffers, one sin, one old tubb		2s	0d

In the chichine

Item	£	s	d
Item, one pare of barres, one pare of racke of iron, one reckon croke, one spit, two iron potts, two pott hocks, one treedinge knife, j pare bellowes		13s	4d
Item, one iron ketle, one earthen pott, 3 payles, j collender, iij small runlets, iij dozen trenchers, vj wooden dishes		8s	0d
Item, one old spence, v old chaires, one old forme		6s	0d

In the backsid

Item	£	s	d
Item, five old casks and a longsetle		4s	6d
Item, one gray mare	1	19s	6d
Item, one cow with the haye	3	0s	0d
Item, in the house, where William Nicholson now dwelleth, two cupbords, one old lead furnace	1	8s	4d
Item, one quarter of a shipe or barke called the Useter	14	0s	0d
Item, the value of the interest of one lease of a house in Sunderland aforsaid	13	6s	8d
Soms	61	16s	10d

Depts owinge to him			
Item, by Henry Kirkinsonne, being desperat dept	1	9s	0d
Item, by Widdowe Baude		13s	0d
Item, by Robert Horsley		10s	0d
Item, by John Read		15s	0d
Item, by Robert Creaswell	1	0s	0d
Item, by Lanslott Swinbourne, desperate dept	1	10s	0d
Item, by Henry Sargison		5s	0d
Som is	6	2s	0d
Houshold stuffe the som is	61	18s	10d
Som total is	67	18s	10d
Som of depts owinge by him is	60	16s	7d
Remaininge of the goods in the inventorye more than the depts	7	2s	3d

Wee whose names are above specified have heare to sette our hands
as praysser of these goods <above> ben set downe
Robert Collingwood
George Humble
Thomas Atkinson
John Hardcastell

Depts owinge by him			
Item, legacies give by his will	2	8s	4d
Item, to Mr William Cadwell	11	13s	0d
Item, to William Watt	10	16s	0d
Item, to Gorge Humble	7	0s	0d
Item, to Mr Gorge Libourne	4	14s	3d
Item, to Mrs Saray ffreman	3	15s	0d
Item, to Robert Newlove		10s	0d
Item, to William Potts		3s	2d
Item, to John Scurfeild	1	16s	10d
Item, to Marye Dickinson, daugher to Thomas Dickinson	2	12s	0d
Item, to Thomas Atkinsonne		12s	0d
Item, to John Cutfourth	2	6s	6d
Item, to Humphrey Harissonne	1	0s	0d
Item, to the five children of Thomas Dickinson	5	0s	0d
Som is	54	8s	1d
Item, ffor funeral charges	6	8s	6d
Som totallis	60	16s	7d

Source: DPR1/1/1639/D3/1–3, paper 2ff.

72. John Hilton of Bishopwearmouth, yeoman, 1639

The last will and testament of John Hilton of Bishoppwarmoth in the county of Durham, yeoman, who is sicke in body but perfect in remembrance, praised be God, made the second day of August, 1639. ffirst, I bequeath my soule to my savior Jesus Christ, through whose merits I hope to be saved, and my[40] body to the earth from whence it came. Item, I give to my sonne John 8 oxen, 4 horses and mares, and six kine, and 2 whyes and a stirke, and 24 sheepe, and 5 swine, and all my plow geare and waine geare, and my croppe of wheat growing upon the ground. Item, I give to my wife the one halfe of my land after my death, for her life, and the other halfe to my sone John, and, after my wife's death, all to my sonne. Item, I give to my sone 3 calves in the fallow. Item, I give to my sister Elsabeth foure pounds a yeare dureing her life and a rood of land in every feald, to be wrought according to the custome of the towne. Item, I give to the poore twenty shillings. In witnes of the same, I have hereunto set my hand, the day and yeare above written.

John Hilton's marke [marked with a scratch]

Witnes hereof
Adam Burden [full name signed]
William Thompson, his marke [marked with a symbol]
John Scurfeild [full name signed]

An invatory of the goods and catels of John Hilton of Bishopp-warmouth, praysed by us whose names are under, this 14 day of August, 1639.

Item, his apparell and purse	3	6s	8d

In the fore house

Tenn pece of puter doblers		17s	0d
One quart pote & one pinte pote and drinking pots		4s	6d
Thre candlestickes and one salt		2s	6d
One litle pote and one litle ketle and tow ould pans		10s	0d
One recken croke with tongs, pors & broyling irons and one spete		5s	0d
Tow skeles, tow canns, foure chese fats and one peck		4s	0d
Tow cuberts, one table, tow formes and one chare	1	10s	0d

---

40 The manuscript has 'by'.

In the chamber

One bedstede, one table, one cauell, tow stands, one flackett	12s	0d

In the loft

One horle bed, one chest, tow tubs, foure pookes, foure seves & ridles, one timses, one covering, one shet, one blankett	11s	0d

The crop one the ground with the hay	60	0s	0d
Eight oxen	37	0s	0d
Six kine	13	0s	0d
Thre young beasts	4	0s	0d
Thre calfes	1	10s	0d
One hors, tow mares, & one stagg	13	0s	0d
Foure tene eyes & elleven lambes	5	0s	0d
Foure swine	1	13s	4d
Tow long waynes & wheles	3	15s	0d
Tow coup wanes & wheles	2	0s	0d
Seven yokes, five somes	1	0s	0d
Thre plowes & tow pare of plow irons		13s	0d
One oxe harrow & tow hors harrowes		13s	4d
Tow pare of hors geare		3s	0d
Thre muck forkes and foure corne forkes & five rakes		5s	4d
Corne in the leath, threshed & unthreshed, valyed to	1	10s	0d
One coke and 4 henes		2s	6d

The sum totall is 153^{li} 8^s 2^d

Raphe Hollme [*full name signed*]
Robart Pattisone [*full name signed*]
Edward Harper [*full name signed*]

Debts oweing by the testator

Imprimis, ffunerall expences & maintienance	3	3s	0d
Item, owing to Mr Johnson	5	0s	0d
Item, Ann Lambe	1	0s	0d
Item, Mr Lilburne	1	0s	6d
Item, to Edward Anderson	6	8s	0d
Item, to Mr Gray		18s	0d
Item, to John Shepperson		18s	0d
Item, to Thomas Snowdon	1	1s	0d
Item, to Peter Greene		9s	4d

Item, to Humphrey Harrieson		15s	0d
Item, to Richard Martindale		6s	0d
Item, to Ann Basnet		2s	6d
Item, to Merill ffletcher		7s	0d
Item, to Mrs Burgaine		4s	6d
Item, to William Caldwell		9s	6d
Item, to Elizabeth Snowdon		1s	6d
Item, to Mr Lilburne		6s	0d
Item, to Sisley Robinson	1	3s	0d
Item, to Robert Moodie		5s	4d
Item, to Mr Nichallson of Hartlepool	2	10s	0d
Item, to John Miller	2	10s	0d
Item, to John Marshall	3	5s	0d
Item, to George Whitehead	2	0s	0d
Item, Marget Humble		11s	0d
Item, to Mr Wright	1	7s	0d
Item, Mr Robert Porrett		9s	0d
Item, to Niminie Hodgson		5s	4d
Item, to Widdow Ferriebie		16s	0d
Item, to Thomas Turbut		14s	0d
Item, Ralph Greene upon a bill		[no entry]	
Sum	36	2s	4d

Source: DPR1/1/1639/H7/1, 3–4, paper 3ff.

73. Reginald Fawcett of Fulwell, yeoman, 1639

In the name of God, amen, the eleaventh day of October in the yeare of the reigne of our Soveraigne Lord 1639, I, Reginald ffawcett of ffulwell in the countie of Durham, yeoman, being of good, whole & perfect remembrance, all laud and prayse be to almightie God, doe make this my last will & testament in manner & forme following, videlicet: ffirst, I commend my soule to almightie God, my maker & redeemer, & my bodie to be buryed in the church of Monck-warmouth. I will that my goods, chattels & debts be devyded into three equall parts, whereof I will that Ann ffawcett, my wife, shall have one equall parte to hir owne proper use, in manner & purpote & reasonable to hir, of all my goods & chattels. And the second equall parte of all my said goods & chattels I bequeath and give unto John ffawcett, my sonne. Item, I give and bequeath unto Willyam Matthew, my wyve's sonne, tenn pounds of the other thirde parte or proporcion of my goods & if he returne forth of the Low Countrie with his life to the place where he was borne, and to be paid by my executor within one yeare after his said returne. Item, I give to everye one of the children of William Roxbie five shillings. Item, I give to everye one of the children of George Craggs five shillings. Item, I give to everye one of the children of Richard Matthew, deceased, fyve shillings. Item, I gyve to everye one of the children of John ffawcett five shillings. Item, I gyve to the poore of the parishe ffortie shillings. Item, I gyve unto John Kitchin tenn shillings. Item, I gyve to everye one of my servants two shillings. Item, I give to Ann ffawcett, my wife, two of my best oxen. Item, I gyve unto Mr Richard Hicks, curatt of the sayd parishe, tenn shillings. Item, I give unto Thomas Taylor of Warmouth and Raiphe Lumley of ffulwell, eyther of them, tene shillings, and doe maike them supervisors[41] of this my last will and testament. Item, I give all the rest of my goods & chattels, my debts, legaces & funeral expenses[42] discharged. Item, all the rest of my good and chattel unbequeathed, unto John ffawcett, my sonn, who I doe appoint and make him my executor of this my last will and testament. In witness whereof, I have setto my hand & seale the day and yeare first above written.

Reginald ffawcett [*signature and seal*]

Selled and signed in the presence of
John Kitchin, William ffawcett, Raph Lumley, Thomas Tayler [*full names signed*]

October the 22th day,
An inventorye of all the goods and chattlels, moveable and immoveable of Reignald ffawcett of ffulwell, deceased, & praised by fower indifferrent men, Anthonye Younge, Thomas Taylor, Christopher Shipperdson, Raphe Lumley, 1639

In primis, one yoke of oxen given to his wife	10	13s	4d
Item, two yoke of oxenn prised at	20	0s	0d
Item, four younge steers prised at	12	0s	0d
Item, tenn kine and two whyes prised at	35	0s	0d
Item, eight younge steers and whyes prised at	11	0s	0d
Item, seaven stirkes prised at	4	10s	0d
Item, seaven horsse and meares prised at	29	0s	0d

41 The manuscript repeats 'and doe make them supervisors'.
42 'expepenses' in MS.

Item, ffortie nine ould sheepe with fourteene hoggs prised at	19	0s	0d
Item, corne and haye in the barne and stakyard prised at	70	0s	0d
Item, wheate one the grounde growinge	32	0s	0d
Item, twente swine prised at	7	10s	0d
Item, plowe and ploughe geare, wayne and waine geare prised at	8	0s	0d
Item, ffive geece with other pultree prised at		13s	0d
Item, in the hall house, two cubbords, one cawells, one table, two ffurmes with other implements	3	15s	0d
Item, in the parlor, one presse, one table, two bed-steads with one hure bedd, thre chists, thre chaires, thre stooles prised at	5	15s	0d
Item, in the hey chamber, two bedsteeds, fours chists with other implements prised at	1	10s	0d
Item, in brasse vessel with other implements	3	15s	0d
Item, one chimnee, one paire of barres with other irone implements prised at	1	10s	0d
Item, two feathere beds with thre boulsters and tenn shorte kodds, five mattrisses, sixe coverledds, eighte hapinges, thre paire of blankets, prised at	12	6s	0d
Item, seaven lininge sheets with aleaven pair of strakinge sheets and other lininge prised at	5	6s	8d
Item, tubbs, skeeles and boules with other woodden vessel prised at	1	4s	0d
Item, two plowe beames prised at		3s	0d
Item, one windowe clothe, one kilne haire, with other implements prised at	1	10s	0d
Item, one longe gune with a shorte gune prised at	1	8s	0d
Item, one musket with hir firniture	1	10s	0d
Item, one grindstone with six stone trowes		12s	0d
Item, in goulde and money	26	13s	0d
Item, one silver belte prised at	1	10s	0d
Item, his apperell prised at	5	0s	0d
Item, thre silver sponnes prised at		16s	0d
Item, two silver rings & two clasps		4s	0d
Item, one steepe stone prised at		10s	0d

The sume of this is 334^{li} 6^s 0^d

DPR1/1/1639/F3/1,3, paper6 ff., part sewn.

74. Richard Halliman of Sunderland, yeoman, 1640

An inventory of the goodes of Richard Halliman of Sunderland in the county of Durham, yeoman, who deseased the 18th day of December, anno Domini 1639 and in the fifteenth yeare of the reigne of our dreade soveraigne lord, King Charles, praysed by Edward Harper, John Johnson, Thomas Halliman & Michael Bryan, as foloweth

The inventory of his goods in Sunderland

Imprimis, his purse & apparrell, priced at	6	6s	8d
Item, a bible & a testament, with other bokes & paper	1	11s	4d
Item, fiften puter dishes & fower lesser platers, two puter basons, six pottingers, five sassors, thre quarte potts, five candelstickes, fower flowerpots, fower saltes & a stone jady	2	1s	6d
Item, a beare bowel & a wine cupe & fower spowens of silver	4	0s	0d
Item, a little table & a forme, a chare & a cradell		10s	0d
Item, a deske & a chare		8s	0d
Item, a musket & a rest		10s	0d
Item, a paire of barres and a paire of tonges & a pore, with other nesesaries		7s	0d
Item, a fether bed, a paire of blankets, a covering and a rauge, two bolsters, two pillow cods, with walons & curtaines	4	0s	0d
Item, five linen shetes & thre paire of scoarse [........], pillibers, tenn nacpkines, nine of a better sort, & two tabell clothes		[........]	
Item, paire of curtaines & vallones & a cerpet cloth		12s	0d
Item, six stoules, fower chares & seaven quisions	1	0s	0d
Item, a litle presser & a table		6s	8d
Item, a paire of iron bares		3s	4d
Item, a flocke bed & a mattris, a paire of shetes, a paire of blankets, two coverlides & two fether codes	1	3s	4d
Item, a litle cubord and a table, a chist & a stoule, two boxes & a voyder and two temeses		13s	0d
Item, a winding cloth & fower pockes		5s	4d
Item, thre bowels of malt and a bushell of wheate	1	6s	8d
Item, thre pottes & five panes, two cettels with other impliments in the cihering	2	13s	4d
Item, two beding of cloth for the servants bedes		13s	4d

Item, twenty hole kaskes & tenn half kaskes	1	15s	0d
Item, an ould bed sted & ould bords, thre sceales, thre washing tubs & an ould flacet		10s	0d
Item, hopes, prised at	2	13s	4d
Item, two wea balcks & a paire of scales with the weaghts		10s	0d
Item, half a hundred dales	1	10s	0d
Item, a bushell tub		2s	0d
Item, a sow & seaven shotes	2	5s	0d
Item, a cow & a peas hay	3	0s	0d
Item, a gray mare	7	0s	0d
Item, a lease of a house in Sunderland	15	0s	0d

An inventorie of the goods in Norton

Imprimis, a bed sted & a table, a cubbord and a cawell, a long setell, two chares, a trinel bed, stockes, two chistes, a litle chare and an iron chimny	2	10s	0d
Item, fower yockes, thre sowmes with other impelmentes		13s	4d

Debtes which others owe to the testator

Item, for beare as doth appeare by the bocke	27	5s	0d
Item, by the cealemen as by the bocke appears	3	19s	5d

Debtes owing by the said testator as foloweth

Imprimis, to John Wheately of Norton	30	0s	0d
Item, to widow Wilson of Norton	14	0s	0d
Item, to my brother Thomas Halliman of <Haswell>	18	0s	0d
Item, to Simond Lackanby of Shadforth	8	0s	0d
Item, to Mistris James of Durham	12	0s	0d
Item, to Edward Gurrat of Scarbrough	26	0s	0d
Item, to Thomas Ayre of Tunstall	3	5s	0d
Item, to Adam Burden of the Panes	46	8s	4d
Item, to John Cocke of Burlinton	1	2s	0d
Item, to Henery Becke of Whitby		12s	0d
Item, to William Haman of Line	5	0s	0d
Item, to Ralph Bericke of Thorpe	1	5s	0d
Item, to my brother William Halliman as by a bond doth appeare	4	[........]	
Item, to William Dossy	1	0s	0d
Item, to my servant John	1	5s	0d
Item, his funerall expences	7	0s	0d

Item, to the poore people		10s	0d
Item, for a mortuary & a larestale		16s	8d

Edward Harper [*full name signed*]
John Johnson [*full name signed*]
Thomas Halliman, mark [*marked with a cross*]
Michaell Bryan [*full name signed*]

Source: DPR1/1/1640/H4/1–4, parchment 3mm. sewn.

75. William Thompson of Sunderland Panns, smith, 1640

Aprile 17th, 1640
The comprisers off the goods off the late deceased William Thomson, smith, off Sunderland Pans, comprised be the persons underwritten, William Blacket, Richard Smith, Thomas Lassie, Richard Wilkinson, James Bently and Richard Johnson

West chamber

One bedstead, one fetherbed one paire off sheets, on coverlet, a rug and courtains		3	10s	0d
One table, a carpet, a chair, 4 stooles			13s	4d
One pair off barrs			5s	0d
	Summa	4	8s	4d

East chamber

One bedstead, a fetherbed and a boulster		2	0s	0d
One trindle bed, with furniture for servants			6s	8d
One table, 2 forms and a chair			6s	0d
One liverie table			10s	0d
One presse			8s	0d
One glasse case with 9 earthen dishes			2s	3d
One pair off barrs, a pair off tongs, a fyre shovell,			5s	0d
5 pound lynt, 2 pounds tow, 2 reeles			4s	0d
	Summa	4	3s	11d

South chamber

36 bouls off white rye		10	0s	0d
1 bushell off wheate			4s	0d
A measureing bushell			2s	0d
One peece off seckweb			3s	0d

One ould bedstead, one ould flockbed		3s	0d
One fetherbed, one matriss, 2 bolsters, 6 pillowes	4	0s	0d
7 blankets	2	0s	0d
4 coverlets, 2 hapings	2	6s	8d
4 cushons		4s	0d
5 lynn sheets	1	0s	0d
9 cod pillowears		9s	0d
7 napkins		5s	0d
5 strakeing sheets		15s	0d
10 course sheets	1	0s	0d
12 yeards off dyper		14s	0d
4 chests and a seai[n]g glasse		10s	6d
1 table cloth		2s	6d
Off linning and harden yarne		10s	0d
Summa	24	13s	8d

High loft

6 dozen off shovells	1	4s	0d
19 scoopes		12s	0d
One bedstead, 2 hapings, on sheete for the servants		8s	0d
40 dozen off shovell irons	4	0s	0d
2,000 hitch naills		16s	0d
2,000 single tack	1	10s	0d
15 pounds spickes		4s	6d
17 set irons, 2 hookes		6s	8d
100 scopper naill, 100 tingle naill			10d
Summa	9	2s	0d

The hall

A eemptie bedstead		8s	0d
A table, 2 formes, 2 stooles, 2 chairs		10s	0d
One cupboord	1	10s	0d
16 peece off peuter	2	0s	0d
3 quart pots		4s	6d
One flagon		6s	0d
3 drinking cups, [........] cellers		3s	0d
A chamber pot		1s	6d
3 pair broyling irons, one choping knyff, one brander		4s	0d
A pair off barrs, 2 recking crookes, a pair off tongs with a porr		16s	0d
2 baccon flecks		10s	0d
Summa	6	13s	0d

The kitchin

	£	s	d
One pair barrs, recking crook, one pair racks, one coal-rack, one dropping pann, 2 pair pot hooks, on peele	1	4s	0d
2 po[........]⁴³		6s	0d
2 brasse pots		10s	0d
2 brew kettles, 3 panns, a <scumer>	1	18s	0d
1 frying pann, a little brasse pann		1s	6d
3 stooles, one table, 1 fou[rme]		4s	0d
One stone trough		1s	0d
7 tubs		5s	0d
3 baskets, 1 pair timps		2s	0d
4 <skeels>		4s	0d
Dishes and bouls		1s	6d
In the backside, 4 tubs		4s	0d
Summa	5	11s	0d

The cellar

		s	d
For 7 barrels, 1 tub, 2 butter kits		9s	0d
A pig		4s	0d
Summa		13s	0d

The shopp

	£	s	d
2 pair off bellowes	1	6s	8d
2 anvils		10s	0d
1 standing bore, 5 small ones		3s	0d
5 pair tongs, 2 scuffers, 2 pors		5s	0d
4 fore hammers		10s	0d
4 up and doun hammers		5s	0d
6 hand hammers		3s	0d
1 chaire, 3 bolsters, one crooke studie		6s	0d
4 hew irons, 2 pinnces			6d
1 pair off scales, one iron balk, 3 hookes		6s	8d
Off <new> iron unwrought	2	18s	4d
For a barr off steele		4s	8d
For [........]	2	9s	6d
[........]⁴⁴	2	0s	0d
6 small anchors	3	6s	8d

---

43 MS faded.
44 Two words illegible and torn.

Off leade a half hundreths ¼ in weights			13s	0d
More in small weights off lead			2s	0d
	Summa	15	10s	0d

In a part off a shopp		36	0s	0d
2 kine		7	0s	0d
In debts		46	0s	0d
In bonds		4	0s	0d
3 hens			1s	6d
In his clothes and his purse		3	6s	8d
	Summa	96	8s	2d

24th April

Prysers, William Black, Thomas Lassie, Richard Johnson, James Bently, [........] houses and shopp with the appertenances thereto belonging		90	0s	0d
	Summa of all	267	3s	1d

Richard Wilkinson, William Blackett [*full names signed*]
Richard Smith, Thomas Lassie [*full names signed*]
Richard Johnson [*full name signed*]
James Bently, [mark] [*marked with a capital initial I*]

Ressaved from William Blacket which was owand		5	0s	0d

Debts owand be the testator

To William Reede		10	0s	0d
To William Pots		5	0s	0d
To Martines Crane		2	10s	0d
To Thomas Anderson		2	0s	0d
	Summa	19	10s	0d
More to Edward Harper		1	1s	0d
	Summa	20	11s	0d

In particular charges

For wyn		1	6s	8d
For cakes		1	14s	0d
For ale and beere		1	4s	0d
For cheeses			14s	0d
For a coffin			6s	0d
For a funerall sermon			12s	0d

For lining and [........]⁴⁵		7s	0d
To the poore		10s	0d
[........] with the prysers		8s	0d
Charges to Durham		4s	0d
Ch [........]		5s	4d
	Summa is	7 11s	0d
	Summa	28 2s	0d

Desperate debts			
Be Mʳ Robert Lampton		2 15s	0d
Be John Thomson in a bonde		10 0s	0d
Be Robert Currisone for one anchor		1 5s	0d
	Summa is	14 0s	0d
[one word illegible] be the testator athwell⁴⁶ for Rye		15 0s	0d

Source: DPR1/1/1640/T2/1–4, paper 4ff.

76. Henry Hilton of Hilton, esquire, 1640

In the name of God, amen, the six and twentieth day of ffebruarie in the sixteenth yeare of the raigne of our soveraigne lord Charles by the grace of God kinge of England, Scotland, ffrance and Ireland, defender of the faith &c., annoque Domini 1640, I, Henry Hilton of Hilton in the countie palatine of Durham, esquire, being sicke in bodie but of an able, perfect and disposeing memory, for which I thanke my lord God, doe make, declare & ordaine my last will and testament in manner and forme following, renounceing hereby all former wills by me made. And herein I willingly give upp & resigne my soule into the hands of almighty God, my maker, and my sweete saviour Jesus Christ, my redeemer, and the Holy Ghost, my sanctifier, nothing doubting but confidently beleeving that by the bitter death and passion of my lord and saviour Jesus I shalbe eternally saved. And I bequeath my body to the earth to be decently interred, without all vaine pompe and glory, in some parte of the cathedral church of St Paule's, London, as neere the place where the tombe of Doctor Dunne is erected as conveniently maybe, in such

---

45 This and the following entries suffer from tearing and fading of the manuscript.
46 Apparently meaning 'as well'.

sort and manner as my executrix and executors hereafter named shall thinke fitt. And wheras I have heretofore by sufficient conveyance & assurance in lawe, bearing date aboute the seaven and twentieth day of June in the twelfe yeare of the raigne of our said soveraigne lord King Charles of England &c., annoque Domini 1636, conveyed and setled on Sr Garret Kempe, knight, and his heires, all my mannors, lands, tenements and hereditaments in the aforesaid county palatine of Durham, which said conveyance and assurance was made to the said Sr Garrett Kempe as a frende in trust to that use, intent and purpose that he and his heires should stand and be seysed thereof, and should convey and assure the same to such person & persons, use and uses, intents & purposes as I should either by my last will & testament or otherwise declare, limit & appoint, which said conveyance I doe hereby ratifie & confirme and doe, by this my last will & testament, declare my intent & purpose concerninge the said use and uses and the said use and uses to be as is hereafter in this my will expressed and declared: that is to saye, of, for and concerning all the said mannors, lands, tenements and hereditaments, with the appurtenances in the same conveyance and assurance mencioned and expressed or any manner of way intended to be by the same conveyed to the lord maior of the cittie of London, for the tyme being and to foure of the senior aldermen of the said cittie of London for the tyme being. And to them I doe by this my will give and bequeath the same to have & to hould to them and their successors the lord maior and foure senior aldermen of the said cittie of London for the tyme being, for and dureing the full tyme and terme of foure score and nyneteen yeares to commence from and ymediatly after my decease, giveing and by this my will graunting unto the said lord maior and foure senior aldermen for the tyme being, full power and authority to demise, graunt & let to farme the said premises by lease or otherwise for the best advantage, rent and proffit they can, and to have, receave and take the rents, yssues and proffits of the said mannors & premises, with the appurtenanc[e]s, for and dureing the said terme of foure score & nyneteene yeares, which said rents, yssues and proffits soe to be by them received, I doe herby appoint, order and declare shalbe by them disposed of, during the said terme of four score and nyneteen yeares, to such person and persons and to such use and uses, intents and purposes as is hereafter in this my will declared: that is to say, unto the church wardens and overseers of the poore of the severall parrishes hereafter named, yearly and every yeare, dureing the said terme of four score and nyneteene yeares, foure and twenty pounds to

everyone of the said parrishes, videlicet in the said county palatine of
Durham to the churchwardens & overseers of the poore of the
parrish of Hilton foure & twenty pounds, of the parrish of ffullwell
foure and twenty pounds, of the parrish of Warmouth foure &
twenty pounds, of the parrish of Ousworth Magna foure and twentie
pounds, of the parrish of Hartlepoole foure and twentie pounds, of
the parrish of Lumly foure and twenty pounds, of the parrish of
Gateside foure and twenty pounds, of the parrish of Chester in the
Streete foure and twenty pounds, of the parrish of Herrington foure
and twenty pounds, of the parrish of fferryhill foure and twenty
pounds, of the parrish of Darleton foure and twenty poundes, of the
parrish of Sunderlande foure and twenty pounds, of the parrish of
Houghton foure & twenty pounds, of the parrish of Renton foure
and twenty pounds, of the parrish of Branspeth foure and twenty
pounds, of the parrish of Lanchester foure and twenty pounds, of the
parrish of Bertly foure and twenty pounds, of the parrish of South
Streete foure and twenty pounds; and in the county of Sussex, where
I now live, unto the churchwarden & overseers of the poore of the
severall parrishes hereafter named, foure & twenty pounds a peece
to everyone of the said parrishes, videlicet of the parrish of Clapham
foure and twenty pounds, of the parrish of Patching foure and
twenty pounds, of the parrish of Subdeanry alias St Peter's the
greater in the citty of Chichester foure and twenty pounds, of the
parrish of Awdon foure and twenty pounds, of the parrish of Tarring
foure and twenty pounds, of the parrish of Palinge foure and twenty
pounds, of the parrish of Arundell foure and twenty pounds, of the
parrish of Angmering foure and twenty pounds, of the parrish of
Selsey foure and twenty pounds, of the parrish of Steanning foure
and twenty pounds, of the parishe of Bramber foure and twenty
pounds, of the parrish of Brighthelinston foure and twenty pounds,
of the severall parrishes in Lewes foure and twenty pounds in the
wholle, and my meaneing is not to give to every parrish in Lewes
foure and twenty pounds but to them all, to be devided amongst
them by equall proporcions, to the parrish of new Shoreham foure
and twenty pounds; and in the county of Surry to the churchwardens and overseers of the poore of the severall parrishes
hereafter named, foure & twenty pounds to everyone of the said
parrishes, videlicet of the parrishe of Walton super Thames foure and
twenty pounds, to the parrish of Richmond foure and twenty
pounds, to the parrish of Lambeth foure & twenty pounds, to the
parrish of Camberwell foure & twenty pounds, to the parrish of
Dorking foure & twenty pounds, and alsoe to the churchwardens &

overseers of the poore of the parish of St Clements Danes in the countie of Middlesex foure and twenty pounds, and also to the maior for the tyme being of the towne of Newcastle upon Tyne foure and twenty pounds, and also to the maior of the cittie of Durham for the tyme being eight and fortie pounds; which said some of foure and twenty pounds soe to to be paied to the maior of Newcastle upon Tyne for tyme being I will order and doe declare my intent and meaning as that he shall yearly pay the same over to the severall churchwardens and overseers of the part in the severall parrishes and overseers of the poore in the severall parrishes of Newcastle upon Tyne; and also that the said eight and fortie pounds soe to be payed to the maior of Durham for the tyme being, I will, order and declare my intent and meaneing is that he shall yearly paye the same over to the severall church wardens and overseers of the poore in the severall parrishes within the said cittie of Durham; and further declare my will and meaneing to be that all the said several sommes of money soe to be payed as aforesaid to the said severall church-wardens and overseers of the poore of all and every the before mencioned severall parrishes yearly and every yeare, dureing the said terme of fourscore & nyneteen years, I will, order, bequeath & direct that the same severall sommes of money shalbe by the said severall churchwardens & overseers of the poore of the said severall parrishes yearly and every yeare forthwith uppon the receipt thereof paied unto and desposed of amongst the poorest inhabitants in the said severall parrishes, geveing to everyone of the said poore inhabitants fortie shillings a peece to every one of them. And I further declare my will and meaneing to be that the churchwardens and overseers of the poore of the said severall parrishes, for the tyme being, shall at the next generall sessions of the peace to be houlden in the severall counties or citties where the said severall parrishes doe lye, after the receite of the said severall sommes of mony and disbursement thereof as aforesaid, give and deliver upp fairly written in parchm[e]nt yearly to the iustices of the peace, then there assembled, a true and perfect note of all the names of such person and persons to whome the said sommes of fortie shillings have beene by them yearly soe payed, which note I desire should be filed upp and kept amongst the records of the same sessions. I further give and bequeath, order and direct to be likewise paied out of the said rents, yssues and proffits of the said mannors and premisses, unto the heire at lawe of my brother John Hylton, one hundred pounds per annum dureing the said terme of fourscore and nyneteene yeares, at two usuall feasts or termes in the yeare, that is to saye at the feast the Annunciacion of the Blessed Virgin Mary and St Michaell the Archangell, by equall porcions, the first payment thereof to begin at which of those feasts first comeing after my decease. Item, I give and bequeath unto the viccar of the parrish church of Monkewarmouth in the countie palatine of Durham and his successors, viccars of the said church, out of the said rents, yssues and proffits of the said mannors, lands & premises, ffyftie pounds per annum, dureing the said terme of forscore and nyneteene years, to be payed at two feasts or termes of the yeare. Item, I give and bequeath to my brother Robert Hylton dureing his n[atu]rall life, and after his decease to his next heire at law, provided alwayes yt be not such a one as is heire at lawe to my said brother John Hylton, ffor yt is my intent that noe such heire shall receave and have both the said sommes of one hundred pounds and of fyftie pounds. And yf it shall happen soe to fall out that any such one shall be heire at law to both my said brothers, where by he maye be intituled to receave both the said sommes of money, then my will and meaneing is that such heire at lawe of my said brother, John Hylton, shall only receave the said somme of one hundred pounds per annum and not the said somme of fyftie pounds per annum but that the said ffyftie pounds per annum shalbe yearly paied dureing the remainder of the said terme of fourscore and nyneteene yeares to the next heire at lawe of my said brother Robert, the said heire of my said brother John Hylton being sett aside. And as concerning the residue of the said rents, yssues and proffits of the said mannors, lands & premisses, the said former payments in this my will appointed to be paied out of the same being first payed and satisffied, my will and meaneing is, and soe I give and bequeath the residue of the said rents, yssues and and proffits to my next heire at lawe, ffor I doe hereby declare to my greife that yf any person shall pretend tobe a childe of my body begotten, which I hope noe body will be so impudent and shameles, I hereby calling God and man to wittnes that I have noe childe liveing of my body begotten and if any such shall pretend soe to be I hereby declare he or she soe doeing to be a very imposture, and I hope noe body will undertake to doe such a shamlesse, dishonest and impudent act. And he or shee soe declareing to be my childe I doe hereby utterly denounce and disclayme them, declareing that noe such childe shalbe reputed to be my heire-at-law or to have any part or porcion of any of my mannors lands, tenements and hereditaments or any of my estate reall or personall. Alsoe, whereas I am seised in fee of and in divers lands, tenements & hereditaments in the countie of Wilteshire, my will and meaneing is and I doe

hereby give and bequeath the same to the said lord maior and foure
senior aldermen of the said cittie of London for the tyme being and
their sucessors for and dureing the said terme of four score and
nyneteene years, to commence from and ymediately after my
decease, giveing them full power & authoritie to demise, graunt, lett
and dispose thereof and to receave, have and take the rents, yssues
and profitts of the same for and dureing the said terme, and out of
the said rents, yssues and profitts to defalcate and allowe to
themselves and their successors, the lord maior and foure senior
aldermen of the said cittie for the tyme being, the somme of one
hundred pounds per annum, to be equally devided amongst them
for their paines and care to be had and taken in the managing,
ordering and disposeing of such thing, as I have in this my will left
unto them to be managed, ordered and disposed hereby, heartily
desireing them not to be scrupulous nor to think much of the takeing
on them the burthen of executing and performing of these things I
have hereby referred to them. And for that I conceave yt necessary
that some one man should be imployed by the said lord maior and
aldermen to keepe their bookes of accompt and reckoninge
concerning their affaires and doeings in the managing of this my
estate unto the said lord maior and aldermen left by this my will to
be managed, I doe hereby give and bequeath unto such person as the
said lord maior and aldermen for the tyme being shall soe imploye in
the said place the somme of tenn pounds per annum dureing the
said terme of fourscore and nyneteene yeares, to be yearly payed
him out of the said rents, yssues and proffits of my said mannors,
lands, tenements and premisses in the said county palatine of
Durham. And as for the residue and remainder of the said rents,
yssues and proffits of my said lands and premisses in the said
county of Wilteshire, I give and bequeath the same to the said lord
maior and fower senior aldermen of the said cittie of London and
their successors for the tyme being, for and dureing the said terme of
foure score and nyneteene yeares, to commence from and
ymediately after my decease, for that use, intent and purpose that
they shall yearly with the same, binde such fyve children of my
kindred as they shall think fitt be be apprentices to some honest
tradesman, therby to learne some honest trade to live in an honest
vocacion. And as concerning the revercion and remainder of all my
mannors, lands, tenements, hereditaments and premisses, as well in
the county palatine of Durham and in the county of Wiltshire as
elsewhere in the realme of England, after that the said terme and
tyme of foure score and nyneteene yeares shalbe fully expired and

determined, I leave the same to discend to my heire at lawe, provided allwayes yt be not such one as shall take on him or her to be a childe of my body begotten. Item, I declare my will and meaneing to be that my executrix and executors, hereafter named, shall, with what conveniencie they may, raise out of my personall estate the somme of foure thousand pounds and paye the same into the chamber of the cittie of London, there to remaine for the space of fourscore and nynteene yeares after that the same shalbe paied in, such persons and persons as shall have the governing, guiding and ordering of the said chamber and stocke, first giving such good and sufficient securetie to my executrix and executors hereafter named, and such person and persons as they shall direct and appoint and by such sufficient conveyance and assurance in the lawe as councell learned in the lawe shall direct and appoint, not only for repayment of the said somme of foure thousand pounds unto my heire at law att the end and expiracion of the said terme of fourscore and nineteen years but alsoe for the yearly payment of foure pounds for the use and interest for every hundred pounds of the said foure thousand pounds unto the said lord maior and fowre senior aldermen of the said citty for the tyme being dureing the said terme, which said use or interest money my will and meaning is that the said lord maior and foure senior aldermen for the tyme being shall therewith binde poore fatherlesse children, whose parents are dead, apprentice to some honest trade whereby they may be able to lyve in a lawfull calling. Item, whereas there is a lease or several leases now in being of the mannor of fford in the parrish of Bishopp Warmouth in the said county palatine and of the mannors of Biddick and Bramstone in the parrish of Washington in the said county palatine, or in whatsoever other parrish or parishes the said three mannors doe lye and extend, in which lease or leases there are divers years yet to come and unexpired, and when the said lease and leases shalbe expired the said mannors and lands in the said leases or leases demised, wilbe improved to a greater yearlie value, my will and meaneing is, and I doe give and bequeath such improvement of rent to my next heire at lawe, provided alwayes yt be not such pretended child, dureing the residue and remainder of the said terme of fourscore and nyneteene yeares. But I declare my will and meaneing is that the said lord maior and foure senior aldermen, for the tyme being, shall lett, sett and dispose of the said mannors, lands and premises dureing the said terme of fourscore and nyneteene yeares & yearly paie the said increase of rent as the same shalbe receaved unto my heire at law. Item, I give and bequeath to Charles Shelly, the only childe of Sr William Shelly, knight, deceased, five hundred pounds to be paied unto his grandfather Sr John Shelly, knight and barronet, the said Sr John first giveing his bonde of one thousand pounds to my executors herafter named to paye the saide Charles the interest thereof yearly towards his maintenance after that he shall have attayned his age of foureteene yeares, and the said fyve hundred pounds when he shall attaine his age of one and twenty yeares. Item, I give to my servant Nicholas Sturt my lease which I holde from the said Sr John Shelley of Clapham farme, dureing the terme yet to come of and in the same, he paying the rentes and performeing the covenants therein reserved and comteyned And alsoe yearely paying to my servant John Cartwright dureing the said lease, yf he shal soe longe leve, the somme of six pounds, thirteene shillings and foure pence, at foure the usuall feasts or termes in the yeare, that ys to saye, at the feast of the Anunciacion of the Blessed Virgin Mary, the feast of St John the Baptist, the feast of St Michaell the archangell and the feast of St Thomas the apostle, by equall porcions, the first payment thereof to begin at which of those feaste shall first come after my decease. And I alsoe give and bequeath to my sayd servant Nicholas Sturt all my horses, geldings, mares and colts and all my apparrell, bookes and plate. Item, I give to all such servants as shalbe dewelling with me at the tyme of my decease, except the said Nicholas Sturt and John Cartwright, twenty pounds a peece. Item, I give to my frend Mr Thomas Bradfold, of the sayd citty of London, one hundred pounds. Item, I give to Lady Jane Shelly, wife of the said Sr John Shelly, fyve hundred pounds, which said fyve hundred pounds I intend to deliver unto her before my decease as alsoe the said fyve hundred pounds soe by this my will formerly given to the said Charles Shelley. Item, I give to Richard Williams of the said citty of Chichester, gent., thirtie pounds and to my said servant Nicholas Sturt thirtie pounds And I make and ordaine the said Ladye Jane Shelly to be executrix, and the said Richard Williams and Nicholas Sturt to be executors of this my will, desireing my said executrix and executors to see this my will performed in all pointes and to cause to made and erected for a memoriall of me in Paule's Church, London, as neere the tombe of Doctor Dunn as conveniently may be, a faire tombe like in fashion to the tombe of the said Doctor Dunn as may be. And I will and direct that my executrix and execators of this my will shall receave and have one thousand pounds for the performance of such things as they shall doe in and about the erecting of the said tombe and executing of this my will. And when my said will shalbe fully executed and performed in all parts, I will that the remainder of the said thousand pounds, yf any shalbe remayning, shalbe paied to such person and persons as I shall hereafter in this my will direct and appoint. Item, all the residue of my goods and chattels in this my will not formerly given and bequeathed in and by this my will, I give and bequeath to my said executrix and executors. Alsoe I doe hereby declare that I have bonds to the value of three thousand pounds money lent in London. In witness of all which I have to this my last will and testament, conteyning eight sheets of paper and fastened together at the lower end with a point and waxe put about the point, set my hand and seale the said six and twentyth day of ffeburarie first before written, 1640. Henry Hilton signed, sealed published and declared before us and wee as witnesses to the same have sett our names with our hand writing to every one of the said eight sheetes. Anthony Howse, John Shelley, Robert Rust, William Smith.

Know all Christian people, by theis presents that whereas I, Henry Hilton of Hilton in the county palatine of Durham, esquire, haveing made my last will and testament in writeing under my hand & seale, bearing date the six and twentyth day of ffebruarij now last past, before the date hereof, that I doe hereby approve of, ratifie and confirme my said will in all points and parts, and in such manner and forme as the same is expressed, specified and declared in my said will. But I desire that this my writeing may be fixed to my said will as a codicell to the said will and be taken, reputed and had as a part of my said will. And first whereas I have in and by my said will given to my next heire at lawe such improved rents as shalbe raysed out of my mannors of fford, Biddick and Bramston, alias Barmston in the parrishes of Bishopp Wearmouth & Washington, or into whatsoever other parrishes or parrish the said three mannors doe lye and extend, after such tymes as the lease or leases now in being of the said mannors shalbe expired and determined, I doe hereby alter my said will concerning the said improved rents for I doe, out of the said improved rents, give and bequeath to my loveing brother John Hilton and his heires forever one hundred pounds per annum out of the said improved rents when the same shalbe soe improved, to be payed to my said brother and his heires at two feasts or termes in the yeare, that is to say, at the feasts of the Annunciacion of the Blessed Virgin Mary and St Michaell the archangel, by equall porcions, the first payment thereof to begin at which of those feasts that shall first happen after the said rents shall soe improved. And the residue of the sayd improved rents, the said one hundred pounds per annum being soe first payd and satisfied to my said brother John Hilton and his heires as aforesaid, I give and bequeath the same to such person and persons and in such manner and forme as I have given, bequeathed and disposed thereof in and by my said will. Alsoe whereas I have sould to severall persons severall quantities of wood, tymber and trees groweing and being on my mannors, lands and tenements, for which I am to receave the somme of eight hundred, threescore and tenn pounds, I doe hereby ratifie and confirme the said sale, hereby declareing my will and meaneing to be that my executrix and executors in my said will named shall receave and have the said eight hundred, threescore and ten pounds and to them, my executrix and executors, I give and bequeath the same accordingly, further declareing my will and meaneing to be that yf those person or persons to whome I have soe sould the said wood shall decline and fall from the said bargaine I have soe made with them and not paie the said eight hundred threescore and ten pounds to my said executrix and executors, then I declare my will and meaneing to be that my said executrix and executors, in my said will named, shall have full power and authority to sell, fell, cutt downe, take, carry awaie and dispose of such quantities of wood, tymber and trees groweing on all or any of my said mannors, lands, tenements and hereditaments whereby they may raise to themselves the said somme of eight hundred, threescore and tenn pounds, which moneys being soe raysed, my will and meaning is shalbe disposed of by my said executors towards the performance of my said will and paying of the legacies therein and thereby given and bequeathed, and soe I give and bequeath the same accordingly. Alsoe, whereas there are certaine rents now in arere and due to me for my lands in the county of Wilteshire, I will give and bequeath the same to my executors in my said will named towards the performance of my said will. And I doe hereby nominate and appoint Robert Doylie of Goring in the county of Sussex, clarke, to be a coexecutor with the said Lady Jane Shelley, Richard Williams and Nicholas Sturt, being by me named and appointed executrix and executors of my said will that said Lady Shelly, Richard Williams and Nicholas Sturt and executors of my said will. And I give and bequeath to the said Robert Doylie the somme of thirtie pounds. In wittnes of all which I have to this my writeing, conteying one shete of paper, sett my hande and seale the thirde day of March in the sixteenth year of the raigne of our Sovereign Lord, Charles, by the grace of God, King of England, Scotland, ffrance and Ireland, defender of the faith &c., annoque Domini 1640. Henry Hylton,

signed, sealed, published and declared in the presence of us,
Anthony Howse, Robert Rast.

Probatum fuit testamentum supracriptum apud London unacum
codicillo eidem annexo, coram magistro, Willielmo James, legum
doctore surrogato, venerabilis viri Domini Henrici Marten, militis,
legum etiam doctoris curie prerogative Cantuariensis, magistri,
custodis sive commissarij legitime constituti, decimo die mensis
Martij, anno Domini, iuxta cursum et computacionem ecclesie
Anglicane, millesimo sexcentensimo quadragesimo, juramentis Jane
Shelley, Richardi Williams, Nicholai Sturt et Roberti Doylie,
executorum in huiusmodi testamento nominatorum, quibus
commissa fuit administracio omnium et singulorum bonorum
inventorie et creditorum dicti defuncti de bene et fideliter
administrando eadem ad sancta dei evangelis juratis

Vicesimo quinto die mensis Maij anno domini millesimo
sexcentesimo sexagesimo quarto emanavit Thome Willielmo
<Genner> principali creditori Henrici Hilton defuncti habentis etc.
ad administrandum bona, jura et credita dicti defuncti iuxta tenorem
et effectum testamenti eius defuncti per dominam Janam Shelly,
Richardum Williams, Nicholam Sturt et Robertum Doylie, iam etiam
decretum non plena administratione de bene et fideliter
administrando eadmen ad sancta Dei evangelia vigore comissionis
juratis

Source: The National Archives, Prob.11/185.

77. Robert Hilton of Hilton, esquire, 1641

The last will & testament of Robert Hilton of Hilton, esquire, within
the county pallytine of Durham, December 23, 1641

In the name of God, amen, I, Robert Hilton, beinge w[e]ake in body
but of perfecte memory (God be praysed) doe make this my last will
& test[am]ent as followeth. First, I bequeath my soule into the hands
of Christ Jesus, my saviour & reedeemer, & my body to the ground
in hope of ioyfull resurrection. Item, for my worldly goods, I
bequeath them as followes. ffor my annuity of 98 yeares, I bequeath
it to my beloved wife Margret Hilton duringe her life, as alsoe, if she
have an other husband or children, to inoye it soe longe as the

tearme of 98 yeares shall continue, & [what]ever [shall] belonge unto me at the hour of my deathe I freely give unto her & make her my sole exequtrix [........] to dispose of the annuity at her death to whome she please. In witnesse whereof I have sett to my hande & seale, December 23, 1641.

Robert Hilton [*no signature or mark*]

In presence of us
Richard Hickes, Thomas Colyer, Thomas Wake [*no signatures or marks*]

This coopy agreeth with the originall beinge [........]
Richard Newhoues
[........]ister

This coppy was [........] examyned [........] agreeth with th[........] [........]eaventh day of [........] 1653 by us.
The [........]

M[aiste]r Newehouse
I shall intreate you to deliver unto my wife the originall will of [........] and Robert Hilton [........] to keepe a true [........] coppy thereof by you, shee discharge [........] to you [........] the same wilbe sufficient, it being [........] here in like cases where la[........] will the executrix or ex[........] all will and only [........] with the legisse[s] [........] orde[........] any [........] Prerog[........] who[........]

assured lovinge [........]
Thomas Helyman

Sex dessim[........]
August 1653

Mr New howse,
These are to certifie you or any other whome it maye concerne that wee whose names are hereunder written subscribed, were swome that the will of Robert Hilton, esquire, deceased, bearinge date the 23th of December, 1641, was the last will of the said Robert Hilton whereunto he sett his hande & seale & which was filed with the register for the probate of wills for the county of Durham.

Richard Hickes [*full name signed*]
Thomas Colyer [*full name signed*]

[........] Newhouse of Durham, Register
being my late [........]to [........] his [........]
exec[........] lastly to
him again with a [........] witnes my hand
Margrate Halyman [*full name signed*]

*Source: DPR1/1/1641/H4/1–8, paper 7ff. The text of the will is badly
damaged by a tear. There are two somewhat careless copies dated 27
February 1834, which have the readings recorded above in square brackets,
but these could have been supplied by inference and it is impossible to say
whether the will was any more legible then than now. A summary of the
will, without the correspondence, is printed in WI Durham, p. 286.*

78. William Read of Silksworth, yeoman, 1642

In the name of God, amen, the seaven and twentieth day of January,
anno Domini 1642, I, William Reade of Silkesworth in the county of
Durham, yeoman, knoweinge the mortalitie of all men and that it is
appointed for all men once to dye, and beinge sicke in bodie but of
good and perfecte remembrance, thanks be given to almightie God,
do heareby make and ordeine this my last will and testament in
manner & forme followinge. ffirst, I give and bequeath my soule into
the hands of almightie God, my maker, hopeinge and beinge fullie
assured by the meritts of the bitter death and passion of our blessed
lord and saviour Jesus Christ, to be saved, and my bodie to be buried
in the parish church yard of Easington. And for my worldlie estate
which almightie God hath endued me withall, I doe heareby dispose
thereof as followeth. Inprimis, I give and bequeath unto my sonne
Thomas Reade and his heires forever all my lands and tenements in
Shotton & in the parish of Easington aforesaid. And, whereas I did
hearetofore give unto my daughter Jane the some of one hundred
pounds, which somme is in the hands of Cuthbert Pepper, esquier,
by bond, which I did give her upon condicion if she marryed with
my likeinge and consent, now, the said Jane haveinge marryed with
one Anthony Wilson against my will and absolutelie without my
consent, I doe, hereby declare, will and sett downe that the said
hundred pounds shall be to her in full of all porcions, legacyes and
child's parte whatsoever issueinge forth of my estate or meanes,
ether reall or personall. Item, I doe give and bequeath to William,
Elizabeth, Sarah and Barbarie Reade, children of my said sonne
Thomas, the somme of ten pounds apeece. Item, I give & bequeath

unto six children of George Hunter's of Sheeles each of them x^s. Item,
I give to my brother Robert the some of fortie shillings. Item, I give to
my wife Barbarie one white mare. Item, I give to my son Thomas a
mare and a fole. Item, I give to thre children of John Smith's each of
them one ewe. Item, I give to two children of Robert Glasenbye each
of them[47] an ewe. Item, I give to the poore of Easington parish the
somme of xx^s. And all my utensells of household stuffe I give unto
Elizabeth Reade, daughter of my said sonne Thomas Reade. And I
do make Thomas Reade the younger, sonne of my said Thomas
Reade, sole executor of this my last will and testament. In witnesse
whereof I, the said William Reade, have heareunto sett my hande &
seale the day and yeare first above written.

William Reade, marke [*marked with a symbol*]
Signed, sealed & delivered
in the presence of us
John Smith, marke [*marked with a symbol*]
James Morre, marke [*marked with a capital initial M*]
Henerie Atkinson, mark [*marked with a symbol*]

Memorandum, that befor the ensealinge heareof, that wheare as John
Smith is oweing unto me the the some of twentie pounds, my will is
that John Smith shall paye it over unto his 3 children Elezabeth,
Barnard & Issabell within one yeare after my death or els the same
shall be lawfull for my executore for to demand & have it.

John Smith, marke [*marked with a symbol*]
James Morre, marke [*marked with a capital initial M*]
Henerie Atkinson, mark [*marked with a symbol*]

Source: DPR1/1/1642/R3/1 paper 1f.

79. William Potts of Sunderland, blacksmith, 1642

In the name of God, amen, I, William Potts of Sunderland by the sea
in the county of Durham, blackesmyth, thanks be to God being in
perfect memorye, thoughe sicke in bodye, makes this my will and
testament in manner and forme followeinge. ffirst, I bequeath my
soule to God that made me, and to his sonne Jesus Christ, my
saviour, by whose death and passion I hope to be saved and by no

---

47 MS repeats 'each of them'.

other meanes, and my bodye [........] the earth where it shall please God, my freinds and children shall burye me. {ffirst} Item, I geve and bequeath to John Potts, my sonne, all that burgage wherein I now dwelleth, with all the houses, ede[........] and buildinges thereunto belongeinge, beinge bounded with a burgage belongeinge to the heires of Tho[........] Dickeson on the west and one wayste peice of grounde on the east and the king's street on the south and the lowe water mark on the northe. Item, I geve, likewise, {geve} unto my said son John Potts, one burgage with one leaz of lande lyeinge upon the south side of the said house and the other end adioyneinge to the towne moore, the said house boundeinge unto the house on Richard Broome on the east and boundeinge of the burgage of the heires of Hary Crapwell on the west, for and dureinge his naturall life. Item, my will and pleasure is that if Barbery Potts, my sonne's wife, shall survive my sonne, that she shall injoye the third parte of all the former bequeathed premisses for and dureing her naturall life. Item, my will is that, after the death of my sonne, John Potts' decease, all the house wherein I now live, with the keay and all other houses, edifices and buildinge thereunto belongeinge shall come unto William Potts, my grandchild, {eldest} sonne to my said sonne John Potts; and the other house and leaz on the south syde of Sunderland likewise, provided alwayes, that if my sonne John Potts dye without issue male, then the said houses, edifices and buildings thereunto belongeinge shalbe equallye devided among the ffemale children of my said sonne John Potts of his bodye lawfullye begotten. Item, I geve and bequeath to my brother Robert Potts twenty shillings. Also, I geve and bequeath to his daughter Jane five shillings. Also, I make George Lilburne of Sunderland, gent., to whome I geve one shilling, supervisor of this my last will and testament. The rest of my goods, mooveable and unmoveable, my debts and ffunerall expences beinge paid and discharged, I make John Potts, my said sonne, sole executor of this my last will and testament. In witness whereof, I have setto my hande and seale the third day of Januarij in the xvij yeare of the raigne of our soveraigne lord, Charles, by the grace of God, kinge of England, Scotland, ffrance and Ireland, annoque Domini 1641. Sealed in the presence of

Wiliam Potts [marked with a symbol]

John Welsh [full name signed]
William Heppell [full name signed]

Item, I geve and bequeath to William Heppell, x^s, and to the poore of the towne, six shillings & to both my servants, Rauf Aude & Raufe

Cave, 5ˢ a peice, to be paid to them when they have served out their
tyme of apprentiship.

Witness hereof,
George Lilburne [*full name signed*]

Aprilis decimo tertio die, 1642
A true inventorie of all the goodes & chattells, moveable and
unmoveable, of William Potts, late of Sunderland in the countie of
Durham, deceased, as followeth, as they were praised by these men
whose names are hereunder written

Imprimis, in the hall, one iron chimney, a fire porr, a pare of tonges & other implements belonging to the fire		13s	4d
Item, one bedstead & feather bed & all other furniture thereunto belonging	3	0s	0d
Item, three chaires & a little table		7s	0d
Item, a long table		13s	4d
Item, the puther		16s	0d
Item, in the kitching, a brewe lead, breweing vessell, an old arke & a paire of small barrs	1	10s	0d
Item, for old iron in the little chamber	4	16s	0d
Item, five doozen of newe shovell irons		8s	4d
Item, for all sorts of nailes in the little chamber	1	6s	8d
Item, newe iron	4	10s	0d
Item, in the parlour, one bedstead with the furniture thereunto belonging	1	10s	0d
Item, for new shovells	2	0s	0d
Item, one coubart, one counter & three chists	2	0s	0d
Item, more, one pare of barrs		3s	0d
Item, newe ironn in the chamber above the shopp	6	6s	0d
Item, for spikes	1	0s	0d
Item, new shovells in the same chamber	1	10s	0d
Item, in the old shopp, a pare of siles & three buntings		10s	0d
Item, three studdies, two of iron & one of drosse	6	0s	0d
Item, bellowes & all furniture belonging the shopp	4	0s	0d
Item, fower anchors	8	0s	0d
Item, his purse & apparell	5	0s	0d
Item, a baye meare	2	10s	0d
Item, two anchors more	6	0s	0d
This summe coms to	64	9s	8d

Debts oweing to the testator as by bondes, bills &
   bookes of accompts & other recconings,
   appeareth the summe of   20   0s   0d
Debts oweing by the testator, the summe of   35   0s   0d

John Hardcastell [*full name signed*]
Houmphrey Harrieson [*marked with a capital initial H*]
Cuthbart Tompson [*full name signed*]
Peter Sharpe, his mark [*marked with the capital initials, P S*]

Source: DPR1/1/1642/P6/1–2 paper 2ff.

80. John Johnson of Bishopwearmouth, rector, 1643

In the name of {the ffather and of the Sonne and of the Holy Ghost}
God, amen, I, John Johnson, rector of Bishopp Weermouth in the
countye of Durham, weake in body but of perfect memory and
minde, doe make and ordeyne this my last will and testament in
manner and forme ffollowinge. ffirst, I commennd my soule into the
hands of almightie God and my body to the earth from whence it
came to be buryed {I give & bequeath unto my welbeloved sister
Mary Johnson of Weremouth the sume of C^{li} to be paid forth of my
goods & personall estate}. Item, I bequeath unto Mrs Elizabeth
ffelton, the daughter of Mr Robert ffelton of Little Gransden in the
countye of Camebridge, six pounds. Item, I bequeath unto my maide
Mary ffisher foure pounds. Item, I bequeath unto my maide Alice ten
shillinges. Item, I bequeath unto John Todd, my servant, tenn
pounds. Item, I bequeath unto the poore of Bishopp Weermouth
parish three pounds. Item, I bequeath unto the ringers of the said
parish tenn shillinges. {And, Item} I dooe {bequeath unto} make my
well beloved {freinde} sister Mary Johnson {spinster} of Bishop
Weremouth aforesaid, spinster, (who will see heis debts & legacies
discharged) {the courte at Durham all my goods, debts, leases and
chattles whatsouever, provided alwaies that the aforesaid Mary
Johnson, whome I make my sole executrix that she pay the aforesaid
debts and legacies and my ffunerall charges} my[48] executrix of this
my last will & testament. And I doe herby make and ordeyne,
constitute & appoint my welbeloved friends Anthony Johnson of

---

48 MS faded.

Haughton, carpenter, and John Hawley, yeoman in the county of
Durham {for overseers} to be supervisors of this my last will and
testament, written this third of October, 1643.
Signed, sealed and pronounced
In the presence of us,
Isaac Basire, clerk [*full name signed*]
Richard Hickes, clerk [*full name signed*]
Thomas Waite, clerke [*full name signed*]

Memorandum, that about nine dayes after the date of this will, the
testator continuing still of perfect minde and memorie, did give and
bequeath the sume of one hundred pounds to his welbeloved sister
Marie as a legacie which he desired might be added to his will, in the
presence and hearing of John Hanley
John Hawkes [*full name signed*]

Source: DPR1/1/1643/J1/1, paper 1f.

81. William Freeman of Sunderland, 1644

A declaracion of the accompt of Sarah Paull alias Freeman, nowe the
wife of Thomas Paull and late the wife & administratrix of the goods,
cattells, chattells and creditts of William Freeman, late of Sunderland
by the sea within the parish of Bishopp Wermouth of the dioces of
Durham, deceased, made upon her administracion of the said
deceased's goods, cattells, chattells, creditts as follweth, *videlice*t:

Inprimis, this administratrix & accomptant chardgeth
herselfe with all and singular the goods, chattells
& credditts of William Freeman, her late
husband, deceased, and conteined in an
inventory thereof formerly exhibited into the
consistory court at Durham, amounting to the
summe of 487¹ 10ˢ 3ᵈ   487   10s   3d

Out of which this administratrix and accomptant
craveth allowance as followeth

ffirst, she craveth allowance of the summe of [*blank*]
for the goods plundered & taken away from her by
the armyes, parte under the command of Sir William

	£	s	d
Armyn and parte by the Scotish army, in & about the month of September in the yeere of our lord, 1644, & conteined in a schedule hereunto annexed, amounting to the summe of 37^{li} 4^s 2^d.	37	4s	2d
Item, one bond entered by [*blank*] Humble to the deceased in the summe of two hundred pounds for the payment of one hundred poundes then taken away alsoe by the said Sir William Armyn as forfeited to the state	100	0s	0d
Item, for a quarter parte of a shipp apprized in the inventory at the summe of 16^{li} which was immediately after the death of the deceased cast away and never came to the hands and possession of this administratrix & accomptant	16	0s	0d
Item, for severall desperate debts oweing to the deceased by severall persons whose names are set downe in a booke of accompts lately belonging to the deceased wherein this administratrix and accomptant hath used her best and utmost indeavours but could never as yet recover the same, in all amounting to the summe of 29^l	29	0s	0d
Et sic computatis computandis, allocatis allocandis et deductis deducendis adhuc restat in manibus dictae administrat*oris* et computan*tis* ad summam	325	6s	1d

[*Schedule of the plundered goods*]

	£	s	d
Inprimis, in the hall, one paire of virginalls with the frame	3	0s	0d
Item, six ioynt stooles and livery cupbord		15s	0d
Item, fower ioynt stooles covered with leather		10s	0d
Item, fower chaires		4s	0d
Item, two watches	4	0s	0d

In the midle chamber

	£	s	d
Inprimis, one bedstead with curtaines and vallance and one greene rugg, two pillowes and one blanckett	4	0s	0d
Item, one feather bed and some bowlster and one coverlitt for a truckle bed	2	0s	0d
Item, one litle drawe table		13s	4d
Item, two small trunckes and two windowe curtaines and iron rodds		13s	4d

Item, one drawe table, one round table, one livery cupbord, and one chist	1	13s	4d
Item, six quishions loome work and other two worse quishions		10s	0d

In the counting house

Inprimis, bookes	1	0s	0d
Item, one chayre, one deske and other small things and one paire of gold weights		16s	0d

In the high chamber

Item, one drawe table, one livery cupbord	1	10s	0d
Item, one great chaire and tenn stooles, all covered with velvett	4	0s	0d
Item, two other chayres, two trunckes and one chist and a litle trunckle & a seller for glasse botles, one lookeing glasse	1	10s	0d
Item, a warmeing pann and irons, fire showell and a paire of tonges		13s	4d
Item, eight quishions, two carpetts, two window courtings and one cupbord cloth	1	16s	0d
Item, one bayson and ure		6s	0d

In the kitching

Item, pewder weighing 23 poundes at 10^d per pound		19s	2d
Item, two flaggons and two other pewder potts		18s	0d
Item, one dozen of pottingers, two candlestickes, one pinte pott, one chamber pott, six sawcers, two pye plates	1	0s	0d
Item, two copper pottes with covers and frames of iron		10s	0d
Item, five brasse pannes, two iron pannes & one chafeing dish of brasse, one ladle, a smouth iron and a shredding knife	1	0s	0d
Item, one jacke for turneing the spitt & one paire of iron rackes, two fryeing pannes, 3 tempses & two sackes	1	0s	0d
Item, one peice or gunn		6s	8d
	37	4s	2d

Source: DPR1/1/1644/F3/1, 3, paper 3ff.

82. Samuel Smaithwaite of Monkwearmouth Hall, gentleman, 1646

An inventory of all the goods & chattels belonging to Mr Samuell Smathwhite, late of Monkwarmoth Hall in the countie of Durham, gentleman, deceased, & his goods prised by us whose names are underwritten as hereafter ffolloweth

Imprimis, a lease or covenant for one cole mine within the grounds and lordshipp of Plessoe wheare of there is to rune and unexpired soe much of the same as by the said covenant will appeare, which is betwixt on & two yeares, prised and vallued at ffortie pownd	40	0s	0d
Item, the remander of a bond of ffiftene pownds oweing by John Read of Sunderland neare the see, marchant & marcer, where of there remaynes to the admme strators of the said Samuel Smathwate the sume of ffive pownds	5	0s	0d
Ittem, two kyne, prised	6	0s	0d
Ittem, two younge swyne		12s	0d
Ittem, too brode gese, with ffife young ons		10s	0d
Ittem, in the hall, on cubbart, one deske & one tresser	1	4s	0d
Ittem, 2 other letle cubarts, on glase case & on letle deske & 2 small boxes, 4 chares, on joynt stoole 2 fformes		17s	0d
Item, one case of botles & payre of playing tables, 1 seing glase		7s	0d
Ittem, one chimney with other iron implaments	1	10s	0d
Ittem, one morter with pestell		2s	0d
Ittem, one craddell		4s	0d
Ittem, 2 iron potts, one litle brase bosnett		8s	0d
Ittem, 3 fflagen potts, 5 candlestickes, 2 salts		13s	4d
Ittem, 2 voyders, 2 great dublers with 3 playne		16s	0d
Ittem, 8 pewther dishes & 13 sassers, 5 bassens, 2 old dublers		12s	0d
Ittem, one table, 4 stooles & one fforme, one litle cubart, One truncke, one chest, 2 chares, one litle rownd table	1	13s	0d
Ittem, one bedstead, ffernished with bedding	3	10s	0d
Ittem, one servant's bed with beding		10s	0d
Ittem one litle chimney		6s	0d

Ittem, one carpitcloth, one dyper table cloth & 8			
napkins, 2 dreser cloths	1	2s	0d
Ittem, one dussen of table napkins		8s	0d
Ittem, tubbs & skeales, with other wood vessele		6s	8d
Ittem, his purse and apparell & ffurnitur	5	0s	0d
	71	11s	0d

Raph Lumley [*full name signed*]
Arthur Crisp [*full name signed*]
William Agar[*full name signed*]

A declaration of the accompt of Mary Smaithwaite, late wife and administratrix of the goods, chattels and credits of Samuell Smaithwayte, gent., late of the parish of Houghton in the Springe, within the diocesse of Durham, deceased, made upon her administringe of the said deceased's goodes, chattells & credits as followeth, v*idelice*t:

The said administratrix and accomptant doth charge			
herselfe with all the goods, chattells and credits of			
the said deceased, conteined in an inventary thereof			
by her formerly exhibited into the consistory court of			
Durham and remaininge there amongst the records of			
that court and amounting to the summe of seaventy			
one pounds eleven shillings	71	11s	0d

And the administratrix and accomptant craveth allowance of the severall summes of monie heereafter mencioned by her, satisfied and paid since the death of the said intestate, being all oweing and due by him the said intestate upon specialties, v*idelice*t:

Inprimis, to George Gray of Suddicke, gent., upon			
bonds, as by the same cancelled, appeareth	20	16s	0d
Item, to John Lambton of West Rainton, yeoman,			
upon bond, as by the same cancelled, appeareth	21	12s	0d
Item, to James Jordan of Great Lumley, yeoman,			
upon bond, as by the same cancelled, appeareth	54	0s	0d
The summe totall satisfied and			
paid as aforesaid amounteth to	96	8s	0d

Et sic computatis computandis, allocatis allocandis,			
d*ic*ta administratrix et computans solvit ultra vires			
bonorum d*ic*ti def*un*cti ad summam	24	17s	0d

Source: DPR1/1/1646/S5/1, 3, paper 2ff.

83. Robert Thompson and Jane, his wife, of Ryhope, 1646

A declaracion of the accompt of William Skurfeild, administrator of the goods, chattels and credits of Robert Thompson and Jane, his wife, late of Rivehop in the parish of Bishopp Wearmouth within the diocese of Durham, deceased, made upon his administringe of the said goods, chattels and credits as followeth

Inprimis, the said administrator and accomptant sayth that all the goods, chattels and credits of the said parties, deceased, conteined in an inventory thereof by him formerly exhibited into the consistory court att Durham and remaineinge there amongst the records of the said court, amounteth to the summe of nine hundred, ffifty and six pounds, seaventeene shillings and one penny (whereof in desperate debts hereafter specified, as in a particular schedule hereunto annexed doth more att large appeare and which the said administrator and accomptant hath used his best diligence and endeavor for the recovery thereof, but as yet in vayne; and wherewithall the said accomptant is willinge to charge himselfe hereafter, if any such shall be by him acquired and gotten, amounteth to the summe of ffifty pounds and eleven pence) so that this administrator and accomptant chargeth himselfe onely with the summe of nine hundred and six pounds, sixteene shillings and two pence, as beinge the cleare estaite of the said parties deceased, which hath as yet comed to his hands

906	16s	2d

Out of which this administrator and accomptant creaveth allowance of the severall summes of mony hereafter mencioned and by him payd and disbursed since the death of the said deceaseds

Inprimis, he craveth to be allowed for his expences in and about the takeing of letters of administracion and letters of tuicion, together with the charges of the court, proctor's ffees and other necessary charges of bondsmen coincident thereunto, the summe of fower pounds, sixteene shillings and tenn pence	4	16s	10d
Item, payd to Mr Collingwood for rent, ffower pounds, seaven shillings and six pence	4	7s	6d
Item, paid to Mr Cante of Houghton for tythes	13	0s	0d
Item, payd to the said deceaseds' servants for wages	2	10s	8d

Item, payd to William Ayre, tutor of the person and
porcion of Jane Thompson, daughter of William
Thompson of Rivehop, the summe of ffifty eight
pounds and eight shillings left in the deceaseds'
hands and payd and discharged by this
accomptant since their deathes   58   8s   0d

Item, payd to Nicholas Thompson, tutor of the person
and porcion of George Thompson, sonne of the
the aforesaid William Thompson, the like summe
of ffifty eight pounds and eight shillings left in
the said deceaseds' hands and payd by this
accomptant since their deathes   58   8s   0d

Item, payd to a councellor att lawe for his opinion   10s   0d

Item, payd to Mr Shawdforth for the rent of a close   7   0s   0d

Item, payd to Mr Easterby for the winter grasse for
two stotts   16s   0d

Item, payd for the tableinge of Robert Thompson,
sonne of the said deceased, together with bookes
and schoole wage   2   11s   0d

Item, payd the bishop's rent att Whitsontide, 1641, due
and payable by the deceaseds in their lifetimes
and discharged by this accomptant since their
deaths   2   10s   3d

Item, payd for the deceased his mortuary to the parson
of Weremouth   10s   0d

Item, payd for two layer-stalls for the said parties,
deceased   13s   4d

Item, payd to William Ayre and George Watson the
summe of one pound and fower shillings, due by
the deceased in their lifetimes, concerning the
porcions of two of William Thompson's children
of Rivehop aforesaid (of whose persons and
porcions they were tutors) being arreared and
behinde of their said porcions, and discharged
by this accomptant since their deaths   1   4s   0d

Item, payd to Margarett Skurfeild of Munkeweremouth,
widow for three yeares tablinge of John Thompson
and Mary Thompson, two of the children of the
said deceased   36   0s   0d

Item, payd then to one John Blaxton of Burden for
lookinge to the grounds there   1   2s   8d

Item, payd to Margery Thompson of Rivehop, mother
    of the said deceased, the summe of twenty two
    pounds, fifteene shillings and seaven pence, beinge
    accordinge to a covenant made betwixt the said
    deceased and the said Margery, his mother in
    their lifetimes, for the for the payment of six pecks
    of corne every twenty dayes, videlicet, two of
    wheate, two of rye and two of pease   22   15s   7d
Item, more to the said Margery in grasse and hay,
    accordinge to a covenant likewise made betwixt
    her and the said deceased, her sonne, the summe
    of eighteene pounds and fifteene shillings   18   15s   0d
Item, payd to one Gabriell Hudspeth of Gateshead,
    barber surgeon, the summe of tenn pounds for the
    bindinge of Robert Thompson, sonne of the said
    deceased, his apprentice   10   0s   0d
Item, payd to John Heighington of Durham, cordwiner,
    the summe of twelve pounds for the bindeinge of
    Andrew Thompson, one of the sonnes of the said
    deceased, an apprentice to him   12   0s   0d
                Summe is   257   18s   10d

Item, this accomptant craveth allowance of such goods and chattels
of the said deceased as were violently taken from him by the severall
armies then resideinge in the county for their present reliefe and
supply, being quartered upon them, as also such necessary summes
and disbursements as were payd by this administrator and
accomptant in asseessements and billettinge since the death of the
said deceased as followeth

Inprimis, ffower fother of hay and one mare taken by
    Colonell Ruthen, one of the Scottish colonels in
    their first expedicion in the yeare one thousand,
    forty and one   9   0s   0d
Item, more the same yeare for assessments and
    billettinge, as by the noates and acquittances
    under the constables' and collectors' hands may
    appeare, whereof, a third part beinge deducted
    as belonginge to the heire, there remaines   11   13s   4d
Item, for assessements and billettinge the yeare
    followeinge, videlicet, 1642, as by noates of
    accompts of the constables and collectors may

appeare, a third part likewise beinge deducted as before	12	13s	4d
Item, violently taken by the Scottish army, part in the yeare 1642 and part in the yeare 1643, ffourteene fothers of hay more, worth 20^s the ffother	14	0s	0d
Item, for assessements and billettinge in the yeare 1643 and for hay and corne delivered to Generall Kinge by his especiall command and directions, as by noates likewise may appeasre, a third part being likewise deducted as due to the heire	10	18s	8d
Item, for sixty sheepe taken by the Scottish army in the said yeare 1643	20	0s	0d
Item, in the yeare 1644 (v*idelicet* when the wholl Scottish army was quartered upon them,upon their second expedicion) six stacks of wheate, consistinge of tenn score thrives, every thrave thereof yeildinge one bushell of wheate, each bushell beinge valewed att eight shillings the bushel, being all seized on by the Scottish army	80	0s	0d
Item, more att the same time to witt, ffower stacks of bigge consistinge of six score and tenn thraves, every thrave yeildinge one bushell of of bigge, and each bushell thereof valewed att ffower shillings, six pence the bushell, seized and taken by the Scottish army as aforesaid	29	4s	0d
Item, att the same time one oatestacke conteyneing by estimacion ffifty thraves of oates, yeildeinge in the wholl ffortie bowles of oates, each bowle thereof worth five shillinges, seized and taken by the Scottish army as aforesaid	10	0s	0d
Item, more then in stacks of pease, estimated to conteyne fforty bowles of pease, each bowle worth tenn shillings, seized and taken by the Scottish army as aforesaid	20	0s	0d
Item, more att the same time, ffive ffoothers of hay, valewed att twenty shillings the ffoother	5	0s	0d
Item, three oxen valewed att thirteene pounds, one cowe att three pounds, two mares att eight pounds, three score sheepe att twenty pounds and twelve swine att twelve pounds, in all ffifty and six pounds, being all seized upon and taken by the Scottish army in the yeare 1644	56	0s	0d

Item, taken away by the said Scottish army att the same time in plough-geare and waine geare	3	0s	0d
Item, paid the same yeare in assesements and billettinge to one Captain fforbus for his use and the cesse att Hartinpoole	10	0s	0d
Item, for assesements and billettinge in the yeare 1645 and 1646, as by severall noates of accompts more att large may appeare	42	0s	0d
Item, he craveth allowance for advice and counsell, for the ffees of the court and other his charges in and about the passing of this his said accompt	2	0s	0d
Summe is	335	10s	4d
Summa allocacionum &c	593	9s	2d
Et sic computatis computandis deductis deducandis, restat in manibus dicti computan[t]is summa	313	7s	0d

A schedule of such debts as this administrator and accomptant conceiveth desperate and wherein he hath used his best diligence and endeavour to recover the same but yett in vayne, neyther hath any of them as yett comed to his hands, videlicet,

Inprimis, from one John Sheapardson, due upon bond	10	16s	0d
Item, from one Mr Henry Wicliffe upon bond likewise	5	8s	4d
Item, from one Richard Sanderson upon bond likewise	25	18s	0d
Item, due from one John Armestronge upon accompt		6s	0d
Item, from one John Burdon upon a noate only	5	4s	1d
Item, from one Thomas Coates upon a noate likewise		18s	0d
Item, from one Robert Corner upon a noate likewise		2s	0d
Item, from one John Rogerson upon a noate likewise		12s	6d
Item, from one Thomas Bittles upon a noate likewise		16s	0d
Summe is	50	0s	11d

This summe of ffifty pounds and eleven pence beinge deducted likewise out of the summe of three hundred and thirteene pounds, seaven shillings remaineinge in his hands, there remaines cleare

	263	6s	1d

DPR1/1/1646/T5/1–3, paper 3ff.

84. William Huntley of Wearmouth Saltpans, ship carpenter, 1647

Memorandum, that William Huntley of Weremouth Saltepanns, shipp carpenter, being very sick but in good and perfect memory, did about twoe dayes before he dyed, being the third of Aprill last, frely declare and say of his owne accorde that his meaning was that Robert Nicholson (who had formerly bene his apprentice & then lived in house with him) should enter of all the estate he had & should call in all his detts, & imploy the same all for and towards the maintenance & educacion of his foure children, & should pay what remained of mainteyning & educating of his said children unto them when they came to age. Of all which, we, ffrancis Readhead[iuratus] of Weremouth Saltepannes and Roger Thornton[iuratus] of the same, both shipp carpenters, were witnesses and in testimony of the truth thereof have thereunto sett our hands, the second day of July, anno Regis Caroli nunc Angliae &c., vicesimo tertio, annoque Domini 1647.

ffrances Readhead[iuratus] [*full name signed*]
Roger Thornton[iuratus], his marke [*marked with a symbol*]

A inventory maid by four men for William Huntley & his children which is left unto Robert Nickelsonn, beinge 4 childerin

John Harrison his worke is	20	0s	0d
John Nicilson his worke is	10	0s	0d
That which is within and without the house come to	10	0s	0d
Thomas Caldwell his worke comes to	20	0s	0d
Thomas Ballie beinge a seae-faringe man	3	0s	0d
The sum	63	0s	0d

Source: DPR1/1/1647/H10/1, 2, paper 2ff. The will and inventory are in different hands.

85. Richard Sharper of Monkwearmouth, yeoman, 1647

In the name of God, amen, I, Rechard Sharper of Monke Warmothe in the countie of Durham, yeman, seike in bodie but in good and pufect remmbrance, thankes be to God, doe make this my last will and testament in manner and forme following. ffirst, I bequeath my sooule to God, my maker and redeemer, and my bodie to be buried in the parish church of Munckwermouth aforesaid. Item, I give and bequeath unto my doughter Eals Houn thre children twenti shiling a peac; also I give unto my son Robart Sharper child twenty shiling. Also I give unto my son in law child, Wiliam Hale twenti shiling, al being in the hand of Mark Watson of Whikem. Item, I give and bequeath unto my doughter Elizabeth Hal, wif is to Wiliam Hal, ten pounds. Item, I give and bequeath unto my doughter Elener Sharper six pounds. Al the rest of my goods mouffabel and unmoufabel, I give and bequeath unto my wife An Sharper. Also she is to resave of my doughter Eals Houn the som of feften pounds. Also I make my wif An Sharper and my son Robart Sharper and my son in law Wiliam Hale my exsexter. Also, I give unto my exsexter al dets, bels and bonds whatsoever.

In witnes hearof, I have set to my hand and seal the twenti seventh day of September, 1644.

Richard Sharper [*marked with scratches*] [*seal*]
Thomas Colyer [*full name signed*]
Richard Watherhead [*marked with a capital initial N*]
Anthony Watherhead [*marked with a capital initial A*]

An inventory of all the goods moveable and unmoveable of Richard Sharper of Monckwermouth, desseassed, praysed by two indifferent men whose names are under written this 8 day of October, 1644

Inprimis, two kine	4	10s	0d
Item, on bond of Emanuell Skorfield and Abigaill Watson	10	0s	0d
Item, on bond of Raph Catcheside and John Catchesyd	10	16s	8d
Item, on bil of Thomas Catchasid	5	8s	4d
Item, on bil of Thomas Haddicke	10	16s	0d
Item, on bil of John Atkinson and Michell Waker	2	3s	4d
Item, on bil of Wiliam Akeland	4	0s	0d
Item, on bil of Thomas Olever's	4	0s	0d
Item, on bond of Katern Rawe and John Harle	20	0s	0d
Item, on bond of An Harle and John Harle	15	0s	0d
Item, on bond of George Erington	6	0s	0d
Item, his wearing apperel	3	0s	0d
	95	14s	4d

Thomas Colyer [*full name signed*]
Owens Redhead, his marke [*marked with a symbol*]

Source: DPR1/1/1647/S4/1, 2, paper 2ff.

86. George Wilson of Silksworth, Bishopwearmouth, 1647

In the name of God, amen, I, George Wilson of Silksworth in the parish of Bishopwearmouth, sick of bodie but perfect in memory, praised be God, doe heare make my last will and testament in manner and forme followinge. Imprimis, I give my soule to almightie God, hopeing to be saved by the onely merits of Christ Jesus, my saviour and redemer. Item, I give my bodie to the earth whence it came and doe desire it may be buryed in the saide Wearemouth church or church yearde, wheather it shall please my frinds. Item, I give to my loveinge mother the one halfe of my lease dureinge the tearme theirof as yet unexpired. Item, I give to my brother Robert Laisonbie, in like manner, the other halfe, dureinge the tearme theirof. Item, I give & bequeath unto Thomas Wilson, my brother's sonne, tenn pounds to be paide him upon his marryage daye or when he shall have accomplished the age of twentie & one years, if he then be living. Item, I give unto Elissabeth and Issabell Smyth, either, fortie shillings. Item, I give unto Barnard Smyth, my neaphew, fortie shillings. And I doe make Robert Lasonbie and George Hunter ioynte executours & also overseers of this my last will and testament. In witnesse whereof I have heare unto set my hand the sixteenth day of Aprill in anno Domini 1643.

Georg Wilson [full name signed]

Witnesses heare of
Henry Atkinson^{iuratus} his marke [*marked with a cross*]
John Lawson [*full name signed*]

DPR1/1/1647/W10/1, paper 1f.

87. John Potts of Sunderland, blacksmith, 1648

In Dei nomine, amen, quarto die Januarij, anno Domini 1642, I, John Potts of Sunderland by sea in the county of Durham, blackesmith, sicke of bodie but of good & perfect memory (God be praysed), doe make this my last will & testament in forme followinge. ffirst, I commend my soule into the hands of God, my maker, hopeing assuredly, through the onely meritts of Jesus Christ, to be made partaker of life everlastinge, and I commend my bodie to the earth whereof it is made. I give & bequeath to my wife Barbary Potts one third part of all my goods dureinge her life. Item, I give & bequeath to my sonne William Potts all that burgage wherein I now dwelleth with all houses, wasts & appurtenances thereunto belongeinge. Item, I give & bequeath to my daughter Ellen Potts ffortie pounds of lawfull English money, to be paid att or before the marriage day of the said Ellene. Item, I give to my daughter Ann Potts ffortie pounds to be paid, likewise, upon her marriage day. Item, I give to Ellen Armestrong tenn shillings. Item, I give to my unkle Robert Potts twenty shillings. Also, I give to his daughter Jane Potts five shillings. Item, I give to the poore of Sunderland tenn shillings. Also, I give to William Heppell, John Heppell & Mary Heppell, every one of them, sixe shillings & eight pence. Also, I make & ordaine John Nicholson & Humfrey Harrison of Sunderland, to whom I give twelve pence to either of them, they beinge supervisors of this my last will & testament. Also, I give to John Hartcastle & John Chapman, either of them, an iron maull. And, I will that my said wife & my sonne William Potts shall be executors of this my last will & testament. In witnes whereof, to this my last will & testament, I have setto my hand & seale the day & yeare first above written.

John Pottes [*full name signed*] [*seal*]

Sealed, signed & delivered in the presence of
John Nicholson, marke [*marked with the capital initials, I N*]
Humphrey Harrason ^{iuratus}, marke [*marked with a capital initial H*]
Richard Browne [*full name signed*]
John Morley [*full name signed*]

A true and perfect inventorie of the goods and chattells of John Potts, laite of Sunderland by sea & county pallatyne of Duresme, deceased, apprized this 3ᵗ day of March, 1643, as followeth, vide*licet*:

Inprimis his worke tooles belongeinge to his shopp for a smythe's craft, and irone	20	0s	0d
Item, spitts, barrs & other iron worke	1	0s	0d
Item, brasse vessells as potts, panns &c		10s	0d
Item, pewter vessell		10s	0d
Item, lyninge	1	0s	0d
Item, beddinge	2	0s	0d
Item, bedsteads, tables, stooles and other wooden vessells	3	0s	0d
Sum	28	0s	0d

Debts oweinge to the testator in particulers amounteinge to 20ˡⁱ or thereabouts	20	0s	0d
Summa totalis	48	0s	0d

Debts oweinge by the testator in particulers
    amounteinge   60   0s   0d

The apprizers' names
Thomas King [*full name signed*]
William Burne [mark] [*marked with a symbol*]
Anthony Armstrong [*full name signed*]
John Dawdson, his marke [*marked with a symbol*]

Source: DPR1/1/1648/P2/1, 3 paper 2ff.

88.   Christoper Shepherdson of Monkwearmouth, yeoman, 1649

January the 16th, 1644

An inventorie of all the goods & chattells, mooveable & unmooveable, of Christopher Shepperson, late of Monkwearmouth in the countie of Durham, yeoman, deceased, estimated & praised by those whose names are hereunder written

	£	s	d
Imprimis, eight oxen praised at	32	0s	0d
Item, tenn kyne praised at	20	0s	0d
Item, one two yeare old steare praised	2	0s	0d
Item, one sow prised		10s	0d
Item, six score threave of wheate prised	30	0s	0d
Item, tenn threave of bigg prised	2	0s	0d
Item, plough & plough geare, waine and wainegeare prised	6	0s	0d
Item, in househould stuffe & beding prised	20	0s	0d
Item, his purse & apparell prised at	5	0s	0d
	117	10s	0d

Debts oweing to the testator

	£	s	d
Oweing by Thomas Atkinson of Sunderland nere the sea the summe of	16	0s	0d
Sum total	133	10s	0d

Thomas Taylor [*full name signed*]
Thomas Colyer [*full name signed*]
William ffawcett [*full name signed*]
William Robinson [*full name signed*]

Vicesimo sexto die mensis ffebruarij & anno Domini 1649 administratio bonorum &c. Christoferi Shepperdson nuper de Wermouth Monachorum, defuncti, comissa Anne vidue, relicte d[i]c[t]i defuncti, petenti

There are three children but all at age.

Source: DPR1/1/1649/S2/1, paper 1f.

89. Bernard Crosby of Sunderland, mariner, 1649

In the name of God, amen, I, Bernard Crosby of Sunderland neare the sea, marriner, sick and weak of bodie but of a good and perfect memory, praised be God for the same, doe constitute and ordayne this my will and testament in manner and forme followinge. ffirst, I give and bequeath my soule to almightie God and my bodie to the earth; secondlie, my last will is that my goods be disposed on as followeth. ffirst, I give to my brother William Crosby two hundred waight of currands. I doe likewise give to my sister Barbary Crosby three hundred waight of currands, and I doe give the remaynder to my sister Anne. I desire that the currands which I gave awaie maie by distributed accordinge to the waight which I bought at Zant ffor Anthony ffoster. I doe give the best suite and coate that is in my chest and likewise my hatt. I doe likewise desire that my clothes at home and my clothes at sea bee distributed to the aforesaid William, Barbarie and Anne, every one an equal share, and in this my last will and testament I doe likewise give my wages that is due to mee in the shipp freely to my sister Anne. Witness, William Johnes, Alexander Annis, Thomas Coleson, Anthony ffoster.

Decimo quarto die mensis Julij, anno domini millesimo sexcentesimo quadragesimo nono, emanavit commissio Thome Snawdon et Barbare eius uxori, sorori naturali et Anne, legatariis principalibus nominatis in testamento Bernardi Crosbie defuncti, habentibus &c, ad administrandum bona, jura et credita dicti defuncti iuxta tenorem et effectum testamenti ipsius defuncti, eo quod nullum in eodem nominaverit executorem, de bene et fideliter administrando eadem ad sancta Dei Evangelia juratis

Source: The National Archives, Prob.11/208.

90. William Bowes of Barnes, 1649

In the name of God, amen, I, William Bowes, perfect in health and memorie but as considering the chances of war, unto which I now am or may be addressed, doe as followeth make and constitute my last will and testament. My soule I most fervently betake to the mercie of God the ffather, the Sonne and the Holy Ghost, in the merritts and by the passion of Christ Jesus, my redeemer, and onely saviour. My bodie I require to be interred in the buriall place of my mother, within the chancell of the church of Bishop Wearmouth. Unto my deare and most true deserving wife I give all my goods, my moveables, all and everie parte of my personall estate, and totally whatsoever I possess or am owner of which by the lawes of England I have power to dispose and maie conferr upon her. And for a further legacie and token of my truest affection, I give entierly to her and charge her with the breeding and education of her and my onlie sonne, William, requireing her therefore to use all possible diligence that the condition of wardshipp maie make necessarie in her and soe good and worthie a mother as I perfectly know her to bee. I doe alsoe declare and hereby confirme and ratifie that betweene mee and her, my said faithfull and loveinge wife, it hath bene and is covenanted that as long as shee shall remaine in widdowhood or unmarried, her provision or joycture shall be yearelie and everie yeare the full and iust somme of one hundred and fiftie poundes, the same in waie of rentcharge to be issueing out of all the landes of the manors of Barnes, Hamilden and Clowcroft, or at her owne choyce shee to have and hould soe much of the said landes in occupation as shall indifferently be estimated to beare the same value, together with the mansion house of Barnes and all the appurtenances thereof whatsoever, as gardens, orchards, yardes, barnes, stables, outhouses &c., for her use, comoditie and habitacion, but if shee happen againe to enter into wedlocke, her joyncture or dowrie as aforesaid thenceforth to be retracted or limitted to the rate or measure onelie one hundred poundes per annum. This I have here expressed which was my promise to her before our marrage as well as frequently since acknowledged to be due (due both as in regard of the faire quantitie of her portion and in the ample meritts of her greate affection to mee). And therefore in the presence of allmightie God I absolutely enjoyne all and everie one whom it may concern to answer and attend itt with most iust performance. I nextly require my heirs and executors that my debts be rightly discharged, the which debts are foure hundred and fiftie pounds to my brother in lawe Mr John Jackson, parson of Marsk, for the which hee hath a rentcharge issueing out of all my lands in such manner as by indenture betweene us are manifested; one hundred poundes to the executors of Mr Sharpe, late of Westminster, for which I am engaged by obligacion; fiftie pounds to Mr Henrie Willson of the said Westminster, due also by bond; and one hundred poundes to my mother in law, M^rs ffrances Ventrys, which shee wilbe pleased to allowe in the three hundred poundes due from her, my said mother, unto mee, my heirs or executors as parte of my wife's portion, not payable untill she, my said wife, come to the age of one and twentie yeares, the which age wilbee compleated and the said three hundred poundes then due aboute six weekes before the daie or ffeast of Saint Michaell the archangell next comeing, ffor the satisfaction of which debts there is due to mee of rents yet behind and unpaid, first from Robert Mason, Thomas Bee and William Snawden thirtie and odd poundes, the said persons all of Bishop Wearmouth. There is due from Robert Jervis and his partners of the said Wearmouth, nyneteene poundes odd money. There is due from William Bird about thirteen poundes, ten shillings. There is due from Roger Stradman fiftie and foure poundes, seaventeene shillinges, six pence. There is due from Sir William Lambton for halfe a yeare's rent of the saltpans thirtie-five poundes. There is due from Cicilie Yool of Sunderland fortie pound, and from Ann Holydaye of Sunderland and Robert Aier of Wearmouth, about 3^li. There wilbe due as aforesaid from my mother, Mrs Ventrys, three hundred poundes, whereof one is to be allowed for the hundred poundes I owe her as above acknowledged. All which sayd summes amount to three hundred, sixtie and odd poundes, unto the which sayd summe I require to be added the whole price of all my wastes or shores along the River Wear, soe soone as they can be sould, and for the which I have bene heretofore offered above two hundred poundes, as also I will and direct that the tythe corne of the towneship of Ryop be for soe long let and farmed out as to raise such summe of money, as together with the above specified, shalbe sufficient to discharge & pay all my said debts in the best and speediest manner that can be effected. To my brother Robert I give onelie an annuitie dureing his life, at equall payments halfe yearely of ten poundes per annum. To my brother Toby, whose right worthy behaviours will I hope lett him stand in noe need of any yearelie provision out of my estate, I give onelie the summe of fortie poundes to buy him a good horse, the same duelie to be paid to him at six monethes time after hee shall demand it. To my brother Richard, if hee be living, I give alsoe as aforesaid, the annuitie of ten pounds per annum. To my brother George I give an annuitie of twentie poundes the yeare dureing his life, paieable also by equall portions everie halfe yeare as aforesaid, requesting my wife that shee will alwaies respect him as a kind brother, and at whose handes shee will ever find retume of the like. To my sister Elinor I give an annuitie dureing her life of tenn poundes per annum, to be paid to her halfe yearelie in equall portions. To my servant John Hollis I give an annuitie or yearelie rent of twentie poundes to be paied unto him or his assignes at the place of his dwellinge, and in equall portions, every halfe yeare from the time of my decease for and during his naturall life, enioyning him that soe long as pleaseth my wife to accept his service, hee shall constantlie and dutifully depend upon her and be principally by her directed in all his courses. To my old servant Henrye Wicliffe I give an annuitie or yearelie pension of six poundes for & dureinge his life, soe that also hee continues in domestique service to my wife soe long as shee pleaseth. To Anne Collingwood, servant to my wife and my kinswoman, I give at her owne choyce either an annuitie of six poundes, thirteene and foure pence, paieable to her or her assignes halfe yearelie by equall portions for and dureing her life, or els the summe of three score poundes, the which said somme, if shee shall chouse to have rather than the annuitie, I will that the one halfe thereof be paied her or her assignes at the next May Daye after shee shall have fullfilled the age of one and twentie yeares and the other halfe at the next ensueing daye of Saint Martyn the Bishop in Winter, provided allwayes that shee, the said Anne Collingwood, doe dutifully remaine in service with my wife untill, with my wife's consent and allowance, shee shall hap to be married. To my servant and kinsman Gilbert Ayneley I give the summe of six poundes, thirteen foure pence to be paid to him within three monthes after my decease. To my servant William Richmond I give the wage or allowance of fortie shillings the yeare, entreating my wife to keepe him in the same way and manner as hath bene my custome. Also I require of whomesoever it maie anyway refeer unto that a pattent deed or covenant by mee made to Margaret Ourd and the severall persons therein expressed (whereof for the substance there is a counterpart among my evidences with onelie the difference or want of a few wordes, (but litle importance) especially towardes the end) maie bee fullfilled iustlie and trulie and that noe defect of any legall forme or errour of orthographie maie impayre the validitie thereof but that in all and everie parte it be whollie observed & performed, according to honest and plaine meaneing. Finallie, it is to be

understood that all the annuities, pensions and legacies aforesaid are
to be issueing out of the landes of the manors of Barnes, Humilden &
Clowecroft, all which the premisses I here declare and establishe
under my hand and seale, to bee my absolute and most determinate
will, the 3° day of January 1648. William Bowes. Signed and sealed in
the presence of Henry Widiffe, John Hollis.

Tertio die mensis Decembris, anno domini millesimo sexcentesimo
quadragesimo nono, eminavit commissio ffrancisco Ventris, avo ex
materno latere Willielmi Bowes, minoris filii dicti defuncti, habenti
dum vixit et mortis sue[49] tempore bona, iura sive credita in diversis
diocesibus sive juribus, ad administrandum bona, iura et credita
dicti defuncti iuxta tenorem et effectum testamenti huiusmodi
durante minori etate dicti Willielmi Bowes minoris, de bene et
fideliter administrando eadem ad sancta Dei evangelia jurato, literis
administratoriis bonorum, iurium et creditorum dicti defuncti
tanquam ab intestato decedenti alias mense Martii, anno Domini
millesimo, sexcentesimo, quadragesimo octavo iuxta &c. cuidam
Johanni Short et Elianorae eius uxori concessis, revocatis proque
nullis et invalidis pronuntiatis etc.

Decimo tertio die mensis Maij, anno Domini 1676, emanavit
commissio Johanni Wilkinson de Furnivall Inne, London, generoso ad
administrandum bona, jura et credita dicti defuncti iuxta tenorem et
effectum testamenti ejusdem defuncti eo quod nullum omnino
nominaverit executorem, de bene &c. jurato, literis administratoriis
cum dicto testamento anexis [de] bonis ipsius defuncti durante minori
etate Willielmi Bowes, junioris, filij dicti defuncti eiusdem, Francisco
Ventris concessis racione mortis dicti minoris [........] et expiratis.

Source: The National Archives, Prob.11/210.

---

49 MS sua

GLOSSARY

This glossary seeks to explain the more obscure terms that occur in the documents. They include words no longer in use, such as 'porr' for poker or 'voider' for waste-bin, and they include words still current, especially in animal husbandry, which have become less familiar as farming has declined as a source of employment: for example, 'gimmer' for a ewe between the first and second shearing and 'stirk' for a young bullock. Other words may seem quite other than they are: a 'stag' is a young colt and a 'window cloth' is a winnowing-cloth. 'Boot hose tops', 'buckinnes', 'jady', 'nodie stick', 'prent' and 'searffers' have eluded satisfactory definition, and readers will find others to challenge. The best work of reference is of course the online edition of the *Oxford English Dictionary*, which enables definition of almost all words sought. In addition, Joseph Wright's six-volume *English Dialect Dictionary* (London, 1898–1905) is of assistance. Rosemary Milward, *A Glossary of Household, Farming and Trade Terms from Probate Inventories* (Chesterfield, 1982) is also valuable.

Accomptant Accountant.
Addes Adze: a tool like an axe with the blade set at right angles to the handle used for shaping.
Adnihilate Annihilate: make null and void.
Akers Acre: a measure of land, originally as much as a yoke of oxen could plough in a day; later limited by statute to a piece 40 poles long by 4 broad (= 4840 yards), or its equivalent.
Alderman A life appointment to the government of a municipality.
Almery, ammery, almerie, ammrie, ambery, aumrie Ambry: a cupboard.
Annuitie Annuity: A yearly allowance or income.
Apparan Apron.
Apparell Apparel: clothing.
Appertinance, appurtenance Appurtenance: an attached property, right or privilege.
Aquavitae Any form of ardent spirits taken as a drink, as brandy etc.
Arke A chest or coffer.

Arne Iron.

Arrow boules Harrow and bolls?

Assill, assell Axle: the centre-pin or spindle upon which a wheel revolves.

Axeltree The spindle or axle of any wheel.

Babling Baubling, trifling, contemptible.

Backsid Backside: the back premises of a house or building; frequently applied to a curtilage, back yard, farmyard, or the garden or fields adjoining.

Baie Bay: a reddish brown colour.

Baising Basin: a circular vessel of greater width than depth, used for holding water for washing and other liquids.

Balke, balcks Balk: a roughly squared beam of timber.

Band boxe Bandbox: a slight box of cardboard or chip, for collars, bands, ruffs, hats, caps, and millinery.

Bandeller Bandoleer: usually a broad belt carried over the shoulder and across the breast worn by soldiers, originally to support the musket and carry cases containing charges for it; later, a shoulder-belt for cartridges.

Barke Bark, barque: any small sailing vessel.

Barre, barres A grate; the iron bars used to make a grate.

Basinge Basin: a circular vessel of greater width than depth, used for holding water for washing and other liquids.

Batten A bundle of straw consisting of two or more sheaves.

Battledoor Battledore: a wooden bat for smoothing out; also (when made cylindrical) for smoothing out or mangling linen clothes.

Beasttyne A little beast or animal?

Beatment A measure of capacity holding a quarter of a peck.

Bedsteade The framework of a bed.

Beig, bigg Barley.

Bels Bills.

Bering cloth A bearing cloth, a child's christening robe.

Besome Besom: an implement for sweeping, usually a bunch of broom or other reeds or small branches, tied around a handle; a broom.

Binding money Money paid for making and confirming an apprentice-ship.

Boale, bole, bowle, boule Boll: a measure of quantity used exclusively in Scotland and northern England varying from an 'old' measure of six bushels to a 'new' of two.

Boardecloathe Table cloth.

Bocher, boocher Butcher.

Bodies Bodice (originally a pair of bodies), a corset.

Bodkine 1. A dagger. 2. A small pointed instrument used for piercing holes in cloth etc. 3. A long pin used by women to fasten up the hair.

Bole *See* Boale.

Boot hose tops An article of clothing for the legs?

Bouder Pewter?

Boulster, bowlster Boulster: a long stuffed pillow or cushion used to support the sleeper's head.

Bounden Made fast by a tie, confined; bound as an apprentice.

Bowe Bow.

Bowell *See* Boale.

Brake, braike 1. A toothed instrument for breaking flax or hemp. 2. A framework intended to hold anything steady, e.g. a horse's foot while being shod.

Branded The natural colouration of a beast, patched or striped red or brown.

Brane A brawn, a boar.

Brazen Made of brass.

Bread grate Wooden slatted crate suspended from the ceiling for bread storage.

Breeches Trousers.

Breede Brede: a piece of stuff of the full breadth.

Brew lead *See* Lead.

Brode Brood or breeding.

Broyleing yrons Broiling iron: support for a cooking pot, like a gridiron.

Buckinnes Buckets?

Buffet stool A low footstool of any kind, three-legged etc.

Buned, bunne *See* Bounden.

Bunting A piece of squared timber.

Burgage A freehold property in a borough.

Bushell A measure of capacity containing 4 pecks or 8 gallons.

Butterie Buttery: a store-room for liquor; also, for provisions generally.

Butterkitts Butterkits: square boxes for carrying butter to market on horseback.

Byer Byre: a cow-house.

Byndage Binding as of an apprentice.

Cadrone Cauldron.

Calle *See* Cawell.

Callever Caliver: 1. A draught horse collar. 2. A light musket.

Callinder Colander: a vessel, usually of metal, closely perforated at the bottom with small holes, and used as a drainer in cookery.

Candellmes Candlemas: the feast of the purification of the Virgin Mary celebrated with many candles, 2 February.

Canhooke Canhook: a short rope or chain with a flat hook at each end, used for slinging a cask.

Capcase Travelling bag or case; basket.

Capon A castrated cock.

Carde Card: an instrument used to part, comb out and set in order the fibres of wool, hemp etc.

Carpett, carpin Carpet: a thick fabric, commonly of wool, used to cover tables, beds, etc.

Cauell Cowl: 1.A large tub or vessel with two ears. 2. A large cask in which malt, liquor, milk etc. is cooled and in which meat is salted; a bucket.

Cawell, cawle Cawl: a basket.

Cealemen Keelman: one who works on a keel or barge to transport coal.

Ceave Sieve.

Cettles Kettle.

Chaffing dishe Chafing dish: dish containing food to be placed on a chafer. Chafer: small dish with a lid used for containing hot ashes or charcoal for heating food.

Chalder An dry measure of capacity for coal and lime varying from 32 to 40 bushels.

Chamber pot A domestic vessel for urine and slops.

Chapman, chapeman A man who buys and sells; a merchant, trader, dealer.

Chattels, chattles, chatilles Goods, money, possessions.

Cheanye China: porcelain, china-ware.

Cheastrough Creeling trough, also a knocking trough: a large stone mortar used for creeing or taking off the husks of barley or wheat preparatory to boiling them for broth.

Cheches The context suggests cheeses.

Checker worke Work chequered in patterns.

Cheese fats The vessel or mould in which the curds are pressed and the cheese shaped in cheese-making.

Cheswood A cheese vat.

Chichine Kitchen.

Chimley Chimney: commonly a detachable or moveable type of smoke vent.

Chirne Churn: a vessel or machine for making butter.

Chist Chest.

Choussins Cushion.

Cihering Kitchen.

Cite *See* Kitt.

Cladinge deske Clothing desk?

Clipes Pot-clip: an iron hook in the chimney on which the pots were hung.

Close, cloase Enclosed piece of ground.

Closett Closet: a room for retirement; a private room.

Clouted Patched.

Coate house Cote-house: 1. A small cottage. 2. A shed, outhouse etc.

Cobble Coble: a sea fishing-boat with a flat bottom, square stern, lug-sail, and a rudder extending 4 or 5 feet below the bottom.

Cod, codde, coode Cod: a pillow, cushion.

Codicell Codicil: a supplement to a will.

Codwares A pillowcase.

Cofferr Coffer: a box, chest, especially a strong box in which money or valuable are kept.

Coll holle Coal-hole: a small store place for coals.

Comoditie Commodity, convenience, amenity.

Compasse Compost, manure.

Conscionable 1. Of conscience. 2. Reasonable, fair, moderate.

Consistorie Court Consistory court: the diocesan court, held by the chancellor of the diocese.

Coope, coupe, cowpe Cart or wagon with closed sides and end, for carting dung, lime etc.

Coove A ditch or hollow.

Copt Copped, tufted.

Cordwainer Shoemaker.

Cote house *See* Coate house.

Coulter Ploughshare: the iron blade fixed in front of the share in a plough, cutting the soil vertically.

Coumferts Comfit: a sweetmeat made of some fruit, root etc., preserved with sugar.

Counter Table or desk used for counting.

Counter Counter, as above.

Covenant A formal agreement.

Coverleed, coverlett Coverlet: the uppermost covering of a bed.

Cowters *See* Coulter.

Crakes Crick: an instrument composed of a toothed wheel which gives motion to a notched bar.

Crankes Crank: a handle or treadle to turn a revolving shaft by hand or foot.

Craveth Crave: to ask earnestly.

Croakes Crooks.

Crooke studie Crook-studie or steady: a cross-beam of wood or an iron bar in the chimney of a cottage on which the crook is hung.

Crosclothes, crosse clothes Cross-cloth: a linen cloth worn across the forehead.

Cubard Cupboard: a closet or cabinet with shelves for keeping cups, dishes, provisions etc.

Cuff A wristband.

Cupstoyll Cup-stool, a small table for placing of cups or glasses.

Currall stalke A coral stem (jewellery).

Currand Currant: a dried berry.

Curtch A covering for the head; a kerchief; formerly worn instead of a cap.

Custorde plate Custard: an open pie containing meat or fruit in a spiced or sweetened sauce thickened with eggs.

Dagg A kind of heavy pistol or hand gun.

Daile, Deyle Deal, a piece of sawn wood.

Dance Danzig: furniture and pottery of Danzig style or provenance.

Darnix Dornick: a fabric named after the Flemish town where it originated or was made.

Defalcate To cut or lop off (a portion from a whole).

Desperate Hopeless, irretrievable.

Diaper The name of a textile fabric.

Dide bread Diet bread: a special bread prepared for invalids and others.

Dioces Diocese: the district under the pastoral care of a bishop.

Draffe Draff: refuse, lees, dregs.

Drafte Draught: the action or an act of drawing or pulling, especially of a vehicle or plough.

Draw table An extending table made in three parts, the end leaves sliding under the centre when not in use.

Drawne Drawn-work: ornamental work done in textile fabrics by drawing out some of the threads of warp and woof so as to form patterns.

Dreeping pan, droppin pan Dripping pan: vessel placed beneath meat roasting on spits to catch the fat.

Dressing Weaving term: the preparation of a warp for the loom; the length of warp which can be dressed at one time.

Drosse Dross: the scum thrown off from metals in smelting.

Dubler Doubler: a large plate or dish.

Dublett Doublet: a close fitting body garment with or without sleeves worn by men from the fourteenth to the eighteenth centuries.

Duresme Durham.

Durtie Dirty: of colour, inclining to black, brown or dark grey.

Each *See* Addes.

Earthen Earthen: made of baked clay.

Ell father Eld father: forefather, grandfather or father-in-law.

Exsexter Executor.

Falling chaire A collapsible chair?

Fallow Ground ploughed and harrowed but left uncropped for a year or more.

Fan-lid A sheath for a fan?

Farment, farmett Farmhold.

Fatt A vat, a vessel.

Faugh Fallow land; ground not under crop.

Feast of the Annunciaton of the blessed Virgin Mary Lady-day, 25 March.

Feast of St John the Baptist 24 June.

Feast of St Michaell the Archangell Michaelmas, 29 September.

Feast of St Thomas the Apostle 21 December.

Fellows, fellyes, felfes Felloes: the curved pieces of wood which, joined together, form the rim of a wheel.

Ffick Flitch.

Filiall, filliall Filial: of or pertaining to a son or daughter.

Fill pott A vessel.

Finiall Finial: final.

Firkine Firkin: a small cask for liquids, fish, butter etc., originally holding a quarter of a barrel.

Firre, fur Fir or pine wood.

Firsparrs Spar: a pole or piece of timber of some length and moderate thickness, especially an undressed stem of fir.

Flacet, flackitt Flacket: a flask or bottle.

Flanders chest Chest ornamented in the Flemish style.

Flasket, flaskett A long, shallow basket.

Flech Fleach: one of the portions into which timber is first cut by a saw; a plank.

Fleers The context suggests a type of table- or bed-cloth.

Fleshe crooke Flesh crook: a kind of fork with hooked prongs.

Flitche Flitch: side of an animal, salted and cured. One side of a pig, when killed, minus legs, thighs and ribs, i.e. bacon.

Flocke bedd Flock: a material consisting of the coarse tufts and refuse of wool or cotton, used for stuffing beds, cushions, mattresses etc.

Flower a spelling for flour.

Footeboate Foot boat: a ferry boat for foot passengers only?

Foothers Fother: a weight of coals, 17 2/3 cwt.

Forehouse The principal room of a house; often the only room in a small house.

Foreside The front side or edge.

Forinter, fornetor Furniture.

Freeleage Freelage: 1. Privilege, immunity; franchise, the freedom or privilege of a burgess in a corporation. 2. A heritable property as distinguished from a rented farm.

French crown The English name for the French coin called an Ecu.

Fudder Fother: a cart-load.

Funle Funnel.

Fyne Fine: sum of money paid by the tenant on the commencement or renewal of his tenancy.

Gailtre Gantry, a stand for barrels.

Gamashes Gamash: a kind of leggings or gaiters worn to protect the legs from mud and wet.

Gammon The ham or haunch of a swine.

Gang of felfes A set of wheel rims (felloes or fellys).

Ganntree Gantry: a four-footed wooden stand for barrels.

Garner A storehouse for corn, granary.

Garthe Garth: a piece of enclosed ground, usually beside a building, a yard, garden or paddock.

Gate A stint or allotment upon a pasture or a common.

Gavelocke Gavelock: an iron crowbar or lever.

Geirt The context suggests geared or linked.

Geld, gelde Castrated.

Gelding A gelded animal.

Gimer, gimmer Gimmer: a ewe between the first and second shearing.

Gird iron Grid-iron.

Girdner The context suggests a garner.

Girkenes Jerkin.

Givelack *See* Gavelocke.

Grappe The context suggests a tool, perhaps a hook or grip.

Gressinge Grazing; grazing ground, pasture land.

Grote Groat: the English groat coined in 1351–2 was made equal to 4 pence.

Guilded Gilded: golden.

Guyl fatt Gyle-fat: the vat in which the wort is left to ferment.

Hacke Hack: 1. Tool rather like a pickaxe or hoe. 2. Rack to hold fodder. 3. Horse let out for hire.

Halbert Halberd: combination of spear and battle axe, consisting of an edged pointed blade and a spearhead mounted on a handle 5 to 7 feet long.

Halver Halver: one who fishes with a halve-net, i.e., a fishing net set or held so as to intercept the fish as the tide ebbs.

Happyng, happing A covering, wrapping, coverlet; in plural, bedclothes.

Harden, harne, hearme Coarse fabric made from hards (the coarser parts of flax or hemp).

Harrowe Harrow: a heavy frame of timber (or iron) set with iron teeth or tines, which is dragged over ploughed land to break clods, pulverise and stir the soil, root up weeds or cover in the seed.

Haver, hawver Oats.

Head peece 1. A cap. 2. A halter.

Heardes Herd: a keeper of a herd or flock of domestic animals.

Hearme Harden, a coarse cloth made from the hards of flax.

Hecke, heck Hatchet.

Heckle, heckel Hackle: a comb for splitting and combing out the fibres of flax or hemp.

Hereditament Any property that can be inherited.

Hespe A hank of yarn, worsted or flax, generally a definite quantity.

Hew irons A tool or tools used in hewing or mowing.

Heyffer Heifer: a young cow that has not had a calf.

Hinde Hind: a farm servant.

Hitch nails A strong nail, sometimes called a pit-hitch nail. It was about 2 inches long with a flat point and a rose head.

Hodge Hog.

Hogget 1. A young boar of the second year. 2. A yearling sheep. 3. A year-old colt.

Hogshead A large cask for liquids.

Holland sheetes A linen fabric from the province of Holland in the Netherlands.

Hopp sack Hop-sacking: a coarse fabric of hemp and jute of which hop-sacks are made.

Hopper A basket, especially that in which the sower carried his seed.

Hop-seane Hop-sieve.

Horle Hurl: to wheel or trundle. *See* Trindle bed.

Horsement Horse mint, wild mint.

Hossat Hassock, cushioned with straw or rushes.

Houle dishes Howl: hollow, deep.

Houre glasse Hour-glass: a contrivance for measuring time, consisting of a glass vessel with obconical ends connected by a constricted neck through which a quantity of sand (or sometimes mercury) runs in exactly one hour.

How Hoe.

Hoy A small vessel, usually rigged as a sloop, and employed in carrying passengers and goods, particularly over short distances on the sea coast.

Hure bed, Hurle bedd Hurl: to wheel or trundle. *See* Trindle bed.

Husbandman Farmer.

Hynd Hind, a farm worker.

Ieast Joist.

Imprimis Latin for firstly, at first.

Indifferent Unbiased, impartial, disinterested.

Ingeare Household goods.

Ingrossing Engross: 1. To write in large letters. 2. To include in a list. 3. To complete a legal document.

Inke standish Inkstand: a stand for holding one or more ink bottles or ink glasses.

Intestate Not having made a will.

Issue, isshew Offspring: a child or children.

Jack Name for various contrivances consisting of a roller or winch, e.g., a machine for turning the spit in roasting meat.

Jack pott A leather tankard or drinking vessel.

Jady, a stone jady Possibly a jad, a tool for working stone but the context suggests an item of table-ware; a jade-stone seems unlikely.

Jeaste Gist, agistment, right or allotment of pasture.

Jemall Gemel: a kind of double ring.

Joycture Jointure: an estate reserved to the wife, to take effect upon the death of her husband for her own life at least.

Joynt stooles Joint-stool: a stool made of parts joined or fitted together; a stool made by a joiner.

Kann Can: a vessel for holding liquids.

Kawell *See* Cawell.

Keale men Keelmen: workers operating flat bottomed vessels, especially used on the Tyne and the Wear for loading colliers.

Keay Quay: a wharf.

Keeling Transporting by means of a keel, usually of coal.

Kerne Kern: a churn.

Kersey Coarse, narrow cloth woven from long wool and usually ribbed.

Kett Small tub or bucket with a handle.

Key Kye: plural of cow.

Kilne Kiln: a building containing a furnace for drying grain, hops etc for making malt.

Kilne haire Kiln hair/hair cloth: a horsehair cloth which holds malt in the kiln.

Kimes Part of a harrow.

Kine, kyen, ky Cows, cattle.

Kitt Kit: a circular wooden vessel made of hooped staves, especially a tub or pail shaped vessel, often with a lid, for carrying milk, butter, fish, etc.

Kneding sheet Kneading: butter, dripping or lard used in making pastry or cakes etc.

Knocke tubb Knock: a bundle of heckled flax.

Knop knob.

Koop *See* Coupe.

Lairstall, larestall, layre stalle Grave inside a church.

Lamas Lammas, 1 August.

Lanthome Lantern.

Larum Alarm, a watch with this function.

Latten, latyne A mixed metal of yellow colour, either identical with or very like brass; often hammered into thin sheets.

Lavere, laver, levere A vessel, basin or cistern for washing.

Leadinge Leading: carting to and from the fields.

League An itinerary measure of distance, varying in different countries, but usually estimated at about three miles.

Leath Leet, a stack.

Leaz Lease, leaze: pasture, pasturage, meadow-land, common.

Leepe Leap: a basket.

Lettres of administration Letters of Administration: authorisation for the management and disposal of the estate of a deceased person by an executor or administrator.

Leven tubb Leaven tub, a fermentation vessel.

Li Abbreviation of libra, Latin for pound.

Line, lyne, linne Linen thread or cloth.

Linne Linn: a plank of wood, a sleeper.

Linsey woolsey A textile material of mixed wool and flax.

Lint Flax prepared for spinning.

List A stripe of colour.

Liverie cubbart Livery cupboard: 1. Cupboard for keeping clothes. 2. Cupboard with perforated doors for the storage of food. 3. Cupboard used for bread and wine in sleeping quarters.

Lode Load.

Lynneing Linen.

Lyons The context suggests a vessel, perhaps a type named after the city.

Maior Mayor.

Malte Barley or other grain prepared for brewing or distilling.

Mannors Manor: land belonging to a lord; a unit of land in feudal times over which the owner had full jurisdiction.

Marcer Mercer: a dealer in textile fabrics; also a small ware dealer.

Marke In England, 13s 4d or two thirds of the pound sterling.

Martinmes Martinmas: The feast of St Martin, 11 November.

Mashing tub A tub in which malt is mashed.

Maske Mash: a hammer for breaking stones.

Masking fatt Mashfatt/vat: tub in which malt is mashed, i.e. mixed with hot water to form the wort in the first stages of brewing.

Masterswingletre Swingletree: 1. A board used in dressing flax or hemp. 2. In a plough, carriage etc. a cross bar pivoted at the middle to which the traces are fastened, giving freedom of movement to the shoulders of the horse or other draught animal.

Mattacke Mattock: an agricultural tool used for loosening hard ground, grubbing up trees etc.

Maull Maul: a massive hammer.

Maunde Maund: a wicker or other woven basket having a handle or handles.

Meade Probably a meadow.

Meare Mare.

Medle Meddle: to concern oneself; to take part in.

Meele, mell Mell: 1. The last cut of corn in the harvest field. 2. A heavy hammer.

Merits, merites Good works deserving reward from God.

Michallmas Michaelmas: the feast of St Michael, 29 September, an English quarter day.

Milche Milk.

Milksile Sile: a strainer or sieve, especially for milk.

Moitie Moiety: a half.

Morter & pestell Mortar: a vessel of hard material (e.g. marble) having a cup-shaped cavity in which ingredients are pounded with a pestle.

Mortis The context suggests a cooking vessell.

Moud, moult bord Mould-board: the board or metal plate in a plough which turns over the furrow slice.

Muckhack A fork for spreading farmyard manure.

Musket rest A forked staff to support a musket.

Musterseede Mustard seed.

Mylne Mill.

Naff Nave: the central part or hub of a wheel into which the ends of the axletree are inserted and from which the spokes radiate.

Nagge Nag: a small riding horse or pony.

Night railes Night-rail: a loose wrap, dressing-gown or negligée.

Noble Gold coin worth 6s 8d.

Nodie sticke A tool for a game?

Nuncupative By word of mouth, orally.

Oge Hog-sheep: a young sheep that has not yet been shorn.

Ordeyne Ordain: to put in order.

Orthographie Orthography: correct spelling.

Overen Overing: 1. The top framework of a wagon. 2. Odds and ends, remnants.

Overseale A coverlet?

Oversear Overseer: 1. A person (formerly) appointed by a testator to supervise the executor of the will. 2. A parish officer (appointed annually) to perform various administrative duties mainly connected with the relief of the poor.

Oxtree Tree: a pole, post, stake, beam, wooden bar etc.

Pallatine County Palatine: a county of which the earl or lord originally had royal privileges with exclusive civil and criminal jurisdiction.

Pallete Pallet: a straw bed; a mattress.

Pannyer Pannier: a basket, especially a large basket for carrying provisions, fish etc.

Parlor, pairler Parlour: room, chamber.

Pastors Pasture.

Patclothes A petticoat? A neck cloth?

Pattent deed Patent: a document conferring some privilege, right, office, etc.

Pecke Peck: the fourth part of a bushel, or two gallons.

Peuther Pewter.

Phisick Physic, medicine.

Pillion seate A kind of saddle, especially a woman's light saddle; also, a pad or cushion attached to the hinder part of an ordinary saddle for a second person.

Pillowe beares, piliberes, pillevers, pelowbers, pillowber Pillow beer: pillow case or slip.

Pinne A small cask or keg holding half a firkin or 4½ gallons.

Plaister Plaster.

Plate A flat sheet of metal.

Poake, pooke Poke: a bag, a small sack.

Podich pot, podin dish *See* Pottin.

Poodere Powdering-tub: a tub in which animal flesh is powdered, or salted and pickled.

Poor, por, porr Purr: 1. An iron bar or pole for stirring the fire or furnace; a poker. 2. A long pole for pushing sheep about when being washed.

Porrenger Porringer: a small basin or the like from which soup, porridge, children's food etc. is eaten.

Portall A frame or frontage for wall furniture such as a cupboard?

Posnet, posnoote Posnet: a small metal pot or vessel for boiling, having a handle and three feet.

Posset A drink composed of hot milk curdled with ale, wine or other liquor, often with sugar, spices etc.

Potle Pottle: a measure of capacity for liquids etc. equal to half a gallon.

Pott kelp/kilp Pot clip: an iron hook in the chimney on which the pots were hung; also a detachable handle used to suspend a pot from the gallows.

Pottin Potting: the preserving of butter, meat, fish etc. in pots or other vessels.

Praysed, priced Praise: to set a price or value upon.

Premisses Premises: the subject of a conveyance or bequest, specified in the premises of the deed; the houses, lands or tenements before-mentioned.

Prent Prunt?: glass ornamentation or means thereof.

Prentise Apprentice.

Presentes Presents: the present document or writing; these words or statements.

Presse Press: a large (usually shelved) cupboard, especially one placed in a recess in the wall, for holding clothes, books etc.

Presser, pressor An apparatus for pressing or squeezing.

Prike Prick: a goad for oxen.

Print A stamp or die.

Puder, puter Pewter.

Pullen, pulleine, pulleyne, pullyne Pullen, poultry.

Pyllewbeers, pyllowbearersr Pillow beer: pillow case or slip.

Quaife Coif: a close-fitting cap covering the top, back and sides of the head worn by both sexes.

Quart Two pints.

Quern A small hand-mill.

Quick Living, alive.

Quishing Cushion.

Quye *See* Why.

Rack A bar, or set of bars, used to support a spit or other cooking utensil.

Rackett The context suggests a fire-iron or a cooking iron, perhaps a small grate.

Racking croke, racking crooke, rakene rukes, rakkencrouks, recken-crooks, reckencrouks Reckon crook: iron hook in a chimney for suspending a pot over an open fire.

Reckoning Reckon: to render an account.

Rector A clergyman, minister of a church whose tithes are not appropriated.

Remembrance Memory or recollection.

Rentcharge A rent forming a charge upon lands etc. granted or reserved by deed to one who is not the owner.

Rigge The context suggests a bed covering, perhaps a rug differently spelt.

Rood, roode, roude Rood: a quarter of an acre.

Rouke Rick: a stack.

Ruddells Riddle: a large, coarse sieve.

Rugg A type of coarse woollen cloth.

Rundlets Runlet: a cask or vessel.

Russett Russet: coarse home-spun wool cloth of a reddish brown, grey or neutral colour.

Safeguard An outer skirt or petticoat worn by women to protect their dress when riding.

Saint Martyn the Bishop in Winter 11 November.

Sallet Salad.

Salme Psalm.

Salt seller Salt cellar: a small vessel placed on the table for holding salt.

Saltepanns Salt-pan: a shallow vessel in which brine is evaporated in salt making; a salt works.

Salter A manufacturer or dealer in salt.

Sassor, sausser, sawcer Saucer: a dish or deep plate in which salt or sauces were placed upon the table.

Sawles Sole: a rope, chain or wooden yoke put round the necks of cattle to fasten them in a stall.

Saye Say: a cloth of fine texture resembling serge; formerly partly of silk, subsequently entirely of wool.

Scopper Scopper: a tool used for hollowing out portions of the surface worked upon.

Scuffers Scuffler: an implement for scarifying and stirring the surface of the ground especially between the rows of crops.

Scuttle Large shallow open basket or wickerwork bowl used for carrying corn, earth, vegetables etc.

Sea Say: fine cloth like serge, made of twilled worsted.

Seai[n]g glasse Seeing glass: a looking glass, mirror.

Searffers The context suggests fishermen or seamen's footwear.

Seat house Residence.

Seeve Sieve.

Seggerston Sacristan: a parish church official.

Seised Put in possession of a feudal holding; to be invested or endowed with a property.

Sessions of the peace The periodic sittings of justices of the peace.

Set irons A bar of soft iron.

Setting sticks A dibble, a sharp pointed implement used to make holes in planting.

Settle A long wooden bench usually with arms and a high back and having a locker or box under the seat.

Shalle Shall: part of an oil lamp.

Sheepe pluck Wool.

Shilling Twelve pence, one twentieth of a £ sterling.

Shott Shoat: a young weaned pig.

Shott sayles The context suggests equipment of a fishing boat.

Showteinge shaftes Shooting shafts, arrows.

Sile, syle Strainer or sieve, especially for milk.

Silling dishe Sile dish: a milk strainer.

Sin Sine: a strainer, a sieve.

Skeele, skele Skeel: a wooden bucket.

Skellett Skillet: a cooking utensil of brass, copper or other metal, for boiling liquids, stewing meat, etc.

Skepp, skeppe Skep: 1. A basket or hamper. 2. A beehive.

Skimmer, skummer A shallow vessel, usually perforated, employed in skimming liquids.

Skoppers *See* Scopper.

Sledge A large heavy hammer usually wielded with both hands, especially the large hammer used by a blacksmith; a sledge-hammer.

Sleeve Sleeve: in early use frequently a separate article of dress which could be worn at will with any body garment.

Slipps Slipe: the iron foundation or shoe of a plough.

Smoothing iron A flat-iron; an iron slicker used for smoothing leather.

Snuffer An instrument for snuffing out candles.

Socke Ploughshare.

Sods A rough saddle made of coarse cloth or skin stuffed with straw.

Sole The rim of a wheel.

Soome, some, sowme, soweme Soam: a rope or chain attaching a draught horse etc. to a wagon, plough etc.

Soone Soum? A stint of pasturage?

Sope Soap.

Soyde 1. A sod used as a saddle. 2. A horse shoe.

Spakes Spokes.

Spangde Spane: to wean.

Spence A buttery or pantry; a cupboard.

Spickes Spick: a spike-nail.

Stackgarthe, staggarth A stackyard.

Stafe Staff.

Stagg, stagge A young colt.

Stakin Starken: strong, sturdy.

Stamell Stammel, a coarse woollen cloth.

Stand bed Bed with posts.

Standerchist Stander: an upright support; a supporting pillar, stem etc.

Standing bore The context suggests a smith's tool of large size.

Standish An inkstand, inkpot.

Stane Stone.

Stang A pole or stake, a wooden bar or beam.

Starte Stott: 1. A horse. 2. A young castrated ox. 3. A heifer.

Stedye, stedy A smith's tool, a form of anvil.

Stee 1. Steer, a young ox. 2. A ladder.

Steepe stone, stepe stone 1. A vessel for steeping malt, flesh etc. 2. Stepping stone: a horse block.

Stiltes, stilts Stilt: the handle of a plough.

Stinge Sting: a pole, post, shaft etc.

Stinte, stynte Stint: the number of cattle allotted to a right of common.

Stircke, stirke, stirk Stirk: a young bullock or heifer.

Stock purse A fund for the common purpose of a group of persons.

Stoddie Study.

Stomachers 1. A kind of waistcoat worn by men. 2. An ornamental covering for the chest (often jewelled) formerly worn by women under the lacing of the bodice.

Stone A measure of weight usually equal to 14 pounds.

Stotte, stott Stott: 1. A horse. 2. A young castrated ox. 3. A heifer.

Stottrell, stottrelle Stotterel: a small stot or bullock.

Stowle Stool.

Stoyne Stone.

Straken, strakine Straiken: a kind of coarse linen. *See* Starken.

Strale Strail, a bed-covering, but somewhat out of context here.

Streakinge *See* Straken.

Strong water Any form of alcoholic spirits used as a beverage.

Suffer Suffer: to allow or permit.

Swadlin Swaddling, cloth used in binding, a bandage.

Swill, swil A roughly made large shallow basket.

Swyne Swine, pigs.

Tapp stone A stone plug or stopper.

Taster An implement by which a small portion of anything is taken for tasting.

Teaster Tester: ceiling or canopy over a bed, made with wood or cloth.

Teddar Machine for scattering hay.

Temse, tempse, timpses Temse: a strainer, a sieve.

Thirds, thrids The third of the personal property of a deceased husband allowed to his widow. Also, the third of his real property to which the widow might be legally entitled for her life.

Thong Narrow strip of hide or leather for use as a lace, cord, band, strap.

Threave Thrave: a measure of straw etc.

Thrinne Triple.

Tides Tide of a river or sea, used as the unit of time and work of a keelman.

Tiffeney tempsis Tiffany: 1. A kind of thin transparent silk. 2. A transparent gauze, muslin, cobweb lawn.

Tinder boxe A box that contains any dry inflammable substance that readily takes fire from a spark.

Tingle naill The smallest type of nail, a tack.

Tith Tithe: the tenth part of the annual produce of agriculture etc. being a due or payment for the support of the priesthood and religious establishments and, after the Reformation, a form of rent to the owner of former religious lands.

Touchinge Concerning, with reference to.

Towe Flax or hemp before spinning.

Tramell Trammel: a long narrow fishing net, set vertically with floats and sinkers; consisting of two walls of large meshed netting between which is a net of fine mesh, loosely hung.

Treeding knife A smoothing or squaring tool?

Trenche Trencher: a flat piece of wood on which meat was served and cut up.

Tresser Trusser: strong heavy bench or table.

Trindle bed *See* Truckle bed.

Trowe Trough.

Truckle bed A low bed running on truckles or castors, usually pushed beneath a high or 'standing' bed when not in use.

Tunne Tun: a large cask or barrel.

Tunnells Tunnel: a net for catching partridges or waterfowl, having a pipe-like passage with a wide opening and narrowing towards the end; perhaps too a fishing device.

Tuppe Ram, a male sheep.

Turkie worke Turkey work: woollen material woven in the same way as a Turkish carpet.

Twinter Two-year-old beast, usually a cow.

Tyles Tiles.

Up and doun hammer A smith's tool.

Ure Ewer.

Vallance Curtain round a bed completely enclosing it.

Victualls Victuals: articles of food.

Vidzt, viz Latin: videlicet = that is to say, namely, more precisely.

Visitation Epidemic.

Voyder Voider: a waste container or basket.

Wach Watch.

Waine, wayne Wain: a large open vehicle usually four wheeled, drawn by horses or oxen and used for carrying heavy loads, especially agricultural produce.

Wainscott A superior quality of foreign oak imported from Russia, Germany and Holland, chiefly used for fine panel-work.

Walons Valance.

Wanded Wickerwork.

Wardshipp Wardship: the office or position of a guardian.

Ware Field produce, crops, vegetables etc. intended for sale.

Warming pann Warming pan: a long-handled covered pan of metal, usually of brass, to contain live coals etc., formerly in common use for warming beds.

Wastes, wasts Waste: a piece of land not cultivated or used for any purpose.

Wea balcks, weabaulks Possibly weigh baulk, the beam or beams of a balance or scale.

Weather Wether: male sheep, ram.

Webe Web: a woven fabric; a whole piece of cloth in process of being woven or after it comes from the loom.

Welling yearn Probably wolling yearn, woollen yarn.

Wherne *See* Quern.

Whetstone Shaped stone used to give a smooth edge to cutting tools when ground.

Whinne Whin: the common furze or gorse.

Whitsonday Whit Sunday: the seventh Sunday after Easter Day.

Why, whye, whie Heifer of up to three years or until she has calved.

Wimble A gimlet or auger drill; an instrument for boring in soft ground.

Winding cloth, window cloth 1. A large cloth on which corn was winnowed. 2. A shroud.

Windles Windle: 1. A basket. 2. A measure of corn or other commodities; of wheat usually about three bushels.

Wreath A metal ring forming a holder for a spindle.

Wrought Embroidered.

Wyne The context suggests the verb 'win'.

Yarne Yarn: fibre spun and prepared for use in weaving, knitting etc.

Yeomann Yeoman: a man owning or renting and cultivating a small estate; a freeholder but not ranked as a gentleman.

Yetling, yelling Small iron pan with a bow handle and three feet.

Yocke Yoke: a contrivance by which two oxen or other beasts are coupled together for drawing a plough or vehicle.

Yowe Ewe.

Yron Iron.

INDEX OF PERSONS AND PLACES

Testators whose documents are edited in this collection are indicated with a dagger, and the testamentary documentation relating to them is indexed in bold typeface. Some attempt has been made to distinguish between different men and women with the same name by allocating them separate numbers, though the implied identifications are not always certain. When several people have the same name, the dagger to identify a testator is placed before the allocated number, as in the example of Adam Blakeston of Old Burdon. Where a testator's name is unique to the index, the dagger is placed before the Christian name, as in the example of Sampson Ayre of Monkwearmouth. A date in brackets indicate the year of probate of the will referred to, which may not be the same as the year when the will was composed.

——, Ralph, debtor of Richard Bartram of Sunderland (1612), 31

Anderson (Anerson), Charles, beneficiary of Jane Smart of Sunderland (1637), 170–1

——, Edward, witness of of Edward Dearnley of Sunderland (1626); creditor of John Hilton of Bishopwearmouth (1639), 82, 179

——, Henry, knight, coal owner and landed magnate of Newcastle upon Tyne, debtor of George Shadforth of Tunstall (1617), xxviii, 69

——, Thomas, appraiser of Thomas Page of Bishopwearmouth (1635); creditor of William Thompson of Pans (1640), 152–3, 188

Angmering, Sussex, 191

Annis, Alexander, witness of Bernard Crosby of Sunderland (1649), 221

Aray, Mr, creditor of Robert Huntley of East Burdon (1622), 76

Armstrong (Armestrong), Anthony, appraiser of John Potts of Sunderland (1648), 220

——, Barbara, beneficiary of Matthew Bulmer of Sunderland (1626), 85

——, Ellen, beneficiary of John Potts of Sunderland (1648), 219

——, John, desperate debtor of Robert and Jane Thompson of Ryhope (1646), 215

——, Ursula, beneficiary of Matthew Bulmer of Sunderland (1626), 85

Armyne, Sir William, army commander, alleged plunderer of the goods of William Freeman of Bishopwearmouth in 1644, xviii, 207

Arnold, Robert, creditor and debtor of Ralph Wells of Sunderland (1632), 124, 127

Arnot, Robert, debtor of George Sheperdson of Bishopwearmouth (1635), 157

Arras, Thomas, of Seaham, creditor of Richard Bartram of Sunderland (1612), 31

Arundel, Sussex, 191

Ashenden, John, witness of Edward Lee of Sunderland (1631), 109

Atkinson, Dennis, creditor of Ralph Wells of Sunderland (1632); debtor of George Sheperdson of Bishopwearmouth (1635), 127, 156

——, Henry, witness of William Read of Silksworth (1642); witness and beneficiary of George Wilson of Silksworth (1647), 202, 218

——, James, of Monkwearmouth, debtor of Gabriel Marley of Grindon (1609), 21

——, John, joint debtor with Michell Walker of Richard Sharper of Monkwearmouth (1647), 217

——, Robert, debtor of Robert Huntley of East Burdon (1622), 75

——, Thomas, (1) appraiser and creditor of Christopher Dickinson of Sunderland (1639), 175, 177. (2) of Sunderland, debtor of Christopher Shepherdson of Monkwearmouth (1649), 220

Audere, John, of the Well House, debtor of Thomas Bulbe of Hilton (1616), 64

Awdon, Sussex, 191

Ayneley, Gilbert, servant and beneficiary of William Bowes of Barnes (1649), 224

Sunderland, father of Ann, debtor and creditor of Richard Morgan of Sunderland (1623), 78–80

———, Thomas, (1) creditor of Alice Wilkinson of Bishopwearmouth (1613), 35; (2) of Bishopwearmouth, tenant and debtor of William Bowes of Barnes (1649), 223

Belford, Northumberland, 105

Bell, John, debtor of Thomas Bulbe of Hilton (1616), 64

———, Mary, beneficiary of George Shadforth of Tunstall (1617), 65

———, Thomas, debtor of John Thompson of Bishopwearmouth (1616), 63

Belsay, Northumberland, 20

Belson, Thomas, of Waldridge, creditor of Thomas Kitching of Southwick (1635), 161

Bentley, James, smith, debtor of Richard Bartram of Sunderland (1612); customer of Ralph Wells of Sunderland (1632); appraiser of William Thompson of Pans (1640), 31, 124, 185

———, Randulph, curate, witness of Ralph Fletcher of Bishopwearmouth (1612); witness of Adam Holme (1619), xviii, 28, 71

Berry, Christopher, debtor and creditor of Thomas Morgan of Sunderland, cordwainer (1632), 132

Berwick (Bericke), Ralph, of Thorpe, creditor of Richard Halliman of Bishopwearmouth (1640), 184

Berwick-on-Tweed, Northumberland, 50

Biddick, County Durham, xxx, 78

Bird (Byrd), Hugh, debtor of Edward Burne of Sunderland (1606), 12

———, William, of Bishopwearmouth, debtor of William Bowes of Barnes (1649), 223

Birtley, County Durham, 191

Bittles, Thomas, desperate debtor of Robert and Jane Thompson of Ryhope (1646), 215

Blacket, William, appraiser of William Thompson of Pans (1640), 185

Blakeston (Blaxton), Adam, (†1) of Old Burdon, yeoman, father of John Blakeston, Alice Snowdon and Grace Robinson, grandfather of Adam, John and Thomas Blakeston, Thomas Snowdon, Elizabeth, Isabel and Thomas Robinson (1635), 158–9. (2) son of John, grandson and beneficiary of Adam (1635), 158

———, John, (1) son-in-law of Adam of Old Burdon, father of Adam, John and Thomas (1635), 158. (2) son of John, grandson and beneficiary of Adam (1635), 158. (3) of Burdon, creditor of Robert and Jane Thompson of Ryhope (1646), 212

———, Thomas, son of John, grandson and beneficiary of Adam (1635), 158

Blyth, Northumberland, xxxix

Boldon, County Durham, 14, 16, 21

Booth, †Charles, of Silksworth, creditor of Richard Bartram of Sunderland (1612); inventory only (1626), xxxii, xxxvii, 31, 86–8

————, Agnes, widow, beneficiary of Agnes Thompson of Bishopwearmouth (1623), 80

————, Alexander, of Bishopwearmouth, xxiv

————, Barbara, daughter of Thomas Chilton of Monkwearmouth, wife of Thomas, formerly married to [......] Hollalye, mother of William and Margaret Hollalye, and of other children by Thomas Brown (1615), 52–3

————, David of Bishopwearmouth, debtor of Anthony Foster of Fulwell (1627), 92

————, John, **(1)** of Great Chilton, debtor of George Fell of Ryhope (1602), 5. **(2)** of Wearmouth, creditor of Richard Bartram of Sunderland, butcher (1612), 31. **(3)** father of John and William, beneficiaries of Alice Watson of Ryhope (1618), 70. **(4)** son of John, grandson, creditor and beneficiary of Anthony (1614); beneficiary of Alice Watson of Ryhope (1618), 44–5, 70

————, Richard, salter, debtor of Richard Bartram of Sunderland (1612), 31

————, Richard, witness of John Potts of Sunderland (1648), 219

————, Thomas, husband of Barbara née Chilton, formerly Hollalye, 52–3

————, William, son of John, grandson and beneficiary of Anthony (1614); beneficiary of Alice Watson of Ryhope (1618); debtor of Robert Scurfield of Grindon (1631), 44, 70, 105

Bryan (Briant), Barbara, daughter and beneficiary of Nicholas Bryan of Monkwearmouth (1611), 24–6

————, Isabel, daughter and beneficiary of Nicholas Bryan of Monkwearmouth (1611), 24–6

————, Margaret, daughter and beneficiary of Nicholas Bryan of Monkwearmouth (1611), 24–6

————, Michael, **(1)** brother of Nicholas Bryan of Monkwearmouth and guardian of his eldest son, Thomas (1611), 24–6. **(2)** son and beneficiary of Nicholas Bryan of Monkwearmouth (1611); beneficiary of Thomas Roxby of Bishopwearmouth (1619); creditor of Ralph Wells of Sunderland (1632); appraiser of George Shepherdson of Bishopwearmouth (1635); appraiser of Isabel Richardson of Burdon (1636); witness and appraiser of Matthew Kelly of Bishopwearmouth (1636); appraiser of Richard Halliman of Sunderland (1640), 24–6, 73,154, 158, 164–5, 168–9, 183, 185

————, Nicholas, **(1)** appraiser of Robert Watson of Bishopwearmouth (1603), 7. **(†2)** of Monkwearmouth, yeoman, brother of Michael, father of Barbara, Isabel, Margaret, Michael, Nicholas and Thomas (1611); deceased (1619), xxxii, **24–6**, 73. **(3)** son and beneficiary of Nicholas Bryan of Monkwearmouth (1611); beneficiary of Thomas Roxby of Bishopwearmouth (1619), 24–6, 73

————, Thomas, son and beneficiary of Nicholas Bryan of Monkwearmouth (1611), 24–6

———, John, **(1)** custodian of goods of George Fell of Ryhope (1602), 3–4. **(2)** debtor of Robert Scurfield of Grindon (1631); debtor of Ralph Wells of Sunderland (1632), 105, 124. **(3)** tailor, creditor of Ralph Wells of Sunderland (1632), 128

———, Robert, **(1)** of Ryhope, debtor of George Fell of Ryhope (1602); creditor of Anthony Watson of Ryhope (1614), 5, 45. **(2)** beneficiary of Elizabeth Burdon of Ryhope (1612), 32. **(3)** of Wearmouth, debtor of Robert Watson of Bishopwearmouth (1603), 9. **(4)** debtor of Thomas Hilton of Bishopwearmouth (1616), 57

———, Thomas, **(†1)** of Burdon, appraiser of Thomas Wilson of Bishopwearmouth (1614); debtor of Robert Huntley of East Burdon (1622); father of George, Thomas, William and three other sons and two daughters (1626), xix, xxii, xxix, 39, 75, **88–90**. **(2)** eldest son, heir, witness and sole executor of Thomas Burdon of Burdon (1626), 89. **(3)** supervisor, guardian, witness and supervisor of Elizabeth Burdon (1612), 32

———, William, **(1)** creditor of Robert Watson of Bishopwearmouth (1603), 9. **(2)** witness of Margaret Goodchild (1610); supervisor, witness and appraiser of Elizabeth Burdon of Ryhope (1612), 23, 32–3. **(3)** son of Thomas Burdon of Burdon, apprenticed (1626), 88. **(†4)** of Ryhope, yeoman (1627), xxvii, xxxviii, **92–3**. **(5)** supervisor, tutor and witness of Elizabeth Burdon (1612), 32

Burgoyne (Burgaine, Burgoine, Burgone, Borgon, Burgine), [......], Mr, creditor of Adam Holme of Bishopwearmouth (1619), 72

———, [......], Mrs, creditor of John Hilton of Bishopwearmouth (1639), 180

———, Francis, rector of Bishopwearmouth, creditor of Robert Scurfield of Grindon (1631), xviii, 105

———, †George, of Sunderland, alderman of Sunderland, creditor of Ralph Wells of Sunderland (1632); creditor of George Shepherson of Bishopwearmouth (1635); alderman of Sunderland, inventory only (1635), xxxii, xlii, 128, **150–2**, 154

———, Magdalen, creditor of George Shepherson of Bishopwearmouth (1635), 157

Burlington (Burlinton, Byrlington), 126, 184

Burne, †Edward, of Sunderland, yeoman, husband of Margaret, uncle of John Hall and Mark Watson (1606), xxiv–xxxv, xxxii, **10–12**

———, Margaret, wife and sole executor of Edward (1606), xxiv–xxv, 10

———, Matthew, witness of Edward Burne of Sunderland (1606), 11

———, William, appraiser of John Potts of Sunderland (1648), 220

Burton, William, appraiser of Matthew Kelly of Bishopwearmouth (1636), 169

Burwell, Edward, court official (1635), 161

Byers, Ann of Southwick, creditor of Thomas Kitching of Southwick (1635), 161

Chester-le-Street, County Durham, 126, 191
Chester Moor, County Durham, 112
Cheyne, Mr, debtor of Ralph Wells of Sunderland (1632), 124
Chichester, Sussex, 191, 196
Chilton, Margaret, (1) witness of Elizabeth Smith of Fulwell (1613), 37.
  (2) wife of Thomas, mother of Margaret, father of Margaret Hollalye
  formerly Browne, Jean Hutchinson, Elizabeth Huntley (1615), 52–3
——, Robert, of Newbottle, witness of Robert Watson (1603), 7
——, †Thomas, of Fulwell, husband of Margaret, father of Barbara
  Hollalye formerly Browne, Jean Hutchinson, Elizabeth Huntley
  (1615), xxvii, xxxvii, xl, **52–5**
Chipchase (Chipchis), Philip, debtor of Agnes Thompson (1623), 82
Clapham, Sussex, 191
Clark (Clarke, Clerk), Ann, daughter and beneficiary of Elizabeth Smith
  of Fulwell, sister of Elizabeth Lumley, Grace Maddison, Jenett Peel
  and Thomas Smith (1613), 36
——, William, of Warden Law, debtor of Robert Scurfield of Grindon
  (1631), 105
Claxheugh? (Clapworthe, Clapheugh), County Durham, 5, 161
Claxton, Sir John, knight, debtor of Elizabeth Smith of Fulwell (1613),
  xxviii, 38
——, Robert, of Chester-le-Street, desperate debtor of Ralph Wells of
  Sunderland (1632), 126
Cleadon, County Durham, 91, 160
Clement, Richard, Mr, curate of Bishopwearmouth, witness and facili-
  tator of George Middleton of Silksworth (1601); witness of Robert
  Watson of Bishopwearmouth (1603); witness of Anthony Gefferson of
  Ryhope (1606), xvi, 2, 7, 10, 13
Clowcroft, manor of, 222
Coates, Thomas, deperate debtor of Robert and Jane Thompson of
  Ryhope (1646), 215
Cock, John, of Burlinton, creditor of Richard Halliman of Bishopwear-
  mouth (1640), 184
Cockfield, County Durham, xxvi
Cold Hesledon, County Durham, 5
Collier (Coilyer, Colyer), Ann, daughter and beneficiary of George
  Collier of Monkwearmouth (1629), 94
——, †George, of Monkwearmouth, appraiser of Elizabeth Smith of
  Fulwell (1613); appraiser and debtor of Anthony Foster of Fulwell
  (1627); yeoman, husband of Jane, father of Margaret Brack and
  Thomas Collier, godfather and father-in-law of Ralphe Brack (1629),
  xix, 37–8, 91, **93–6**
——, Jane, wife and joint executor of George Collier of Monkwear-
  mouth, mother of Margaret Brack and Thomas Collier (1629), 94
——, Thomas, (1) son of George and and Jane Collier of Monkwear-
  mouth, beneficiary and joint executor to his father (1629), 94. **(2)**

witness of Robert Hilton of Hilton (1641); witness and appraiser of Richard Sharper of Monkwearmouth (1647); appraiser of Christopher Huntley of Monkwearmouth (1649), 200, 217, 220

Collingwood, [......], Mr, creditor of Robert Scurfield of Grindon (1631); creditor of Robert and Jane Thompson of Ryhope (1646), 105, 211

——, Ann, kinswoman and beneficiary of William Bowes of Barnes, and his wife's servant (1649), 224

——, George, (1) Mr, of Eppleden, supervisor, creditor and beneficiary of George Shadforth of Tunstall (1617), xxviii, 65–6, 69. (2) witness and writer of the will of Thomas Burdon of Burdon (1626), 89

——, John, debtor of Robert Huntley of East Burdon (1622), 75

——, Robert, (1) Mr, custodian of goods of George Shadforth of Tunstall (1617), 68. (2) appraiser of Christopher Morgan of Sunderland (1639), 175, 177

Colson (Coleson, Coolson), Elizabeth, sister-in-law and beneficiary of John Thompson of Bishopwearmouth (1616), 61

——, John, witness to John Rand's power of attorney for Henry Rand's estate (1614), 43

——, Ralph, whose wife was a customer of Ralph Wells of Sunderland (1632), 125

——, Thomas, (1) whose children were beneficiaries of Thomas Chilton of Monkwearmouth (1615), 53. (2) witness of Bernard Crosby of Sunderland (1649), 221

——, Thomasin, beneficiary of John Thompson of Bishopwearmouth (1616), 61

Comen, Timothy, of Durham, debtor of Edward Dearnley of Sunderland (1626), 84

Cooke, Margaret or Marjory, beneficiary of Jane Smart of Sunderland (1637), 170

——, Thomas, of Durham, customer of Ralph Wells of Sunderland (1632), 124

——, William, witness and appraiser of William Scurfield of Grindon (1607), 19

Cooper, Robert, Mr, of Durham, attorney-general to the bishop of Durham, debtor of George Shadforth of Tunstall (1617), xxviii, 69

Corner, Robert, desperate debtor of Robert and Jane Thompson of Ryhope (1646), 215

Cossen, George, debtor of Thomas Dickinson of Sunderland (1632), 132

Cotterill, Richard, creditor of Thomas Dickinson of Sunderland (1632); creditor of Maurice Prescott of Sunderland (1635), 132, 160

Cowling, Richard, creditor ofThomas Dickinson of Sunderland (1632), 132

Cradocke, Dr John, chancellor of the bishopric of Durham (1627), 91

Cragge, George, creditor of Ralph Wetslett of Barnes (1615), 91

Craggs, George, whose children were beneficiaries of Reginald Fawcett of Fulwell (1639), 181

———, William, debtor of Matthew Bulmer of Sunderland (1626), 85

Fell, [......], of Ryhope, widow, creditor of Richard Bartram of Sunderland (1612), 31

———, Ann, widow and beneficiary of George of Ryhope, mother of Edward, George and John (1602), 3

———, Edward, **(1)** creditor of Anthony Watson of Ryhope (1614); witness of Alice Watson of Ryhope (1618); appraiser of Adam Holme (1619); creditor of Robert Huntley of East Burdon (1622); debtor and appraiser of William Burdon of Ryhope (1627); appraiser of Thomas Roxbye of Ryhope (1633); appraiser of Alison Holme of Bishopwearmouth (1634), 45, 70, 76, 93, 135. **(2)** son of and beneficiary of George Fell of Ryhope (1602), 3

———, George, **(†1)** of Ryhope, husbandman, husband of Ann, father of Edward, George and John (1602); his executors debtors of Robert Watson of Bishopwearmouth (1603), xxvii–xxviii, xxxii, xxxvi, **3–6**, 9. **(2)** eldest son and beneficiary of George Fell of Ryhope (1602), 3

———, John, **(1)** of Ryhope, father of Richard Fell, appraiser of Anthony Watson of Ryhope (1614); witness of Alice Watson of Ryhope (1618); witness, beneficiary and appraiser of Richard Morgan of Sunderland (1623); creditor of Edward Dearnley of Sunderland (1626); supervisor, witness and appraiser of Thomas Roxby of Ryhope (1633), 45, 70, 77–8, 84, 134–5. **(2)** the elder of Ryhope, beneficiary and executor of William Burdon of Ryhope (1627); witness of Alison Holme of Bishopwearmouth (1634), 93, 139. **(3)** son and beneficiary of George Fell of Ryhope (1602), 3. **(4)** of Newcastle, debtor to Charles Booth of Silksworth (1626), 88

———, Richard, son of John, beneficiary of Richard Morgan (1623), 77

Felton, Elizabeth, Mrs, daughter of Mr Robert Felton of Little Gransden, Cambridgeshire, beneficiary of John Johnson, rector of Bishopwearmouth (1643), 205

———, Robert, Mr, of Little Gransden, Cambridgeshire, father of Elizabeth Felton, 205

Ferriebie, [......], widow, creditor of John Hilton of Bishopwearmouth (1639), 180

Ferryhill, County Durham, 191

Fetherston, Ralph, Mr, gentleman, debtor of George Shadforth of Tunstall (1617), xxviii, 69

Fisher, Mary, maid and beneficiary of John Johnson, rector of Bishopwearmouth (1643), 205

Fletcher, George, son of Elizaneth Ousnet, grandson and beneficiary of Matthew Kelly of Bishopwearmouth (1636), 168

———, Isabel, daughter of Isabel Ousnet, granddaughter and beneficiary of Matthew Kelly of Bishopwearmouth (1636), 168

———, John, son and beneficiary of of Ralph Fletcher of Bishopwearmouth (1612), 28

———, Merill, creditor of John Hilton of Bishopwearmouth (1639), 204

Gefferson, †Anthony, of Ryhope, brother of Robert, nephew of Christopher Pattinson (1606), xvi, xviii, xx, **13**

―――, Christopher, uncle of Anthony, xvi, 13

―――, Robert, brother and beneficiary of Anthony Gefferson of Ryhope (1606), 13

Gest, Matthew, debtor of Thomas Dickinson of Sunderland (1632), 132

Gibson (Gybscon, Gybscone, Gipson), Agnes, daughter of John Goodchild, sister of Jane Huntley, Joan Shepherdson and of Margaret and Robert Goodchild, beneficiary of his sister Margaret (1610); creditor of Gabriel Marley of Hilton (1609), 22–3

―――, Edward, debtor of Thomas Bulbe of Hilton (1616), 64

―――, Henry, appraiser, beneficiary and witness of Edward Dearnley of Sunderland(1626); debtor of Robert Scurfield of Grindon (1631); creditor of Ralph Wells of Sunderland (1632); debtor of John Harrison of Sunderland (1633), 82, 105, 127, 137

―――, John, tenant of George Middleton of Silksworth (1601), 1

―――, John, of Herrington, creditor of Robert Scurfield of Grindon (1631), 105

―――, Richard, **(1)** appraiser of Gabriel Marley of Grindon (1609), 20. **(2)** of Hilton, debtor of Agnes Thompson (1623), 82

―――, Thomas, debtor of Thomas Bulbe of Hilton (1616), 64

Glasenbye, Robert, whose two children were beneficiaries of William Read of Silksworth (1642), 202

Glen, John, tenant of George Middleton of Silksworth (1601), 1–2

―――, Thomas, of Seaton, appraiser of Adam Blakeston of Old Burdon (1635), 158–9

Glover, Christopher and Gillian, xxiii

Goodchild, John, of Ryhope, deceased, father of Robert and Margaret Goodchild, Agnes Gibson, Jane Huntley and Joan Shepherdson (1610), 23

―――, †Margaret, of Ryhope, daughter of John, fosterchild of George and Mary Shepherdson, sister of Agnes Gibson, Agnes Gibson, Jane Huntley and Joan Shepherdson (1610), xxi, xxv, xxvii, xxxii, **23–4**

―――, Robert, **(1)** son of John Goodchild, brother of Agnes Gibson, Jane Huntley, Joan Shepherdson, and Margaret Goodchild and beneficiary of his siter Margaret (1627); witness of and appraiser of Edward Burne of Sunderland (1606); appraiser of Anthony Watson of Bishopwearmouth (1614); debtor of George Shadforth of Tunstall (1617); appraiser of Adam Holme (1619); appraiser of William Burdon of Ryhope, 11–12, 23, 45, 69, 71, 93. **(2)** of Boldon, father of Robert (1634), 139. **(3)** younger son of Robert Goodchild of Boldon, beneficiary of Alison Holme of Bishopwearmouth (1634); debtor of Thomas Page of Bishopwearmouth (1635), 139, 153

Goring, Sussex, 198

Goslinge, James, of Richmond, creditor of Richard Bartram of Sunderland (1612), 31

Henry Hilton and Robert Hilton, and heir-at-law of Henry (1640), 99. 160, 192–3

———, Margaret, wife and sole executor of Robert of Hilton, Esq. (1641), 199

———, Ralph, debtor of Edward Burne of Sunderland (1606), 12

———, †Robert, of Hilton, Esq., appraiser and creditor of Gabriel Marley of Grindon (1609); appraiser of Thomas Bulbe (1616); brother of Henry and John, husband of Margaret (1641), 20, 22, 63, 65, 193, **199–201**

———, Thomas, **(†1)** of Bishopwearmouth, husband of Elizabeth, father of John and Ann, grandfather of Thomas (1616), xxvii, **56–8 (2)** son of John, grandson and beneficiary of Thomas Hilton of Bishopwearmouth (1616), 56. **(3)** appraiser of Nicholas Bryan (1611), 26

Hirdman, Henry, appraiser of Thomas Whitehead of Sunderland (1635), 163

Hobson, John, of Ryhope, occupier of house bequeathed by Anthony Watson of Ryhope (1614), 44

Hodgson, Ann, wife of Thomas, daughter and beneficiary of Thomas Watt of Sunderland (1635), xxix, 148

———, Niminie, creditor of John Hilton of Bishopwearmouth (1639), 180

———, Thomas, husband of Ann, daughter of Thomas Watt of Sunderland (1635), 148

———, William, creditor of Thomas Dickinson of Sunderland (1632), 133

Hogg, Ralph of Sunderland, desperate debtor of Ralph Wells of Sunderland (1632), 126

Holbourne, Richard, creditor of Thomas Hilton of Bishopwearmouth (1616), 58

Hollalye, Margaret, daughter of Barbara Browne, formerly Hollalye, sister of William Hollalye; beneficiary of her grandfather Thomas Chilton of Monkwearmouth (1615), 52

———, William, son of Barbara Browne, formerly Hollalye, brother of Margaret Hollalye; beneficiary of his grandfather Thomas Chilton of Monkwearmouth (1615), 52–4

Hollis, John, servant, witness and beneficiary of William Bowes of Barnes (1649), 224–5

Holme (Holline, Holm, Holmes, Home), †Adam, of Bishopwearmouth, debtor of George Fell of Ryhope (1602); appraiser of John Thompson of Bishopwearmouth (1616); father of Ralph, George and Agnes (1619), 5, 61, **70–2**

———, Agnes, daughter and beneficiary of Adam Holme of Bishopwearmouth (1619), 71

———, [......],wife of Adam of Bishopwearmouth, mother of Ralph, George and Agnes, beneficiary and sole executor of her husband (1619), 71

———, Anthony, of Haughton, carpenter, supervisor and beneficiary of John Johnson, rector of Bishopwearmouth (1643), 205

———, Christopher, deceased, son of John Johnson the elder, father of Elizabeth and John (1629), 96

———, Elizabeth, **(1)** debtor of Robert Huntley of East Burdon (1622), 75. **(2)** daughter of Christopher Johnson, beneficiary of her grandfather John (1629), 96

———, Isabel, daughter of Richard Johnson, granddaughter of John Johnson the elder (1629), 96

———, John, **(†1)** of Bishopwearmouth, blacksmith, appraiser of Nicholas Bryan (1611); appraiser and creditor of Alice Wilkinson of Bishopwearmouth (1613); appraiser of William Pattinson of Bishopwearmouth (1615); appraiser of Ralph Wetslett of Barnes (1615); creditor of William Pattinson of Bishopwearmouth (1615); witness, creditor and appraiser of Thomas Hilton of Bishopwearmouth (1616); appraiser of John Thompson of Bishopwearmouth (1616); appraiser of Adam Holme (1619); witness and appraiser of Thomas Roxby of Bishopwearmouth (1619); witness and appraiser of Agnes Thompson of Bishopwearmouth (1623); 'the elder', father of Christopher, John and Richard (1629), xviii–xx, xxvii, xxxii, xli, 26, 35, 46, 49, 51, 57–8, 61, 71, 73, **96–8**. **(2)** of Wearmouth, creditor of Richard Bartram of Sunderland (1612), 31. **(3)** son and co-executor of John Johnson the elder (1629), 97. **(4)** son of Christopher Johnson, beneficiary of his grandfather John, 96. **(5)** creditor of Thomas Dickinson (1632); appraiser of George Shepherdson of Bishopwearmouth (1635); appraiser of Richard Halliman of Sunderland (1640), 132, 154, 183, 185. **(†6)** rector of Bishopwearmouth, brother of Mary (1643), xvii, xl, **205–6**

———, Mary, spinster, sister, sole executrix and beneficiary of John Johnson, rector of Bishopwearmouth (1643), 205–6

———, Ralph, creditor of Robert Watson of Bishopwearmouth (1603), 9

———, Richard, **(1)** son, witness and debtor of John Johnson the elder, father of Alice, Isabel, Richard and Thomas (1629), 96–8. **(2)** son of Richard Johnson, grandson of John Johnson the elder (1629), 96. **(3)** debtor of Alison Holme, widow, of Bishopwearmouth (1634), appraiser of William Thompson of Pans (1640), 140, 185

———, Thomas, **(1)** yeoman, appraiser of Robert Huntley of East Burdon (1622); witness and appraiser of John Johnson the elder of Bishopwearmouth (1629), 74. **(2)** nephew, witness and appraiser of Thomas Burdon of Burdon (1626), 89. **(3)** witness of John Johnson the elder of Bishopwearmouth (1629), 97–8. **(4)** son of Richard Johnson, grandson of John Johnson the elder (1629), 96

Johnes, William, witness of Bernard Crosby of Sunderland (1649), 221

Jordan (Jordone), Elizabeth, wife and creditor of Thomas of Barnes Ferry, mother of John and Francis, xxiii, 13–14, 16

of Fulwell (1627); appraiser of Samuel Smaithwaite of Monkwear-
mouth Hall, 17, 90–1, 210
————, Roger, desperate debtor of George Shadforth of Tunstall (1617),
69
Lyell (Liell), George, debtor and creditor of Richard Morgan of
Sunderland (1623), 77, 79
————, James, of Barmeston, debtor of Edward Burne of Sunderland
(1606), 12

Maddison (Madison), [......], Mr, partner with Mr Langley, creditor of
Ralph Welles of Sunderland (1632), 126, 128–9
————, Grace, daughter and beneficiary of Elizabeth Smith of Fulwell
(1613), sister of Jennet Peel, Elizabeth Lumley, Ann Clark and
Thomas Smith, 36
————, Lionel, son of Ralph, beneficiary of Elizabeth Smith of Fulwell
(1613), 36
————, Ralph, father of Lionel, beneficiary of Elizabeth Smith of Fulwell
(1613), 36
Maltby, Cuthbert, debtor of Thomas Burdon of Burdon (1626), xxix, 90
Manning, Arthur, appraiser of Edward Burne of Sunderland (1606), 12
March, [......], Mr, creditor of Ralph Wells of Sunderland (1632), 127
Marley (Merley, Morley), Agnes, wife and executrix of Peter Marley of
Hilton, mother of Henry, Isabel, George and Margaret Marley (1630),
101
————, Alice, daughter of Elizabeth, beneficiary of Gabriel (1609), 20
————, Cuthbert, witness of Peter Marley of Hilton (1630), 102
————, Dorothy, wife and beneficiary of Gabriel (1609), 20
————, Elizabeth, mother of Alice, Gabriel, Peter, Samuel and Thomas,
creditor and beneficiary of Gabriel (1609), 20, 22
————, Frances, a minor, daughter and beneficiary of William, sister of
Jane (1609), 20
————, †Gabriel, of Hilton, beneficiary or creditor of Percival Vipond of
Monkwearmouth (1607); son of Elizabeth Marley, husband of
Dorothy, father of Frances and Jane (1609), xxi–xxii, xxvii, xli, 17, **20–2**
————, George, son of Peter and Agnes, beneficiary, witness and
appraiser of his father (1630), 101–2
————, Henry, son of Peter and Agnes, beneficiary of his father (1630),
101
————, Isabel, daughter of Peter and Agnes of Hilton, beneficiary of her
father (1630), 101
————, Jane, a minor, daughter and beneficiary of William, sister of
Frances (1609), 20
————, John, witness of John Potts of Sunderland (1648), 219
————, Margaret, daughter of Peter and Agnes, beneficiary of her father
(1630), 101
————, †Peter, of Hilton, son of Elizabeth, beneficiary of Gabriel (1609);

husband of Agnes, father of George, Henry, Isabel and Margaret (1630), xxiv, xxxii, 20, **101–3**

———, Samuel, son of Elizabeth, witness and beneficiary of Gabriel (1609), 20

———, Thomas, son of Elizabeth, beneficiary of Gabriel (1609), 20

Marshall, John, creditor of John Hilton of Bishopwearmouth (1639), 180

———, Paul, of Scarbrough, desperate debtor of Ralph Wells of Sunderland (1632), 126

———, Ralph, debtor of Ralph Wells of Sunderland (1632), 125

———, Richard, appraiser of Thomas Burdon of Burdon (1626), 89

———, Robert, of Cold Hesledon, debtor of George Fell of Ryhope (1602), 5

———, Walter, clerk, appraiser of John Johnson the elder of Bishopwearmouth (1629), xviii, 97–8

Marske, Yorkshire, North Riding, 223

Martin, Ralph, creditor of Ralph Watson of Barnes (1629), 101

Martindale (Martindaile), [......], wife of, creditor of Ralph Wells of Sunderland (1632), 128

———, Richard, creditor of John Hilton of Bishopwearmouth, yeoman (1639), 180

Martine, William, appraiser of Robert Scurfield of Grindon (1631), 103

Mason, Robert, creditor and debtor of Ralph Wells of Sunderland (1632), 124, 127

———, Robert, of Bishopwearmouth, tenant and debtor of William Bowes of Barnes (1649), 223

Mathew, [......], Mr, creditor of Ralph Wells of Sunderland (1632), 127–8

Maultland, Thomas, witness of William Scurfield of Grindon (1607), 19

Maven, Robert, creditor of Robert Watson of Bishopwearmouth (1603), 9

Mayer, Lancelot, desperate debtor of Matthew Bulmer of Sunderland (1626), 86

Mempis (Mempris), Elizabeth, of Monkwearmouth, creditor of Thomas Kitching of Southwick (1635), 161

———, John, debtor of Ralph Wells of Sunderland (1632), 124

Menorie, William, tenant of Edward Lee (1631), xxix, 112

Merrington, County Durham, 126

Middleton, Adam, son and beneficiary of George Middleton of Silksworth (1601); joint tenant of Tunstall farm; debtor of George Shadforth of Tunstall (1617); appraiser of Charles Booth of Silksworth (1626), 1, 56, 69, 86

———, Barbara, daughter and beneficiary of George Middleton of Silksworth (1601), 1

———, Constance, sister and beneficiary of George Middleton of Silksworth (1601), xxii, 2

———, Edward, appraiser of Peter Marley of Hilton (1630), 102

———, Elizabeth, daughter and beneficiary of George Middleton of Silksworth (1601), 1–2

———, George, (†1) of Silksworth, brother of Constance, husband of Margaret, father of Adam, Barbara, Elizabeth, George, Gilbert and Susan (1601), xxii–xxvi, 1–2. **(2)** eldest son and heir of George of Silksworth (1601), 1–2. **(3)** witness of Isabel Richardson of Burdon (1636), 164

———, Gilbert, son of George Middleton of Silksworth (1601), 1–2

———, Margaret, wife and beneficiary of George of Silksworth (1601), xxiv, 1–2

———, Richard, Mr, of Tunstall, supervisor of the will of George Middleton of Silksworth (1601); debtor of George Fell of Ryhope (1601), 2, 5

———, Susan, daughter of George Middleton of Silksworth, 1

Milbourne, Francis, debtor of Robert Scurfield of Grindon (1631), 141

Miles (Myles), David, Mr, creditor of Ralph Wells of Sunderland (1632), 127

Miller, John, creditor of John Hilton of Bishopwearmouth (1639), 180

———, Richard, debtor of Richard Bartram of Sunderland (1612), 31

Moody, Robert, debtor of John Harrison of Sunderland (1633); creditor of John Hilton of Bishopwearmouth (1639), 138, 180

Morgan (Morgane, Morgine), Elizabeth, beneficiary and creditor of Richard Morgan of Sunderland (1623), 77, 79

———, Francis, son of George, beneficiary of Richard Morgan of Sunderland (1623), 77

———, George, father of Francis and John (1623), 77

———, John, beneficiary of Richard Morgan of Sunderland (1623), 77

———, Margery, wife, beneficiary and executrix of Richard Morgan of Sunderland (1623), 77

———, †Richard, of Sunderland, creditor of Richard Bartram of Sunderland, butcher (1612); yeoman, husband of Margery (1623), xxv, xxvii, xxxii, 31, **76–80**

Morpeth, Northumberland, xix, 49

Morre, James, witness of William Read of Silksworth (1642), 202

Morton, County Durham, 4, 68, 139

Morye, Robert, debtor of George Fell of Ryhope (1602), 5

Mounton, Murton? County Durham, 4

Moverlie, John, debtor of George Shepherdson of Bishopwearmouth (1635); witness of Thomas Watt of Sunderland (1635), 149, 156

Moyser, Alice, daughter of Anthony Watson and Alice, sister of George Watson, wife of Ambrose, mother of Eleanor, Francis and Samuel, and aunt of William and John Brown; beneficiary of father's will (1614); beneficiary of her mother (1618), 44, 70

———, Ambrose, husband of Alice, father of Eleanor, Francis and Samuel, beneficiary of Anthony Watson (1614); beneficiary and joint executor of Alice Watson (1618); debtor of John Harrison of Sunderland (1633), 44, 70, 137

Offerton, County Durham, xxxviii, 77, 79, 105

Ogle, Cuthbert, appraiser of William Oliver of Monkwearmouth (1615), 49

Oliver (Olever), Robert, of Clapheugh, creditor of Thomas Kitching of Southwick (1635), 161

———, Thomas, debtor of Richard Sharper of Monkwearmouth (1647), 217

———, †William, chapman, of Monkwearmouth and Morpeth, inventory only (1615), xix, xxxii, xxxvii, **49–50**

'Ooldes' (unidentified), 4

Ourd (Hourd, Ourde, Aude, Awd), Anthony, of Offerton, debtor and creditor of Richard Morgan of Sunderland (1623), 77, 79

———, Barthram, debtor of George Shadforth of Tunstall (1617), 69

———, Margaret beneficiary of William Bowes of Barnes (1649), 224

———, Ralph, servant and beneficiary of William Potts of Sunderland (1642), 203

———, Robert, witness of Anthony Watson of Ryhope (1614), 44

Ousnet (Ousenet), Anthony, of Bishopwearmouth, tailor, husband of Elizabeth and stepfather of George and Isabel Fletcher, son-in-law and appraiser of Mathew Kelly of Bishopwearmouth (1636), 168–9

———, Elizabeth, daughter of of Matthew Kelly of Bishopwearmouth, labourer, wife of Anthony, mother of George and Isabel Fletcher (1636), 169

Oxnarde, Thomas, of Mounton, debtor of George Fell of Ryhope (1602), 5

Oxnett, Thomas, debtor of Thomas Roxby of Ryhope (1633), 134

Page, Ambrose, appraiser of Thomas Page of Bishopwearmouth (1635), 152–3

———, Anthony, son and appraiser of Thomas (1635); debtor? of Thomas Roxby of Ryhope (1633), 134, 152–3

———, Henry, son of Thomas (1635), 152

———, Thomas, (†1) of Bishopwearmouth, labourer, father of Anthony, Henry, Thomas, William and two daughters (1635), xxviii, **152–3**. **(2)** son of Thomas (1635), 152

———, William, son of Thomas (1635), 152

Paling, Sussex, 191

Palleser, Ralph, debtor of Ralph Wetslett of Barnes (1615), 51

Palmer, Bess, debtor and creditor of Ralph Wells of Sunderland (1632), 124, 127

Parkinson, Henry, Mr, debtor of Edward Burne of Sunderland (1606), 12

Partis, [......], of Ryhope, widow, debtor of George Fell of Ryhope (1602), 5

Partridge, Michael, creditor of Thomas Dickinson of Sunderland (1632), 133

Pasmore (Pasmoure), Alice, debtor of Robert Watson of Bishopwearmouth (1603), 9

Shadforth (Shawdfurth, Shawefurth, Shotforthe, Shotfurthe) [......],
widow, creditor of Robert Huntley of East Burdon (1622), 76

———, [......], Mr, creditor of Robert and Jane Thompson of Ryhope
(1646), 212

———, Anthony, second son and beneficiary of George of Tunstall
(1617), 65

———, George, (†1) of Tunstall, nephew of John Shadforth, brother of
Isabel, husband of Isabel, father of Anthony, an elder son and a
daughter (1617), xxviii, xxxii–xxxiii, xxxviii, 65–9. (2) appraiser of
Thomas Wilson of Bishopwearmouth (1614); witness and appraiser of
Anthony Smith of Tunstall (1616), 39, 59

———, Isabel, wife, beneficiary and sole executor of George, mother of
Anthony, and of another son and a daughter (1617), 65

———, John, (1) uncle of George of Tunstall, 65. (2) of Morton, overseer
of the will of George Fell (1602), 41. (3) of Warden, whose children
were beneficiaries of George Shadforth of Tunstall (1617), 65

———, Thomas, (1) of Tunstall, executor and beneficiary of Edward Lee
of Sunderland (1631), 107–8. (2) of Eppleton, appraiser of Adam
Blakeston of Old Burdon (1635), 158–9

Shaftoe, Ann, beneficiary of Jane Smart of Sunderland (1637), 170

Sharpe, [......], Mr, of Westminster, creditor of William Bowes of Barnes
(1649), 223

———, John, creditor of Robert Watson of Bishopwearmouth (1603), 10

———, Peter, appraiser of William Potts of Sunderland (1642), 205

———, Thomas, customer and creditor of Ralph Wells of Sunderland
(1632); appraiser of Thomas Dickinson of Sunderland (1632), 124, 127,
130

———, William, appraiser of Robert Huntley of East Burdon (1622), 74

Sharper, Ann, wife of Richard Sharper, of Monkwearmouth, yeoman,
mother of Alice Houn, Eleanor Sharper, Elizabeth Hall and Robert
Sharper, and executor of her husband (1647), 217

———, Eleanor, daughter of of Richard and Ann, sister of Alice Houn,
Elizabeth Halland and Robert Sharper (1647), 217

———, †Richard, of Monkwearmouth, yeoman, husband of Ann, father
of Alice Houn, Elizabeth Hall, Eleanor Sharper and Robert, father-
in-law of William Hall (1647), xxviii, **216–17**

———, Robert, son of Richard and Ann, yeoman, brother of Alice Houn,
Eleanor Sharper and Elizabeth Hall and executor of his father (1647),
217

Shawe, Christopher, appraiser of Peter Marley of Hilton (1630), 102

Sheale, John, of Shirwinford, Weardale, lessor to Matthew Bulmer of
Sunderland (1626), 85

Shelley (Shelly), Charles, son of Sir William, beneficiary of Henry Hilton
of Hilton (1640), 195–6

———, Jane, Lady, wife of Sir John, beneficiary and executrix of Henry
Hilton of Hilton (1640), 196, 198–9

————, Ann, daughter of John Smith, the elder, butcher, beneficiary of Nicholas Bryan (1611), 25

————, Anthony, (†1) of Tunstall, father of Hugh, Lucy, Margaret and Richard, grandfather of William Thompson (1616), **59–60**. **(2)** friend of George Gray of Southwick, xxxvii.

————, Barnard, son of John and beneficiary of William Read of Silksworth (1642); nephew and beneficiary of George Wilson of Silksworth (1647), 202, 218

————, Elizabeth, (†1) of Fulwell, mother of Ann Clark, Elizabeth Lumley, Jennet Peel and Thomas Smith (1613), xxviii–xxix, xxxiii, **36–8**. **(2)** daughter of John and beneficiary of William Read of Silksworth (1642); beneficiary of George Wilson of Silksworth (1647), 202, 218

————, Gawen, appraiser of William Oliver of Monkwearmouth (1615), 49

————, Hugh, son and beneficiary of Anthony Smith of Tunstall (1616), 59

————, Isabel, **(1)** daughter of Richard Smith of Tunstall, beneficiary of John Johnson the elder (1629), 96. **(2)** daughter of John and beneficiary of William Read of Silksworth (1642); beneficiary of George Wilson of Silksworth (1647), 202, 218

————, John, **(1)** the elder, butcher, 'ell father' of Nicholas Bryan, husband of Margaret, father of Ann, supervisor and witness of Nicholas Bryan of Monkwearmouth and guardian of his daughter Margaret (1611); creditor of Robert Huntley of East Burdon (1622), 25, 76. **(2)** creditor of Thomas Chilton of Fulwell (1615), 55. **(3)** creditor of Ralph Watson of Barnes (1629), 101. **(4)** debtor of Isabel Richardson of Burdon (1636), 165; **(5)** keelman, debtor of Matthew Kelly of Bishopwearmouth (1636), 168; **(6)** father of Bernard Elizabeth and Isabel, witness, debtor and beneficiary of William Read of Silksworth (1642), 202; **(7)** husband of Alice, xxxiii.

————, Lucy, daughter and beneficiary of Smith, Anthony, of Tunstall, 59

————, Margaret, daughter and beneficiary of Smith, Anthony, of Tunstall, 59

————, Nicholas, debtor of Charles Booth of Silksworth (1626), 87

————, Richard, **(1)** of Hartlepool, debtor of George Fell of Ryhope (1602), 5. **(2)** salter, debtor of Richard Bartram of Sunderland (1612), 31. **(3)** herd of Bishopwearmouth, debtor of Matthew Kelly of Bishopwearmouth (1636), 168. **(4)** yeoman, son and beneficiary of Anthony Smith of Tunstall (1616); father of Isabel, witness and appraiser of John Johnson the elder of Bishopwearmouth (1629); appraiser of Elizabeth Lee of Sunderland (1632); witness of Thomas Roxby of Ryhope (1633); creditor of George Shepherdson of Bishopwearmouth (1635); appraiser of William Thompson of Pans (1640), 59, 96, 114, 134, 157, 185. **(5)** appraiser of Ralph Watson of Barnes (1629), 100–1

———, Robert, herd of Bishopwearmouth (1636), 168

———, Thomas, **(1)** appraiser of Thomas Jordan of Barnes Ferry (1606), 14. **(2)** son and beneficiary of Elizabeth Smith (1613), brother of Elizabeth Lumley, xxix, 36. **(3)** of Waldridge, debtor of Elizabeth Smith of Fulwell (1613), 38. **(4)** creditor of Ralph Wetslett of Barnes (1615), 52. **(5)** knight, governor of East India Company, debtor of Henry Rand of Sunderland (1614), 42

———, William, **(1)** of Wearmouth, debtor of George Fell of Ryhope (1602); debtor of Robert Watson of Bishopwearmouth (1603), 5–6, 8. **(2)** of Sunderland, witness of Robert Watson (1603), 7. **(3)** debtor of Ralph Wells of Sunderland (1632), 124, 127. **(4)** witness of Henry Hilton of Hilton (1640), 197

Snowdon (Snaden, Snadone, Snawden, Snawdon) Alice, daughter of Adam Blakeston of Old Burdon, sister of Grace Robinson, wife of Thomas Snowdon, mother of Thomas (1635), 158

———, Barbara, sister, beneficiary and administrator of Bernard Crosby and wife of Thomas Snowdon (1649), 221

———, Elizabeth, creditor, beneficiary and administrator of John Hilton of Bishopwearmouth (1639), 180

———, Margaret, creditor of Gabriel Marley of Grindon (1609), 22

———, Thomas, **(1)** debtor of John Thompson of Bishopwearmouth (1616), 63. **(2)** creditor of Ralph Wells of Sunderland (1632); appraiser of George Thompson of Sunderland (1636), 124, 127, 166. **(3)** son-in-law and witness of Adam Blakeston of Old Burdon, husband of Alice, father of Thomas (1635), 158. **(4)** son of Thomas and Alice, grandson and beneficiary of Adam Blakeston of Old Burdon (1635), 158. **(5)** creditor of John Hilton of Bishopwearmouth (1639), 179. **(6)** husband of Barbara Crosby, joint administrator of Bernard Crosby (1649), 221

———, William, **(1)** debtor of Ralph Wells of Sunderland (1632); creditor of George Shepherdson of Bishopwearmouth (1635), 124, 127, 157. **(2)** of Bishopwearmouth, tenant and debtor of William Bowes of Barnes (1649), 223

Sommer, Stephen, 1

Sones, Richard, of Seaham, appraiser, debtor and creditor of Richard Morgan of Sunderland (1623), 78–9

Sothren, William, of Heworth, debtor of Gabriel Marley of Grindon (1609), 21

South Shields, County Durham, 92; *see also* Shields

Southwick (Suddicke), 90, 160–1, 210

Sparrow (Sparro), Richard, debtor and witness of Percival Vipond of Monkwearmouth (1607); creditor and appraiser of Gabriel Marley of Hilton (1609); appraiser of Thomas Bulbe (1616), 17–18, 20, 22, 63, 65

———, Thomas, debtor of Richard Bartram of Sunderland (1612); witness of Thomas Hilton of Bishopwearmouth (1616), 31, 57

Stafford, Thomas, of Sunderland, debtor and creditor of Richard Morgan of Sunderland (1623), 77, 79

and William (1636), 167. **(3)** a minor, son of William Thompson of Ryhope (1646), 212

————, Jane, **(1)** wife of Robert Thompson of Ryhope, mother of Anthony, John, Mary and Robert (1646), xiv, xviii, 211. **(2)** minor, daughter of William Thompson of Ryhope (1646), 212

————, Jasper, creditor of William Pattinson of Bishopwearmouth (1615), 49

————, Joan, daughter of Thomas of Sunderland, beneficiary of George Thompson (1636), 165–6

————, John, **(1)** witness and appraiser of Ralph Fletcher of Bishopwearmouth (1612), 28. **(2)** husband of Ellen Scurfield, son-in-law and debtor of William Scurfield of Grindon, 19. **(3)** witness and appraiser of Robert Watson (1603), 7. **(4)** appraiser of Nicholas Bryan (1611); appraiser of Alice Wilkinson of Bishopwearmouth (1613); witness and appraiser of William Pattinson of Bishopwearmouth (1615); appraiser of Thomas Hilton of Bishopwearmouth (1616), 26, 34, 46, 57. **(5)** keelman, debtor of William Pattinson of Bishopwearmouth (1615), 48. **(†6)** of Bishopwearmouth, yeoman, husband of Agnes, brother-in-law of Elizabeth Coulson, uncle of Agnes Sanderson, employer of William Curtis (1616), xxvii, **60–3**. **(7)** of Wearmouth, debtor of Thomas Wilson of Bishopwearmouth (1614), 40. **(8)** of Southwick, creditor of Thomas Kitching of Southwick (1635), 161. **(9)** debtor of Thomas Bulbe of Hilton (1616), 64. **(10)** son of Richard, grandson and beneficiary of Nicholas Thompson the elder of Ryhope and of John Rutter (1636); desperate debtor of William Thompson of Pans (1640), 167, 189. **(11)** a minor, son of Robert and Jane Thompson of Ryhope (1646), 212

————, Margaret, creditor of Thomas Chilton of Fulwell (1615), 55

————, Margery, **(1)** of Ryhope, creditor of Anthony Watson of Ryhope (1614), 45; **(2)** creditor of Robert Scurfield of Grindon (1631), 105; **(3)** of Ryhope, mother of Robert Thompson of Ryhope (1646), 213

————, Mary, a minor, daughter of Robert and Jane Thompson of Ryhope (1646), 212

————, Nicholas, **(1)** witness of Anthony Watson of Bishopwearmouth (1614), 45. **(†2)** the elder, of Ryhope, father of George and Richard, grandfather of Elizabeth, John, Robert, William and three other girls (1636), xxvii, **167–9**. **(3)** guardian of George, son of William Thompson of Ryhope (1646), 212

————, Richard, **(1)** the elder, debtor of Nicholas Thompson the elder of Ryhope (1636), 168. **(2)** creditor of Gabriel Marley of Grindon (1609); debtor of Thomas Bulbe of Hilton (1616), 22, 64. **(3)** witness and appraiser of Ralph Fletcher of Bishopwearmouth (1612), 28. **(4)** father of John and son-in-law of John Rutter, son and executor of Nicholas Thompson the elder of Ryhope, father of Elizabeth and three other daughters, 167

———, Robert, **(1)** of Ryhope, son of George Thompson, creditor and appraisor of Robert Scurfield of Grindon (1631); grandson, beneficiary and appraiser of Nicholas Thompson the elder of Ryhope (1636), 103, 105, 167–8. **(†2)** perhaps the same as (1), son of Margery Thompson, husband of Jane, father of Anthony, John, Mary and Robert, inventory only (1646), xiv, xviii, xli, **211–15**. **(3)** a minor, son of Robert and Jane Thompson of Ryhope, apprenticed to Gabriel Hudspeth of Gateshead (1646), 212–13

———, Thomas, late of Sunderland, fisherman, father of Joan beneficiary of George Thompson (1636), 165–6

———, William, **(1)** appraiser of George Fell of Ryhope (1602); appraiser of Elizabeth Burdon of Ryhope (1613), 4, 33. **(2)** grandson, beneficiary, witness and appraiser of Anthony Smith of Tunstall (1616), 59. **(3)** joint occupier of a Tunstall farm bequeathed to Thomas Ayre by Thomas Hilton of Bishopwearmouth (1616), 56. **(4)** of Silksworth, debtor of Charles Booth of Silksworth (1626), 88. **(†5)** of the Pans, smith, town councillor of Sunderland, creditor of George Shepherdson of Bishopwearmouth (1635); inventory only (1640), xxvii, xxxii, xlii, 157, **185–9**. **(6)** witness and appraiser of Isabel Richardson of Burdon (1636), 165. **(7)** the younger, son of George Thompson, grandson, beneficiary and appraiser of Nicholas Thompson the elder of Ryhope (1636), 167. **(8)** the elder, appraiser of Nicholas Thompson the elder of Ryhope (1636), 167. **(9)** appraiser of James Rider of Sunderland (1638), 173. **(10)** witness of John Hilton of Bishopwearmouth (1639), 178. **(11)** of Ryhope, deceased, father of George and Jane (1646), 212

Thornton (Thorntonn), John, debtor of Robert Scurfield of Grindon (1631), 105

———, Roger, of Wearmouth Salt Pans, witness of Willisam Huntley, of Wearmouth Saltpans (1647), 216

Thorpe, *see also* Little Thorpe, 184

Todd (Tod, Tood, Toode) Elizabeth, debtor of Charles Booth of Silksworth (1626), 88

———, Francis, witness of Sampson Ayre of Monkwearmouth (1634), 141

———, John, servant and beneficiary of John Johnson, rector of Bishopwearmouth (1643), 205

———, Michael, debtor of Thomas Bulbe of Hilton (1616), 64

———, Nicholas, **(1)** of Houghton, appraiser of Richard Morgan of Sunderland (1623); appraiser of Adam Blakeston of Old Burdon (1635), 78, 158. **(2)** appraiser of Ralph Watson of Barnes (1629), 100–1

———, Thomas, creditor of Matthew Bulmer of Sunderland (1626), joint debtor with William Dawson of Thomas Dickinson of Sunderland (1632), 86, 132

———, William, of Washington, witness of a debt of Henry Storie of Gateshead to Charles Booth of Silksworth (1626), 87

Tow, [......], of Sunderland, debtor of Robert Scurfield of Grindon (1631), 105

Towers, Oswald, debtor of John Harrison of Sunderland (1633), 167

Townerawe, William, dwelling in Lord Darcy's park, debtor of Thomas Bulbe of Hilton (1616), 64

Travers, Thomas of Selby, desperate debtor of Ralph Wells of Sunderland (1632), 126

Turbut, Thomas, creditor of John Hilton of Bishopwearmouth (1639), 180

Urpeth, County Durham, xxxviii, 112

Ursie, William, custodian of property of Edward Lee (1631), 1112

Ushaw, Thomas of Ufferton, creditor of Robert Scurfield of Grindon (1631), 105

Usworth, County Durham, 21

Vasye, Thomas, debtor of Thomas Bulbe of Hilton (1616), 64

Ventris (Ventrys), Frances, Mrs, mother-in-law, creditor and debtor of William Bowes of Barnes (1649), 223

———, Francis, maternal uncle of and administrator of William Bowes (1649), 225

Vipond (Vepont), †Percival, of Monkwearmouth (1607), xxxiv, xxxvii, xl, **17–18**

———, Richard, brother and administrator of Percival Vipond of Monkwearmouth (1606), 17–18

Waike (Wake), Richard, of Cleadon, debtor of Anthony Foster of Fulwell (1627); witness of Sampson Ayre of Monkwearmouth (1634), 91, 142

———, Thomas, witness of Robert Hilton of Hilton, Esq. (1641), 200

Waite, Thomas, clerk in holy orders, witness of John Johnson, rector of Bishopwearmouth (1643), xvii, 206

Waldridge, County Durham, 36, 161

Walker (Waker), Michael, with John Atkinson debtor of Richard Sharper of Monkwearmouth (1647), 217

———, [......], Mr, of Littlethorpe, debtor of George Fell of Ryhope (1602), 5

———, William, of Silksworth, debtor of George Fell of Ryhope (1602), 5

Waller (Wauller), [......], Mr, creditor of Gabriel Marley of Grindon (1609), 22

Walton (Waultone), Anthony, of Nenthall, debtor of Percival Vipond of Monkwearmouth (1607), 18

———, George, **(1)** creditor of Gabriel Marley of Grindon (1609), 22. **(2)** of Nenthall, debtor of Percival Vipond of Monkwearmouth (1607), 18

———, John, of Durham, creditor of Gabriel Marley of Grindon (1609), 22

———, Nicholas, creditor of Gabriel Marley of Grindon (1609), 22

———, Florence, who received a testament bought from the estate of Ralph Wells of Sunderland (1632), 127

———, George, brother and creditor and desperate debtor of Ralph Wells of Sunderland (1632), 126, 128

———, John, Ralph Wells of Sunderland, debtor of Adam Burdon (1632), 127–9

———, Mary, daughter of Ralph, sister of Elizabeth, beneficiary of Thomas Roxby of Bishopwearmouth (1619); maintained from her father's estate (1632), 128

———, Peter, Mr, creditor of Ralph Wells of Sunderland (1632), 127

———, †Ralph, of Sunderland, father of Elizabeth and Maty, witness of Thomas Roxby of Bishopwearmouth (1619); appraiser of Edward Lee of Sunderland (1631); inventory only (1632), xx, xxxix, 73, 109, 113, 114–29

Welsh (Welshe), John, witness of William Potts of Sunderland (1642), 203

———, Richard, debtor of Ralph Wells of Sunderland (1632), 124

Westwood, Ann, beneficiary of Mathew Bulmer of Sunderland (1632), 51–2

Wetslett, †Robert, of Barnes, Bishopwearmouth, inventory only (1615), xxviii, **51–2**

Wharton, Mr Christopher, witness of Robert Watson (1603); appraiser of Thomas Wilson of Bishopwearmouth (1614); supervisor and witness of Anthony Watson of Bishopwearmouth (1614); creditor of William Pattinson of Bishopwearmouth (1615), 7, 39, 44, 49

———, Humphry, Mr, creditor of Ralph Wetslett of Barnes (1615), 52

Wheately, John, of Norton, creditor of Richard Halliman of Bishopwearmouth (1640), 184

White, Robert, appraiser of Elizabeth Smith of Fulwell (1613), 37–8

Whitehead (Whytthed), **(1)** George, Mr, debtor of Robert Watson of Bishopwearmouth (1603), debtor of Thomas Hilton of Bishopwearmouth (1616), 9, 57–8. **(2)** George, creditor of John Hilton of Bishopwearmouth (1639), 180

———, Henry, supervisor of the will of George Middleton of Silksworth (1601), 2

———, Hugh (died before 1601), father of James, 2

———, James, son of Hugh, 2

———, Jane, widow of Thomas of Sunderland, fisherman (1635), 163

———, †Thomas, fisherman, of Sunderland, husband of Jane, inventory only (1635), xxxii, **162–3**

———, William, **(1)** Mr, debtor of Robert Watson of Bishopwearmouth (1603), 9. **(2)** of Brighouse, debtor of Edward Burne of Sunderland (1606), 12

Whitton (Whittan, Whittans), Jane, wife of John, witness of William Burdon of Ryhope, yeoman (1627); witness of Nicholas Thompson the elder of Ryhope (1636), 92, 167